Frommer's

Washington, D.C. with Kids

Here's what the critics say about Frommer's:

"Amazingly easy to use. Very portable, very complete."
—Booklist

♦

"The only mainstream guide to list specific prices. The Walter Cronkite of guidebooks—with all that implies."
—Travel & Leisure

♦

"Complete, concise, and filled with useful information."
—New York Daily News

♦

"Hotel information is close to encyclopedic."
—Des Moines Sunday Register

♦

"Detailed, accurate, and easy-to-read information for all price ranges."
—Glamour Magazine

Other Great Guides for Your Trip:

Frommer's Washington, D.C.

Frommer's Washington, D.C., from $70 a Day

Frommer's Portable Washington, D.C.

Frommer's Memorable Walks in Washington, D.C.

Frommer's Irreverent Guide to Washington, D.C.

The Unofficial Guide to Washington, D.C.

Frommer's Virginia

Frommer's Maryland & Delaware

Frommer's®   5th Edition

Washington, D.C. with Kids

by Beth Rubin

IDG Books Worldwide, Inc.
An International Data Group Company
Foster City, CA • Chicago, IL • Indianapolis, IN • New York, NY

ABOUT THE AUTHOR

Beth Rubin has written extensively on family topics for 20 years and has lived in the Washington, D.C., area since the early 1960s. During that time, she has played tour guide to her own two children and grandson as well as the offspring of numerous relatives and friends. Her experience and tell-it-like-it-is style make this well-researched book indispensable to anyone living in or visiting the nation's capital with kids in tow.

IDG BOOKS WORLDWIDE, INC.

An International Data Group Company
919 E. Hillsdale Blvd.
Suite 400
Foster City, CA 94404

Find us online at **www.frommers.com**

ISBN 0-02-863670-8
ISSN 1058-4978

Editor: David Gibbs
Production Editor: Donna Wright
Photo Editor: Richard Fox
Design by Michele Laseau
Staff Cartographers: John Decamillas, Roberta Stockwell
Page Creation: John Bitter, Pete Lippincott, and Kendra Span

SPECIAL SALES

For general information on IDG Books Worldwide's books in the U.S., please call our Consumer Customer Service department at 1-800-762-2974. For reseller information, including discounts, bulk sales, customized editions, and premium sales, please call our Reseller Customer Service department at 1-800-434-3422.

Manufactured in the United States of America

5 4 3 2 1

Contents

10　Easy Excursions　263

Index　299

List of Maps

For Rachel, Tony, Josh, Eric, and Lisa, for the love,
inspiration, and good times.

ACKNOWLEDGMENTS

To my loved ones and friends, thanks for putting up with me through the fifth edition. I can come out and play now. To my publisher, Mike Spring, thank you for another vote of confidence. To my editor, David Gibbs, thanks for giving me a push when I needed it and for keeping me honest. To the many relatives, friends, and readers of past editions who shared their experiences, thank you for your input. And to everyone at the Smithsonian, the National Park Service, Washington Metropolitan Area Transit Authority, airlines, Amtrak, independent museums and other attractions, tour operators, hotels, restaurants, shops, performing arts organizations, and anyone else who contributed to this book (you know who you are!), thank you for sharing your time and your knowledge.

An Invitation to the Reader

In researching this book, we discovered many wonderful places—hotels, restaurants, shops, and more. We're sure you'll find others. Please tell us about them, so we can share the information with your fellow travelers in upcoming editions. If you were disappointed with a recommendation, we'd love to know that, too. Please write to:

Frommer's Washington, D.C. with Kids
IDG Travel
1633 Broadway
New York, NY 10019

An Additional Note

Please be advised that travel information is subject to change at any time—and this is especially true of prices. We therefore suggest that you write or call ahead for confirmation when making your travel plans. The author, editors, and publisher cannot be held responsible for the experiences of readers while traveling. Your safety is important to us, however, so we encourage you to stay alert and be aware of your surroundings. Keep a close eye on cameras, purses, and wallets—all favorite targets of thieves and pickpockets.

What the Symbols Mean

✪ Frommer's Favorites

Our favorite places and experiences—outstanding for quality, value, or both.

The following abbreviations are used for credit cards:

AE	American Express	EURO	Eurocard
CB	Carte Blanche	JCB	Japan Credit Bank
DC	Diners Club	MC	MasterCard
DISC	Discover	V	Visa
ER	EnRoute		

Find Frommer's Online

Arthur Frommer's Budget Travel Online (**www.frommers.com**) offers more than 6,000 pages of up-to-the-minute travel information—including the latest bargains and candid, personal articles updated daily by Arthur Frommer himself. No other Web site offers such comprehensive and timely coverage of the world of travel.

Planning a Family Trip to Washington, D.C.

Kids and Washington, D.C., go together like peanut butter and jelly. Little wonder that children of all ages come to know and love the fascinating international playground that is the nation's capital. Packed into the 69¼-square-mile parcel of former swampland, "the District" or "D.C." offers a host of attractions, historic and new, waiting to be discovered and rediscovered. With its broad tree-lined boulevards, numerous parks and recreational areas, and multiethnic shops and restaurants, it's a natural as a family vacation destination. For those of us living here, it is not surprising that visiting families have been flocking to Washington in increasing numbers over the years. In fact, the capital city, which celebrated its bicentennial in 1991, attracts about 21 million visitors per year. Not bad for a spruced-up swamp! Rest assured, the District pulls out all the stops to extend a friendly hand to families. Local hotels bend over backward to cater to families by offering special rates and perks to those with kids in tow. And restaurants go out of their way to please pint-size patrons with kids' menus, half portions, crayons—and sometimes, free food.

Not by accident do thousands of bus and planeloads of schoolchildren arrive annually from all over the world. Where else can kids visit the president's house, touch a moon rock, view the city from atop a 555-foot obelisk, and cruise the Potomac all in the same day? And that's just for openers!

Despite the staggering number of federal buildings and museums, much of downtown Washington resembles an enormous park. First-time visitors are quick to note the abundance of greenery cozying up to all the marble and granite. In fact, grassy knolls, gardens, fountains, and parks hug most major sightseeing attractions. The area known as the National Mall stretches for 2 miles from the U.S. Capitol to the Lincoln Memorial—the perfect site for chasing pigeons or a family jog. The open spaces are a boon to children, who typically become bored and antsy after an hour in a museum. The same kids, cranky from being cooped up and longing for physical activity, can exit almost any museum onto a glorified yard and let loose.

Compared to other urban areas here and abroad, Washington's skyline is surprisingly and refreshingly uncluttered. We can thank the founding fathers for that: Because the original city planners declared that no building could be higher than the dome of the U.S.

Capitol, the height of commercial buildings is strictly regulated to 110 feet. And if you've visited other major cities recently, you'll be pleased to discover that Washington's major tourist areas are squeaky clean. Of course, we're not talking politics here. That's a topic for another day.

Getting around D.C. is a breeze. All major attractions are accessible by Metro, the public rail/bus system. The subways are clean, efficient, safe, and surprisingly graffiti-free. They are also quiet.

Prices for food, lodging, and entertainment compare favorably to those of other tourist meccas both here and abroad. If you've recently been to New York, Boston, Los Angeles, or San Francisco, you'll find Washington a relative bargain—even if you can't sleep for free in the White House. Families find they can eat well in a variety of more than 3,500 Washington restaurants without breaking the bank. Best of all, almost all the major attractions are free. Try that in New York or Paris!

Except for a few neighborhoods, where you're not apt to be in the first place, you can unleash older children to wander on their own. Teenagers will enjoy exploring areas such as Georgetown and Old Town, Alexandria, which are uniquely appealing to this age group.

Tourism is the second largest industry in D.C. The first, as you may have guessed, is the federal government. The "natives" (sort of an inside joke, since so many residents come from somewhere else) are friendly, helpful, and eager to make visitors feel at home. Washington is, after all, everyone's home and engenders a sense of belonging to short-term guests as well as longtime residents.

Although D.C.'s citizens enjoy many perks, they have suffered, one way or another, because of local politics. Here's why. According to the Constitution, Congress has the power to "exercise exclusive legislation . . . over the seat of the Government of the United States." Believe it or not, before 1961 and the passage of the 23rd Amendment, residents of the District could not vote in national elections. Under the Reorganization of 1967, the president appointed a mayor and nine-member council to govern the District.

In 1970, Congress okayed legislation for a delegate to represent the District in the House of Representatives but, and here's the catch, this rep can vote on committees but *not* on the House floor. And, although Washington has had an elected mayor and city council since 1975, Congress continues its tight reign over the D.C. budget, which has been grossly mismanaged by several administrations.

It must be true that adversity builds character, because, despite the ongoing problems of the D.C. government, those who live and work in the District share an immense feeling of pride. Chances are it will rub off on you and yours during your visit.

1 Visitor Information

Nothing beats careful planning for a smooth-running, fun-filled vacation, especially when traveling with kids. Step one in the planning process hasn't changed over the years: It is always helpful to familiarize yourself with your destination. And since you're traveling to the nation's capital, practice the precepts of a democracy and include your children in the planning process. Digest as much information as you can. Then gather everyone around the kitchen table and discuss your priorities. Some families make a list of sights that are must-sees followed by backups they can live without. While I admit to having a type A personality, the practice served us well when my kids were growing up. I've found that it's wise not to leave anything but the weather (and, if you're not fussy, where to eat) to chance.

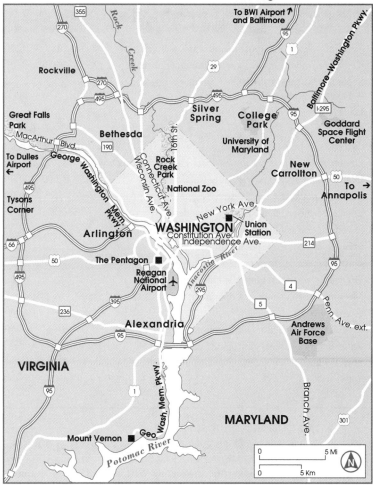

Rehearse well—do some advance research and planning and make the necessary reservations—and your vacation will be a stellar performance.

For admittance to either gallery when the Senate or House is in session, to eat lunch in the members' dining room, or to take VIP tours of the Capitol, White House, and FBI, contact your congressional representatives. Passes are limited, and 6 months before your visit is not too soon to write. Send your request, with the dates of your trip, to your senator, C/O U.S. Senate, Washington, DC 20510, or your representative, C/O U.S. House of Representatives, Washington, DC 20515. If you're not sure whom to write to, visit the Web site: www.capweb.net.

Besides combing the travel shelves of your local library and bookstores, I strongly suggest ordering brochures from the following sources: **Washington, D.C., Convention and Visitors Association,** 1212 New York Ave. NW, Suite 600, Washington, DC 20005 (☎ 202/789-7000; www.washington.org); **Washington, D.C. Reservations,** 1201 Wisconsin Ave. NW, Washington, DC 20007 (☎ 800/554-2220; www.dcaccommodations.com); **Capitol Reservations,** 1730 Rhode Island Ave. NW,

What Things Cost in Washington, D.C.	U.S. $
Taxi from National Airport to a downtown hotel	14.00–15.00
Taxi from Dulles Airport (Virginia) to downtown	40.00–45.00
Super Shuttle from Baltimore–Washington International to Downtown Hotel (J.W. Marriott)	28.00
Local telephone call	.35
Metro ride	1.10–3.25
Taxi	4.00 (within same zone) and up
Double room at Loews L'Enfant Plaza Hotel (very expensive)	189.00–299.00
Double room at the Carlyle Suites (moderate)	79.00–149.00
Double room at the Best Western Capital Beltway (inexpensive)	69.00
Lunch for one at Hard Rock Cafe (moderate)	20.00
Lunch for one at Flight Line cafeteria (inexpensive)	8.00
Lunch (hot dog, soda, potato chips) from street vendor	3.00
Dinner for one at America (moderate)	25.00
Dinner for one at Hogs on the Hill (inexpensive)	14.00
Medium-size soft drink in a restaurant	1.30–1.75
Ice-cream cone	2.00
Roll of Kodak 100 film, 36 exposures	6.50
Admission to National Zoological Park	Free
Movie ticket	
Adult	5.00 (matinee before 6pm) 7.50
Child	4.50

Washington, DC 20036 (☎ 800/847-4832); **Bed 'n' Breakfasts of Washington, D.C.,** P.O. Box 12011, Washington, DC 20005 (☎ 202/328-3510; www.bnbaccom.com); **DC Committee to Promote Washington (D.C. Government),** 1212 New York Ave., Suite 200, Washington, DC 20005 (☎ 202/724-5644.

If you're planning to visit during the **National Cherry Blossom Festival** that runs for 2 weeks from late March into April, write for a schedule of events to **National Cherry Blossom Festival,** P.O. Box 33224, Washington, DC 20033-0224 or call the hot line (☎ **202/547-1500;** www.nps.gov).

Internet surfers can obtain information on all museums that are part of the Smithsonian Institution at www.si.edu.

For information on Metrorail service, write to the **Washington Metropolitan Area Transit Authority,** 600 5th St. NW, Washington, DC 20001 (☎ **202/637-7000**), and request the free "Metro Pocket Ride Guide."

2 When to Go

THE CLIMATE   For obvious reasons, you'll probably plan your visit for spring or summer, when the kids are out of school. That's fine, but understand that the warm-weather months are when Washington is most crowded. Although summer is the best time to take advantage of numerous free outdoor events and reduced hotel rates, the heat and humidity can wilt a cactus. But if you dress appropriately and sightsee early or late in the day, you'll fare well.

July and August are the warmest months, with average highs in the mid-80s. This is not to say it won't heat up to the mid-90s—it does with disturbing regularity and oppressively high humidity. Fortunately, all the public buildings, restaurants, and hotels in Washington are air-conditioned, and most hotels have swimming pools, making a summer visit tolerable.

If your kids are preschoolers or budding geniuses who can afford to miss school, fall is a lovely time to visit. The weather is usually pleasant and mild, and you can enjoy the city while the rest of the world is at home, work, or school. In winter, hotel prices are lowest and lines are shortest. So if you hate crowds and love bargains, pack your galoshes and come see Washington when it is decked out for the holidays.

Highs in December, January, and February are in the mid-40s, with lows around 30°F. Again, these are averages. The rainfall is evenly distributed throughout the year, so don't leave home without a raincoat.

Average Monthly Temperatures (°F)

	Jan	Feb	Mar	Apr	May	June	July	Aug	Sept	Oct	Nov	Dec
Avg. High	45	44	53	64	75	83	87	84	78	68	55	45
Avg. Low	27	28	35	44	55	63	68	66	60	48	38	30

HOLIDAYS   On the following legal national holidays, banks, government offices, and post offices are closed. Subways (Metrorail) and buses (Metrobus) operate less frequently, usually on a Saturday or Sunday schedule (☎ **202/ 637-7000** for information). Museums, stores, and restaurants vary widely in their open/closed policy. To avoid disappointment, call before you go.

January 1 (New Year's Day); third Monday in January (Martin Luther King Jr.'s Birthday); third Monday in February (Presidents' Day); last Monday in May (Memorial Day); July 4 (Independence Day); first Monday in September (Labor Day); second Monday in October (Columbus Day); November 11 (Veterans' Day/Armistice Day); last Thursday in November (Thanksgiving Day); and December 25 (Christmas Day).

The Tuesday following the first Monday in November is Election Day. It is a legal holiday in presidential election years (2000, 2004, and so on).

Kids' Favorite Events

Whether you decide to visit Washington in June or in January, or any time in between, you'll find a wide range of special events to enhance your sightseeing. Most are free. For the latest information before you leave home, contact the **Washington, D.C., Convention and Visitors Association,** 1212 New York Ave. NW, Washington, DC 20005 (☎ **202/789-7000**), and request the quarterly "Calendar of Events" brochure.

The **White House Visitors Center,** in the Department of Commerce's Herbert Hoover Building at 1450 Pennsylvania Ave. NW (between 14th and 15th streets), distributes tourist information daily from 7:30am to 4pm, sometimes with extended summer hours (☎ **202/208-1631**). Also consult the "Weekend" magazine of the *Washington Post* every Friday. Before you attend a special event, it's smart to call and verify the time and location. Some changes and cancellations are inevitable.

January

○ **Martin Luther King Jr.'s Birthday.** This national holiday is celebrated the third Monday in January with speeches, dance performances, and choral presentations citywide and a wreath-laying ceremony at the Lincoln Memorial. Check local newspapers for free commemorative events.(☎ **202/619-7222**).

○ **Washington Boat Show.** Kids love boats—in or out of the water. Consider the experience a healthy exercise in fantasizing for the entire family. The weeklong show is held midmonth at the Washington Convention Center, 900 9th St. NW (☎ **703/569-7141**).

• **Robert E. Lee's Birthday Bash.** Lee's birthday is observed January 19 at Arlington House in Arlington National Cemetery and features 19th-century music, food, and memorabilia (☎ **703/557-0613**). Free. Visit Lee's boyhood home at 607 Oronoco St. and the Lee-Fendall House at 614 Oronoco St. in Old Town, Alexandria (☎ **703/548-1789**).

○ **Inauguration Day.** This monumental event is held on January 20 of every fourth year when the president is sworn in at the West Front of the Capitol. The next presidential inauguration will be January 20, 2001. A colorful and *very* lengthy parade follows the ceremony from the Capitol to the White House along Pennsylvania Avenue. Free.

February

• **Black History Month.** This is observed by museums, libraries, and recreation centers with special exhibits, events, and performances to celebrate African American contributions to American life. Check local newspapers and magazines for events (☎ **202/357-2700**).

• **Abraham Lincoln's Birthday.** A moving wreath-laying ceremony and reading of the Gettysburg Address at the Lincoln Memorial on February 12 commemorates the birthday of the 16th U.S. president. It's truly inspiring (☎ **202/619-7222**).

• **Chinese New Year Parade.** Although younger kids may be frightened by the firecrackers announcing the Chinese lunar New Year, the colorful street parade of lions and dragons, dancers, and music-makers through Chinatown (H Street NW, between 5th and 7th streets) is great family fun. After the parade, fill up on dumplings and duck (Peking, of course) at one of Chinatown's many restaurants. *Note:* Sometimes the Chinese New Year is in early March. Blame it on the moon.

○ **George Washington's Birthday.** The father of our country's birthday is celebrated with a parade through Old Town, Alexandria's historic district on the Saturday closest to his February 22 birthday. The parade begins at Wilkes and St. Asaph streets. Wear your cleanest white stockings and powdered wig (☎ **703/838-5005**). Free. On February 22, a ceremony is held at the Washington Monument cosponsored by the National Park Service and Washington National Monument Society (☎ **202/783-6832**). Free. George Washington's Mount Vernon estate features a family celebration on Presidents' Day, on the third Monday of the month (☎ **703/780-2000**). Free.

March

• **Washington Flower & Garden Show.** This harbinger of spring gives you the opportunity to get a jump on the season at the Washington Convention Center, 9th and H streets NW (☎ **202/789-1600**).

• **St. Patrick's Day Parades.** On the Sunday closest to St. Paddy's Day, it's top o' the mornin' at the festive afternoon parade down Constitution Avenue, from 7th to 17th streets NW, with floats, bagpipes, bands, and dancers (☎ **202/**

637-2474). Old Town, Alexandria, also celebrates the wearin' of the green with a procession down King Street (☎ **703/549-4535**).

○ **Ringling Bros. and Barnum & Bailey Circus.** The world's only three-ring circus pitches its tent at the D.C. Armory for 2 weeks of thrills and chills extending into April. Treat your kids if they've never been. It's still the greatest show on earth (☎ **703/448-4000**).

○ **Smithsonian Kite Festival.** Breeze on down to the Washington Monument grounds for this annual event that draws kite makers from all over the country. Prizes and trophies are awarded for homemade kites, but you must register between 10am and noon. (☎ **202/357-2700**). Free.

April

○ **National Cherry Blossom Festival.** If you hit this right—no snow, no gale winds, no August-in-spring weather—the vision of thousands of cherry trees blooming around the Tidal Basin will take your breath away. There's a parade of floats with cherry-blossom princesses from each state, free concerts, a marathon, Japanese lantern lighting ceremony, and fireworks (☎ **202/619-7222;** www.nps.gov). For parade information, call the D.C. Downtown Jaycees (☎ **202/728-1137**). See "Parks, Gardens & Other Wide-Open Spaces" in chapter 7 for more about the famed trees.

○ **White House Easter Egg Roll.** Children 8 and under, accompanied by an adult, are invited on Easter Monday to the South Lawn of the White House, where free eggs (hard-boiled or wooden, depending on the activity) and entertainment are dished out. Although there's a crunch of people and eggshells, your kids may find the event "egg-citing." No yolk! Line up early at the southeast gate of the White House on East Executive Avenue (☎ **202/456-7041**). Free.

• **Thomas Jefferson's Birthday.** On April 13, gather at the Jefferson Memorial to honor the birthday of this Renaissance man and third U.S. president with military drills and a wreath-laying ceremony (☎ **202/619-7222**). Free.

○ **White House Garden Tour.** Tour the Children's Garden, with its bronze impressions of the hands and feet of White House children and grandchildren among the tulips and azaleas, and the executive mansion's public rooms. Line up at least an hour before the weekend event (☎ **202/456-7041**). Free.

• **Emancipation Day Celebration.** The anniversary of the Emancipation Proclamation (April 16, 1862) is observed with choral music, oratory, and displays of slave memorabilia at the Anacostia Museum, 1901 Fort Place SE, and Freedom Plaza, 14th Street and Pennsylvania Avenue NW (☎ **202/357-2700**). Free.

• **Smithsonian Craft Show** (☎ **202/357-2700**). For 4 glorious days at the Andrew W. Mellon Auditorium, 1301 Constitution Ave. NW, this show of fine crafts features one-of-a-kind works from more than 100 exhibitors from all over the country. Strollers are not allowed, but backpacks are available. Watch little hands; you break, you pay!

• **William Shakespeare's Birthday.** The bard's birthday is celebrated the Saturday closest to April 23 at the Folger Shakespeare Library, 201 E. Capitol St. SE, with music, theater, children's events, and food (☎ **202/544-7077**). Free.

• **Trolley Car Spectacular.** Take a trip down memory lane and ride an antique trolley at the National Capital Trolley Museum in Wheaton, Maryland. Bring your camera (☎ **301/384-6088**). Free.

May

• **Friendship House Market Day Street Festival.** On the first Sunday in May, the streets around Eastern Market, 7th and C streets SE, are filled with vendors selling clothes, jewelry, and artifacts to benefit Friendship House. Enjoy carnival rides, crafts, music, and food while you browse (☎ **202/546-7600**). Free.

- **National Cathedral Flower Mart.** Children's games, flower booths, entertainment, and food spring up everywhere on the grounds of the majestic National Cathedral, Wisconsin Avenue and Woodley Road NW. There's also an extensive selection of herbs for sale (☎ **202/537-6200**). Free.

○ **Air Show at Andrews AFB.** Go ballistic over the Army's Golden Knights parachute team and aerial show by the Air Force Thunderbirds in their F-16s at this weekend open house at Andrews Air Force Base in Camp Springs, Maryland. Kids can climb aboard aircraft and tanks. Go early, allow plenty of driving time, and bring earplugs (☎ **301/981-6681**). Free.

- **Greek Spring Festival.** Gorge on Greek souvlaki and baklava while enjoying music, games, clowns, and arts and crafts at Saints Constantine and Helen Greek Orthodox Church, 4115 16th St. NW (☎ **202/829-2910**). Free.

- **Memorial Day Concert.** The Sunday of Memorial Day weekend, Washington's own National Symphony Orchestra will serenade you on the West Lawn of the Capitol (☎ **202/416-8100**). Bring a blanket. Free.

- **Memorial Day Ceremonies.** Witness wreath-laying ceremonies in Arlington Cemetery at the Kennedy grave site and Tomb of the Unknowns and services at the Memorial Amphitheater accompanied by military bands (☎ **202/685-2851**). Free.

- **Wreath-laying ceremonies.** These ceremonies also take place at the Vietnam and Korean War Veterans Memorials, just south of 21st Street and Constitution Avenue NW (☎ **202/619-7222**), and the Navy Memorial, Pennsylvania Avenue between 7th and 9th streets NW (☎ **202/737-2300,** ext. 768). Free.

June

- **American Sailor.** From the third Wednesday in June, and every Wednesday thereafter through early September, a multimedia presentation showcases the history of the U.S. Navy at the Washington Navy Yard waterfront at 9pm (☎ **202/433-2218**). Free, but reservations are required.

- **Dupont-Kalorama Museum Walk Day.** Textile demonstrations, video programs, house tours, hands-on art, music, and street food provide fun for the whole family at this neighborhood event (☎ **202/387-2151**). Free.

○ **Alexandria Red Cross Waterfront Festival.** Tall ships berth at Alexandria's historical waterfront during this family-oriented weekend featuring games, refreshments, entertainment, arts and crafts, and the blessing of the fleet (☎ **703/549-8300**). Free.

- **Juneteenth Jubilee.** Storytellers, infantry reenactment groups, clowns, and magicians commemorate the day Texas slaves learned of the Emancipation Proclamation. Call for the festival location, which changes from year to year (☎ **202/287-2060**). Free.

○ **Festival of American Folklife.** One of the most popular annual events in the nation's capital, the folklife festival on the Mall is filled with music, crafts, and ethnic foods reflecting America's rich multicultural heritage (☎ **202/357-2700**). Free. *Note:* The festival spills over into July.

- **National Capital Barbecue Battle.** Bring your appetites to the grandest pork barrel of them all, the third weekend of the month at Pennsylvania Avenue NW between 9th and 12th streets. Local restaurants pit their pork against each other for a rib-roaring good time sauced with cooking demonstrations and music (☎ **301/939-2444**).

July

○ **Independence Day Celebration.** The nation celebrates its birthday in grand style, beginning with a 12:30pm parade along Constitution Avenue, from 7th to 17th streets NW (☎ **202/619-7222**). See the Declaration of Independence at the National Archives, then enjoy entertainment all afternoon at the Sylvan Theatre on the Washington Monument grounds (☎ **202/426-6841**). At 8pm the National Symphony plays on the Capitol's West Lawn (☎ **202/416-8100**), and a fantastic fireworks display starts about 9:20pm (☎ **202/619-7222**). Bring something soft and dry to sit on. Check newspapers July 3 and 4 for details. Free.

- **Bastille Day Waiters Race.** Behold the waiters scurrying down Pennsylvania Avenue with trays of champagne glasses on July 14. The race for a grand-prize trip to Paris begins at 20th Street and Pennsylvania Avenue NW at noon. Free.

- **Virginia Scottish Games.** One of the largest Scottish festivals in the United States features Highland dancing, fiddling competitions, a heptathlon, animal events, and plenty of puffed-cheeked bagpipers. It's held at Episcopal High School, 3901 W. Braddock Rd., Alexandria, Virginia (☎ **703/838-4200**). Free.

- **Greater Washington Soap Box Derby.** Drivers between 9 and 16 years old coast down Capitol Hill in their aerodynamic vehicles at the traffic-stopping event that has taken place annually for more than 50 years (☎ **301/670-1110**). Free.

- **Latin American Festival.** A parade along Constitution Avenue caps the weekend celebration featuring entertainment, arts and crafts, and delicious international snacks. The festival radiates in all directions from Freedom Plaza at 14th Street and Constitution Avenue NW. Free.

- **Farm Tours.** About 20 Montgomery County, Maryland, farms open their doors and stalls to visitors for one Saturday this month. If your kids think eggs hatch in little corrugated cartons, bring them here. It's great fun, but leave your Sunday shoes at home (☎ **301/217-2345**). Free.

August

○ **Renaissance Festival.** Crownsville, Maryland (about 30 miles from downtown), is the site for a 16th-century fair with jousting matches, magicians, wandering minstrels, and crafts. A special children's area has pony rides, a zoo, and Tudor-era amusements. Armor up on weekends from late August to mid-October (☎ **800/296-7304**). Free for kids under 12 on Children's Weekend.

- **U.S. Army Band's 1812 Overture.** The Salute Gun Platoon of the 3rd U.S. Infantry provides the noisy finale to this patriotic concert by the U.S. Army Band at the Sylvan Theatre, Washington Monument grounds (☎ **202/619-7222**). Free.

- **Civil War Living History Day.** Take a torchlight tour of Union and Confederate camps and watch "soldiers" in Civil War uniforms reenact a battle and perform drill competitions at Fort Ward Museum and Park, 4301 W. Braddock Rd., Alexandria, Virginia (☎ **703/838-4848**). Free.

- **Children's Day.** Puppeteers, music-makers, mimes, and face-painters enchant and entertain kids at the Capital Children's Museum, 800 3rd St. NE (☎ **202/675-4120**). September

- **Labor Day Concert.** The National Symphony bids adieu to summer, even though it's usually still hot as blazes, with a concert on the West Lawn of the Capitol (☎ **202/619-7222**). Free.

○ **International Children's Festival.** Rain or shine the sun will be out at Wolf Trap Farm Park in Vienna, Virginia, where craft, music, and dance workshops and performances delight families annually over Labor Day weekend (☎ **703/642-0862**).

- **College Park Airport Open House and Air Fair.** Fly over here with your crew for airplane and helicopter rides, an air show, and exhibits at the area's oldest airport, at 1909 Corporal Frank Scott Dr., College Park, Maryland (☎ **301/864-5844**). Free.
- **National Frisbee Festival.** Disk-catching dogs are but one highlight of the annual World Frisbee Championship that's also well attended by noncompetitive champions of the two-legged variety. It's held on the Mall near the Air and Space Museum and sometimes things get ruff (☎ **301/645-5043**). Heads up! Free.
- **Adams-Morgan Day.** Visit Washington's most diverse neighborhood and enjoy crafts, music, and cuisine from Central America, Africa, and Europe along 18th Street NW between Florida Avenue and Columbia Road (☎ **202/789-7000**). Free.
- **National Capital Trolley Museum Fall Open House.** Take a trip down memory lane and ride an antique trolley at the National Capital Trolley Museum in Wheaton, Maryland. Bring your camera (☎ **301/384-6088**)
- **Constitution Day Commemoration.** On September 17 at the National Archives, Constitution Avenue at 8th Street NW, pay your respects to the Constitution on the anniversary of its signing. A naturalization program and honor guard ceremonies are part of the day's events (☎ **202/501-5215**). Free.
- ✪ **Rock Creek Park Day.** Children's activities, environmental and recreational exhibits, foods, crafts, and music highlight the celebration of Washington's largest park, which reached the ripe old age of 100 in 1990. The event is usually held on the Saturday closest to September 25, the park's birthday (☎ **202/426-6829**). Free.
- **Folger Open House.** Here's a chance to go behind the scenes. Inspect costumes and scenery and watch a rehearsal in the Shakespeare Theatre (an authentic model of an Elizabethan theater) at the Folger Library, 201 E. Capitol St. SE (☎ **202/546-4000**). Free.
- **Kennedy Center Open House Arts Festival.** Treat your senses to a musical celebration by more than 40 entertainers who appear in every nook and cranny of the Ken Cen (☎ **202/467-4600**). Free.
- **Black Family Reunion Celebration.** Gospel music, ethnic treats, dancing, and craft demonstrations liven the Washington Monument grounds (☎ **202/619-7222**). Free.

October

- ✪ **Kinderfest.** A fall festival for the 6-and-under set at Watkins Regional Park in Upper Marlboro, Maryland, features games, rides, pumpkin painting, and scarecrow making (☎ **301/249-9220**). Free admission, but bring money for rides and food.
- **Zoo Arts Festival.** Free workshops and demonstrations by local artists, a wildlife art exhibit and sale, and a kids' "Creation Station" take place at the National Zoo the first weekend of the month (☎ **202/673-4961**). Free.
- **Greek Fall Festival and Christmas Bazaar.** Games for kids, a Greek buffet, arts and crafts, jewelry, and Oriental rugs are featured at this lively bazaar at Saint Sophia Cathedral, 36th Street and Massachusetts Avenue NW (☎ **202/333-4730**). Music and dancing after 5pm. Free.
- **U.S. Navy Birthday Concert.** Wear your dress blues to the Kennedy Center on the second Monday in October for the concert celebrating the navy's birthday (225 in 2000) (☎ **202/433-6090**). Free, but tickets must be ordered in September. Send a self-addressed stamped envelope to: Navy Birthday

Tickets, U.S. Navy Band, Building 105, Washington Navy Yard, Washington, DC 20374-5054.

- **White House Fall Garden Tour.** One weekend this month (all day Saturday, Sunday afternoon only) the public is invited to visit the Rose Garden, South Lawn, and beautiful beds of multihued chrysanthemums, as well as some of the White House's public rooms, while enjoying the upbeat sounds of military bands. Line up at the southeast gate, E Street and East Executive Avenue, an hour before the tour starts (☎ 202/456-7041). Free.

- **Taste of D.C. Festival.** Saturday through Monday on Columbus Day weekend sample food from about 50 diverse restaurants while enjoying crafts, entertainment on two stages, and special kids' activities along Pennsylvania Avenue, between 9th and 14th streets NW (☎ 202/724-5430). Free admission; food and beverage tickets $6 for a strip of nine.

- **Corcoran Gallery of Art's Fall Family Day.** Films, storytellers, mime, and dance highlight the fall celebration at the Corcoran, 17th Street and New York Avenue NW (☎ 202/639-1700). Free.

- **Oxon Hill Farm Park's Fall Festival.** Visit this working farm where you can enjoy a hayride, try your hand at cider pressing, and watch a blacksmith demonstration (☎ 301/839-1177). Free.

- **Theodore Roosevelt's Birthday.** Even if you forgot to send a card, on the Saturday closest to T. R.'s birthday (142 on October 27, 2000) you can celebrate with nature programs, island tours, and special kids' entertainment. No food on the island but you can picnic outside. The island is off the G. W. Parkway, north of Roosevelt Bridge (☎ 703/285-2225). Free.

- ❂ **Halloween Monster Bash.** Come to a costume party October 31 at the Capital Children's Museum, 3rd and H streets NE (☎ 202/675-4125).

November

- **Veterans' Day Ceremonies.** Military music accompanies a solemn ceremony honoring the nation's war dead. The Memorial Amphitheater at Arlington National Cemetery is the service site, where the president or another high-ranking official lays a wreath at the Tomb of the Unknown Soldier (☎ 202/619-7222). Free.

- ❂ **Sugarloaf's Autumn Crafts Festival.** Puppet shows, storytelling, and a petting zoo will keep the youngsters happy while grown-ups shop for holiday gifts and souvenirs sold by 400 artists and craftspeople at the Montgomery County Fairgrounds in Gaithersburg, Maryland (☎ 301/963-3247; www.mcagfair.com).

- **Seafaring Celebration.** Have a "nauti" but nice time watching boat-building demonstrations and enjoying sea chanteys and sailing lore at the Navy Museum, Washington Navy Yard, 9th and M streets SE (☎ 202/433-4882). Free.

December

- ❂ **Festival of Music and Lights.** More than 200,000 twinkling bulbs sparkle and gleam on the greenery at the Washington Mormon Temple in Kensington, Maryland, through Twelfth Night. Concerts are held nightly until New Year's Eve (☎ 301/587-0144). Free.

- ❂ **Woodlawn Plantation Christmas.** Get a taste of Christmas, old Virginia style, as musicians and carolers serenade you at this historic estate, which was a wedding gift from George Washington to his foster daughter, Nelly Custis, and her husband (who was Washington's nephew), Lawrence Lewis. Wagon rides and refreshments are part of the holiday fun (☎ 703/780-4000).

- ✪ **Scottish Christmas Walk.** A parade through historic Old Town, Alexandria, Virginia, includes Celtic activities for children, tartan-clad bagpipers and Highland dancers, and house tours (☎ **703/549-0111**). Free.
- **"A Soldier's Gift."** This holiday offering of seasonal music from the U.S. Army Band is held at DAR Constitution Hall, 1776 D St. NW (☎ **202/628-4780**). Free, but tickets are required. Write to "A Soldier's Gift," P.O. Box 24074, Washington, DC 20024 (☎ **202/638-2661**).
- **Old Town Christmas Candlelight Tours.** Several historic homes, dressed up with period decorations, open their doors to visitors. Music, colonial dancing, and refreshments add to the festive atmosphere (☎ **703/838-5005**).
- **Holiday Celebration.** Decorated Christmas trees, holiday crafts, ethnic food, stories, and music at the Smithsonian's National Museum of American History demonstrate how Americans celebrate Christmas, Hanukkah, Kwanzaa, and the New Year. Join the holiday fun at the Smithsonian (☎ **202/357-2700**). Free.
- ✪ **People's Christmas Tree Lighting.** The People's Christmas Tree, towering some 60 feet, is lighted each year on the west side of the Capitol to herald the holiday season. There's music, too (☎ **202/224-3069**). Free.
- ✪ **National Christmas Tree Lighting and Pageant of Peace.** Every year on the Ellipse (between the White House and Constitution Avenue) one or more members of the First Family throws the switch that lights the nation's blue spruce Christmas tree and 57 Scotch pine siblings, representing the 50 states, the District of Columbia, and the six U.S. territories. Musical and choral performances take place every evening from 6 to 9pm, except Christmas, through December 30 (☎ **202/619-7222**). Free.
- **U.S. Navy Band Holiday Concert.** A free concert awaits all holiday revelers at DAR Constitution Hall, 1776 D St. NW (☎ **202/433-6090**). Free, but reservations are required.
- ✪ **Children's Hanukkah Festival.** Games, music, entertainment, and food celebrate the Festival of Lights at the B'nai B'rith Klutznick Museum, 1640 Rhode Island Ave. NW (☎ **202/857-6583**).
- ✪ **Family Hanukkah Celebration.** Sing the popular Hanukkah song "Dreidel, dreidel, dreidel" with your loved ones, watch puppet shows, play dreidel games, and nosh at the Jewish Community Center, 1529 16th St. NW (☎ **202/ 518-9400**).
- ✪ **Kennedy Center Holiday Celebrations.** Since its opening in 1971, the Kennedy Center has been celebrating the holidays in grand style. The festivities include a "Messiah" Sing-Along, Hanukkah Festival, Christmas Eve and New Year's Eve programs, and concerts by local children's choruses (☎ **202/467-4600**). Many events are free.
- ✪ **White House Christmas Candlelight Tours.** If seeing the White House dressed up in holiday finery doesn't put you in a ho-ho-ho mood, nothing will. Maybe you'll catch the First Lady leaving a "Dear Santa" note and milk and cookies. In recent years, the tour was held three post-Christmas evenings from 5 to 7pm, and anyone in line before 7pm was admitted. Dress warmly and be prepared for a long wait. Gather at the Park Service's kiosk on the Ellipse, south of the White House, or you'll be left out in the cold (☎ **202/208-1631**). Free.
- **Audubon Holiday Fair.** Get into the Yuletide spirit with model railroad displays, crafts, and nature talks at the Audubon Naturalist Society, 8940 Jones Mill Rd., Chevy Chase, Maryland (☎ **301/652-9188**). Admission is charged to anyone over age 12.

3 What to Pack

FOR YOU   You can leave your tux and gown at home unless you're attending a state occasion at the White House. This is the nation's capital, however, so a bit of decorum is prescribed when it comes to dress. Any time of the year casual attire—jeans, sweat suits, and your most comfortable walking shoes—is recommended for sightseeing. If you're planning on dining in an elegant restaurant, include something dressier. A few of the fancier places require men to wear jackets. (But why in the world would you be taking your kids to a place like that?)

It's easy to pack for summer. Bring the lightest clothing you own and double the number of T-shirts, sport shirts, or blouses you normally wear on a summer day. Washingtonians measure the heat by the number of shirts they soak, as in "Yesterday was a real scorcher, a three-shirter!" Leave short-shorts and tank tops at home where they belong, unless you're planning a side trip to the beach.

Fall, winter, and spring frequently blur, so prudent packing means bringing clothing that can be layered. In fall, warm weather is the rule, often lingering well into October or November. But every rule has an exception, so don't forget a jacket. In the winter, you'll need a heavy topcoat, even though a mild day occasionally surfaces, to everyone's pleasure. Some years spring sneaks by while everyone is asleep; sometimes it lasts several weeks. Be prepared and bring a mix of winter and summer things.

Be sure to include a sweater or sweatshirt, no matter what the season. In summer, the overly air-conditioned public buildings and restaurants can deliver a cruel shock to your overheated system. Since precipitation is spread fairly evenly throughout the year, follow my mother's advice and always take a raincoat. Mother still knows best. And carry a collapsible cup with you and reduce all those back-breaking lifts at water fountains.

FOR THE KIDS   Layering is the name of the game when it comes to packing for children. Unless you're traveling with an infant or toddler, packing for them is the same as packing for you, except their stuff takes up less space. Remind teenagers that nobody in Washington has seen their clothes before, so they don't have to pack every stitch they own.

A raincoat and rain hat make sense in any season, but I suggest leaving umbrellas at home. I think they're a hazard and too easy to lose. Waterproof boots, warm gloves, and a hat with earflaps are wintertime necessities.

As every parent knows, the younger the child, the more clothes he or she will mess up. Since a washer and dryer may not be handy, plan two or three outfits per day for kids under 5 and throw in a few extra shirts for good measure. Take at least one extra outfit for little ones in a carry-on bag. If all their gear is stowed in the cargo hold, overhead rack, or trunk, you won't be a happy parent if you have to change their wet, smelly clothing in a hurry. Include enough diapers—and then some—to keep the baby's bottom dry until you can get to your suitcase or a store.

Consider tucking in a "Snoozle" for your toddler. The colorful stuffed pillow is designed as a headrest for naps in cars, buses, planes, and trains. Snoozles sell for about $10 at toy, travel, and map stores.

If your kids are flying alone, contact the individual airline or request a copy of "When Kids Fly," from Massport, Public Affairs Department, 10 Park Plaza, Boston, MA 02116-3971 (☎ **617/973-5500**), or "Kids and Teens in Flight," from the U.S. Department of Transportation, I-25, Washington, DC 20590 (☎ **202/366-2220**).

When traveling by plane, make sure everyone has a sweatshirt or sweater. It can get downright chilly once you're airborne, and airline blankets disappear quickly. Ask your pediatrician about oral decongestants and nasal sprays, especially if your kids have colds. Changes in cabin pressure, especially during takeoffs and landings, can cause excruciating inner-ear pain in some ultrasensitive kids.

Don't forget two laundry bags or a couple of pillowcases for dirties. Most hotels have laundry and/or dry cleaning services, but they can be costly. There are Laundromats in D.C., but they may not be convenient to where you're staying, and watching the family wash tumble dry is probably a low-priority item on your list of things to do in Washington. Pack liquid Woolite or fill a couple of small resealable plastic bags with powdered laundry soap so you can do emergency washing in the sink.

4 Tips for Travelers with Disabilities

Call ahead for general information about special arrangements that various Washington sites make for people with disabilities. The Washington, D.C., Convention & Visitors Association publishes a fact sheet detailing general accessibility of Washington hotels, restaurants, shopping malls, and attractions. For a free copy, call ☎ **202/ 789-7093** or write to WCVA, 1212 New York Ave. NW, Suite 600, Washington, DC, 20005.

The Washington Metropolitan Transit Authority also publishes a free guide on Metro's bus and rail system accessibility for the elderly and physically disabled. Call ☎ **202/962-0128** to order the guide, or check out Metro's Web site at **www.wmata.com**. Each Metro station is equipped with an elevator (complete with Braille number plates) to train platforms, and rail cars are fully accessible. Metro is now installing 24-inch sections of punctuated rubber tiles leading up to the granite-lined platform edge to warn visually impaired Metro riders that they are nearing the tracks. Train operators make station and onboard announcements of train destinations and stops. Most of the district's Metrobuses have wheelchair lifts and kneel at the curb (this number will increase as time goes on). The TDD number for Metro information is ☎ **202/638-3780.** For other questions about Metro services for travelers with disabilities, call ☎ **202/962-6464.** In fact, it's probably a good idea to call this number to verify that the elevators are operating at the stations you'll be traveling to.

Regular **Tourmobile** trams (see "Organized Tours" in chapter 6 for info about this sightseeing company) are accessible to visitors with disabilities. The company also operates special vans for immobile travelers, complete with wheelchair lifts. Tourmobile recommends that you call a day ahead to ensure that the van is available for you when you arrive. For information, call ☎ **202/554-5100.**

All Smithsonian museum buildings are accessible to wheelchair visitors. A free, comprehensive publication called Smithsonian Access lists all services available to visitors with disabilities, including parking, building access, sign language interpreters, and more. To obtain a copy, call (☎ **202/357-2700** or TTY 202/ 357-1729). You can also use the TTY number to obtain information on all Smithsonian museums and events.

You may also find it helpful to know about the arrangements available at these specific sites:

For tours of the White House, visitors in wheelchairs should come to the East Visitors' Gate (along East Executive Ave) between 10:30am and noon, and you will be allowed to go to the head of the line; visitors arriving in wheelchairs, and their companions (up to four people), do not need tickets. For details, call ☎ **202/456-2322.**

The Lincoln, Jefferson, and Vietnam Memorials and the Washington Monument are also equipped to accommodate visitors with disabilities and keep wheelchairs on the premises. There's limited parking for visitors with disabilities on the south side of the Lincoln Memorial. Call ahead to other sightseeing attractions for accessibility information and special services: ☎ **202/619-7222** or TDD 202/619-7083.

Call your senator or representative to arrange wheelchair-accessible tours of the Capitol; they can also arrange special tours for the blind or deaf. If you need further information on these tours, call ☎ **202/224-4048.**

Shoppers should know that places well equipped with wheelchair ramps and other facilities for visitors with disabilities include Union Station, the Shops at National Place, the Pavilion at the Old Post Office, and Georgetown Park Mall.

And if you're a theater-goer, be assured that Washington theaters are handily equipped: The John F. Kennedy Center for the Performing Arts provides headphones to hearing-impaired patrons at no charge. A wireless, infrared listening enhancement system is available in all theaters. Some performances offer sign-language and audio description. A public TTY is located at the Information Center in the Hall of States. Large print programs are available at every performance; a limited number of Braille programs are available from the house manager. All theaters in the complex (except the Terrace) are wheelchair accessible. The 1997 renovation of the Concert Hall has made it the most accessible venue in the city; improvements include ingenious wheelchair seating, increased to 4% of the seats, and enhanced acoustics. To reserve a wheelchair, call ☎ **202/416-8340.** For other questions regarding patrons with disabilities, including information about half-priced tickets (you will need to submit a letter from your doctor stating that your disability is permanent), call ☎ **202/416-8727.** The TTY number is ☎ **202/416-8728**.

The Arena Stage (☎ **202/554-9066**) has a wheelchair lift and is otherwise accessible. It offers audio description and sign interpretation at designated performances as well as infrared and audio loop assisted-listening devices for the hearing-impaired, plus program books in Braille and large-print. The TTY box office line is ☎ **202/484-0247.** You can also call ahead to reserve handicapped parking spaces for a performance.

Ford's Theatre is wheelchair-accessible and offers listening devices as well as special signed and audio-described performances. Call ☎ **202/347-4833** for details. The TTY number is ☎ **202/347-5599.**

The National Theatre is wheelchair-accessible and features special performances of its shows for visually and hearing-impaired theatergoers. To obtain amplified-sound earphones for narration, simply ask an usher before the performance. The National also offers a limited number of half-price tickets to patrons in wheelchairs; seating is in the orchestra section and you may receive no more than two half-price tickets. For details, call ☎ **202/628-6161.**

5 Health & Other Precautions

HEALTH If you or your children require **medication,** pack plenty, preferably in a carry-on bag. Be prepared for **motion sickness.** Make sure you have a bottle of liquid Dramamine close at hand. Kids who are fine in a car may get sick on a boat, plane, or train, and vice versa.

You'll want a **first-aid kit.** A small basic kit is available at most pharmacies and supermarkets, or call your physician or local Red Cross chapter for a recommendation.

In addition, remember grown-up– and children's-strength aspirin or Tylenol, a thermometer, cough syrup, a plastic cup, flexible straws, baby wipes, a plastic spoon, nightlight, and pacifiers.

If you or the kids wear **eyeglasses,** by all means bring backups. If extra pairs are unavailable, bring the prescriptions. You can't sightsee if you can't see!

Before you leave, get a list of your **kids' inoculations** and the dates they were administered from your pediatrician. In an emergency, you're not apt to remember this information, and your hometown doctor might be out on the golf course without a beeper.

If possible, before you leave home obtain the name of a **Washington, D.C., pediatrician** from your hometown physician or relatives or friends in the Washington area. If your child spikes a fever of 102° in the middle of the night, you won't feel like flipping through a couple of hundred unfamiliar names in the yellow pages.

If you are caring for someone else's child, make sure the child's parent or guardian has filled out and signed a **notarized letter** giving you the legal right to authorize medical and surgical treatment. Basically, it should say, "So-and-So has the right to authorize medical/surgical treatment after all attempts to reach parents fail." Although, according to one hospital spokesman, "No invasive treatment will be done unless a parent can be notified; in case of a life-threatening emergency, doctors will take responsibility until the parent can be notified." Doctors and lawyers say these forms will "facilitate treatment," even though they may not be legally binding. If you have custodial care of a child with divorced parents, it's wise to get forms from both parents.

If you've never taken a first-aid course or earned a Boy Scout or Girl Scout first-aid badge, pick up a copy of *A Sigh of Relief* by Martin I. Green (Bantam Books). It'll tell you everything you need to know about the most common childhood emergencies and how to treat them.

SAFETY   There are a few general safety precautions that should be discussed ahead of time, and one that especially applies to sightseeing.

If You Become Separated   Discuss with your kids what they should do if they get separated from you during the trip. Some parents dress their kids in bright colors when they're sightseeing. Probably because I put the fear of God in them every time we entered a crowded museum, my kids rarely wandered off for long. The few times they strayed, I heard them before I saw them. You may want to take a tip from preschool groups on field trips and have your very young ones wear a name tag that includes the name and phone number of your hotel.

Fire   When you check into your room, give the kids a little time to settle in before rushing off to an activity. Find the nearest fire exits and discuss the do's and don'ts of fire safety. If there isn't a card in the room describing emergency procedures, ask for one at the front desk. Before turning in, some families pack a small bag or sack with emergency items: a flashlight, extra room key, wallets, and the like. If there's a fire drill in the middle of the night, you'll be good to go in a matter of seconds.

6 Getting the Kids Interested

Successful family vacations don't just happen serendipitously. If you follow these simple guidelines, your family should have a good time and fill several scrapbooks with happy memories:

- Help your children gather information about the nation's capital.
- Plan ahead and allow them input in organizing your sightseeing schedule.
- Think small. Prioritize your sightseeing objectives, leaving time for recreational and spontaneous activities such as chasing squirrels and eating ice cream.

For more detailed information, check out chapter 6.

Preschoolers have probably learned something about Washington, D.C., from watching TV. Supplement their sketchy knowledge by purchasing a basic book about the city and reading it with them nightly. Those old enough to read and write will know it's the home of the president of the United States and they may have heard about the giant panda in the National Zoo. Still, they might badger you with, "Why can't we go to Walt Disney World again instead of dumb old Washington?"

SPECIAL PROJECTS   Of course, as a family vacation destination, Washington is *anything* but boring and yucky. Your mission, should you decide to accept it, is to get your kids so fired up about the impending trip that they probably won't sleep the night before you leave home.

Here are some suggestions to accomplish this end. First, ask them to jot down every time they see or hear something about Washington, D.C., or its residents. If they listen to the radio, watch TV, or pick up a newspaper occasionally for something other than the comics and sports scores, this will be a snap. You can discuss their lists at mealtime and "fill in the blanks." They may shock you and learn the details of the latest government scandal completely on their own.

Again, I suggest that you borrow from your local library or purchase one or more of the many books on Washington to help familiarize your kids with the city. Then they'll be better able to participate in planning the family's sightseeing activities. If they have a say in what they see and do, everyone will have a more enjoyable vacation.

Encourage them to write to the **Washington, D.C., Convention and Visitors Association,** 1212 New York Ave. NW, Washington, DC 20005, for free brochures and maps. They should also read chapter 6 and write down the attractions that most interest them. They can request information about any of the **Smithsonian's** museums by writing to the Public Affairs Office, Smithsonian Institution, Washington, DC 20560 (Attention: *Name of specific museum*), or log on to their Web site: www.si.edu.

Under your supervision, your children can also send away for maps and guidebooks. The widest selection I've ever seen is available at **Travel Books and Language Center,** 4437 Wisconsin Ave. NW (☎ **800/220-2665** or 202/237-1322). Request the catalog, which comes with an order form. They ship worldwide and accept major credit cards. Kids love getting mail.

Washington, D.C.: A Capital Adventure, part of the Video Visits series, is a marvelous 50-minute tape with drop-dead photography and well-paced informative narration. The tape gives a wonderful overview of the city's history and major sightseeing highlights while delivering a sugarcoated mini-lesson in American history and government. It's available for rent at many video stores or by mail order for $24.95 plus $5 shipping (outside the D.C. area) from Travel Books and Language Center (see above). If this doesn't whet your family's travel appetite, nothing will.

7 Getting There

BY PLANE
THE MAJOR AIRLINES

Scheduled domestic airlines flying into Washington's three airports include **Air-Tran** (☎ 800/825-8538), **America West** (☎ 800/235-9292), **American** (☎ 800/433-7300), **Continental** (☎ 800/525-0280), **Delta** (☎ 800/221-1212), **Northwest** (☎ 800/225-2525), **Southwest** (☎ 800/435-9792), **TransWorld Airlines—TWA** (☎ 800/221-2000), **US Airways and US Airways Shuttle** (☎ 800/428-4322), and **United** (☎ 800/241-6522).

For a quarterly guide to flights in and out of National and Dulles, write to **Metropolitan Washington Airports Authority,** P.O. Box 17045, Washington Dulles

International Airport, Washington, DC 20041. To receive a similar guide for BWI, write to **Maryland Aviation Administration,** Marketing and Development, P.O. Box 8766, BWI Airport, MD 21240-0766.

SHUTTLES TO & FROM NEW YORK   The shuttles are convenient because you can just show up, buy a ticket, and hop on the next plane out. But to save money, if you will be traveling at least one way on a Saturday or Sunday, book at least 3 days ahead.

The **Delta Shuttle** (☎ **800/221-1212**), which flies out of La Guardia's Marine Terminal in New York and Washington National Airport, has hourly flights leaving daily on the half hour. To Washington, departures are weekdays from 6:30am to 8:30pm, plus an extra 9pm flight; Saturday from 7:30am to 8:30pm; and Sunday from 8:30am to 8:30pm plus an extra 9pm flight. From Washington to New York, departures are hourly on the half hour from 7:30am to 9:30pm. Because the schedule has been known to change, please call for the latest information.

As we go to press the shuttle is $202 one way with no advance purchase. With a 3-day advance purchase, weekends (all day Saturday and Sunday from 8:30am to 2:30pm) the fare is $60 one way. But before you book your ticket, ask about special advance purchase and promotional fares.

The **US Airways Shuttle** (☎ **800/428-4322**) runs from a separate terminal at La Guardia Airport in New York to Washington National Airport. Weekday departures from New York are hourly from 7am to 9pm Saturday from 7am to 8pm, and Sunday from 9am to 9pm. Washington to New York hourly departures on weekdays and Saturday are from 7am to 9pm and Sunday from 9am to 9pm. Ask about student (12 to 24 years old) and senior (age 62 and over) discounts.

FINDING THE BEST AIRFARE

If you've ever flown, you know there is no such thing as a "typical" or "normal" fare. For every flight there are usually several fares available under three main categories: first class, coach, and discount. Although visitors to Washington benefit from a wide choice of flights, they may grow dizzy deciphering the ever-changing fare structure.

Generally, midweek fares ticketed 21 days or more in advance are the lowest. Holidays are often subject to blackout restrictions, as in "no bargains spoken here." Winter fares are usually lowest and summer fares highest. But, as you know, fare wars spread like swamp fever. Watch for ads announcing special promotions. They pop up unexpectedly throughout the year and can save you big bucks. If you don't qualify for a promotional or other reduced fare, you could pay substantially more for your ticket. To get the most for your travel dollar, plan well in advance and do a bit of comparison shopping by calling the airlines or consulting an accredited travel agent.

Also inquire about money-saving packages that include hotel accommodations, car rentals, tours, and so on, with your airfare.

Consolidators, also known as bucket shops, are a good place to find low fares, but you must expect the most basic seating. Consolidators buy seats in bulk from the airlines and then sell them back to the public at prices below even the airlines' discounted rates. Their small ads usually run in the Sunday travel section at the bottom of the page. Before you pay, however, ask for a confirmation number from the consolidator and then call the airline itself to confirm your seat. Be prepared to book your ticket with a different consolidator—there are many to choose from—if the airline can't confirm your reservation. Also be aware that bucket shop tickets are usually nonrefundable or rigged with stiff cancellation penalties, often as high as

50% to 75% of the ticket price. **Council Travel** (☎ **800/226-8624;** www. counciltravel.com) and **STA Travel** (☎ **800/781-4040;** www.sta.travel.com) cater especially to young travelers, but their bargain basement prices are available to people of all ages. **Travel Bargains** (☎ **800/AIR-FARE;** www.1800airfare.com) was formerly owned by TWA but now offers the deepest discounts on many other airlines, with a four-day advance purchase. Other reliable consolidators include **1-800-FLY-CHEAP** (www.1800flycheap.com); **TFI Tours International** (☎ **800/745-8000** or 212/736-1140), which serves as a clearinghouse for unused seats; or "rebators" such as **Travel Avenue** (☎ **800/333-3335** or 312/876-1116) and the **Smart Traveller** (☎ **800/448-3338** in the U.S., or 305/448-3338), which rebate part of their commissions to you.

The airlines frequently offer special family fares as well. Children under 2 who do not occupy a seat usually travel free and, depending on the airline, various discounts apply to kids between the ages of 2 and 12. If you will be traveling with an infant, toddler, or active preschooler, when you make your reservation, request the seats behind the bulkhead, where you'll have more legroom and they'll have more play room. Many planes have special fittings for bassinets and some will allow you to use your child's car seat. To find out if your particular brand of car seat is approved by the Federal Aviation Administration, request "Child/Infant Safety Seats Acceptable for Use in Aircraft" from the Community and Consumer Liaison Division, APA-400 Federal Aviation Administration, 800 Independence Ave. SW, Washington, DC 20591 (☎ **202/267-3479**). Also ask about special meals for the kids. The worst hamburger or hot dog should taste better than rubbery chicken. If you fly United, ask if the McDonald's Friendly Skies Meals for kids are available on your flight.

THE D.C. AREA'S AIRPORTS

If you're arriving by commercial airline, you will land at one of Washington's three major airports: Washington National, Dulles, or Baltimore–Washington (BWI).

The **"Super Shuttle"** (☎ **800/258-3826** "blue van"; 410/859-0800 in Baltimore) offers door-to-door service between Dulles, Reagan National, and BWI airports and the Metropolitan D.C. area. Shuttles operate on an as-needed basis, usually every 20 minutes or less. Call for pricing, which is based on zip code. To give you an example, the fare from Reagan National Airport to the White House and other downtown hotels is $9 per person. Kids 2 and under ride for free. On arrival, board the Super Shuttle blue van at the airport. Reservations are required 24 hours ahead for transit to the airport.

The **Montgomery Airport Shuttle** (☎ **301/990-6000**) operates from all three airports to D.C., Montgomery County, Maryland, and suburban Virginia 24 hours a day. The fare from Reagan National Airport to downtown Bethesda is $16; to Gaithersburg it's $19. Call at least 3 hours ahead of time to reserve.

WASHINGTON NATIONAL AIRPORT (NATIONAL)   Just across the Potomac River in Virginia, it is about a 15- to 30-minute taxi ride from downtown in nonrush-hour traffic; less via Metro, depending on where you're staying. It is the most convenient airport to downtown, but also the most congested.

After a 10-year, $1 billion renovation, the airport unveiled its new face in July 1997. As part of the massive project, new approach roads were built, old ones were rehabilitated.

A new glass-and-steel main terminal has 35 gates. The Cesar Pelli–designed terminal is a stunner, with 54 skylighted domes and a five-story glass wall overlooking the Potomac River. My sources tell me the view from Gate 43 is primo.

CyberDeals for Net Surfers

It's possible to get some great deals on airfare, hotels, and car rentals via the Internet. So go grab your mouse and start surfing—you could save a bundle on your trip. The Web sites we've highlighted below are worth checking out, especially since all the services are free.

Microsoft Expedia (www.expedia.com)   The best part of this multipurpose travel site is the "Fare Tracker": You fill out a form on the screen indicating that you're interested in cheap flights to wherever from your hometown and once a week they'll e-mail you the best airfare deals. The site's "Travel Agent" will steer you to bargains on hotels and car rentals, and you can book everything, including flights, right on line. This site is even useful once you're booked: Before you go, log on to Expedia for oodles of up-to-date travel information, including weather reports and foreign exchange rates.

Preview Travel (www.reservations.com and www.vacations.com)   Another useful travel site, "Reservations.com" has a "Best Fare Finder" that will search the Apollo computer reservations system for the three lowest fares for any route on any days of the year. Just fill out the form on the screen with times, dates, and destinations, and within minutes Preview will show you the best deals. If you find an airfare you like, you can book your ticket right on-line—you can even reserve hotels and car rentals on this site. If you're in the preplanning stage, head to Preview's "Vacations.com" site, where you can check out the latest package deals for D.C. and other destinations around the world by clicking on "Hot Deals."

Travelocity (www.travelocity.com)   This is one of the best travel sites out there. In addition to its "Personal Fare Watcher," which notifies you via e-mail of the lowest airfares for up to five different destinations, Travelocity will track the three lowest fares for any routes on any dates in minutes. You can book a flight right then and there, and if you need a rental car or hotel, Travelocity will find you the best deal via the SABRE computer reservations system, a huge database used by travel agents worldwide. Click on "Last Minute Deals" for the latest travel bargains, including a link to "H.O.T. Coupons" (**www.hotcoupons.com**), where you can print out electronic coupons for travel in the United States and Canada, including Hawaii.

Metro accessibility was greatly improved (it could only get better!), and covered pedestrian bridges now connect the Metro station and the terminal. Thank heavens, the 15-minute hikes to Metro are now history. Of course, the best parking spaces—112 of them right next to the terminal—are reserved for VIPs.

In the vast commercial space, 40 shops, 25 eateries, and 30 retail carts vie for travelers' wallets. There's even a meditation room near the baggage claim area, so you can compose yourself if your flight out is canceled or delayed.

It remains to be seen whether the airport will be more successful than it was in the past in meeting its primary mission: to transport passengers safely and efficiently. Despite the airport's pretty new face, there are still only three runways (and short ones at that) on the 90-acre site. Call me a skeptic, but I'll stick with BWI. For airport information, call ☎ **703/419-8000.**

Trip.Com (www.thetrip.com)   This site is really geared toward the business traveler, but vacationers-to-be can also use Trip.Com's valuable fare-finding engine, which will e-mail you every week with the best city-to-city airfare deals on your selected route or routes.

Discount Tickets (www.discount-tickets.com)   Operated by the ETN (European Travel Network), this site offers discounts on airfares, accommodations, car rentals, and tours. It deals in flights between the United States and other countries, not domestic U.S. flights, so it's most useful for travelers coming to D.C. from abroad.

E-Savers Programs   Several major airlines offer a free e-mail service known as **E-Savers,** via which they'll send you their best bargain airfares on a weekly basis. Here's how it works: Once a week (usually Wednesday) subscribers receive a list of discounted flights to and from various destinations, both international and domestic. Now here's the catch: These fares are only available if you leave the very next Saturday (or sometimes Friday night) and return on the following Monday or Tuesday. It's really a service for the spontaneously inclined and travelers looking for a quick getaway (if you are traveling with kids, this may not be the site for you). But the fares are cheap, so it's worth taking a look. If you have a preference for certain airlines (in other words, the ones you fly most frequently), sign up with them first. Another caveat: You'll get frequent-flier miles if you purchase one of these fares, but you can't use miles to buy the ticket.

Here's a list of airlines and their Web sites, where you can get on the e-mail lists as well as book flights directly:

American Airlines: www.americanair.com

Continental Airlines: www.flycontiental.com

TWA: www.twa.com

Northwest Airlines: www.nwa.com

US Airways: www.usairways.com

Epicurious Travel (travel.epicurious.com), another good travel site, allows you to sign up for all of these airline e-mail lists at once.

—Jeanette Foster

Shuttle service is provided by some hotels. Check to see if yours is one of them. A taxi from National to downtown Washington, D.C., should cost about $15. Trains on **Metro's Blue and Yellow lines** stop at National. Metro is the quickest way to get to many locations in the District and beyond since local roads are notoriously bottlenecked. Count on a 15- to 20-minute ride into D.C. To help you, maps, fares, and traveling times are posted at every stop. Trains run Monday through Thursday and Sunday from 5:30am to midnight and Friday and Saturday from 8am to 1am (☎ **202/637-7000** from 6am to 11:30pm).

The Super Shuttle (☎ **800/258-3826**) departs Reagan National every 20 to 30 minutes for D.C. Hotels. The fare is $9 per person. You must make a reservation, however, for the return trip to the airport.

The **Washington Flyer** (☎ **800/258-3826** or 703/685-1400) provides daily bus service between National Airport and several downtown hotels. During the week there are two departures per hour from 6:05am to 10:35pm. Call ahead for weekend and holiday schedules, when service is less frequent The all-inclusive one-way fare is $8; round-trip is $14. Kids under 6 ride free; families of three or more, $6 per adult.

WASHINGTON DULLES INTERNATIONAL AIRPORT (DULLES)   Located in Chantilly, Virginia, a 35- to 45-minute ride to downtown D.C. in nonrush-hour traffic. Construction on the main I. M. Pei–designed terminal to double its size was completed in 1996. A second midfield terminal opened early in 1998; a third is on the drawing board. The building of a wider, more efficient road system is nearly complete. For airport information, call ☎ **703/419-8000;** www.wmaa.com.

A taxi from Dulles to downtown Washington costs from $40 to $45. The **Washington Flyer Shuttle** (☎ **703/685-1400**) is designed primarily for business travelers and provides daily bus service between Dulles to several downtown hotels and the convention center. Buses leave Dulles for downtown Washington daily. Monday through Friday departures are every 30 minutes at 15 and 45 minutes past the hour from 6:15 to 10:15pm. On Saturday, Sunday, and holidays, departures are at 20 minutes past the hour from 5:20am to 12:20pm, then at 20 and 50 minutes past the hour until 10:20pm. The all-inclusive price is $16 one-way, $26 round-trip. Children 6 and under ride free.

The **Super Shuttle** (☎ **800/258-3826**) serves downtown D.C. from Dulles (also from BWI and Reagan National). The fare from Dulles to the J. W. Marriott, for example, is $20 for the first person, $10 for each additional. Vans hold up to 7 persons, and you can rent an entire van for $65. Vans depart the airport on demand, about every 20 to 30 minutes. Travel is by reservations only to the airport. Check the Web site: www.supershuttle.com.

BALTIMORE–WASHINGTON INTERNATIONAL AIRPORT (BWI)   BWI is a few miles south of Baltimore, Maryland, and about a 45-minute ride from downtown Washington. It, too, has undergone massive renovation; road improvement and expanded parking make BWI the most user-friendly of the three airports serving Washington. Take your pick, but don't say I didn't warn you.

BWI sports a two-level observation gallery, with computerized interactive displays and a Smithsonian Museum Shop. If you have time to kill, this is a great place to do it. Sink into one of the comfortable leatherette chairs in front of the 147-foot-wide window, where you can marvel at the takeoffs and landings. By punching a flight number into one of the computer displays, your kids can learn the altitude, speed, and location of the plane of their choice.

Taxi fare from BWI to downtown Washington is about $50 per family. Super Shuttle from BWI to downtown D.C. (Marriott) is $28 for first person, $5 for each additional person. Departures are every 20 to 30 minutes. Reservations are needed for return to the airport. The **Airport Connection** (☎ **800/284-6066** or 301/261-1000) operates a door-to-door van service between BWI and Washington, D.C., Prince George's County, Maryland, and Montgomery County, Maryland; a minimum of 24 hours' notice is suggested. For a family of four, the fare will be $55. Train service is available daily on **Amtrak** (☎ **800/USA-RAIL**) and weekdays on **MARC** (☎ **800/325-RAIL**) at the **BWI Rail Station,** 5 minutes from the airport. A **courtesy shuttle** runs between the airport and the train station weekdays between 5:20am and 11:30pm. Weekend service may be less regular.

INTERAIRPORT TRANSFERS

An **Interairport Express** bus operates daily between Dulles and National. Departures from Dulles are Monday through Friday on the hour from 5am to 11pm; Saturday, Sunday, and holidays every 2 hours between 5 and 11am, every hour between 1 and 11pm (*Note:* no noon bus). From National to Dulles, buses depart Monday through Friday on the hour from 6am to 11pm; Saturday, Sunday, and holidays every 2 hours from 6am to noon, every hour from 1 to 11pm. The ride is 45 minutes under optimum conditions. The fare is $16 one way, $26 round-trip. Kids 6 and under ride free.

FOOD PRICES AT THE AIRPORT

Be forewarned: If hunger strikes in any of the area airports, you'll be a captive audience and will pay dearly. Prices are often at least 20% higher than they would be at the same restaurants off airport premises. So, when flying into the nation's capital, you may want to consider a brown bag from home.

BY CAR

Most visitors arrive in Washington by car. Although a car is necessary if you wish to take excursions to many points outside the city, it can be a real liability in the downtown area. You might want to consider leaving the car at home and renting one for day trips outside the city.

Washington's streets are congested and its drivers—many of whom learned to drive elsewhere or not at all—follow many different rules of the road. The result can be less than pleasant. In addition, parking in most sectors is expensive or nonexistent. (At some hotels, parking is included in the room rate. Find out ahead, or you may be unpleasantly surprised by having to shell out up to $15 a day. Also ask if there is a reparking charge every time you use the car.) If your sightseeing plans are restricted to the city and close-in environs, leave the family buggy at home; you'll have a far better time. The District's efficient subway system will transport your brood to within a short walk of all the major attractions.

Like it or not, whether you are arriving from the north (I-270, I-95, I-295), south (I-95, Route 1, Route 301), east (Route 50/301, Route 450), or west (Route 7, Route 50, I-66, Route 29/211), you will run into the **Capital Beltway** (hereinafter known as the **Beltway**). This 66-mile road encircles Washington, D.C., and has 56 interchanges that intersect with all the major approach routes to the city. Sometimes more than 600,000 cars per day travel the Beltway, and gridlock is not uncommon, especially between 7 and 9am and 3 and 7pm. The eastern segment of the Beltway is part of I-95, which joins Baltimore, Maryland, to the north and Richmond, Virginia, to the south. To confuse you, the rest is designated I-495, but mercifully dual I-495/I-95 signs are posted. Before you leave home, study a map; make sure you have directions from the intersection of the Beltway and whichever interstate or road you will be traveling to your destination. To further challenge those driving into the D.C. metropolitan area, Maryland's exits correspond to the nearest milepost. Virginia's are numbered consecutively. Go figure. People have been known to drive the entire 66 miles of the Beltway before realizing that they've missed their exit. You don't want to spend your vacation this way; there's no room service and not much of a view.

North of the city, **I-270** links the Maryland suburbs with **I-70** at Frederick. To the southwest, **I-66** and **U.S. 50** connect with the Virginia segment of **I-495.** If you're a member of **AAA,** request a Trip-Tik and other pertinent information (☎ **800/222-4357** or 703/222-6000) before you depart.

To help you plan your car trip, some approximate driving distances (in miles) from several cities follow.

Atlanta	634	Montréal	544
Boston	471	Miami	1,070
Chicago	712	New York	236
Los Angeles	2,727	Pittsburgh	251

BY TRAIN

Amtrak offers daily service to Washington from several East Coast, Midwest, and West Coast cities. Travelers from the far West change trains in Chicago or New Orleans. At the end of 1999, Amtrak unveiled its high-speed Acela trains, which travel as fast as 150 miles per hour, along the Northeast Corridor, linking Boston, New York, and Washington. The Acela cuts up to 30 minutes off the usual 4-hour ride between New York and Washington, and as much as an hour off the trip between Boston and Washington.

Disabled passengers are entitled to a 25% reduction on regular one-way coach fares. Disabled children between the ages of 2 and 15 can travel for 50% of the disabled adult fare. The discount does not apply to the Metroliner.

The cheapest one-way fare between New York and Washington is $64 for an unreserved seat at off-peak times. At peak times, the fare is $79. Bear in mind that some weekend and holiday blackouts may apply, so check when you call for scheduling information. On the faster, more streamlined Metroliner, with reserved seating, the fare is $115 (Monday to Friday) or $93 (weekends).

Between Boston and Washington the one-way unreserved fare is $65; Friday and Sunday between 11am and 11pm it jumps to $82. Between Chicago and Washington all seats are reserved, and the lowest fare is $92; the highest is $113. Ask about special All-Aboard fares and promotions. As you probably guessed, sleeping accommodations are extra. Kids up to 15 pay half the adult rate when accompanied by a fare-paying passenger 18 or older. Every adult passenger is allowed two children's fare tickets. For information and reservations, call Amtrak (☎ 800/872-7245). Seniors 62 and older are entitled to a 15% discount. AAA members get a 10% discount. Call for details.

Amtrak also offers **Great American Vacations** (☎ 800/321-8684), a plan whereby travelers arrive by rail and return by United Airlines.

If you arrive by Amtrak, your first glimpse of Washington will be **Union Station,** at Massachusetts Avenue NE and North Capitol Street, a stone's throw from the U.S. Capitol. The kids may want to spend their entire vacation here. No doubt they'll have a swell time at the food court, movies, shops, and restaurants. There's Metro service right in the building, and taxis are plentiful. MARC (Maryland Rural Commuter System) and Virginia Railway Express arrive and depart from here, too. The grand scale of Union Station does much to heighten the excitement of arrival.

Many Amtrak trains also stop at the **New Carrollton Station** in Lanham, Maryland, about 10 minutes by rail and 20 minutes by car from Union Station. Long-term parking is available at New Carrollton. If you're staying in the Maryland suburbs, this may be more convenient than Union Station.

Kids usually enjoy train travel because it's less confining than a car or plane, and it's fun visiting the snack bar. You may want to consider giving your children a food allowance to last the entire trip so they don't bug you every few minutes. Also, Amtrak is not known for its snack bar cuisine. What worked best when my kids were younger was bringing sandwiches from home and letting them buy drinks and snacks.

Maryland Rural Commuter System (MARC) operates trains between Union Station in Washington, BWI Airport, and downtown Baltimore on Monday through Friday (☎ **800/325-RAIL**).

Between New York and Washington, Amtrak (which has stations in New Jersey, Pennsylvania, Delaware, and Maryland) is still the most efficient means of transportation, despite some disappointments.

BY BUS

Greyhound buses connect just about the entire country with Washington, D.C. They pull in at a terminal at 1st and L streets NE (☎ **800/231-2222;** www.greyhound.com). The closest Metro station is Union Station, 4 blocks away. The bus terminal area is not what you'd call a showplace neighborhood, so a taxi is advisable.

If you're staying in the suburbs, note that Greyhound also has service to Silver Spring, Maryland, and Arlington and Springfield, Virginia.

When you call to make your reservation, be sure to ask about advance purchase or supersaver fares, especially during the summer months. In fall 1999, the lowest one-way fare between New York City and Washington, D.C., was $35; between Chicago and Washington, $78. The good news is that when you call Greyhound, they'll always give you the lowest fare options. Since some discount fares require advance purchase, always call ahead.

8 Keeping the Kids Entertained While Traveling

Keeping kids entertained while traveling can be a challenge, especially if the trip is long and they are cold, hot, hungry, tired, restless, or just plain ornery. So pack a few age-appropriate toys, games, artsy-craftsy items, and books. If you're traveling with toddlers, be sure to bring their favorite stuffed animal or security blanket. Between naps and feedings, a couple of small dolls or toys without sharp edges should amuse a wee one—that and climbing all over everything within a 6-mile radius. I've heard that the motion of riding in a car, train, or plane lulls little children to sleep. Unfortunately, my kids didn't know this until they were about three years old, so if this doesn't work, try bribing them with a snack or toy, then turn up the volume on your headset and tough it out.

School-age kids might be easier to deal with and are usually content with a bag of crayons, colored pencils, or nonpermanent markers and plenty of paper. Depending on the child's age, supplement the art supplies with some of the following: books, magnetic games, Colorforms, write-and-wipe boards, cassette tapes, travel-size board games, and a deck of cards. Forget jigsaw puzzles and games with lots of little pieces. If they're really bored, you can always regale them with a story about your youth. Guaranteed they'll fall asleep in 2 minutes.

Interest older kids in starting a travel diary. All it takes is a blank notebook and pen. Traveling with teenagers? You don't have to entertain them. You're not even supposed to act like you know them. They'll probably be hooked up to some kind of offensive noise before you've backed out of the driveway.

You may want to borrow or rent age-appropriate books on tape for your trip. I can't think of a better or more worthwhile way to keep youngsters (and parents) entertained (and quiet) during a long trip. You may want to pick up *Kids Travel,* a book filled with games, craft kits, and other time-fillers for kids over 6.

Let kids pack their own entertainment bag or backpack. They'll learn to be selective if you limit what they can bring, either by the number of items or tonnage.

Even if you forget the crayons, books, and video games, you'll be forgiven if you have food. Don't travel *anywhere* without food, even if you're just driving from Baltimore. Easily stowable snacks such as nuts, fruit, pretzels or chips, yogurt, and juice will keep a hungry or irritable crew from mutiny. Eating gives everyone something to do and helps pass the time. This is no time to count calories. You're on vacation. If there's a chance you'll miss a meal en route (and who among us has traveled and not missed a meal?), take sandwiches. They don't have to be fancy but, believe me, your family will think you're Mother Teresa for remembering. Pack perishables in a small plastic cooler and toss in some of those cute little artificial ice cubes. Oh, and don't forget paper towels and moist towelettes for quick cleanups.

Getting to Know Washington, D.C.

2

Welcome! You and your family are about to embark on an adventure in one of the most inspiring and captivating cities in the world. The nation's capital is distinguished by an eclectic style, where Old South mixes with high-tech, marble and granite blend with cherry blossoms and magnolias, ethnic festivals meld with presidential inaugurals, and the nation's history bumps noses with tomorrow's headlines. Have fun discovering with your children the many facets of this enchanting and enigmatic city.

1 Orientation

IMPORTANT INFORMATION RESOURCES

The White House Visitors Center, at 1450 Pennsylvania Ave. NW, in the Herbert Hoover Building of the Commerce Department (☎ **202/208-1631**), has brochures and maps listing attractions, activities, restaurants, and accommodations, and also distributes tickets for White House tours. It is open daily from 7:30am to 4pm, sometimes with extended summer hours. Also check the front section of the Bell Atlantic telephone book Yellow Pages, available at most (if not all) hotels. The more than 30 pages of valuable information and maps will help you get your bearings. For information on Maryland, call ☎ **800/543-1036.** Virginia has a tourism office at 1629 K St. NW (☎ **202/872-0523**). Hours are 8:30am to 5pm Monday through Friday.

If you need help sorting out mixed-up tickets, retrieving lost baggage, or locating lost family members, the **Travelers Aid Society** will come to the rescue. Besides maintaining desks at all the airports and Union Station, a central office at 512 C St. NE is open weekdays from 9am to 5pm. An emergency phone line operates 24 hours a day (☎ **202/546-3120**).

To find out what's going on day by day, see Washington's two daily newspapers, the *Washington Post* (the Thursday "Weekly" section and Friday "Weekend" magazine are especially helpful) and the *Washington Times. City Paper,* a spirited weekly, is published every Thursday and is available at downtown shops and restaurants. *Jewish Week* comes out every Thursday. If you're staying in the suburbs, the Friday *Journal* newspapers (no relation to the *Wall Street Journal*) are chockablock with things to do and see.

Washington, D.C. at a Glance

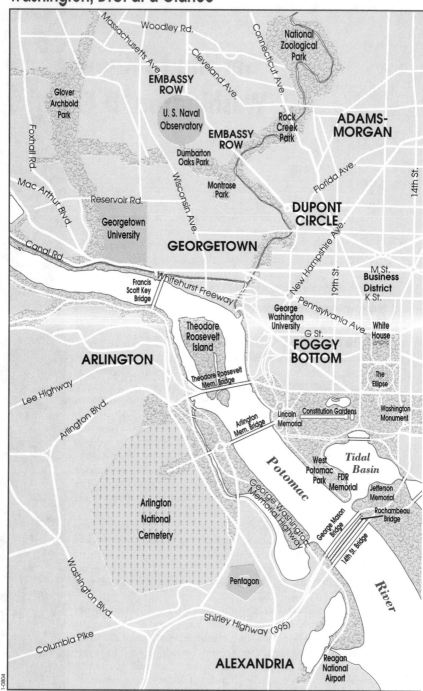

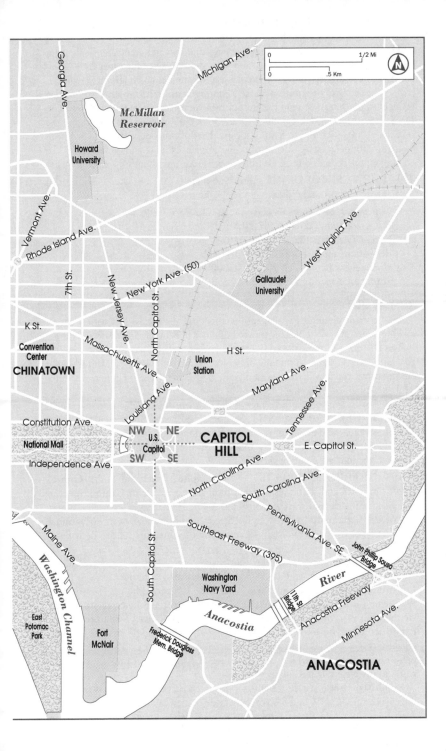

The *Washingtonian,* a popular monthly magazine, lists area events, previews major happenings, and reviews restaurants; also look for *Washington Flyer* magazine (available free at the airports) and *Here!* (available at downtown hotels and newsstands).

For a free copy of the Smithsonian's **"Planning Your Smithsonian Visit,"** which is full of valuable tips, write to the Smithsonian Information Center, 1000 Jefferson Dr. SW, Washington, DC 20560 (☎ **202/357-2700;** www.si.edu), or stop at the "Castle," 1000 Jefferson Dr. SW, for a copy. The Information Center is open from 9am to 5:30pm daily. A calendar of Smithsonian exhibits and activities for the coming month appears during the third week of each month in the *Washington Post.*

TELEPHONE RECORDINGS *(Note:* Washington's 202 area code is not needed if you are in D.C.) Local calls are 35¢.

>Convention & Visitors Association (☎ **202/789-7000**)
>Dial-a-Museum (☎ **202/357-2020**)
>National Archives (☎ **202/501-5402**)
>Recreation and Parks (☎ **202/673-7660**)
>Skywatcher's Report (☎ **202/357-2000**)
>Tourist Information (☎ **202/789-7038**)

CITY LAYOUT

The District of Columbia is shaped like a baseball diamond—but with a chunk missing, as if someone took a big bite out of the field between third base and home.

The District was originally laid out on a grid, and if you pay attention to a few general rules, you should have little difficulty finding your way around. It will help enormously if you consult the "Washington, D.C., at a Glance" map in this chapter while digesting the following.

The U.S. Capitol marks the center of the city, which is divided into quadrants: **Northeast (NE), Northwest (NW), Southeast (SE),** and **Southwest (SW).** All addresses are followed by one of the four designations. Pay attention to them, as the same address can (and often does) appear in all four quadrants of the city. Most tourist attractions are either in the NW or SW quadrants.

MAIN ARTERIES & STREETS   **North Capitol Street** and **South Capitol Street** run north and south, respectively, from the Capitol. **East Capitol Street**—you guessed it—divides the city north and south. Here the plot thickens. Where you would expect to find a West Capitol Street lies the area known as the **National Mall.** The north side of the Mall is Constitution Avenue; the south side is Independence Avenue.

Lettered streets above and below (north and south if you prefer) East Capitol Street run east and west and are named **alphabetically,** beginning with A Street. Just to keep things interesting, there is no B or J Street, although Constitution Avenue on the north side of the Mall and Independence Avenue on the south side are the equivalent of B Street. I understand L'Enfant omitted J Street because the I and J too closely resembled each other in old-style printing. After W Street, one-syllable, two-syllable, and three-syllable street names come into play. There are many exceptions, but don't lose sleep over them. Chances are your travels won't take you into three-syllable territory very often.

Numbered streets run north and south, so, theoretically at least, there's a 1st Street (NE and SE; NW and SW) on either side of the Capitol. Here comes the fun part. Radiating from the Capitol, like so many wheel spokes, are a bunch of **avenues** bearing state names. They slice diagonally through the numbered and lettered streets, creating a host of circles and sometimes havoc. If you're new in town,

it is possible to drive several times around these circles before finding the continu-
ation of the street you were on.

The primary artery is **Pennsylvania Avenue,** scene of parades, inaugurations,
and other splashy events. Pennsylvania runs between the Capitol and the White
House. In the original plan, the president was supposed to have an uninterrupted
view of the Capitol Building from the White House. But Andrew Jackson placed
the Treasury Building between the White House and the Capitol, blocking off the
presidential vista. Pennsylvania Avenue continues on a northwest trajectory from
the White House to Georgetown.

Pennsylvania Avenue between 15th and 17th streets NW, fronting the White
House, has been closed to cars for security reasons since 1995. To handle the traffic
snarls caused by the 2-block closing, H Street is one way eastbound between 13th
and 19th streets NW; I Street is one way westbound between 11th and 21st streets
NW. If you're driving, good luck—you'll need it.

Constitution Avenue parallels **Independence Avenue** to the south. It runs east-
west, flanking the U.S. Capitol and the Mall with its many major museums (and
important government buildings to the north and south), the Washington Monument, the Ellipse, and the White House (to the north), and continues on past the
Reflecting Pool to the Lincoln Memorial and the Potomac River. Until the late
1800s, when Tiber Creek ran through town (down what is now Constitution
Avenue) to meet the Potomac, the entire area was a malaria-infested swamp. You
can be sure they had trouble drawing the tourists then. In fact, they had trouble
drawing anyone, and D.C. was considered a hard-luck post. For many politicians,
it still is.

Washington's longest avenue, **Massachusetts Avenue,** runs north of and parallel
to Pennsylvania Avenue. Along the way you'll find Union Station, Dupont Circle,
and Embassy Row. Farther out are the Naval Observatory (the vice president's residence is on the premises), Washington National Cathedral, and American University. Then Massachusetts Avenue just keeps going, right into Maryland.

Connecticut Avenue, running more directly north, starts at Lafayette Square
near the White House. Heading north, it cuts through Dupont Circle and Rock
Creek Park, past the National Zoo's main entrance, through a mostly residential
neighborhood, and on well into suburban Maryland. It's the city's equivalent to
New York's Fifth Avenue, the boulevard lined with elegant eateries, shops, hotels,
and high-rise apartment buildings.

Wisconsin Avenue, from the point where it crosses M Street, creates Georgetown's main intersection. Antique shops, trendy boutiques, discos, restaurants, and
pubs all vie for attention. Yet, on the side streets, lined with lovely Georgian and Federal homes, Georgetown manages to maintain its almost European charm. Wisconsin Avenue continues into Chevy Chase and Bethesda, Maryland. In Rockville it
becomes Rockville Pike/Route 355. Farther north it is Frederick Avenue/Route 355.

FINDING AN ADDRESS   Finding an address in Washington, D.C., is easy,
once you get the hang of it. In any four-digit address, the first two digits indicate
the nearest lower-numbered cross street. For example, 1750 K Street NW is
between 17th and 18th streets in the northwest quadrant of the city. In a three-digit
address, look at the first digit. A restaurant at 620 H Street NW would be between
6th and 7th streets.

Finding an address on a numbered street is a little stickier. Your kids may want
to remove their socks when they run out of fingers in this exercise. Suppose you're
looking for 808 17th Street NW. First, assume that the addresses between A and B

streets are numbered in the 100s, between B and C in the 200s, C and D in the 300s, and so on. Following this line of reasoning, the first digit in 808 signifies eight letters or blocks away from A Street. I am not making this up, so start counting! If you come up with H, you're a winner, as 808 17th Street is between H and I streets. This will become a game to your kids, who will find your destination while you're still deciding if you're in SW or NW. When they were youngsters, my own kids thought I made this up. They had their own method for finding their way around D.C., and you may want to try it. Repeat these two magic words, "Where is?" Works like a charm.

The Neighborhoods in Brief

To help you get acquainted with the city, the following alphabetical rundown will give you a fix on Washington's major sightseeing areas.

Adams–Morgan　Centered around 18th Street and Columbia Road NW, colorful, vibrant, multiethnic Adams–Morgan is host to many international shops, restaurants, and music clubs. Whether you hunger for Ethiopian, Italian, Latin American, or any other cuisine that comes to mind, family appetites will be well satisfied. You'll encounter fewer briefcases and button-down shirts and minds here than in any other sector of the city. Parking, however, is a problem, especially on weekends. Although the 15- to 20-minute walk from the nearest Metro is fine in nice weather, I don't recommend it after dark. Be safe and take a taxi.

Capitol Hill　Known affectionately as "the Hill," this area encompasses much more than the awe-inspiring U.S. Capitol. Bounded by the western side of the Capitol to the west, H Street NE to the north, RFK Stadium to the east, and the Southwest Freeway to the south, it is home to the Library of Congress, the Folger Shakespeare Library, Union Station, the U.S. Botanic Garden (closed until the year 2000), and the Capital Children's Museum. The restaurants are especially kid-friendly.

Convention Center　There are few sights around here. It's mostly businesses and hotels in one of D.C.'s less attractive areas. It is, however, convenient to Metro Center (transfer station for all lines), within walking distance of the FBI Building, Chinatown, Ford's Theatre, and numerous restaurants. Several large hotels serve the businesspeople in town for events at the convention center.

Downtown　Critics like to argue that Washington has no downtown. See for yourself. The area is centered around Connecticut Avenue and K Street NW and extends east to about 7th Street, west to 22nd Street, north to P Street, and south to Pennsylvania Avenue. The heart of the business community beats here, and you'll find such diverse attractions as the White House, downtown department stores and shops, Chinatown, the Convention Center, street vendors hawking everything from soft pretzels to designer knockoffs, and many of the city's finest restaurants. Within this parcel you'll find the New Downtown (7th Street between E and I), where many of the city's art spaces and trendy eateries are located.

Dupont Circle　Dupont Circle (the neighborhood) surrounds Dupont Circle (the traffic circle and park). The park—and by extension the neighborhood—is distinguished by an abundance of squirrels and pigeons, young people with multipierced body parts, and ongoing chess games between seniors. Radiating from the intersection of Connecticut and Massachusetts avenues NW lies an area colored by the many artistic types and free spirits who reside there. Several of the city's better-known art galleries, diverse restaurants, boutiques, and bookstores abound. It's a great place for browsing and people-watching.

Foggy Bottom   An industrial center in the 18th century, Foggy Bottom lies west of the White House and stretches about 10 blocks to the foot of Georgetown. Pennsylvania Avenue and Constitution Avenue are its northern and southern perimeters. The area is villagelike, with turn-of-the-century (that is, 18th to 19th century!) homes with postage-size gardens fronting brick-walked, tree-lined streets. Foggy Bottom derives much of its panache and international flavor from the State Department, Kennedy Center for the Performing Arts, and George Washington University.

Georgetown   Long a favorite tourist draw, this bustling enclave that was once a prosperous tobacco port radiates from the intersection of Wisconsin Avenue and M Street NW. The population of about 11,000 swells nearly threefold on weekends. Georgetown's riverfront setting, Federal and Victorian architecture, boutiques, and wealth of restaurants draw visitors of all ages. Sightseeing attractions include the C & O Canal, the pre-Revolutionary Old Stone House, and magnificent Dumbarton Oaks Gardens and Museum. On this picturesque parcel you'll find the Washington Harbor Complex with outdoor restaurants and a scenic promenade. The Georgetown University campus perches on a hill in the western corner of this vibrant neighborhood. Walking, biking, or renting a boat on the canal are all popular warm-weather respites.

The Mall   Your kids will think you're crazy when you tell them they can't buy anything at this "Mall." They can, however, visit several of the Smithsonian museums and galleries, the Lincoln Memorial, Washington Monument, Vietnam and Korean War Veterans Memorials, and take a ride on an antique carousel. This lush parklike rectangle between the Capitol and Lincoln Memorial attracts kite fliers, joggers, Frisbee-tossers, in-line skaters, and picnickers.

2 Getting Around

BY PUBLIC TRANSPORTATION

Getting around Washington is child's play, with one glaring exception: Unless you absolutely have to, don't drive in D.C. If you don't swallow anything else in this guidebook, please accept on blind faith (and my nearly 40 years of living in the area) that you'll waste precious time crawling through Washington's heavily trafficked downtown streets. There is little commercial parking in the Smithsonian/ Mall area, and when it's available, it's very expensive. Washington's Metrorail subway system is so reliable, efficient, clean, and quiet (it's even carpeted!) that your kids may want to spend their whole visit riding underground. Many of the major sightseeing attractions stand shoulder to shoulder on the Mall, so your own feet are often the best means of getting around. And walking is the one sure way to savor small unexpected sights and pleasures that you might otherwise miss.

DISCOUNT PASSES   For $5 per person, Metro offers a **1-Day Rail pass.** This is a good deal! It can be used after 9:30am weekdays and all day Saturday and Sunday. You can purchase the pass at any station or at the Washington Metropolitan Area Transit Authority, 600 5th St. NW (☎ **202/637-7000**). Kids 4 and under always ride free on Metro. Senior citizens (65 and older) and handicapped persons with valid proof ride Metrorail and Metrobus for a reduced fare.

BY SUBWAY   Metrorail (Metro) is Washington's subway system. Longtime Washington residents will tell you that the quality of life vastly improved when

Metro Stops in Georgetown & Downtown

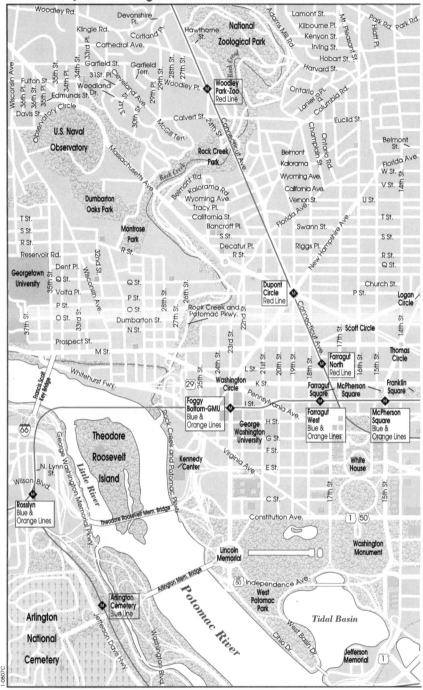

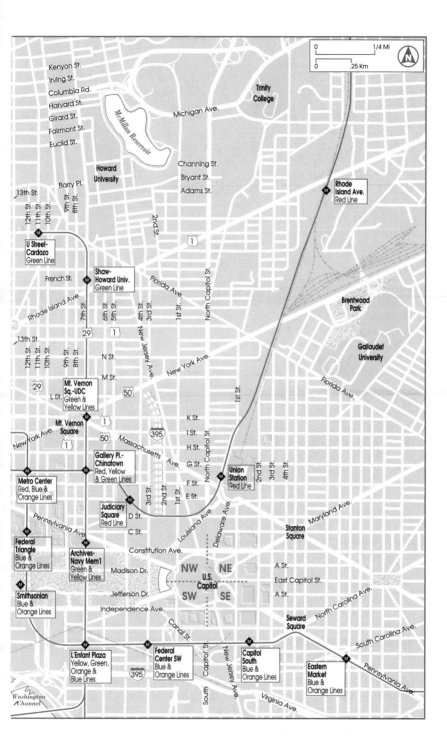

0 | 1/4 Mi
0 | .25 Km

Kenyon St.
Irving St.
Columbia Rd.
Harvard St.
Girard St.
Fairmont St.
Euclid St.

McMillan Reservoir

Michigan Ave.

Trinity College

Howard University

Channing St.
Bryant St.
Adams St.

Rhode Island Ave.
Red Line

Barry Pl.

13th St.
12th St.
11th St.
10th St.
9th St.
8th St.

2nd St.

U Street-Cardozo
Green Line

French St.

Shaw-Howard Univ.
Green Line

Florida Ave.

Brentwood Park

Rhode Island Ave.

6th St.
5th St.
4th St.
3rd St.
1st St.

North Capitol St.

Gallaudet University

13th St.
12th St.
11th St.
10th St.
9th St.
8th St.
7th St.

N St.

New Jersey Ave.

New York Ave.

Florida Ave.

M St.

Mt. Vernon Sq.-UDC
Green & Yellow Lines

L St.

Mt. Vernon Square

K St.
I St.
H St.
G St.
F St.
E St.

1st St.

Gallery Pl.-Chinatown
Red, Yellow & Green Lines

Massachusetts Ave.

North Capitol St.

Union Station
Red Line

2nd St.
3rd St.
4th St.

New York Ave.

Metro Center
Red, Blue & Orange Lines

Judiciary Square
Red Line

3rd St.
2nd St.
1st St.

D St.
C St.

Pennsylvania Ave.

Louisiana Ave.

Delaware Ave.

Stanton Square

Maryland Ave.

Federal Triangle
Blue & Orange Lines

Archives-Navy Mem'l
Green & Yellow Lines

Constitution Ave.

Madison Dr.

NW | NE
U.S. Capitol
SW | SE

A St.
East Capitol St.
A St.

Smithsonian
Blue & Orange Lines

Jefferson Dr.

Independence Ave.

North Carolina Ave.

Canal St.

Seward Square

South Carolina Ave.

Washington Channel

L'Enfant Plaza
Yellow, Green, Orange & Blue Lines

Federal Center SW
Blue & Orange Lines

Capitol St.

New Jersey Ave.

Capitol South
Blue & Orange Lines

Eastern Market
Blue & Orange Lines

Pennsylvania Ave.

South Capitol St.

Virginia Ave.

35

Metro began operating in 1976. The system's more than 100 miles of track blanket the metropolitan area, reaching deeply into the Maryland and Virginia suburbs. The cars, surprisingly graffiti-free, are streamlined and attractive with air-conditioning and comfortable upholstered seats. For a view of the operator's compartment, kids can sit in the front window seat of the first car, where they'll be able to note the train's speed and eye the control panel.

You can forget the shrill, grinding noises you may have endured in other cities' subways. Metro is quiet. With stations just 2 or 3 minutes apart, you're never more than a short walk from all the major attractions. Metro was designed with safety in mind. There are no dark nooks and crannies in the stations to shelter criminals, and Metro Transit Police (MTP) constantly monitor and patrol the trains and stations. Late nighters were happy when, in September 1999, Metro extended the weekend hours to 1am. By the time you read this it could be 2am.

Even if you have no reason to ride Metro during your visit, invent one for the kids' sake. It's definitely one of life's kinder, gentler rides. When riding the escalator, I urge you to stand in the center of the step and hold your child's hand, and don't allow your youngster to sit on the step. Unattended kids are accidents waiting to happen, and unfortunately they occasionally do.

Pick up a Pocket Guide in any station and tuck it in your backpack or use it as a bookmark for easy retrieval. Call with your questions (☎ **202/637-7000**) or go to www.wmata.com.

The five Metro lines **Red, Blue, Orange, Yellow,** and **Green**—operate Monday through Friday from 5:30am to midnight, and Saturday and Sunday from 8am to midnight. Even though talk is cheap, especially in Washington, there is a rumor floating around that Metro will extend its weekend hours to 1am. Although the folks at Metro would not confirm this, I think it's a done deal. Stay tuned! A weekend schedule is usually adopted on holidays, and evening hours are sometimes extended for special events such as the Fourth of July festivities on the Mall. Trains run about every 12 minutes, more frequently (every 3 to 6 minutes) during rush hour. Marking the entrance to every Metro station is a narrow brown column inscribed with the letter *M*. Below the *M* is a colored stripe or stripes that tell you which line or lines operate there. Station names also appear in Braille on the columns at all Metro stops. The kiosk attendant will answer any routing or fare card questions you may have.

Your ticket to ride is a computerized fare card from the intimidating-looking machines near the entrance. Under the distance-based fare system, you pay the minimum during nonrush hours (9:30am to 3pm and after 7pm weekdays and all day Saturday and Sunday and holidays) and the maximum during rush hours (5:30 to 9:30am and 3 to 7pm weekdays). The minimum fare is $1.10; the maximum is $3.25 (during rush hour). Save by riding between 9:30am and 3pm and again after 7pm. Fares are posted beneath the large colored map, and the machines take nickels, dimes, quarters, $1 bills, $5 bills, $10 bills, and $20 bills. On fare cards valued at $20 or more, you'll receive a 10% discount. If you arrive at a destination and your fare card comes up short, add what's necessary at an Addfare machine near the exit gate. *Warning:* Change is returned in coins. If you feed the machine a $10 bill for a $1.10 fare, you'll be walking around with mighty heavy pockets.

Because you need a fare card to enter and exit each station, keep it handy for reinsertion at your destination. If you will be transferring to Metrobus, pick up a transfer on the mezzanine level when you enter the system (*not* your destination station). With the transfer ticket, it will cost you only 25¢ when boarding the Metrobus. Otherwise, you'll pay the full fare.

Purchase a round-trip fare card when possible to save time. On your last day in D.C., plan carefully. There are no cash refunds on amounts showing on your fare card.

The **Bike-on-Rail program** permits riders to take their bikes on Metro after 7pm Monday through Friday and all day Saturday, Sunday, and holidays (but never on July 4). You must first pass a written test to get the required $15 permit (☎ **202/962-1116**).

BY BUS   You don't have to be a genius to figure out the **Metrobus** system, but it helps. The 13,000 stops on the 1,500-square-mile route (operating on all major D.C. arteries and in the Virginia and Maryland suburbs) are indicated by red, white, and blue signs. However, the signs at best just tell you what buses pull into a given stop, not where they go. For routing information, call ☎ **202/637-7000.** Using a computer, a transit information agent can tell you the most efficient route from where you are to where you want to go (using bus and/or subway) almost instantly. Calls are taken daily between 6am and 11:30pm, but the line is often busy.

If you travel the same route frequently and would like a free map and time schedule, ask the bus driver or call ☎ **202/637-7000** and request one. Information about free parking in Metrobus fringe lots is also available from this number.

Base fare in the District is $1, and transfers from Metrorail to Metrobus are 25¢. (*Note:* You will pay the going fare when transferring from bus to rail. No special deals here!) There are additional charges for travel into the Maryland and Virginia suburbs. Bus drivers are not equipped to make change, so be sure to *carry exact change or tokens.* The latter are available at 250 ticket outlets (call the above number for locations and hours of operation). If you're going to be in Washington for a while and plan to use the buses a lot, consider a 2-week pass such as the $21 **D.C. Only Pass,** good for unlimited Metrobus rides within the District and $4 worth of Metrorail rides. These are also available at ticket outlets. Other passes include zones in Virginia or Maryland.

Most buses operate daily almost around the clock. Service is very frequent on weekdays (especially during rush hours), less so on weekends and late at night.

There's a full bus information center (the Metro Sales Facility) at the Metro Center Station (12th and F streets) where tokens, special bus tickets, and all else is available.

Up to two children 4 and under ride free with a paying passenger on both the Metrorail and the Metrobus, and there are reduced fares for senior citizens (☎ **202/962-1245**) and the disabled (☎ **202/962-1245**). Finally, should you leave something on a bus, on a train, or in a station, call **Lost and Found** (☎ **202/962-1195**).

BY CAR

Within the District a car is a luxury and a headache, as public transportation is so comprehensive and D.C.'s many one-way streets and circles confound motorists. Having a car can be a major inconvenience, especially during rush hour (weekdays from 6 to 10am and 2 to 8pm), and spring and summer, when traffic jams are the norm. At *all times*, street parking is almost nonexistent and parking lots are ruinously expensive. The only exception is on weekends, when the bureaucrats are home cutting the grass. If you're driving into D.C. for the day, you may want to park in Union Station's ample garage then board Metro for your destination. On the other hand, you will need wheels to see most attractions in Virginia and Maryland.

All the major car-rental companies are represented here. Some handy phone numbers are: **Budget** (☎ **800/527-0700**); **Hertz** (☎ **800/654-3131**); **Thrifty** (☎ **800/367-2277**); **Avis** (☎ **800/331-1212**); and **Alamo** (☎ **800/327-9633**).

BY TAXI

Surprise! In many cases, you can take taxis in Washington without busting your budget. District cabs work on a zone system. If you ride within one zone, the fare is $4. A two-zone trip is $5.50; three zones is $6.90. The maximum, eight zones, is $12.50. If you wish to hire a taxi for an hour or more, the hourly rate is $20 for the first hour and $5 for each additional quarter hour. Bear in mind that you're unlikely to travel more than three zones unless you're staying in some remote section of town. The driver's identification card must, by law, be displayed on the cab's right-side sun visor.

Be careful: The fares can add up. There's a rush-hour surcharge of $1 between 7 and 9:30am and 4 and 6:30pm. Also, there's a $1.50 charge for each additional passenger after the first. If you want to stop en route, it'll cost you $1 for under 5 minutes, and the stop can't be more than 5 blocks from your destination (honest). The baggage handling rate for one piece of luggage is 50¢. Trunks and large articles are $2. Tipping is up to you, but the going rate is 10% to 15% of the fare.

What can a sane person say about a system with so many variables? Believe it or not, if you exit or enter the cab at a zone boundary, your fare could jump to the next level, depending on which side of the street you are on (the zone line goes down the middle of some streets). After living in the area for close to 40 years, I still find it confusing, and I don't envy visitors trying to figure out the cockamamie fares. There's talk of converting to a meter system, but I'm not holding my breath. The not-so-hidden message: Take Metro or walk whenever possible. The fares are printed plainly in each station and you won't need a calculator to tally the fare.

The zone system is not used when your destination is an out-of-district address (like the airport); the fare is then based on mileage covered—$2 for the first mile or part of a mile and 70¢ for each additional half mile or part. You can call ☎ **202/331-1671** to find out what the rate should be between any point in D.C. and an address in Virginia or Maryland. Call ☎ **202/767-8380** for inquiries about fares within the District.

If you decide to go for broke, it's generally easy to hail a taxi; there are about 9,000 cabs, and drivers are allowed to pick up as many passengers as can comfortably fit (provided the new passenger doesn't take the first passenger more than 5 blocks out of the way). If your group is small, you can count on sharing the taxi. You may also call a taxi, though there is a charge for doing so. Try **Diamond Cab Company** (☎ **202/387-6200**), **Yellow Cab** (☎ **202/544-1212**), or **Capitol Cab** (☎ **202/546-2400**). They're three of the oldest and most reputable companies.

For a copy of "The Consumer Guide to Taxicabs," write to the **D.C. Taxicab Commission,** 2041 Martin Luther King Jr. Ave. SE, Washington, DC 20020 (☎ **202/645-6010**). If you have a complaint, note the driver's name and cab number, and call the **Taxicab Complaint Office** (☎ **202/727-5401**).

BY TOURMOBILE

If you're visiting Washington for the first time, consider the Tourmobile, a National Park Service concession. It's an ideal way to get an overview of the major attractions. The open-air, blue-and-white sightseeing trams run on routes along the Mall and as far out as Arlington Cemetery and even (with coach service) Mount Vernon.

You may take the full-day **American Heritage Tour** (Washington and Arlington Cemetery) or tour Arlington Cemetery only. The former visits 17 different sites on or near the Mall and four sites at Arlington Cemetery: the Visitor Center, the grave sites of John and Robert Kennedy and Jacqueline Kennedy Onassis, the Tomb of the Unknowns, and Arlington House.

Taxicab Zones

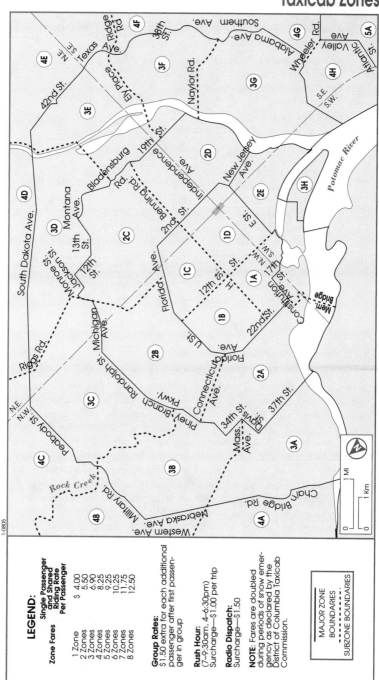

LEGEND:

Zone Fares	Single Passenger and Shared Riding Rate Per Passenger
1 Zone	$ 4.00
2 Zones	5.50
3 Zones	6.90
4 Zones	8.25
5 Zones	9.25
6 Zones	10.25
7 Zones	11.75
8 Zones	12.50

Group Rates:
$1.50 extra for each additional passenger after first passenger in group

Rush Hour:
(7–9:30am, 4–6:30pm)
Surcharge—$1.00 per trip

Radio Dispatch:
Surcharge—$1.50

NOTE: Fares are doubled during periods of snow emergency as declared by the District of Columbia Taxicab Commission.

———— MAJOR ZONE BOUNDARIES
- - - - SUBZONE BOUNDARIES

1-0805

You may board vehicles at any of the following locations (* indicates that a ticket booth is located near the site):

Arlington Cemetery Visitor Center *
Kennedy Gravesites
Tomb of the Unknowns
Arlington House
Kennedy Center
Lincoln, Vietnam & Korean War Memorials *
White House *
Washington Monument *
Arts & Industries Bldg./Smithsonian Castle *
Air & Space Museum *
U.S. Botanic Gardens
Union Station/National Postal Museum *
U.S. Capitol/Library of Congress/Supreme Court
National Gallery of Art
Museum of Natural History
Museum of American History *
Bureau of Engraving and Printing/U.S. Holocaust Memorial Museum
Jefferson Memorial
FDR Memorial *
Old Post Office Pavilion
Ford's Theatre/FBI
National Archives/U.S. Navy Memorial
National Law Enforcement Memorial

You pay the driver when you first board the trams. Along the route, you may get off at any stop to visit monuments or buildings. When you finish exploring each area, you step aboard the next Tourmobile that comes along. The trams travel in a loop, serving each stop about every 20 to 30 minutes. One **fare** allows you to use the trams for a full day. *Note:* Payment is accepted in travelers' checks or cash *only.* For the full-day American Heritage tour (D.C. and Arlington Cemetery) The cost is $16 for age 12 and older, $7 for children 3 to 11. For Arlington only, adults pay $4.75; children, $2.25. Trams follow "figure-8" circuits from the Capitol to Arlington and back. Children under 3 ride free. In past years, you could buy a ticket after 3pm (June to Labor Day; after 1pm Labor Day to May) good for the rest of the afternoon and the following day. Call to see if this is available during your visit. The savvy guides pepper their descriptions of the sights with anecdotes along the route and will answer your questions. It may seem like a lot of money to plunk down at one time, but I think it's well spent. (In today's parlance, the Tourmobile is "cost effective.") With kids in tow, you can cover a lot of ground with comfort and ease.

Tourmobiles operate year-round, daily from approximately 9am to 4:30pm. Summer hours are usually extended to 6:30pm, but you can expect seasonal and year-to-year variations. For further Tourmobile information, call ☎ **202/554-5100** or visit the Web site at www.tourmobile.com.

Tourmobile also runs round-trip tours to Mount Vernon. Coaches depart from the Arlington National Cemetery Visitors Center at 10am, noon, and 2pm, and from the Washington Monument at 10am, noon, and 2pm. The price is $22 for those 12 and older, $11 for children 3 to 11, including admission to Mount Vernon. For the Mount Vernon tour, I was told that you must show up at least half an hour before the departure time. A combination tour of Washington, Arlington

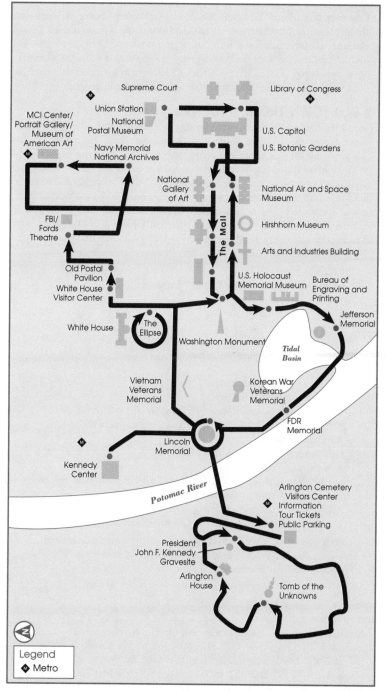

Cemetery, and Mount Vernon is $28 for 12 and older, $14 for children—much cheaper than the Gray Line equivalent. Another offering is the **Frederick Douglass National Historic Site Tour,** including a guided tour of Douglass's home, Cedar Hill. Departures are from the Washington Monument and Arlington Cemetery at noon. Adults pay $7; children, $3.50. It's advisable to make a reservation at least an hour in advance. Call for information on other combination tours.

BY OLD TOWN TROLLEY TOURS

Similar to Tourmobile, and very competitive in terms of price and quality, is the Old Town Trolley (☎ 202/832-9800; www.historictours.com). For a fixed price, you can get on and off these green-and-orange open-air vehicles as many times as you like at 19 locations (listed below) in the District. Most of the stops are at or near major sightseeing attractions, including Georgetown and the National Zoo. The trolley is not licensed to stop directly on the Mall, and that is the primary difference between it and Tourmobile. The trolleys operate daily between 9am and 4:30pm, later in summer. Cost is $24 for adults 12 and older, $11 for kids 4 to 11, free for children 3 and under. The full narrated tour takes about 2¼ hours, and trolleys come by every 20 to 30 minutes beginning at 9am. The following stops are made:

> Union Station
> Capitol Arboretum (Hyatt Regency Capitol Hill)
> Pavilion at the Old Post Office
> Museum of Women in the Arts
> Chinatown/MCI Center
> FBI Building/Ford's Theatre
> Freedom Plaza/National Aquarium
> The White House
> Lafayette Park/Decatur House
> National Geographic Society
> Dupont Circle Neighborhood (Washington Hilton Hotel)
> Kalorama/Adams–Morgan (Calvert and 24th streets NW)
> National Cathedral
> Georgetown (Georgetown Park Mall)
> Arlington Cemetery
> Lincoln/Vietnam Veterans/Korean Veterans/FDR memorials (*reboarding only*)
> Smithsonian Castle (*reboarding only*)
> Air & Space Museum (*reboarding only*)
> U.S. Capitol/Library of Congress (Neptune's Fountain on 1st Street SE)

Tickets can be purchased at all stops except the Lincoln Memorial, the U.S. Capitol, the Washington Monument, and Arlington Cemetery.

For additional tour information, see chapter 6.

Fast Facts: Washington, D.C.

American Express   There is an American Express Travel Service office downtown at 1001 G St. NW (☎ **202/393-2368**), 1150 Connecticut Ave. NW (☎ **202/457-1300**), one uptown near Chevy Chase, Maryland, at 5300 Wisconsin Ave. NW (☎ **202/362-4000**), and several in the Maryland/Virginia suburbs; call ☎ **800/528-4800** for exact locations.

Area Codes   If you are calling a D.C. number from somewhere else, dial **202.** If you are in D.C. and calling D.C., no area code is needed. In D.C., dial **301**

for the close-by Maryland suburbs; **410** for Baltimore, Annapolis, and the Eastern Shore of Maryland; and **703** for suburban Virginia.

Baby-Sitters   Most hotels will secure a bonded sitter for your brood. **Wee Sit,** operating out of Burke, Virginia, has been providing hotel child care to visiting families for many years (☎ **703/764-1542**). You may also call Georgetown University (☎ **202/687-4187**), American University (☎ **202/885-1800**), George Washington University (☎ **202/994-6495**), or look in the Yellow Pages under "Sitting Services."

Congressional Representatives   To locate your senator or congressional representative, call the Capitol switchboard (☎ **202/224-3121**).

Deaf Emergency   Call ☎ **202/727-9334.**

Dentist   Call ☎ **800/DOCTORS** or Dental Referral Service at ☎ **202/723-5323.** You can also call the D.C. Dental Society at ☎ **202/547-7615,** Monday through Friday from 8am to 4pm. Pediatric dentists (for children) are listed in the Yellow Pages under "Dentists, Grouped by Practice."

Disabled Visitors   Washington welcomes visitors with physical disabilities with open arms and relatively few obstacles. Most of the museums, monuments, and public buildings—as well as many theaters and restaurants—are accessible to travelers with disabilities. Metro, the public transportation system, is rated among the nation's best for accommodating the disabled. For information, call ☎ **202/962-1245.**

Doctor   Physicians Home Service (PHS), Suite 401, 2311 M St. NW (☎ **202/331-3888**), makes house calls 24 hours a day and will come to your hotel if you are staying in the District. Kids who are not too sick are seen in the downtown office during regular hours. PHS accepts credit cards, traveler's checks, personal checks with adequate identification, and cash. You can also call Prologue (☎ **800/DOCTOR**).

Drugstores   For free same-day delivery, call **Tschiffely Pharmacy,** 1330 Connecticut Ave. NW (☎ **202/331-7176**), or Union Station (☎ **202/408-5178**). The **CVS** chain has two 24-hour locations: 7 Dupont Circle NW (☎ **202/785-1466**) and 1211 Vermont Ave. NW (☎ **202/628-0720**). Two of CVS's suburban all-night stores are at Bradley Boulevard and Arlington Road, Bethesda, Maryland (☎ **301/656-2522**), and Lyon Village Shopping Center, 3133 Lee Hwy., Arlington, Virginia (☎ **703/522-0260**).

Emergencies   Call ☎ **911** for fire, police, or ambulance. For poison control, call ☎ **202/625-3333.** Also see "Health & Other Precautions" in chapter 1.

Eyeglasses   For same-day service on most prescriptions, call **Atlantic Optical,** 1747 Pennsylvania Ave. NW (☎ **202/466-2050**), or **Sterling Optical,** 1900 M St. NW (☎ **202/728-1041**).

Hairdressers & Barbers   If you want a new look and can't wait until you return home, ask your concierge to recommend a hair stylist (there are 11 pages of beauty salons in the Yellow Pages). For a quick cut, wash, and blow-dry that's reasonable, with no appointment necessary, the whole family can try the **Hair Cuttery** at 1645 Connecticut Ave. NW near Dupont Circle (☎ **202/232-9685**), L'Enfant Plaza (☎ **202/863-9400**), and several suburban locations.

Hospitals   In case of a life-threatening emergency, call ☎ **911.** For those emergencies not requiring immediate ambulance transportation but requiring emergency-room treatment, call one of the following hospitals. To save time and aggravation, call first and get directions; you or your taxi driver may need them.

- **Children's Hospital National Medical Center,** 111 Michigan Ave. NW (☎ 202/884-5000 for emergency room and general information).
- **George Washington University Hospital,** 901 23rd St. NW (☎ 202/994-3211 for emergency room; 202/994-1000 for general information).
- **Georgetown University Hospital,** 3800 Reservoir Rd. NW (☎ 202/784-2118 for emergency room; 202/687-2000 for general information).
- **Howard University Hospital,** 2041 Georgia Ave. NW (☎ 202/865-1131 for emergency room; 202/865-6100 for general information).
- **Providence Hospital,** 1150 Varnum St. NE (☎ 202/269-7910 for emergency room; 202/269-7000 for general information).
- **Sibley Memorial Hospital,** 5255 Loughboro Rd. NW (☎ 202/537-4080 for emergency room; 202/537-4000 for general information).
- **Washington Hospital Center,** 110 Irving St. NW (☎ 202/877-5515 for emergency room; 202/877-7000 for general information).

Laundry & Dry Cleaning   If you are looking for a self-service, coin-operated laundry, try **Washtub Laundromat,** 1511 17th St. NW (☎ 202/332-9455). For complete laundry and dry-cleaning services with pickup and delivery, contact **Bergmann's** (☎ 202/737-5400). For same-day dry-cleaning service, try **MacDee Quality Cleaners** at 1639 L St. NW (☎ 202/296-6100) or 1822½ N St. NW (☎ 202/457-0555), open Monday through Saturday. Most hotels provide laundry and dry-cleaning services and/or have coin-operated laundry facilities.

Liquor Laws   The minimum drinking age is 21. Establishments can serve alcoholic beverages Monday through Thursday from 8am to 2am, Friday and Saturday until 2:30am, and Sunday from 10am to 2am. Liquor stores are closed on Sunday.

Newspapers & Magazines   See "Important Information Resources," earlier in this chapter.

Police   In an emergency, dial ☎ 911. For a nonemergency, call ☎ 202/727-4326. For the location of the nearest district headquarters, call ☎ 202/727-1000.

Post Office   The **National Capital Post Office** (next to Union Station), at North Capitol Street and Massachusetts Avenue NE (☎ 202/682-9595), is open Monday through Friday from 7am to midnight, Saturday and Sunday from 7am to 8pm. For the location of the post office nearest your hotel, ask at the front desk. For **ZIP code information,** call ☎ 202/682-9595.

Safety   I wish I could tell you that there is no crime in Washington, but I'd be lying. Despite adverse media hype, the areas in which you'll be spending most, if not all, of your time are relatively safe. And violent crimes are down in recent years. To help ensure that your family has a safe visit, stay out of dark and deserted areas and don't wander aimlessly. Always have a destination in mind. Criminals are known to prey on those who appear defenseless, so be alert to what's going on around you and walk purposefully. If your children are very young, hold their hands. Make sure you have a plan if you are separated. Kids old enough to understand should know the name and address of their hotel.

Always lock your hotel room, car doors, and trunk. Wear a money belt and keep a close eye on your pocketbook, camera, and wallet. Hold onto your purse in a restaurant; don't drape it over a chair back or put it on an empty seat. When you buy something, put your money and credit cards away and secure your wallet before you go out on the street. Leave expensive jewelry at home, and what you do bring, don't flash. For a copy of "Take a Bite Out of Crime," by the Crime Prevention Coalition, contact the **U.S. Government Printing Office** (☎ **202/512-1993**).

Taxes   The sales tax on merchandise is 6% in D.C., 5% in Maryland, and 4.5% in Virginia. The restaurant tax is 10% in D.C., 5% in Maryland, and 4.5% in Virginia. The hotel sales tax is 13% in D.C. plus a $1.50-per-night occupancy tax, 5% (plus 5% to 7% local or city tax) in Maryland, and 10% in Virginia.

Time   Washington, D.C., is on **eastern standard time,** except when **daylight saving time** is in effect from the first Sunday in April (clocks are moved ahead 1 hour) to the last Sunday in October (clocks are moved back 1 hour). When it's noon in Washington, it's 11am in Chicago, 10am in Denver, and 9am in Los Angeles. To find out the local time, dial ☎ **202/844-2525.**

Useful Telephone Numbers   You might find the following telephone numbers useful during your stay:

Amtrak (☎ **800/872-7245**)
Convention and Visitors Association (☎ **202/789-7000**)
Daily Calendar of Events (☎ **202/789-7000**)
Dental Referrals (☎ **202/547-7613**)
Dial-a-Museum (☎ **202/357-2020**)
Dial-a-Park (☎ **202/619-7275**)
Dial-a-Story (☎ **202/638-5717**)
D.C. Rape Crisis Center (☎ **202/333-7273**)
Medical Referrals (☎ **202/362-8677**)
Metro Information (☎ **202/637-7000**)
Physically Disabled Visitors Information (☎ **202/388-0033**)
Poison Control (☎ **202/625-3333**)
Public School Information (☎ **202/724-4044**)
Smithsonian Information Center (☎ **202/357-2700**)
Time of Day (☎ **202/844-2525**)
Travelers Aid Society (☎ **202/546-3120**)
Visitors Information Association (☎ **202/789-7000**)
Weather (☎ **202/936-1212**)

Weather   For the local weather forecast, call ☎ **202/936-1212.** If you want the extended outlook for the area, call ☎ **202/899-3240.** To check the weather back home, call ☎ **703/260-0107.** For the air quality, call ☎ **202/682-0677.**

3

For Foreign Visitors

Entering a foreign country for the first time can be bewildering at best, especially if you don't speak the language. When you're traveling with kids, your difficulties multiply. Not only do you have to deal with your own uncertainties and frustrations, but you must reassure your little ones, who may be overwhelmed by the baffling strangeness of new sights, sounds, and smells. This chapter is designed to ease your transition by answering your most immediate questions. For help in planning your visit, read chapters 1 and 2 and share the information with your children. Knowing something about the city will help them to feel involved, lessen their anxieties, and stimulate their curiosity.

Although you're bound to feel strange at first, you won't be alone. In 1996, 21 million tourists from around the world visited Washington, D.C., and many who now call the nation's capital home began or spent portions of their lives elsewhere. If you have any doubt, wait until you hear all the foreign languages and accents spoken on Washington's streets. Regardless of their origins, the residents of the nation's capital are friendly and eager to help visitors. Don't be shy. Ask lots of questions, even if your English is less than perfect. Your family is in for a real treat. Remember to put film in your camera and take a tip from the natives: "Go with the flow!"

1 Preparing for Your Trip

ENTRY REQUIREMENTS

Immigration laws are a hot political issue in the United States these days, and the following requirements may have changed somewhat by the time you plan your trip. Check at any U.S. embassy or consulate for current information and requirements. You can also plug into the **U.S. State Department** site at **www.state.gov**.

VISAS The U.S. State Department has a **Visa Waiver Pilot Program** allowing citizens of certain countries to enter the United States without a visa for stays of up to 90 days. At press time these included Andorra, Argentina, Australia, Austria, Belgium, Brunei, Denmark, Finland, France, Germany, Iceland, Ireland, Italy, Japan, Liechtenstein, Luxembourg, Monaco, the Netherlands, New Zealand, Norway, San Marino, Slovenia, Spain, Sweden, Switzerland, and the United Kingdom. Citizens of these countries need only a valid passport and a round-trip air or cruise ticket in their possession upon arrival. If they first enter the United States, they may also visit Mexico, Canada, Bermuda, and/or the Caribbean islands and return to the United States without a visa. Further information is available from any U.S. embassy or consulate. Canadian citizens may enter the United States without visas; they need only proof of residence.

Citizens of all other countries must have (1) a valid passport that expires at least 6 months later than the scheduled end of their visit to the United States, and (2) a tourist visa, which may be obtained without charge from any U.S. consulate.

OBTAINING A VISA   To obtain a visa, the traveler must submit a completed application form (either in person or by mail) with a 1½-inch-square photo, and must demonstrate binding ties to a residence abroad. Usually you can obtain a visa at once or within 24 hours, but it may take longer during the summer rush from June through August. If you cannot go in person, contact the nearest U.S. embassy or consulate for directions on applying by mail. Your travel agent or airline office may also be able to provide you with visa applications and instructions. The U.S. consulate or embassy that issues your visa will determine whether you will be issued a multiple- or single-entry visa and any restrictions regarding the length of your stay.

British subjects can obtain up-to-date passport and visa information by calling the **U.S. Embassy Visa Information Line** (☎ **0891/200-290**) or the **London Passport Office** (☎ **0990/210-410** for recorded information).

IMMIGRATION QUESTIONS   Telephone operators will answer your inquiries regarding U.S. immigration policies or laws at the **Immigration and Naturalization Service's Customer Information Center** (☎ **800/375-5283**). Representatives are available from 9am to 3pm, Monday through Friday. Also, access the Web site at www.ins.usdoj.gov.

MEDICAL REQUIREMENTS   Unless you're arriving from an area known to be suffering from an epidemic (particularly cholera or yellow fever), inoculations or vaccinations are not required for entry into the United States. If you have a disease that requires treatment with narcotics or syringe-administered medications, carry a valid signed prescription from your physician to allay any suspicions that you may be smuggling narcotics (a serious offense that carries severe penalties in the United States).

For up-to-the-minute information concerning HIV-positive travelers, contact the Center for Disease Control's **National Center for HIV** (☎ **404/332-4559;** www.hivatis.org) or the **Gay Men's Health Crisis** (☎ **212/367-1000;** www. gmhc.org).

DRIVER'S LICENSES   Foreign driver's licenses are mostly recognized in the United States, although you may want to get an international driver's license if your home license is not written in English.

PASSPORT INFORMATION

Safeguard your passport in an inconspicuous, inaccessible place like a money belt. If you lose it, visit the nearest consulate of your native country as soon as possible for a replacement. Passport applications are downloadable from the Internet sites listed below.

For Residents of Canada

You can pick up a passport application at one of 28 regional passport offices or most travel agencies. The passport is valid for 5 years and costs $60. Children under 16 may be included on a parent's passport but need their own to travel unaccompanied by the parent. Applications, which must be accompanied by two identical passport-sized photographs and proof of Canadian citizenship, are available at travel agencies throughout Canada or from the central **Passport Office, Department of Foreign Affairs and International Trade**, Ottawa, ON K1A 0G3 (☎ **800/567-6868;** www.dfait-maeci.gc.ca/passport). Processing takes 5 to 10 days if you apply in person, or about 3 weeks by mail.

For Residents of the United Kingdom

To pick up an application for a regular 10-year passport (the Visitor's Passport has been abolished), visit your nearest passport office, major post office, or travel agency. You can also contact the London Passport Office at ☎ **020/7271-3000** or www.open.gov.uk/ukpass/ukpass.htm. Passports are 21£ for adults and 11£ for children under 16.

CUSTOMS
What You Can Bring In

Every visitor over 21 years of age may bring in, free of duty, the following: (1) 1 liter of wine or hard liquor; (2) 200 cigarettes, 100 cigars (but not from Cuba), or 3 pounds of smoking tobacco; and (3) $100 worth of gifts. These exemptions are offered to travelers who spend at least 72 hours in the United States and who have not claimed them within the preceding 6 months. Foreign tourists may bring in or take out up to $10,000 in U.S. or foreign currency with no formalities; larger sums must be declared to U.S. Customs on entering or leaving, which includes filing form CM 4790.

You may bring in certain food products, such as bakery items and all cured cheeses. To bring fruits, vegetables, plants, cuttings, seeds, unprocessed plant products, and certain endangered plant species into the country, you must obtain an import permit, or else you will not be allowed to carry those things into the United States. The only meat you may bring in is canned meat that the inspector can determine has been commercially canned, cooked in the container, hermetically sealed, and requires no refrigeration; you are otherwise prohibited or restricted from bringing any other meat, livestock, poultry, or their by-products into the country.

For more specific information regarding U.S. Customs, call your nearest U.S. embassy or consulate, or the **U.S. Customs** office at ☎ **202/927-1770** or www.customs.ustreas.gov. Ask for copies of "Visiting the United States," which offers travelers more information about what U.S. Customs allows you to bring in. You can also call the U.S. Department of Agriculture's Animal and Plant Health Inspection Service (☎ **301/734-8455**) and ask for a copy of "Traveler's Tips," which provides detailed information on bringing food, plant, and animal products into the United States.

WHAT YOU CAN TAKE HOME

U.K. citizens returning from the United States have a customs allowance of: 200 cigarettes; 50 cigars; 250 grams of smoking tobacco; 2 liters of still table wine; 1 liter of spirits or strong liqueurs (over 22% volume); 2 liters of fortified wine, sparkling wine or other liqueurs; 60 cubic centimeters (ml) perfume; 250 cubic centimeters (ml) of toilet water; and £145 worth of all other goods, including gifts and souvenirs. People under 17 cannot have the tobacco or alcohol allowance. For more information, contact HM Customs & Excise, Passenger Enquiry Point, 2nd Floor Wayfarer House, Great South West Road, Feltham, Middlesex, TW14 8NP (☎ **020/8910-3744;** from outside the U.K. 44/181-910-3744), or at www.open.gov.uk.

For a clear summary of Canadian rules, write for the booklet *I Declare,* issued by **Revenue Canada,** 2265 St. Laurent Blvd., Ottawa, ON K1G 4KE (☎ **613/993-0534**). Canada allows its citizens a $500 exemption, and you're allowed to bring back duty-free 200 cigarettes, 2.2 pounds of tobacco, 40 imperial ounces of liquor, and 50 cigars. In addition, you're allowed to mail gifts to Canada from abroad at the rate of Can$60 a day, provided they're unsolicited and don't contain alcohol or tobacco (write on the package "Unsolicited gift, under $60 value"). All valuables should be declared on the Y-38 form before departure from Canada, including serial numbers of valuables you already own, such as expensive foreign cameras. *Note:* The $500 exemption can only be used once a year and only after an absence of 7 days.

INSURANCE

Although it's not required of travelers, health insurance is highly recommended. Unlike many European countries, the United States does not usually offer free or low-cost medical care to its citizens or visitors. Doctors and hospitals are expensive, and in most cases will require advance payment or proof of coverage before they render their services. Policies can cover everything from the loss or theft of your baggage and trip cancellation to the guarantee of bail in case you're arrested. Good policies will also cover the costs of an accident, repatriation, or death. Packages such as **Europ Assistance** in Europe are sold by automobile clubs and travel agencies at attractive rates. **Worldwide Assistance Services** (☎ **800/821-2828**) is the agent for Europ Assistance in the United States.

Though lack of health insurance may prevent you from being admitted to a hospital in nonemergencies, don't worry about being left on a street corner to die: The American way is to fix you now and bill the living daylights out of you later.

INSURANCE FOR BRITISH TRAVELERS   Most big travel agents offer their own insurance and will probably try to sell you their package when you book a holiday. Think before you sign. **Britain's Consumers' Association** recommends that you insist on seeing the policy and reading the fine print before buying travel insurance. **The Association of British Insurers** (☎ **020/7600-3333**) gives advice by phone and publishes the free *Holiday Insurance,* a guide to policy provisions and prices. You might also shop around for better deals: Try **Columbus Travel Insurance Ltd.** (☎ **020/7375-0011**) or, for students, **Campus Travel** (☎ **020/7730-2101**).

INSURANCE FOR CANADIAN TRAVELERS   Canadians should check with their provincial health plan offices or call **HealthCanada** (☎ **613/957-2991**) to find out the extent of their coverage and what documentation and receipts they must take home in case they are treated in the United States.

MONEY

CURRENCY   The U.S. monetary system is painfully simple: The most common bills (all ugly, all green) are the $1 (colloquially, a "buck"), $5, $10, and $20 denominations. There are also $2 bills (seldom encountered), $50 bills, and $100 bills (the last two are usually not welcome as payment for small purchases). Note that a newly redesigned $100 and $50 bill were introduced in 1996, and a redesigned $20 bill in 1998. Expect to see redesigned $10 and $5 notes in the year 2000. Despite rumors to the contrary, the old-style bills are still legal tender.

There are six denominations of coins: 1¢ (1 cent, or a penny); 5¢ (5 cents, or a nickel); 10¢ (10 cents, or a dime); 25¢ (25 cents, or a quarter); 50¢ (50 cents, or a half dollar); and, prized by collectors, the rare $1 piece (the older, large silver dollar and the newer, small Susan B. Anthony coin). A new gold $1 piece will be introduced by the year 2000.

Note: It's best not to change foreign money (or traveler's checks denominated in a currency other than U.S. dollars) at a small-town bank, or even a branch in a big city; in fact, leave any currency other than U.S. dollars at home—it may prove a greater nuisance to you than it's worth.

TRAVELER'S CHECKS   Though traveler's checks are widely accepted, make sure that they're denominated in U.S. dollars, as foreign-currency checks are often difficult to exchange. The three traveler's checks that are most widely recognized— and least likely to be denied—are **Visa, American Express,** and **Thomas Cook.** Be sure to record the numbers of the checks, and keep that information separately in case they get lost or stolen. Most businesses are pretty good about taking traveler's checks, but you're better off cashing them in at a bank (in small amounts, of course) and paying in cash. Remember: you'll need identification, such as a driver's license or passport, to change a traveler's check.

CREDIT CARDS & ATMS   Credit cards are the most widely used form of payment in the United States: **Visa** (BarclayCard in Britain), **MasterCard** (EuroCard in Europe, Access in Britain, Chargex in Canada), **American Express, Diners Club, Discover, and Carte Blanche.** You must have a credit or charge card to rent a car. There are, however, a handful of stores and restaurants that do not take credit cards, so be sure to ask in advance. Most businesses display a sticker near their entrance to let you know which cards they accept. (*Note:* Often businesses require a minimum purchase price, usually around $10, to use a credit card.)

It is strongly recommended that you bring at least one major credit card. Hotels, car-rental companies, and airlines usually require a credit-card imprint as a deposit against expenses, and in an emergency a credit card can be priceless. You'll find automated-teller machines (ATMs) on just about every block—at least in almost every town—across the country.

SAFETY

GENERAL SAFETY SUGGESTIONS   While tourist areas are generally safe, crime is on the increase everywhere, and U.S. urban areas tend to be less safe than those in Europe or Japan. You should always stay alert. It is wise to ask your hotel front desk staff or the city's tourist office if you're in doubt about which neighborhoods are safe.

Avoid deserted areas, especially at night, and don't go into public parks at night unless there's a concert or similar occasion that will attract a crowd.

Avoid carrying valuables with you on the street, and don't display expensive cameras or electronic equipment. If you are using a map, consult it inconspicuously— or better yet, try to study it before you leave your room. In general, the more you "look" like a tourist, the more likely someone will try to take advantage of you. If you're walking, pay attention to who is near you as you walk. If you are attending a convention or event where you wear a name tag, remove it before venturing outside. Hold onto your pocketbook, and place your billfold in an inside pocket. In theaters, restaurants, and other public places, keep your possessions in sight.

Remember also that hotels are open to the public, and in a large hotel, security may not be able to screen everyone entering. Always lock your room door.

DRIVING SAFETY   Question your rental agency about personal safety and ask for a traveler-safety brochure when you pick up your car. Obtain written directions—or a map with the route clearly marked—from the agency showing how to get to your destination. (Many agencies now offer the option of renting a cellular phone for the duration of your car rental; check with the rental agent when you pick up the car.) And, if possible, arrive and depart during daylight hours.

Recently, more and more crime has involved cars and drivers. If you drive off a highway into a doubtful neighborhood, leave the area as quickly as possible. If you have an accident, even on the highway, assess the situation or wait until the police arrive before you get out of the car. If you're bumped from behind on the street or are involved in a minor accident with no injuries and the situation appears to be suspicious, motion to the other driver to follow you. Handle the situation at the nearest police precinct, well-lit service station, or 24-hour store.

Always try to park in well-lit and well-traveled areas if possible. Never leave any packages or valuables in sight. If someone attempts to rob you or steal your car, don't try to resist—report the incident to the police department immediately by calling ☎ **911.**

2 Getting to the United States

BY AIR International airlines with scheduled flights into **National** are Air Canada (☎ **800/776-3000;** www.aircanada.ca) and Canadian Airlines (☎ **800/426-7000;** www.cdnair.ca). International airlines with scheduled flights into **BWI** include Air Canada, British Airways (☎ **800/247-9297;** www.british-airways.com), El Al Israel (☎ **800/223-6700;** www.elal.co.il), and Icelandair (☎ **800/223-5500;** www. icelandair.com). International airlines with scheduled flights into **Dulles** include Air Canada, Air France (☎ **800/237-2747;** www.airfrance.com), All Nippon Airways (☎ **800/235-9262;** www.allnipponairways.com), British Airways, KLM Royal Dutch (☎ **800/374-7747,** www.klm.nl); Lufthansa (☎ **800/645-3880;** www. lufthansa.com); Saudi Arabian Airlines (☎ **800/472-8342;** www. saudiarabian-airlines.com), Swissair (☎ **800/221-4750;** www. swissair.com), and Virgin Atlantic (☎ **800/862-8621;** fly.virgina.com).

See the box "CyberDeals for Net Surfers" in chapter 1. If you are coming from Europe, you will want to know about Discount Tickets, www.discount-tickets.com, a Web site operated by the European Travel Network, which offers discounts on airfares, accommodations, car rentals and tours. It deals with flights between the United States and other countries, so it's most useful for travelers coming to Washington from abroad.

Travelers from overseas can take advantage of the APEX (advance purchase excursion) fares offered by all the major U.S. and European carriers.

BY TRAIN Amtrak (☎ **800/USA-RAIL;** www.amtrak.com) operates two trains between Canada and Washington: The Vermonter travels from Montreal to Washington and Washington to Montreal daily, stopping in Vermont, Massachusetts, Connecticut, New York, and so on; the Maple Leaf operates in both directions, Washington to Toronto and Toronto to Washington daily, via stops in New York State, Philadelphia, and Ontario. See chapter 2, "Getting There," for more information on train travel.

3 Getting Around the United States

BY PLANE Some large American airlines, for example, American, Northwest, United, and Delta, offer travelers on their trans-Atlantic or trans-Pacific flights special discount tickets allowing travel between U.S. destinations at minimum rates. (Two such programs are American's **Visit USA** and Delta's **Discover America.**) These tickets are not on sale in the United States and must, therefore, be purchased before you leave your foreign point of departure. This arrangement is the best, easiest, and fastest way to see the United States at low cost. You should obtain information well in advance from your travel agent or the office of the airline concerned, since the conditions attached to these discount tickets can be changed without advance notice.

If you are arriving by air, allow lots of time to make connections between international and domestic flights—an average of 2 to 3 hours at least.

In contrast, air travelers from Canada, Bermuda, and some places in the Caribbean can sometimes go through Customs and Immigration at the point of departure, which is much quicker and less painful.

BY TRAIN   International visitors, except Canadians, can buy a **USA Railpass**, good for 15 or 30 days of unlimited travel on Amtrak (☎ **800/USA-RAIL**). The pass is available through many foreign travel agents. Prices in 1999 for a 15-day pass were $285 off-peak, $425 peak; a 30-day pass cost $375 off-peak, $535 peak. (With a foreign passport, you can also buy passes at some Amtrak offices in the United States, including locations in Chicago, New York, Boston, and Washington, D.C.) Reservations are generally required and should be made for each part of your trip as early as possible.

If your travel plans include visiting both the United States and Canada, you need to purchase a **North American Railpass.** Also available through Amtrak is an **Airail** pass, a joint venture of United Airlines and Amtrak that's available as part of **Amtrak Vacations packages** (☎ **800/321-8684**). The pass allows you to arrive in Washington (from a location within the U.S.) by one mode, plane or rail, and return via the other. During the train portion of your trip, you can make up to three stops along the way at no extra charge.

BY BUS   Although bus travel is often the most economical form of public transit for short hops between U.S. cities, it can also be slow and uncomfortable—certainly not an option for everyone (particularly when Amtrak, which is far more luxurious, offers similar rates). **Greyhound/Trailways** (☎ **800/231-2222**), the sole nationwide bus line, offers an **Ameripass** for unlimited travel for 7 days at $199, 15 days at $299, 30 days at $409, and 60 days at $599. Passes must be purchased at a Greyhound terminal. Special rates are available for senior citizens and students.

Fast Facts: For the Foreign Traveler

Automobile Organizations   Auto clubs will supply maps, recommended routes, guidebooks, accident and bail-bond insurance, and, most important of all, emergency road service. The leader, with 850 offices and 28 million members, is the **American Automobile Association (AAA),** with national headquarters at 1000 AAA Dr., Heathrow, FL 32745 (☎ **407/444-7000**). Check the telephone book for local offices. Membership for both U.S. citizens and foreign visitors ranges from $37 to $57, depending on which particular local office you join. AAA also has a 24-hour emergency number (☎ **800/222-4357**). AAA can provide you with a "Touring Permit" validating your foreign driver's license. Members of some foreign auto clubs that have reciprocal arrangements with AAA enjoy AAA's services at no charge.

Auto Rentals   To rent a car you need a major credit card, or you'll have to leave a sizable cash deposit ($100 or more for each day). Minimum driver age is usually 21 (but depending on the car-rental company the minimum age limit can be as high as 25), and you'll need a valid driver's license.

The best way to find the lowest rate is to shop around—prices vary from company to company, from location to location (airport versus downtown, Florida versus New York City). In addition, companies offer unlimited-mileage options vs. per-mile charges and also special discounts on weekends, for example. So it pays to check out many different companies. Use the major companies' toll-free 800 numbers to do this. Other variable costs to research include drop-off charges if you're picking up the car in one city and leaving it in another, as well as the cost of daily collision damage and personal accident insurance. And always return your car with a full tank—the rental companies charge excessive prices for gasoline.

The major companies are **Hertz** (☎ 800/654-3131), **Avis** (☎ 800/331-1212), **National** (☎ 800/227-7368), **Budget** (☎ 800/527-0700), and **Dollar** (☎ 800/421-6868). Also check the smaller local companies and **Rent a Wreck** (☎ 800/535-1391), if there is one in a particular city.

Business Hours   Public and private offices are usually open Monday through Friday from 9am to 5pm, but U.S. government offices have staggered hours.

Banking hours: in D.C., most banks are open from 9am to 3pm; some are open until 4pm; many stay open until 6pm Friday. In the Maryland and Virginia suburbs, banks typically have lobby hours until 6 or 7pm, as well as drive-thrus that remain open until 6 or 7pm.

Post offices are open Monday through Friday from 8 or 8:30am to 5:30 or 6pm and Saturday from 8 or 8:30am to noon.

Store hours are Monday through Saturday from 9:30 or 10am to 5:30 or 6pm, though often until 9pm one or two evenings a week. Shopping centers, drugstores, and supermarkets are open 9 or 9:30am to 9pm 6 days a week (sometimes 7 days, and in some cases even 24 hours).

Museum hours vary widely. The norm is 10am to 5:30pm daily (a few close on Monday). See chapter 6 for details about days and hours of individual museums.

Climate   See "The Climate," in chapter 1.

Currency & Exchange   See "Money" above.

Customs & Immigration   See "Customs" above.

Drinking Laws   As with marriage and divorce, every state, and sometimes every county and community, has its own laws governing the sale of liquor. The only federal regulation (based on a judgment of the U.S. Supreme Court on June 23, 1987) restricts the consumption of liquor in public places anywhere in the country to persons age 21 or over (states not respecting this rule may be penalized by a withdrawal of federal highway funds). In D.C., establishments can serve alcoholic beverages Monday through Thursday from 8am to 2am, Friday and Saturday until 2:30am, and Sunday from 10am to 2am. Liquor stores are closed on Sunday.

Electric Current   U.S. wall outlets give power at 110 to 115 volts AC (60 cycles), compared to 220 volts AC (50 cycles), in most of Europe. Besides a 110-volt converter, small appliances of non-American manufacture, such as hair dryers and shavers, will require a plug adapter with two flat parallel pins.

Embassies & Consulates   All embassies are located in Washington, D.C., as it's the nation's capital, and many consulates are located here as well. Among the embassies here are those for **Australia,** 1601 Massachusetts Ave. NW, Washington, DC 20036 (☎ 202/797-3000); **Canada,** 501 Pennsylvania Ave. NW, Washington, DC 20001 (☎ 202/682-1740); **Ireland,** 2234 Massachusetts Ave. NW, Washington, DC 20008 (☎ 202/462-3939); **New Zealand,** 37 Observatory

Circle NW, Washington, DC 20008 (☎ 202/328-4800); and **Great Britain,** 3100 Massachusetts Ave. NW, Washington, DC 20008 (☎ 202/ 462-1340). You can get the telephone numbers of other embassies and consulates by calling "Information" in Washington, D.C. (dial ☎ **411** within D.C.'s 202 area code; elsewhere, dial ☎ **202/555-1212**). Or consult the phone book you'll find in your hotel room.

Emergencies   In Washington, D.C., as in all major cities, you can call the police, an ambulance, or the fire department through the single emergency telephone number ☎ **911.** For a deaf emergency, dial ☎ **202/727-9334;** for a nonemergency situation, dial the police at ☎ **202/727-4326.** Another useful way of reporting an emergency is to call the telephone company operator by dialing 0 (the number *zero,* not the letter "O"). Outside major cities, call the local police department or the fire department at the number you will find in the local telephone book.

If you encounter such travelers' problems as sickness, accident, or lost or stolen baggage, it will pay to call the **Travelers Aid Society,** 512 C St. NE (☎ **202/ 546-3120**), an organization that specializes in helping distressed travelers.

Gasoline (Petrol)   One U.S. gallon equals 3.75 liters, while 1.2 U.S. gallons equals one imperial gallon. You'll notice there are several grades (and price levels) of gasoline available at most gas stations. And you'll also notice that their names change from company to company. The unleaded ones with the highest octane are the most expensive (most rental cars take the least expensive "regular" unleaded), and leaded gas is the least expensive (but only older cars can take this, so check if you're not sure).

Holidays   On the following legal national holidays, banks, government offices, post offices, and many stores and museums are closed (some restaurants are closed Christmas Day):

> January 1 (New Year's Day)
> Third Monday in January (Martin Luther King Jr.'s Birthday)
> Third Monday in February (Presidents' Day, Washington's Birthday)
> Last Monday in May (Memorial Day)
> July 4 (Independence Day) If July 4 falls on a weekend, the Friday before or
>   the Monday afterward will be considered a holiday
> First Monday in September (Labor Day)
> Second Monday in October (Columbus Day)
> November 11 (Veterans' Day/Armistice Day)
> Last Thursday in November (Thanksgiving Day)
> December 25 (Christmas Day)

Finally, the Tuesday following the first Monday in November is Election Day and is a legal holiday in presidential election years (2000, 2004, and so on).

Individual listings in the appropriate chapters will tell you when an establishment is closed.

Legal Aid   The foreign tourist, unless positively identified as a member of the Mafia or of a drug ring, will probably never become involved with the American legal system. If you are pulled over for a minor infraction (for example, of the highway code, such as speeding), never attempt to pay the fine directly to a police officer; you may wind up arrested on the much more serious charge of attempted bribery. Pay fines by mail or directly into the hands of the clerk of the court. If accused of a more serious offense, it is wise to say and do nothing before consulting a lawyer. Under U.S. law an arrested person is allowed one telephone call to a party of his or her choice. Call your embassy or consulate.

Generally mailboxes, which are blue with a white eagle logo, can be found at intersections; they carry the inscription "U.S.MAIL." If your mail is addressed to a U.S. destination, don't forget to add the five-figure postal code or ZIP (zone improvement plan) code after the two-letter abbreviation of the state to which the mail is addressed (CA for California, MA for Massachusetts, NY for New York, and so on).

The National Capitol branch of the post office (☎ **202/523-2628**) is located opposite Union Station at Postal Square, 2 Massachusetts Ave. NE. It's open weekdays from 7am to midnight, Saturday and Sunday until 8pm.

Newspapers & Magazines   National newspapers include *The New York Times, USA Today,* the *Wall Street Journal,* and the *Christian Science Monitor.* There are also innumerable national news weeklies including *Newsweek, Time,* and *U.S. News & World Report.*

The local paper in D.C. is the *Washington Post.*

Foreign newspapers and magazines are available at the Newsroom, 1753 Connecticut Ave. NW (☎ **202/332-1489**).

Radio & Television   Audiovisual media, with four coast-to-coast broadcast networks—ABC, CBS, NBC, and Fox—joined by the Public Broadcasting System (PBS), which broadcasts a wide range of educational programs specifically geared toward children, and the cable network, CNN, play a major part in American life. In big cities such as Washington, D.C., televiewers have a choice of about a dozen channels (including the UHF channels), many of them transmitting 24 hours a day, without counting the pay-TV channels showing recent movies or sports events. All options are usually indicated on your hotel TV set. You'll also find a wide choice of local radio stations, each broadcasting talk shows and/or a particular kind of music—classical, country, jazz, pop, gospel—punctuated by news broadcasts and frequent commercials.

Safety   Whenever you're traveling in an unfamiliar city, stay alert. Be aware of your immediate surroundings. Wear a money belt—or better yet, check valuables in a safe-deposit box at your hotel. It's your responsibility to be careful even in the most heavily touristed areas. See "Safety" in section 1, "Preparing for Your Trip."

Taxes   In the United States, there is no VAT (value-added tax) or other indirect tax at a national level. Every state, and each city in it, has the right to levy its own local tax on all purchases, including hotel and restaurant checks, airline tickets, and so on. It is automatically added to the price of certain services such as public transportation, cab fares, phone calls, and gasoline. It varies from 4% to 10%, depending on the state and city, so when you are making major purchases such as photographic equipment, clothing, or high-fidelity components, it can be a significant part of the cost.

The sales tax on merchandise is 6% in the District, 5% in Maryland, and 4.5% in Virginia. The tax on restaurant meals is 10% in the District, 5% in Maryland, and 4.5% in Virginia.

Each locality also has the right to levy its own separate tax on hotel occupancy. Since this tax is in addition to any general sales tax, taken together these two taxes can add a considerable amount to the basic cost of your accommodations.

In the District, in addition to your hotel rate, you pay 13% sales tax and $1.50-per-night occupancy tax. The state sales tax on a hotel room is 10% in suburban Virginia and 5% in Maryland (where you can expect an additional 5% to 7% in city or local taxes).

Foreign visitors must also pay a $10 Customs tax on entry to the United States and a $6 departure tax.

Telephone & Telegraph   Pay phones are an integral part of the American landscape. You will find them everywhere: at street corners; in bars, restaurants, public buildings, stores, service stations; along highways; and elsewhere. Outside the big metropolitan areas, public telephones are more difficult to find. Stores and gas stations are your best bet.

Unlike the mail and the railroads, the telephone is not a public-service system. It is run by private corporations, which perhaps explains its high standard of service. In the District local calls cost 35¢.

For long-distance or international calls, stock up with a supply of quarters; the pay phone will instruct you when, and in what quantity, you should put them into the slot. For direct overseas calls, first dial 011, followed by the country code (Australia, 61; New Zealand, 64; United Kingdom, 44; and so on), and then by the city code and the number of the person you wish to call. For Canada and long-distance calls in the United States, dial 1 followed by the area code and number you want.

Before calling from a hotel room, always ask the hotel phone operator if there are any telephone surcharges. They will often charge you for making an outside call, even if you bill the call to a credit card. These charges are best avoided by using a public phone.

For reversed-charge or collect calls, and for person-to-person calls, dial 0 (zero, *not* the letter "O") followed by the area code and number you want; an operator will then come on the line, and you should specify that you are calling collect, or person-to-person, or both. If your operator-assisted call is international, ask for the overseas operator.

For local directory assistance ("information"), dial 411; for long-distance information, dial 1, then the appropriate area code and 555-1212.

Like the telephone system, telegraph and telex services are provided by private corporations such as ITT, MCI, and above all, **Western Union,** the most important. You can bring your telegram in to the nearest Western Union office (there are hundreds across the country) or dictate it over the phone (a toll-free call, ☎ **800/325-6000**). You can also telegraph money or have it telegraphed to you very quickly over the Western Union system.

Telephone Directory   See "Yellow Pages," below.

Time   The United States is divided into four time zones (six, if Alaska and Hawaii are included). From east to west, these are eastern standard time (EST), central standard time (CST), mountain standard time (MST), Pacific standard time (PST), Alaska standard time (AST), and Hawaii standard time (HST). Keep these time zones in mind if you are traveling (or even telephoning) long distances in the United States. For example, noon in New York City (EST) is 11am in Chicago (CST), 10am in Denver (MST), 9am in Los Angeles (PST), 8am in Anchorage (AST), and 7am in Honolulu (HST). Washington, D.C., is EST.

Daylight saving time is in effect from the first Sunday in April until the last Sunday in October (actually, the change is made at 2am on Sunday) except in Arizona, Hawaii, part of Indiana, and Puerto Rico. Daylight saving time moves the clock 1 hour ahead of standard time.

Tipping   This is part of the American way of life, on the principle that you must expect to pay for any service you get. Here are some rules of thumb:

  Bartenders: 10% to 15%
  Bellhops: at least 50¢ per piece; $2 to $3 for a lot of baggage
  Cab drivers: 15% of the fare
  Cafeterias, fast-food restaurants: no tip
  Chambermaids: $1 a day
  Checkroom attendants (restaurants, theaters): $1 per garment
  Cinemas, movies, theaters: no tip
  Doormen (hotels or restaurants): not obligatory
  Gas-station attendants: no tip
  Hairdressers: 15% to 20%
  Parking-lot attendant: $1
  Redcaps/porters (airport and railroad station): $1 per piece; $2 to $3 for a
    lot of baggage
  Restaurants, nightclubs: 15% to 20% of the check

Toilets   Washington reminds many visitors of Paris, but with one striking exception: You won't find a public facility on every street corner. Fortunately, you won't see as many men relieving themselves publicly either. Museums, hotels, and department stores have clean, well-lighted bathrooms, some with tables for changing babies. While restaurant rest rooms are *supposed* to be for patrons only, those in hotel lobbies, shopping malls, and department stores are fair game. If you or your child have an emergency and you're near a restaurant, ask the maître d' if you can use the pay phone. Usually there's a rest room a few feet away. If there's an attendant, it is proper to leave 50¢ or $1.

Yellow Pages   There are two kinds of telephone directories available to you. The general directory is the so-called White Pages, in which private and business subscribers are listed in alphabetical order. The inside front cover lists the emergency numbers for police, fire, and ambulance, and other vital numbers (such as the poison-control center and crime-victims hot line). The first few pages are devoted to community service numbers, including a guide to long-distance and international calling, complete with country codes and area codes.

The second directory, printed on yellow paper (hence its name, Yellow Pages), lists all local services, businesses, and industries by type of activity, with an index at the back. The listings cover not only such obvious items as automobile repairs by make of car, or drugstores (pharmacies), often by geographical location, but also restaurants by type of cuisine and geographical location, bookstores by special subject and/or language, places of worship by religious denomination, and other information that the tourist might otherwise not readily find. The Yellow Pages also includes city plans or detailed area maps, often showing postal ZIP codes and public transportation routes.

4

Family-Friendly Accommodations

When it comes to choosing a place to stay with your kids, look for a hotel that is convenient to the Metro, sightseeing attractions, restaurants, and amusements. While you may be turned on by complimentary terry-cloth robes and 24-hour room service, such amenities are of little consequence to most youngsters. What's important to them is whether there's a refrigerator, restaurant, or snack machine, and whether there's a pool, video games, or shopping close by. Good news for families: Many of the large hotel chains have added lobby coffee bars, fast-food kiosks—Burger King, Sbarro, and I Can't Believe It's Yogurt, to name a few—as well as shops that carry snacks and light fare. This is a boon to tired and budget-minded travelers who may opt to enjoy a light bite in their rooms rather than dine in a restaurant.

Depending on your budget, the selection of places to stay in Washington, D.C., is wide indeed. For those who like to exit the city at night, I've included several hotels in the Maryland and Virginia suburbs. The following suggestions cover a broad spectrum, from superduper luxury hotels to budget alternatives. All, with a few exceptions, are within easy walking distance of the Metro, and all have something (in most cases, several somethings) that make them attractive to kids. If you can't swing a $2,000-a-night Presidential Suite or room with a view of the Capitol, don't despair. You won't be spending that much time in your room anyway. At day's end, flopping into a bed—even one with a few lumps—will spell relief.

GETTING THE MOST FOR YOUR DOLLAR

To get the best value for your travel dollar, here are a few tips from the experts. You'll pay top dollar during the high season, which runs from late March to mid-June. Rates typically fall in summer when Congress is on vacation and during the winter months. January is especially slow. If you can live without cherry blossoms, avoid the 2-week festival in late March and early April; it's an expensive and crowded time to visit D.C.

Your kids may be your ticket to special room rates and weekend packages. Hotels clamor for family business, especially on weekends and during the summer. At most places, children under a certain age (usually 16 or 18) stay free in their parents' room. Weekday rates may drop 30% to 50% on weekends and, depending on occupancy, you may cash in on weekdays as well. Hotels sometimes run unadvertised special promotions, but you won't find out about them if you don't ask.

Many experienced travelers believe you'll be quoted a better rate if you call the hotel directly rather than reserving through the toll-free number. Don't be afraid to ask (as if you're hard of hearing), "Don't you have something for less?" In some circles, this is considered chutzpah, but in most it's considered just plain good sense. There's probably no point trying this around cherry blossom time, but it's amazing what reservations clerks will come up with when you tell them you're going to shop around.

And when you're budgeting your vacation, don't forget the hotel tax. The tax on hotel rooms in the District is 13%. That's $19.50 per night (plus a $1.50 room tax) on a $150 room.

It's no secret that in most cases accommodations in the suburbs are less expensive than in D.C. But, as the old saying goes, "You pays your money and you takes your choices." Many disagree, but I think there's a lot to be said for waking up in the city and having the attractions at your fingertips and, perhaps, a view of the Potomac or U.S. Capitol rather than a highway or shopping mall.

HELPING HANDS

For information on accommodations, try the **Washington, D.C. Convention and Visitors Association,** 1212 New York Ave., Suite 600, Washington, DC 20005 (☎ 202/789-7000; www.washington.org). Down the hall is the **D.C. Committee to Promote Washington,** 1212 New York Ave. NW, Suite 200, Washington, DC 20005 (☎ 202/754-5644).

Washington D.C. Reservations, 1201 Wisconsin Ave., NW, Washington, DC 20007 (☎ 800/554-2220; www.dcaccmomodations.com) offers free advice and reservations. If you're more comfortable with someone else doing the negotiating for you, write or call **Capitol Reservations,** 1730 Rhode Island Ave. NW, Suite 302, Washington, DC 20036 (☎ 800/847-4832). They handle hotels in all price ranges and are privy to discounts because of their high-volume business, and, important to families, they've been screened for cleanliness and they're in safe neighborhoods.

Groups who will occupy 10 or more rooms should know about **U.S.A. Groups** (☎ 800/872-4777 or 202/861-1900). The free service represents hotel rooms at almost every property in the Washington, D.C., and suburban Virginia/Maryland region and will work hard to find the best accommodations at the rates you request, saving your group valuable time and money.

Note: A few of the hotels listed below allow pets. For a complete list of pet-friendly accommodations in the D.C. area, don't leave home without **"Touring with Towser."** To get a copy of this helpful booklet, send a check or money order for $3 made payable to Quaker Professional Services, 585 Hawthorne Court, Galesburg, IL 61401.

Presented below are those establishments in all price categories that are "kid-friendly" and offer the best value for the money in the D.C. area.

1 Best Bets

- **Best Historic Hotel: Morrison-Clark Inn,** 1015 L St. NW (☎ 202/898-1200). The original twin buildings of this downtown B&B were erected in 1865, and the inn, exquisitely decorated in the Victorian style, is on the National Register of Historic Places.

- **Best Hotel Lobby for Pretending That You're Rich: Omni Shoreham,** near the National Zoo at 2500 Calvert St. NW (☎ 202/234-0700), is overdone, glitzy, and cavernous, but it's still a head-turner. Keep an eye on your spouse and kids here, or you might lose them.
- **Best Moderately Priced Hotel: Days Inn Premier Hotel,** 1201 K St. NW (☎ 202/842-1020; fax 202/289-0336; www.DaysInnwashdc.com), near Metro Center and the Convention Center, has a rooftop pool with sundeck and family restaurant. It offers families especially low weekend rates.
- **Best Inexpensive Hotel: Best Western Capital Beltway,** 5910 Princess Garden Pkwy., Lanham, Maryland (☎ 301/459-1000), is nicely furnished and has an indoor pool with a retractable roof. Van service is provided to the New Carrollton, Maryland, Metro station, a mile away.

  Near the Convention Center, **Hosteling International—Washington, D.C.,** 1009 11th St. NW (☎ 202/737-2333), keeps a handful of family rooms (the other dorm-style rooms are segregated by sex) for those who book early. Towels and soap are strictly BYO.
- **Best Campgrounds:** Both **Aquia Pines Resort Camp,** 3071 Jefferson Davis Hwy., Stafford, Virginia (☎ 800/726-1710-3447), and **Cherry Hill Park,** 9800 Cherry Hill Rd., College Park, Maryland (☎ 800/801-6449), are about a half hour from the heart of D.C. Open to RVers, these two campgrounds have pools and offer family activities and transportation to downtown. At Aquia, a family of four can rent a cabin for $40 a night.
- **Best Service:** The **Four Seasons** in Georgetown, at 2800 Pennsylvania Ave. NW (☎ 202/342-0444), hasn't won all those service awards for nothing. Whether you need a toothbrush, truffles, tuxedo, or tickets to a show, the staff delivers 24 hours a day.
- **Best Location:** The **J. W. Marriott Hotel,** 1331 Pennsylvania Ave. NW (☎ 202/626-6991), is within walking distance of many attractions and a block from Metro Center. Also downtown, **Loew's L'Enfant Plaza,** 480 L'Enfant Plaza SW (☎ 202/484-1000), is mere blocks from the Air & Space Museum and other Mall attractions, but if you're feeling lazy you can take the Metro from the station in the basement.
- **Best Overall Facilities:** The **J. W. Marriott,** downtown at 1331 Pennsylvania Ave. NW (☎ 202/626-6991), has three restaurants, a health club (with exercise room, indoor swimming pool, hydrotherapy pool, and game room), connecting mall with 85 shops and restaurants, car-rental service, gift shop, and business center.
- **Best Health Club:** In Georgetown, the **Four Seasons,** 2800 Pennsylvania Ave. NW (☎ 202/342-0444), has an indoor pool and whirlpool (wrap up in an oversized terry robe) and fully equipped state-of-the-art fitness club. If you forgot your workout clothes or a bathing suit, they'll loan 'em to you.
- **Best Fitness Facilities:** Near the National Zoo, the **Omni Shoreham,** 2500 Calvert St. NW (☎ 202/234-0700), is a logical choice for family fitness freaks, with a state-of-the-art health club/spa, oversized outdoor pool, and extensive grounds for power walks or jogs. The hotel's back door opens onto Rock Creek Park's 10 miles of hiking and biking trails and 1½-mile par course with 18 exercise stations.
- **Best Hotel Pool:** In downtown, **Loews L'Enfant Plaza,** 480 L'Enfant Plaza (☎ 202/484-1000), features an attractive outdoor pool (covered in the winter), which is surrounded by potted flowering plants, plenty of seating, and, best of all, a snack bar.
- **Best Views:** Some rooms at the **Loews L'Enfant Plaza,** 7th & D streets SW (☎ 202/484-1000), enjoy views of the Potomac River, Arlington, Virginia, and Georgetown.

2 Capitol Hill

After living in the D.C. area for more than 35 years, I still get a thrill every time I see the Capitol, especially when it is lighted like a beacon at night. You too can find your thrill on Capitol Hill, and be close to the Hill's attractions and Union Station. *A word of warning:* While my Hill friends accuse me of being overly cautious, I maintain that walking on side streets in this neighborhood after dark is not a smart idea.

EXPENSIVE

Hotel George

15 (unit block) E St. NW. ☎ **800/576-8331** or 202/347-4200. Fax 202/347-4213. www.hotelgeorge.com. 147 units. A/C TV TEL. Weekday $220 and up; weekend from $139. Weekend packages. Kids 16 and under stay free. Crib free; rollaway $20. AE, CB, DC, DISC, MC, V. Valet garage parking $20. Metro: Union Station.

Within spitting distance of the Capitol and Union Station, the eight-story Hotel George opened in 1998 in a pre–Depression era building, formerly the Bellevue Hotel. In 1999, the George was added to the prestigious list of Preferred Hotels and Resorts Worldwide.

Contemporary-style posters of G. W. hang in the hip two-story glass, chrome, and limestone lobby and uncluttered guest rooms. Now I don't think the father of our country was a fox, but *this* George is a definite looker. Stylistically, the hotel is a complete 180° from genteel Mount Vernon. Floor-to-ceiling cherry cabinets conceal dresser drawers, closet space, and a refreshment center. The rooms, spare but soothing in tone, are done in shades of tasteful beige. The upholstered lounge chair with ottoman and arm chair do much to soften the decor's hard edges. Hide the family jewels and loose change in the in-room safes. Business types can request a room with high-speed Internet access. Unwind with a choice movie on one of the complimentary premium stations (Nintendo is extra). Bathrooms (most with tub and shower but some with shower only) are a symphony of gray and white marble and black granite. Standard amenities include a coffeemaker, robe, clock radio, in-room safe dual-line phone system, data/fax modem ports, voice mail, and iron and ironing board. VCRs and CD players are available on request. Families can spread out by booking an adjoining parlor room (the hotel has seven) with double-size Murphy beds. During the day the extra space could be a playroom for the kids and/or office for you. The George Suite is a one-bedroom suite with separate living room, wet bar, powder room, dressing area, Jacuzzi, and shower.

Dining: Chef Jeff Buben (winner of the 1999 James Beard Foundation Mid-Atlantic Chef of the Year) whisks and whips up delectable French bistro fare at **bis.** Like the hotel, bis sports a clean, contemporary look. Open for breakfast, lunch, and dinner, bis is a grown-up kind of place, with such items as escargots, duck foie gras, steak tartare, sweetbreads, and sea scallops regularly on the lunch and dinner menu. The food is exquisite, the setting romantic. At dinner it'd be a shame to waste this on family members who favor meals in under 5 minutes, so although the kitchen will gladly prepare "child-friendly" food for your tots, I suggest trying bis with youngsters at breakfast and lunch. At dinner you'd do better to feed the kids in Union Station with its myriad restaurants and multiple-choice Food Court, then slip downstairs for a quiet dinner for two.

Amenities: Iron and ironing board, coffee maker, refreshment center, robe, in-room safe, dual-line phone system, data/fax modem ports; VCRs and CD players available on request.

Washington, D.C. Accommodations

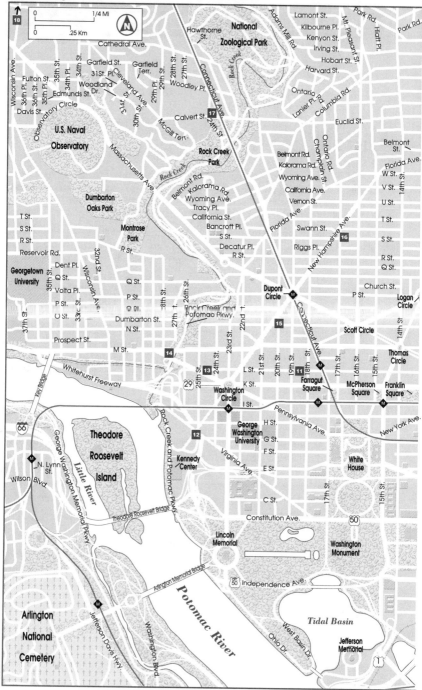

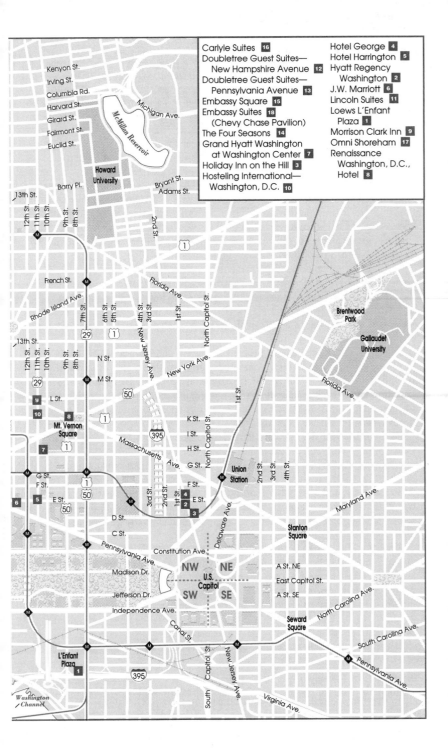

Carlyle Suites **16**
Doubletree Guest Suites—
  New Hampshire Avenue **12**
Doubletree Guest Suites—
  Pennsylvania Avenue **13**
Embassy Square **15**
Embassy Suites **18**
  (Chevy Chase Pavilion)
The Four Seasons **14**
Grand Hyatt Washington
  at Washington Center **7**
Holiday Inn on the Hill **3**
Hosteling International—
  Washington, D.C. **10**

Hotel George **4**
Hotel Harrington **5**
Hyatt Regency
  Washington **2**
J.W. Marriott **6**
Lincoln Suites **11**
Loews L'Enfant
  Plaza **1**
Morrison Clark Inn **9**
Omni Shoreham **17**
Renaissance
  Washington, D.C.,
  Hotel **8**

✪ Hyatt Regency Washington

400 New Jersey Ave. NW, Washington, DC 20001. ☎ **800/233-1234** or 202/737-1234. Fax 202/737-5773. www.regencywashington.com. 865 units. A/C MINIBAR TV TEL. Weekday $225–$290 single, $250–$315 double, $260–$350 Regency Club; weekend from $99 single or double. Children under 18 stay free in parents' room; crib free. Weekend and seasonal packages, Gold Passport and Regency Club available. Ask about AAA discounts. AE, DC, DISC, MC, V. Valet parking $22 (overnight), limited meter parking. Metro: Union Station.

The wonderful Camp Hyatt program was born at this Hyatt on Capitol Hill in 1986. As part of Camp Hyatt, families can book a second room at half price for the kids, and the restaurants and room service have special kids' menus.

The hotel is within walking distance of Metro, the U.S. Capitol, and other Capitol Hill attractions. It's a little farther to the Mall and Smithsonian museums.

This Hyatt caused quite a stir with its five-story atrium lobby and luxurious rooms and facilities when it opened in 1976. Now, of course, the style is as fresh as yesterday's scandal. But it's still attractive. The rooftop restaurant, the Capitol View Club, has a bird's-eye view of the Capitol building.

Standard amenities include a stocked minibar, TV, CNN, Spectravision (charge), hair dryer, and irons. On the 8th and higher floors you'll find two phones and a coffeemaker. Some rooms have showers only, so if you're a bubble bath fan, be sure to ask. With the Business Plan and Regency Club, a continental breakfast is included. The Hyatt has a full line of ADA equipment for disabled guests as well as accessible rooms and suites.

Extras include two restaurants (where kids 15 and under can order smaller portions for half price), and a large pool in a beautiful two-story glass atrium with a poolside juice and snack bar and health club (kids 18 and under must be accompanied by an adult). You'll also find a shoeshine stand and a gift and sundries shop for postcards, snacks, and, we hope, copies of this book. You can arrange an Old Town Trolley Tour at the concierge desk.

Dining/Diversions: The sunny **Park Promenade** is a 200-seat atrium restaurant, which is open for breakfast, lunch, and dinner. Fresh, seasonal dishes are offered at reasonable prices. **NetWorks,** the lobby bar, is the perfect place to have a quick lunch, enjoy a drink, or watch that all-important game on the big screen TV. The rooftop **Capitol View Club** is open to the public for dinner nightly. At lunch it serves hotel guests and club members exclusively (maybe you'll run into your Senator). I wouldn't bring children under 10 here for dinner. Enjoy cocktails (or late-night cordials and cigars) in the adjacent lounge.

Amenities: Room service (6am to midnight), concierge, shoeshine, complimentary newspaper delivery, twice-daily maid service, express check-out; laundry/dry cleaning service (charge), in-room massage (extra), baby-sitting ($10 per hour), secretarial services, Spectravision movies, indoor heated pool with deck and juice/snack bar (kids 16 and under must be accompanied by an adult) located within the health club (fee) with saunas (kids 18 and under must be accompanied by an adult), gift shop, business center, conference rooms.

MODERATE

Holiday Inn on the Hill

415 New Jersey Ave. NW, Washington, DC 20001. ☎ **800/638-1116** or 202/638-1616. Fax 202/638-0707. www.basshotels.com/holiday-inn. 343 units. A/C TV TEL. Weekdays $119–$179; weekends $109–$169, single or double. Ask about Holiday Inn Great Rate. Kids 18 and under stay free in parents' room; crib free; rollaway $20. Kids under 12 eat free with an adult. AE, DC, DISC, MC, V. Self-parking $15 per day. Metro: Union Station.

At this prime Capitol Hill location—the Capitol is only 2 blocks away—the Holiday Inn is a find, especially on weekends, when the rates dip as low as $109. Underground parking is available, and Union Station and Amtrak are less than a 5-minute walk away. Rooms, which were renovated in 1999, are clean, large, and comfortable, with an extra sink or vanity outside the bathroom. If you want more space, request a room with an adjoining parlor—a large TV/sitting room.

Now hear this: Every night from Memorial Day to Labor Day, from 5 to 10pm, guests can drop their kids at the Discovery Zone, a special room set aside just for them. (Of course, an attendant/sitter is on duty.) While the children enjoy movies, Ping-Pong, Nintendo, crafts, and board and card games, you can enjoy a quiet dinner downstairs or at any other restaurant in the city, for that matter. (Where was the Discovery Zone when my kids were growing up?) The fee for all this good fortune is only $5 per child per night.

The remote-control TVs have HBO and Nintendo, and there are soda and ice machines on every floor. In summer, take the young ones swimming in the rooftop pool—one of the largest in the city—with its adjacent sundeck and Skybox snack bar with a view and a hamburger and cold drink. If you forgot toothpaste, purchase some at the front desk.

Senators Sports Grill has a special menu with games and pictures to color for the kids. And, hey, kids 12 and under eat free when dining with an adult. Try that at home! The all-you-can-eat breakfast buffet could be your main meal. Stop in the adjacent cocktail lounge where, during Happy Hour, snacks are $1.

Service is key here; more than half of the employees have been with the hotel for 5 or more years. How many hotels can make that claim? Amenities include room service and a coin-op laundry, which may be history by the time you check in.

3 Convention Center

This may not be the most scenic part of the city, but it is convenient; many attractions—among them Ford's Theatre, the FBI, and the MCI Center, with sports events, concerts, and the Discovery Channel store—are within walking distance. At nearby Metro Center, 12th and G streets NW, you can board trains on all five subway lines.

EXPENSIVE

✪ Renaissance Washington, D.C., Hotel

999 9th St. NW, at K St. NW, Washington, DC 20001. ☎ **800/228-9898** or 202/898-9000. Fax 202/789-4213. www.Renaissancehotels.com. 801 units. A/C TV TEL. Weekday $199 single, $219 club single, $219 double, $239 club double; weekend from $109 (depending on availability) to $199 single or double. Children 18 and under stay free in parents' room; crib free. Seasonal and weekend packages available. Ask about the Renaissance Rendezvous. AE, CB, DC, DISC, MC, V. Parking (valet or self) $14. Metro: Gallery Place or Metro Center.

There are plenty of hustle and bustle weekdays at the 801-room Renaissance, which mainly serves conventioneers attending functions at the Convention Center across the street. The Renaissance is centrally located, convenient to the White House (about 8 blocks via New York Avenue west to Pennsylvania Avenue), Mall, and MCI Center. On weekends, when the place is relatively quiet, families can take advantage of huge savings and enjoy all the extras on a shoestring.

Thanks to recent renovations—new lighting, chairs, drapes, and spreads in guest rooms—everything looks brand spanking new in the 9-year-old property. The attractive, well-equipped rooms have coffeemakers and refrigerators, remote-control color TVs with cable, pay movie options, and CNN, hair dryers, and video message retrieval. There are ice and soft-drink machines on every floor.

An entire six-story tower with 146 rooms constitutes the Renaissance Club, where guests are pampered with extra amenities. Club guests also have a private concierge-staffed lounge, a cozy domain where you may enjoy sharing a complimentary continental breakfast with the kids from 6:30 to 10am. Afternoon hors d'oeuvres are available from 5 to 7pm for grown-ups.

Adjacent to the third-floor health club are a 60-foot pool and juice machines. A minishopping area and a newsstand are right off the large atrium lobby, which is broken up into small sitting areas—ideal for kids who need a little space and want to have a hot game of cards or checkers. The Chinese rock garden outside is something to see and may inspire a game of hide-and-seek. Public areas and several guest rooms are ADA-compliant for disabled guests.

Dining/Diversions: One restaurant, a lounge, and outdoor cafe serve everything from gourmet fare to pizza. **Florentine** is the Renaissance's upscale gourmet restaurant featuring American regional cuisine. For an after-dinner drink, the **Tavern Lounge** and **Lobby Court Bar** offer a pleasing palm-filled setting. In warm weather, the most picturesque dining spot is the family friendly outdoor **Plaza Gourmet,** where breakfast, salads, sandwiches, and finger food are served from 7:30am to 5pm, weather permitting.

Amenities: 24-hour room service, concierge daily from 7am to 11pm, laundry/dry cleaning, baby-sitting (fee), secretarial services (fee), express check-out, valet parking, complimentary *USA Today,* free in-room coffee, indoor heated pool, fully equipped health club (with lap pool, whirlpool, steam rooms, treadmills, Stair-Masters, bikes, rowing machines), aerobics classes, gift shops, business center, conference rooms, tour desk, newsstand.

INEXPENSIVE

○ Days Inn Premier Hotel

1201 K St. NW, Washington, DC 20005. ☎ **800/562-3350** or 202/842-1020. Fax 202/289-0336. www.daysinnwashdc.com. 219 units. A/C TV TEL. Weekday $99–$160 single or double; weekend $99 single or double. Extra person $10. Children under 18 stay free in parents' room. AE, CB, DC, DISC, MC, V. Valet parking (based on availability) $16. Metro: Metro Center.

Note: This hotel is slated to become a Sheraton 4 Point property in April 2000, so prices, decor, and amenities are bound to change.

The Days Inn Premier is convenient to the Convention Center and within walking distance of many downtown attractions.

Standard amenities include air-conditioning (a given in all D.C. hotels!), telephone, TV, coffeemaker, and hair dryer. Most rooms have refrigerators, a second phone, and view of something more pleasing than an elevator shaft. Some have fax machines. Although this isn't the most picturesque block in the city, the location is primo. It's 4 blocks to Metro Center, where you can hop a train for anywhere on Metro's five lines. Walk to Ford's Theatre, the FBI, the Shops at National Place, the Mall, the MCI Center for a sports event or rock concert, and downtown shopping. Stroll a little further and you'll land on the National Mall. A small rooftop swimming pool with a sundeck is more than adequate for cooling off after pounding the summertime pavement. Kids can watch free movies on TV or the channel airing tourism information. There are ice, soda, snack, and candy machines on every floor, and Impressions restaurant welcomes families with open arms. Many favorite, family friendly restaurants—Hard Rock Cafe, Planet Hollywood, T.G.I. Friday's, Capitol City Brewing Co.—are within a few blocks. You can call room service when the spirit moves you or rent a car from one of the agencies across the street. Too tired to dine out? Call Domino's Pizza at 1300 L St. NW (☎ **202/639-8700**).

Impressions is the casual, family friendly restaurant in the Days Inn, serving breakfast, lunch, and dinner daily, except for Saturday lunch. Load up on the $6.95 breakfast buffet, available from 7 to 10:30am, and you may be able to skip lunch altogether. Impressions has a children's menu for kids 11 and under at lunch and dinner (hamburgers, chicken fingers, and the like).

Amenities include concierge, room service, dry cleaning, laundry service, newspaper delivery, in-room massage, secretarial services, express check-out, valet parking, courtesy shuttle service (by prior arrangement), outdoor pool with lifeguard, self-service Laundromat, business center, conference rooms, car-rental desk, tour desk, and an arrangement with nearby fitness center.

✪ Hosteling International—Washington, D.C.

1009 11th St. NW, at K St., Washington, DC 20001. ☎ **202/737-2333.** Fax 202/737-1508. www.hiayh.org. E-mail: dchostel@erols.com. 250 beds. A/C. $20 HI members; $23 nonmembers (yearly membership is $25 per adult). Children 3–11 (with a parent) pay $10 per night, 2 and under free. MC. V. No parking; public lots, some street parking in area. Metro: Metro Center, McPherson Square, Gallery Place.

Hosteling International (HI) offers dorm-style rooms in a renovated downtown building. Lodging is strictly no-frills and I wouldn't call the neighborhood drop-dead gorgeous, but the location just 3 blocks north of the Metro Center stop is extremely convenient. The big question is: Can your family survive without an in-room TV? (There's one in the game room.) The dorm-style rooms—all air conditioned—are comfortable and have from 4 to 18 beds; there are clean, recently renovated bathrooms down the hall, and new curtains are in place. Some family rooms, accommodating four persons, are available. Book early. Although some of the dorm rooms are coed, most are for men or women, so couples are separated, with sons sleeping in the same dorm as fathers and daughters with their mothers.

Guests must provide their own soap and towels. Linens, blankets, and pillows are provided. Sleeping bags are allowed. You can borrow sleep sheets here for a small deposit.

Upon registering, you'll be given a calendar of events. The HI offers special activities for guests—walking tours, concerts, movies, and more. And the knowledgeable staff at the information desk is available to help guests with sightseeing and other travel questions. Movies are shown every evening at 8pm. Conference rooms and a self-service Laundromat are available.

To cut costs further, you can shop for groceries at the Giant supermarket at 9th and P streets NW. Meet some of the international visitors who stay here while preparing meals in the huge self-service kitchen, and eat in the dining room. Just like home! There's a comfortable lounge, storage lockers, and indoor parking for bicycles. All public areas and rooms are accessible to travelers with disabilities.

Reserve as far in advance as possible, especially for a family room. Check-in is anytime; checkout is 11am. Remember, the maximum stay is 29 nights. With the money you save by staying here, you can fund a return visit next year.

4 Downtown

If you stay in this area, you can roll out of bed and onto the White House lawn. Well, *almost.* While you'll usually pay top dollar for accommodations at a downtown hotel, you'll have more time for sightseeing and spend less getting around. If your time is limited, wouldn't you rather spend it *in,* rather than traveling *to,* a museum?

VERY EXPENSIVE

✪ Grand Hyatt Washington at Washington Center

1000 H St. NW, Washington, DC 20001. ☎ **800/233-1234** or 202/582-1234. Fax 202/637-4781. www.washington.grand.hyatt.com. 960 units. A/C MINIBAR TV TEL. Weekday $255 single, $280 double, $500–$1,700 suite; weekend $119–$175 single or double. Children under 18 stay free in parents' room; crib free. Special family weekend rates, and Regency Club and Business Plan available. Ask about AAA discounts. AE, CB, DC, DISC, MC, V. Self-parking $12. Metro: Metro Center.

Your kids may not want to go home after they see this place! Adjacent to Metro Center, the Grand Hyatt is within walking distance of the National Aquarium, National Mall, FBI, Ford's Theatre, Chinatown, the Old Post Office Pavilion, and shopping. The large, well-appointed rooms are located on 12 floors surrounding a stunning glass-enclosed atrium filled with abundant light and greenery. There's plenty of action and razzle-dazzle here for the entire family. Standard amenities include a TV with 44 cable channels, hair dryers, and coffeemakers. The suites have wet bars. Seeing Eye dogs are welcome. The Hyatt has 24 ADA-designated rooms; accessibility devices are available through housekeeping.

As part of the weekend family program, kids 18 and under (traveling with a parent or guardian) get their own room at half price, as well as special room-service and restaurant menus. They can also borrow books, videos, and games at the concierge desk that will allow you to slip off for a little quality adult time. Kids can swim in the indoor pool (accompanied by an adult), play shuffleboard and mini-basketball at Grand Slam (with a parent or guardian), feel the spray from the two-story waterfall, or watch an in-room movie or videos. Board the **Old Town Trolley** outside the 10th Street door. One ticket will buy you a guided tour of 12 attractions, and you'll be allowed to board and reboard as often as you like.

Dining/Diversions: Breakfast or lunch on American fare in the open-air **Grand Café** (open daily from 6:30am to 3pm) surrounding the lagoon. Kids 3 and under eat free; those 12 and under can order smaller portions for half price or items from the children's menu. I'm partial to the delicious club sandwich at lunch. Relax while the pianist at the white baby grand piano (atop a glass-and-stone "lily pad") sends soothing sounds your way.

Sharing is encouraged at dinner in the **Via Pacifica** restaurant, where Italian and Asian fare share billing on the eclectic menu. Enjoy drinks and light fare at the **Via Bar** overlooking the lagoon daily from 4pm to midnight.

The **Zephyr Deli** is open for breakfast, lunch (sandwiches, pizza, salads), and snacks daily from 7am to 3pm. Pick up sandwiches and picnic on the Mall or in your room if you return for a midday siesta. Kids can accompany their parents to the **Grand Slam** sports bar to shoot pool, watch their favorite teams on large-screen TVs, or play miniature hockey and interactive video games while downing burgers, hot dogs, chicken wings, and nachos. Since this is primarily a bar, please don't send your kids here unaccompanied. **Butler's** is the Hyatt's art deco cigar bar, good for a stogie and a martini your way—shaken or stirred. Enjoy live jazz some evenings while soaking up the cigar culture (and smoke).

Amenities: Concierge and 24-hour room service, dry cleaning/laundry service, complimentary newspaper delivery, in-room massage by appointment (charge), baby-sitting, secretarial services, express check-out, courtesy car based on availability, 44 cable channels. **Regency Club Weekend Package** includes breakfast, tea and cookies, cocktails, and hors d'oeuvres served in a private lounge, fully equipped business center, bike rentals, heated indoor pool (kids under 16 must be accompanied by an adult); steam room, sauna, health club, Jacuzzi, sauna, exercise/aerobics room, massage room; car rental/tour desk, business center, conference rooms, gift shop.

EXPENSIVE

✪ J. W. Marriott

1331 Pennsylvania Ave. NW at E St., Washington, DC 20004. ☎ **800/228-9290** or 202/393-2000. Fax 202/626-6991. www.marriotthotels.com. 772 units. A/C MINIBAR TV TEL. Weekday and weekend $119–$259 single or double; ask about Weekend Escape package. Children under 16 stay free in parents' room; crib/rollaway free. Extra person $10. AE, CB, DC, DISC, ER, JCB, MC, V. Valet garage parking $16; self-parking $6 per hr/$25 per day. Metro: Metro Center.

One look at the large, opulent lobby and you know the Marriott family has come a *long* way since opening a root-beer stand on 14th Street in 1927. The expansive space—with crystal chandeliers, towering ficus trees, and fresh flower arrangements—is a sight for sore eyes, as my grandmother used to say. Public areas were recently refurbished and recarpeted. Renovation of the guest rooms began in November 1999 and should be completed by March 2000. If for some reason construction is still going on when you make your reservation, be sure to request a room away from any related noise and dust. Pretty as the Marriott is, it's easy to become disoriented. One end of the lobby flows into the Shops at National Place, making things a bit more confusing, so keep a sharp eye on younger kids. Send them on an errand and they may be gone for days.

Marriott's **"Two for Breakfast"** concept has proved to be a winner. When the package is available on a Friday and/or Saturday night, the next morning's full breakfast is included. Kids stay free, and those 5 and under eat free from the special kids' menu in the hotel restaurants. A late (3pm) checkout may be included. Weekend visitors will want to ask if the Weekend Escape (or some other) package is available.

If you're looking for luxury and location, you've arrived. Metro Center, with trains on all lines, is one block away. Even without the decor update in 2000, the rooms are light and bright. Tasteful furnishings include a king or two double beds, a good-size dresser, desk and chair, two phones, remote-control TV with cable and premium movie channels, and a stocked minibar. The minibar contents, however, are not free. Suites have kitchenettes. Bathrooms are generous in size; a terry robe, hair dryer, and basket of amenities await guests. A limited number of rooms have a view of the Washington Monument or Pennsylvania Avenue, rather than a courtyard. (Be a squeaky wheel if you want one.) Kids will no doubt bypass the health club and maybe the indoor pool in their haste to reach the game room. (For this you traveled to Washington?) While they're playing you can work out, swim 100 laps, or slip into the Garden Terrace lounge for a cocktail in the Pennsylvania Avenue view.

Nobody goes hungry at the Marriott. The four restaurants run the gamut from very elegant to very casual (see below). Children are better served at the **Food Hall** next door in the Shops at National Place. A host of good restaurants are within a short walk or Metro ride.

Dining/Diversions: Continental cuisine, with an emphasis on seafood specialties, is featured at elegant and pricey **Celadon.** Kids over 12 with sophisticated taste buds may like the atmosphere and food; those younger will consider it a punishment. Off the lobby is the **Garden Terrace,** with a window wall overlooking Freedom Plaza (Pennsylvania Avenue). My money is on the Sunday buffet-style brunch accompanied by a jazz combo or trio, 10:30am to 3pm. Try to snag a window table for a primo view of Pennsylvania Avenue. **Allie's American Grille** on the lower level features American cuisine and the atmosphere is more casual than at Celadon. Or you can grab a snack at **SRO,** a New York–style deli next to Allie's. Kids are welcome to watch their favorite team on TV as long as they don't stand at the bar or drink.

Amenities: 24-hour room service, concierge, laundry/valet (extra), complimentary newspaper, health club (with exercise room with Universal equipment, indoor swimming pool, Jacuzzi, sauna), in-room massage (extra), twice-daily maid service, baby-sitting (extra), and video arcade, a connecting mall with 85 shops and restaurants, car rental, gift shop, business center, secretarial services, conference rooms, car rental and tours, express check-out, complimentary coffee and refreshments in lobby.

✪ Loews L'Enfant Plaza Hotel

480 L'Enfant Plaza SW, Washington, DC 20024. ☎ **800/23-LOEWS** or 202/484-1000. Fax 202/646-4456. www.loewshotels.com. 392 units. A/C MINIBAR TV TEL. $209 single/double weekdays; $475 suite. Weekend specials from $109. Children under 18 stay free in parents' room; crib free, rollaway $20. Weekend packages. Ask about daily packages late June–Sept. AE, CB, DC, DISC, MC, V. Valet garage parking $16. Metro: L'Enfant Plaza. Pets accepted.

If you're not on a budget, this hotel is hot. First of all, the location is prime. It's a 5-minute walk to the Air & Space museum, a little longer to other sites on the Mall. Don't feel like walking? The steps off the lobby lead to a Metro transfer station for the Blue, Orange, Yellow, and Green lines. Headed for the Smithsonian? It's one stop away.

I, who descend from less-than-noble stock, think this hotel is Classy with a capital *C.* The lobby is quietly elegant, European in tone. Nicely integrated with the lobby are a lounge, restaurant, and a couple of shops. The staff, from the executive office on down, is professional, gracious, and courteous. As part of the Loews Loves Kids program, children receive a gift on arrival and order from a special kids menu in the restaurant. The Tour for Tots takes a look at the so-called "back of the house." And pets are welcome. In fact, if Spot checks in with you, Loews donates 5% of the room rate to the Washington, D.C., Humane Society.

Guest rooms take up the top four floors of the 15-story office building. The 14th- and 15th-floor rooms have balconies. Take your pick of views: You can overlook the city with a sweep from the Washington Monument to the Washington Cathedral several miles away or the Potomac riverfront, with its restaurants and marinas, across to East Potomac Park and Virginia.

To say the rooms are well appointed is an understatement. There are three phones, one in the bathroom, two in the bedroom, *each* with two lines. If you're traveling with teenagers, you'll recognize the advantage. New spreads and drapes were added in 1999. A large armoire contains a drawer filled with souvenirs, stocked minibar (locked against mischievous hands), hair dryer, coffeemaker, and TV with CNN and on-command movies (for a charge) when you tire of the view outdoors. Most rooms have faxes. Choose a room with two doubles or a king, or upgrade to one of the suites with a kitchenette.

In the bathroom, besides the usual plumbing and amenities, are a small TV and phone. The closet holds a safe for pocket change. The upgraded Club Room comes with a full breakfast and fruit, wine, and cheese daily. And a river view.

The outdoor pool is a knockout, as nice as I've seen at any resort, with plenty of chaises and chairs, and cachepots brimming with flowering plants. In winter, the pool area is covered with a bubble. A lifeguard is on duty from 9am to 8pm, and the snack bar serves drinks, sandwiches, and burgers. It's understandable why many families request a room around the pool.

Adults are invited to make use of the 11th-floor state-of-the-art fitness center. The center features free weights, Nautilus equipment, aerobics classes, and massages.

Although check-in is at 3pm, if your room is ready earlier, the staff will not make you squirm. They'll give you the key.

A 5-minute walk over a pedestrian-only bridge will lead you to the waterfront, where you can board the *Spirit of Washington* cruise to Mount Vernon, inspect the seafood stands along Maine Avenue, eat in one of several riverside restaurants, or ogle the pleasure craft in the marina. The hotel is also within walking distance of the Bureau of Engraving and Printing, the Holocaust Museum, and Tidal Basin.

Besides the restaurants down by the riverside, there are fast-food and sit-down establishments in underground L'Enfant Plaza (down the same steps you take to the Metro).

Dining: Children accompanied by a dining adult eat free from the children's menu between 5:30 and 7:30pm. Poolside from 11am to 7pm during summer months, **Flamingos** features burgers, sandwiches, salads, sweets, and spirits. Let me know what you think of the frozen drinks.

The **American Grill** has three sections. The **Terrace** is for upscale dining inside, and dinner entrees run from $17 to $19. A breakfast buffet, "Monumental Breakfasts" such as the "Judicial" (fresh-squeezed orange juice, waffle or French toast, bacon or sausage, and a beverage), lunch, and dinner are served in the American Grill and **Lobby Café**. At lunch, an assortment of sandwiches, salads, and hot main courses is priced from $8 to $16. The dinner menu includes main dishes from $10 to $25. The Lobby Café, probably the best bet with children, is open for breakfast and lunch. The cute and colorful Kid Cuisine menu, available for lunch and dinner, lists half a dozen main courses such as pizza and burgers ($2.95 to $5.25) and desserts ($2 to $4).

Amenities: Room service from 6:30am to midnight, 24-hour concierge, laundry/valet, twice-daily maid service, baby-sitting arrangements and secretarial services (both at extra charge), express check-out, outdoor pool (bubble September to May) with snack bar; fully equipped health club with Nautilus equipment, weights, aerobic classes, masseuse (no one under 16), boutiques; connecting mall with shops, restaurants, arcade, free lemonade in lobby during summer.

MODERATE

Lincoln Suites

1823 L St. NW, Washington, DC 20036. ☎ **800/424-2970** or 202/223-4320. Fax 202/223-8546. www.lincolnhotels.com. 99 studio suites. A/C TV TEL. Weekday $129–$149 single or double; weekend $109–$119 single or double. Children under 16 stay free in parents' room. Extra person $10. Weekend packages available. AE, DC, DISC, MC, V. Parking $14 (valet), free on-street Fri night through Sun. Metro: Farragut North or Farragut West. Pets allowed.

Walk to the White House, National Geographic, and the Renwick and Corcoran galleries from this rather elegant-looking residential hotel 2 blocks from the Connecticut Avenue business corridor lined with upscale dining and shopping establishments. At the Lincoln Suites, visitors enjoy the comforts of home just four Metro stops from the Smithsonian museums. The heck with proximity to the museums, the Lincoln Suites serves freshly baked cookies, with cold milk to wash 'em down, nightly in the lobby. And weekends, a continental breakfast is included in the rate.

All efficiency suites (for the sake of clarity, that's one room, folks) have air-conditioning, two phones, TV with CNN, sink, refrigerator (unstocked), coffeemaker, cutlery, china, cookware, a microwave, and a wet bar, hair dryer, iron, and ironing board. King studio suites have a desk, two phones, and a computer jack. The bathrooms were renovated and new elevators were installed in 1999. Twenty-four rooms have full kitchens. And you can fill the fridge with dog food, but it'll cost you $15 per day to bring Spot along.

Lincoln Suites' on-premises restaurant, **Mackey's Public House,** serves Irish fare in a setting befitting its name. While youngsters are welcome anytime, the manager says the pub can become a bit rowdy Friday and Saturday nights.

Amenities include concierge, room service (lunch and dinnertime), complimentary *Washington Post* weekdays, complimentary cookies and milk (evenings), laundry and dry cleaning, express check-out, valet parking, video rentals, tour desk, conference rooms, gratis use of the nearby Bally's Total Fitness (2 blocks away) with Nautilus equipment, Lifecycles, an indoor running track, StairMasters, aerobics classes, and more (kids must be accompanied by an adult).

INEXPENSIVE

Hotel Harrington
11th and E sts. NW, Washington, DC 20004. ☎ **800/424-8532** or 202/628-8140. Fax 202/347-3924. www.hotel-harrington.com. E-mail: hotel-harrington.com. 290 units. A/C TV TEL. Weekday from $85 single or double; triples and quads from $95. Family discounts available. Family, weekend, and summer packages available. Cribs and refrigerators free. AE, DC, DISC, MC, V. Garage self-parking $8.50 per 24 hours (cars & minivans only). Metro: Metro Center.

Some things never change, thank heaven. The Harrington is still 6 blocks from the White House, still family owned after more than 75 years, and still one of the best deals around. An easy walk to the FBI, Ford's Theatre, the Shops at National Place, the Old Post Office Pavilion, the National Aquarium, and several Smithsonian museums, it is 2 blocks to Metro Center and all five Metrorail lines. With the money you save by staying here you can splurge at nearby Planet Hollywood and be a hero to your kids. Speaking of kids, at check-in ask for a Harrington Hawk, an unassembled toy airplane.

Make no mistake, you'll know you're in an older hotel, but the high-ceilinged rooms are clean and have been updated recently with new carpets and drapes. The beds are firm; closets and bathrooms are small. Please note that some bathrooms have shower only. All rooms have a desk, chair, and TV with CNN. Take advantage of the refrigerator and stock it with snacks from the CVS Pharmacy at 13th Street and Pennsylvania Avenue NW. Soft drink machines are located on the lobby level and floors one through six; ice machines are on four floors. Triples and quads are ideal for families, with different bed configurations (queen and twin) and two bathrooms. Three restaurants (one a cafeteria), offer reasonably priced fare on site. How can you go wrong and still stay downtown? The neighborhood has taken a turn for the better in the last couple of years, we're pleased to report.

As a Harrington guest, you'll have access to a nearby health club (it'll cost ya') and a car-rental/tour desk. Bus service to Dulles Airport is also available. A self-service guest laundry is on the premises. Parking, at $8.50 per 24-hour period, is in a garage 4 blocks from the hotel that is open around the clock. Hotel Harrington guests have unlimited in-and-out access.

Little wonder this old-timer is still truckin' after so many years. The price is right, and the location is prime. The Harrington doesn't pretend to be something it is not, and it's the only hotel that hasn't succumbed to inflation in this pricey neighborhood.

The **Harrington Café** is a no-frills cafeteria, open year-round for breakfast, lunch, and dinner daily. At lunch if the line is out the door, try **Ollie's Trolley,** a bargain for a quick burger, fries, and shake. **Harry's Pub,** with sidewalk tables in good weather, is open from lunchtime until 1am for drinks, sandwiches, and snacks.

Amenities include cable TV with HBO, gift shop, coin-op laundry (tokens and complimentary soap at front desk).

5 Dupont Circle

Dupont Circle has a free-spirited, residential feel to it, with a real sense of neighborhood. It's definitely less uptight and less homogenous than most of "official" Washington. Stay here if you're into gallery- and boutique-browsing and people-watching, and if you don't mind a few extra minutes on Metro to the Mall attractions.

EXPENSIVE

❂ Embassy Square (A Summerfield Suites Hotel)

2000 N St. NW. Washington, DC 20036. ☎ **800/424-2999** or 202/659-9000. Fax 202/429-9546. www.staydc.com. 278 suites. A/C MINIBAR TV TEL. Weekday $179–$289; weekend $99–$179. AAA, weekly, and monthly rates subject to availability. Rates include continental breakfast. Children 17 and under stay free in parents' room; cribs free. AE, CB, DC, DISC, MC, V. Self-parking $15 (no vans). Metro: Dupont Circle.

First off, the Embassy Square is not to be confused with Embassy Suites—they are different chains. Choose an executive; one-bedroom; or two-bedroom, two-bathroom suite at this property catering to business travelers and relocating families. The accommodations are comfy and roomy, and half the rooms have balconies. It's ideal for families, as everyone is afforded space and privacy. The living room is equipped with a wet bar, refrigerator, coffeemaker, voice mail, data ports, and a second TV to prevent arguments over who watches what. (Spectravision is extra.) The walk-in kitchens come fully equipped, in case you miss cooking.

You want more? The rates include a deluxe continental breakfast, complimentary HBO and Disney channels, coin-operated laundry, iron and ironing board in each suite, and a 24-hour gift shop/convenience store. The pool sits in the center of an open-air courtyard, and adults have free use of the on-premises fitness center. All this, and you're only 2 blocks from the Dupont Circle Metro stop and within walking distance of the White House, Georgetown, and more than 30 art galleries and 75 restaurants. It's one Metro stop to Connecticut Avenue and K Street NW; two to Metro Center, where you can transfer to trains on the other lines.

Amenities: 24-hour front-desk assistance, concierge, complimentary coffee, dry cleaning/laundry service, outdoor pool and sundeck, complimentary use of on-premises fitness center, self-service Laundromat, conference rooms, tour desk.

MODERATE

Carlyle Suites

1731 New Hampshire Ave. NW, between R and S sts., Washington, DC 20009. ☎ **202/234-3200.** Fax 202/387-0085. 170 suites. A/C TV TEL. Weekday $69–$139 single, $79–$149 double, $150 suite; weekend $69 for 1, $79 for 2. Children under 18 stay free in parents' room; crib free. Extra person $10. Weekend packages available. AE, DC, MC, V. Parking free but limited. Metro: Dupont Circle (Q St. exit).

This eight-story all-suite hotel, 3 blocks from the Dupont Circle Metro, sits on a residential street (by D.C. standards) near restaurants, shops, and galleries. One of the top family attractions, the National Geographic Society Explorers Hall—with nourishment for the mind and soul—is 6 blocks away.

The Carlyle Suites, distinguished by its art deco exterior and lobby, has lots going for it besides its location. Rooms (with two double beds and a sofa bed, or a king and sofa bed) are average in size with large closets, a dining and sitting area, and well-equipped kitchenettes. You can even request a microwave for the children's popcorn. A Safeway market is 2 blocks away. Load up on supplies and your family can breakfast in the room if you choose, or snack while enjoying a movie on Spectravision. Do shop, because there's no room service here. Tables and chairs are set in a courtyard off the lobby for relaxing or writing postcards.

Randolph's Grill, created on a glass-enclosed patio, offers year-round outdoor dining, whatever the weather. On mild days the roof retracts to "let the sunshine in." The ample breakfast buffet will fortify your family before you set out. Light fare is served at lunch, and the dinner menu features a wide range of creative main dishes as well as home-style favorites. Randy is happy to cut adult portions to child size, and pizza and hamburgers are staples at lunch and dinner. If you prefer to relax and eat in your room, all items can be packed "to go." The **Wave Bar** serves light fare and cocktails from 4pm until midnight.

Amenities include 24-hour front-desk assistance, food shopping service, baby-sitting sources, and access to the nearby, adults-only **Sporting Club,** 1120 20th St. NW.

6 Georgetown

A small, sophisticated riverfront town within the city, Georgetown draws locals and out-of-towners with its fine Georgian architecture, hundreds of restaurants and shops, and party atmosphere (especially evenings and weekends). Of all D.C.'s neighborhoods, however, it is the least accessible to the Metro. The nearest station, Foggy Bottom, is a good 15-minute walk.

VERY EXPENSIVE

✪ Four Seasons Hotel Washington, D.C.

2800 Pennsylvania Ave. NW, Washington, DC 20007. ☎ **800/332-3442** or 202/342-0444. Fax 202/944-2076. www.fourseasons.com. 575 units. A/C MINIBAR TV TEL. Weekday from $370 single, from $410 double, from $775 suite; weekend from $345 single, from $385 double, from $500 suite. Children under 16 stay free in parents' room; up to 2 rollaways and crib free. Ask about seasonal packages. AE, DC, ER, JCB, MC, V. Valet parking $24, self-parking $10 (complimentary with some packages), some street parking. Metro: Foggy Bottom.

One of my fantasies is to have a suite at the Four Seasons (paid for by an admirer, of course) for spur-of-the moment getaways and days when I just don't feel like going home. I'm surprised the management of this elegantly appointed, yet unpretentious, Georgetown hostelry can coax guests to leave once they've experienced the coddling and TLC the Four Seasons is famous for worldwide. The hotel's staff-to-guest room ratio is two to one, and the concierge staff alone has filled as many as 300 requests a day for everything from 30-dozen long-stemmed red roses to Super Bowl tickets. Some visitors have checked in empty-handed (I don't suggest it) and been outfitted within hours—even at night. General manager Stan Bromley's credo is "You want, I get."

Some recent guests you may have heard of include John Travolta, Sheryl Crow, Nicholas Cage, Tom Hanks, and Val Kilmer. While business and entertainment types, heads of state, and royalty have frequented the hotel regularly since it opened in 1979, a greater number of families are staying here to enjoy the same service afforded sultans of faraway republics and stars of the silver screen.

Distinguishing the Four Seasons—the only AAA five-diamond hotel in Washington—is a lavish attention to details. As it is said, little things mean a lot.

Tips for Bargain Hunters

1. Use reservations services such as **Capitol Reservations** (details at beginning of chapter): They frequently obtain lower rates by booking rooms in volume.
2. Take advantage of **reduced weekend rates,** often offered Friday through Sunday and sometimes off-season weekdays as well. They may be as much as 50% lower.
3. Bargain with the reservations clerk. An unoccupied room nets a hotel zero dollars, and whatever you offer to pay is better than that. This works best on the afternoon of your arrival, when the desk knows there will be empty rooms. Adventurous families may try this approach; less adventurous ones may prefer confirmed reservations.
4. Ask about special discounts for families.

Traveling with an infant? The crib comes furnished with bumpers and a colorful mobile, in addition to bottles and bottle warmer, a change of diapers, and a diaper pail. Children can borrow a Disney video, board game, or Nintendo at the concierge desk, perhaps after taking tea (finger sandwiches, brownies, and milk shakes) in the Garden Terrace while their parents enjoy a more traditional afternoon tea. Families checking into a suite receive "the works": snacks, sodas, balloons, stuffed toys, games, books, and video games. All children under 13 receive a gift-wrapped game or activity book (squeeze toys for babies) and their own menu in the award-winning Seasons restaurant or in the Garden Terrace. They also get milk and cookies at evening turndown. (There'll be no living with them when you get home!)

As for the basics: A $20 million expansion of the hotel and health club took place in 1998. (Hey, I thought it looked pretty good before the facelift.) Every room has a remote-control TV, digital clock radio, combination minibar/refrigerator, hair dryer, three phones with a second line on the desk (handy if there's a teen in your midst), and safes. Hanging alongside the thick, oversized terry robes for Mom and Dad in all family-occupied rooms (and also at the indoor pool) are kid-sized flame-proof robes. While there's nothing novel about ice machines on every floor, a full bucket of ice greets arriving visitors.

Those partaking of such luxury have to follow certain ground rules. Children under 16 must be accompanied by an adult at the pool, whirlpool, and in the fitness club, where complimentary juices, coffee, and fruit are available for all. The recently expanded fitness club is 12,500 square feet of state-of-the-art luxury (what did you expect?). In addition to the lap pool, whirlpool, steam, sauna, Nautilus equipment, and weights, you'll find a Vichy shower, hydrotherapy, aerobics studio, and "quiet rooms." (I'd like to rent one of those!) Water toys are kept poolside for little squirts, and while you work out they can amuse themselves at the computer. You can even borrow a bathing suit or workout clothes if you forget yours. (I told you they think of everything.) Pets are welcomed with a treat and bottled water, served on a silver tray, no less.

The hotel, overlooking Rock Creek Park and the C & O Canal at the edge of Georgetown, with its historic homes and concentration of fine restaurants and shops, is only a few blocks from Washington Harbour, with more restaurants on the Potomac and a lovely park. The nearest Metro stop, Foggy Bottom, is a 15-minute walk or 5-minute bus ride. This might pose a problem if bad weather strikes unexpectedly or you're toting a sleepy toddler and/or cumbersome stroller along with your souvenirs. While a complimentary Four Seasons Lincoln Town Car is available on request, service can't be assured every time you venture out.

Dining/Diversions: The **Garden Terrace** lounge with overstuffed couches and large floral displays overlooks Rock Creek Park and is open for cocktails throughout the afternoon and evening and for tea 3 to 5pm daily. A pianist plays in the afternoon and evening. A Sunday Jazz Brunch (10:30am to 2pm) featuring a New Orleans–style jazz trio is extremely popular. The brunch is $43 and reservations are strongly recommended. **Seasons** restaurant features contemporary American fare in sumptuous surroundings overlooking the greenery (and some traffic) in Rock Creek Park. Open for breakfast, lunch, and dinner, it is not inexpensive; dinner for two with a drink and tip will set you back about $100. The eclectic menu changes seasonally. The restaurant is known for using the freshest in-season ingredients in dishes, including penne pasta and seafood in a pesto cream sauce, fish and seafood, chicken, and alternative cuisine (low-calorie, -sodium, -cholesterol) selections. The children's menu consists of more basic fare. The wine cellar is recognized as one of the country's best. Seasons is open year-round weekdays from 7am to 11am, noon to 2:30pm, and 6 to 10:30pm. Weekend hours are 8am to noon and 6 to 10:30pm (no lunch).

Amenities: 24-hour room service, concierge, twice-daily maid service, complimentary morning newspaper, videotape and compact disc library, complimentary coffee and tea from 6 to 8am in the lobby, complimentary overnight shoe shine, shuttle to Metro, express check-out, dry cleaning, laundry service, in-room massage, baby-sitting, secretarial services, valet parking, indoor heated pool and whirlpool, sauna, sundeck, jogging track, fully equipped state-of-the-art fitness club, children's programs, newsstand, shopping arcade, beauty salon, business center, conference rooms, car rental and tours (through concierge).

7 Foggy Bottom

Foggy Bottom is distinguished by its relatively quiet tree-lined streets and Lilliputian row houses. The sophisticated international air is generated by the State Department, Kennedy Center, and George Washington University. Pinstripers, students, artistic types, and old-timers populate the neighborhood after dark. In the West End of the city, charming Foggy Bottom is within walking distance of Georgetown and accessible to D.C.'s sights via the Metro station at 23rd and I streets NW.

EXPENSIVE

Doubletree Guest Suites—New Hampshire Avenue

801 New Hampshire Ave. NW, Washington, DC 20037. ☎ **800/424-2900** or 202/785-2000. Fax 202/785-9485. 101 suites. A/C MINIBAR TV TEL. Weekday/weekend $129–$199. Children under 18 stay free in parents' room; crib free. Extra person $20. Weekend and special packages available. Monthly rates. AE, DC, DISC, MC, V. Valet garage parking $15 per day. Metro: Foggy Bottom. Pets accepted.

A bag of chocolate chip cookies welcomes visitors to the Doubletree. Nice touch! All rooms have a wet bar, "honor" bar (you drink, you pay), robes, hair dryers, fully equipped kitchen with microwave and refrigerator, and an ironing board and iron. Cribs are free; rollaways are $15 per day. Stock up on snacks at the Safeway in the Watergate where you may run into Elizabeth Dole and her husband. A complimentary breakfast is served in the lobby weekends only. One advantage of this Doubletree over its cousin around the corner is the small rooftop pool and sundeck. It's too small to do laps, but it's big enough for a cooling dunk. If you're combining business with pleasure, the voice mail and two data ports will come in handy. And Fido or Fluffy are welcome here for a $15 daily fee. The big pluses at Doubletree Guest Suites are space and privacy—and those yummy cookies, which you collect at check-in.

Amenities: Room service (6am to 2:30pm and 5 to 10pm), complimentary newspapers (*USA Today* and the *Washington Post*), roof-top pool/sundeck, express check-in and check-out, dry cleaning/laundry service (extra), complimentary coffee in lobby, garage parking ($15 per day), vending and ice machines, meeting rooms, and secretarial services.

Doubletree Guest Suites—Pennsylvania Avenue

2500 Pennsylvania Ave. NW, Washington, DC 20037. ☎ **800/424-2900** or 202/333-8060. Fax 202/338-3818. 124 suites. A/C TV TEL. Weekday/weekend $129–$199. Children under 18 stay free in parents' room; crib free. Extra person $20. Weekend and special packages available. Monthly rates. AE, DC, DISC, MC, V. Valet parking $15 per day. Metro: Foggy Bottom. Pets accepted.

No, you're not seeing double. This Guest Suites is in Foggy Bottom too, and the suites are nearly identical. Walk to Georgetown, the Kennedy Center, the Renwick Museum, and the White House from this location. The Metro is a few short blocks away. The contemporary suites are looking younger than springtime after a major renovation in 1999. Units are spacious, with a living room/dining room, separate bedroom, full kitchen (refrigerator, stove, dishwasher, microwave) and bathroom. Veg out and watch a first-run movie on one of the premium channels or let the kids play Nintendo until they fall asleep. A complimentary continental breakfast is served in the lobby Saturday and Sunday mornings. There's a pleasant tree-lined patio off the rear of the lobby, and numerous restaurants are within a couple of blocks. Kinkead's, one of the best restaurants in the entire city, is a short walk, but I don't recommend it for very young children. And who can resist T.G.I. Friday's, also nearby, for satisfying family fare? The Foggy Dogg and Marshall's are local spots welcoming families. The Safeway in the Watergate is a 10-minute walk. This is also a good choice if you're shopping for colleges. George Washington University is a stone's throw away, Georgetown University a couple of miles to the west.

Amenities: Room service (6am to 10pm), coin-op laundry, laundry/dry cleaning service, complimentary newspaper, vending machines, and complimentary use of an off-premises health club (adults only), microwaves. Pets are welcome ($15 per day).

8 Upper Northwest

EXPENSIVE

✪ Embassy Suites at The Chevy Chase Pavilion

4300 Military Rd. NW, at Wisconsin Ave., Washington, DC 20015. ☎ **800/EMBASSY** or 202/362-9300. Fax 202/686-3405. www.embassy_suites.com. 198 suites. A/C TV TEL. Weekday $199–$289; weekend $159–$219. Rates include breakfast and cocktails. Children 18 and under stay free in parents' room; crib free, rollaway $10. Weekend, AAA, family, and seasonal packages available. AE, DC, DISC, MC, V. Garage self-parking $12 per day. Metro: Friendship Heights (Western Ave. exit).

When my kids were little, our family was on the verge of selling our house and moving to an Embassy Suites. Breakfast alone is sufficient reason to relocate. At this property, which opened its doors in October 1990 at the Chevy Chase Pavilion, guests enjoy a complimentary full, hot breakfast, served daily.

Spacious suites consist of a bedroom with a king-size bed or two doubles and a separate living room with a sofa bed. There are two TVs (ask about HBO and pay-per-view movies and Nintendo) and a wet bar and refrigerator, so the munchkins need never go hungry. Rooms also include a microwave, refrigerator, iron and ironing board, coffeemaker, and hair dryers.

Stay dry with underground access to the Friendship Heights Metro station. From there, it's only a 15-minute ride to downtown. Enjoy shopping downstairs in the multilevel Chevy Chase Pavilion with 50 shops and 5 restaurants. The hotel is within walking distance of scores of restaurants and more excellent shopping at Mazza Gallerie (with Neiman Marcus and Filene's Basement), Lord & Taylor, Saks, and Tiffany & Co.

After a tough day of sightseeing, swim in the indoor pool, unwind in the Jacuzzi, or work out in the fully equipped health club (kids must be accompanied by an adult). Cocktails are complimentary daily from 5 to 7pm.

Dining: Complimentary breakfast and cocktails daily in the hotel's **Café Cino.** Within the Chevy Chase Pavilion are the Cheesecake Factory, with California cuisine and 35 varieties of cheesecake and the California Pizza Kitchen, offering specialty pastas and gourmet pizza baked in a wood-burning oven. Maggiano's, half a block away on Wisconsin Avenue, has super Italian fare and huge portions. The front room is down-home casual for a quick bite with little ones. Several other restaurants are within easy walking distance.

Amenities: Suite service until 10pm, 24-hour front-desk assistance, valet/cleaning Monday through Friday, indoor pool, Jacuzzi, on-premises health club, coin-operated laundry.

✪ Omni Shoreham Hotel

2500 Calvert St. NW at Connecticut Ave., Washington, DC 20008. ☎ **800/THE-OMNI** or 202/234-0700. Fax 202/756-5145. www.omnihotels.com. 825 units. A/C MINIBAR TV TEL. Weekday/weekend $129–$309; $229–$450 suite. Children under 18 stay free in parents' room; crib free, cot $25. Extra person $25. Family and weekend packages available. AE, CB, DC, DISC, ER, JCB, MC, V. Garage self-parking $14; valet $17. Metro: Woodley Park-Zoo.

By the time you read this the dowager queen of D.C. hotels will have a new face. Not only were guest rooms completely redone in 1999, but numerous changes were made to the public areas and grounds. If you think bigger is better, your pockets are deep, and you have a family of fitness freaks who like to jump from sightseeing to jogging to swimming, look no further. The Omni Shoreham, adjacent to Rock Creek Park, is a self-contained 14-acre resort in a residential neighborhood off Connecticut Avenue, about 100 yards from the Metro and less than 15 minutes from downtown. At day's end, cool off in the large outdoor pool, work out in the health club, or stroll through the gardens. If you crave more exercise, the hotel's back door opens onto Rock Creek Park, with hiking, biking, riding, and jogging trails, and a fitness course.

This Omni Shoreham (when it was just the plain-old Shoreham) has in its lifetime provided the setting for Perle Mesta's celebrated parties, numerous inaugural balls, and Harry Truman's poker games. The cavernous lobby is usually filled with conventioneers weekdays.

As you might expect at these prices, the guest rooms are large and elegantly furnished. We hope that snacking kids will avoid picnicking on the bedspreads while they watch in-room movies. The chichi atmosphere, myriad amenities, marble-floored bathrooms, and glitzy lobby are all well and good, but the best thing about the Omni Shoreham is its location—you can walk to the National Zoo.

Dining: At press time the Omni Shoreham's elegant new restaurant was expected to open early in 2000. Stop at **A Little Something,** a European gourmet carry-out in the lobby, for a little something to tide you over to the next big meal. Enjoy your light bite at an outdoor table or in your room. The convenient carryout may be just what the doctor ordered if your little ones are too tired to eat in a proper *restaurant*.

Amenities: 24-hour room service, concierge, laundry/valet, video checkout, limousine rental, baby-sitting arrangement, outdoor pool; on-premises health club/spa with sauna, massage, manicure/pedicure (kids must be accompanied by an adult); 10 miles of jogging, hiking, and bicycle trails, 1½-mile Perrier par course with 18 exercise stations (in Rock Creek Park); newsstand.

9 Suburban Maryland

BETHESDA

Believe it or not, I remember when Bethesda was a sleepy suburban village. (I can't help yearning for those good old days when I'm caught in traffic on Wisconsin Avenue.) The big attractions here are the excellent restaurants in all price ranges. Almost all are within walking distance of the hotels. The Metro ride to downtown D.C. is about 30 minutes. Otherwise the area is overbuilt and overpopulated with people, office buildings, and cars.

EXPENSIVE

✪ Hyatt Regency Bethesda

One Bethesda Metro Center (Wisconsin Ave. and Old Georgetown Rd.), Bethesda, MD 20814. ☎ **800/233-1234** or 301/657-1234. Fax 301/657-6478. www.hyatt.com. 381 units. A/C MINIBAR TV TEL. Weekday $240–$285 single; $265–$295 double, from $400 suite; weekend from $89 single or double, from $175 suite. Children 18 and under stay free in parents' room; crib free. Special weekend, family, Gold Passport, and Camp Hyatt packages available. AE, CB, DC, DISC, MC, V. Self-parking $10; valet parking $14 per day. Metro: Bethesda.

Providing top-notch facilities at a convenient suburban location next to the Bethesda Metro, the Hyatt knows how to deliver the goods to vacationing families. As part of Camp Hyatt, families benefit from 50% savings on a second room. There's a special Camp Hyatt menu, and kids 12 and under can always order smaller portions at reduced rates in the Plaza Café.

As Yogi Berra used to say, you'll get "déjà vu all over again" when you enter the large plant-filled open-atrium lobby with its requisite bar. There is a definite tendency, obviously intentional, toward repetition among Hyatts, and this location is no exception. You have to admit though that it's eye-catching and, refreshingly, the Southwestern look is given a welcome reprieve.

The guest rooms, redecorated in 1999, are large and sumptuous with either a king or two double beds, plenty of closet and drawer space, and marble bathrooms. A one-bedroom suite that goes for $400 during the week may be $175 on weekends, when the rate for a regular room sometimes dips as low as $89. Always ask the reservationist for the best family rate available.

Stocked minibars, coffeemakers, hair dryers, two phones, and Spectravision on the TVs are standard. So are balconies/terraces. Don't be surprised though if your view is of commercial downtown Bethesda—not the pretty picture it once was. The once bucolic small town is a traffic-choked minimegalopolis.

Your kids will spend nary a dull moment here. There's a large glass-enclosed heated indoor pool (open daily during the summer, weekends the rest of the year), fully equipped health club (you'll have to go with them) and workout area, and a family-style restaurant. An 11-screen movie theater is within walking distance, as are more than 150 restaurants and Gifford's ice cream parlor.

Adjacent to the hotel at Bethesda Metro Center is a skating rink (open from Thanksgiving through February), playground and Food Court selling a variety of fast food and snacks. Friday evenings from May to September there's big-band dancing at an outdoor ballroom, and all ages are welcome. Bethesda Metro Center also sponsors special family events throughout the year. Usually once during the summer, 30 tons of sand are dumped on the ice rink for a beach party blast.

Bethesda abounds with more restaurants than you can shake a stick at, representing just about every ethnic persuasion. Mazza Gallerie, Chevy Chase Pavilion, and White Flint Mall (with Bloomies, Lord & Taylor, Border's, and numerous specialty shops) are about equidistant by car or Metro.

Dining: The kid-friendly **Plaza Café,** overlooking the skating rink and playground, is open for breakfast, lunch, and dinner. Half portions are available for kids 12 and under. Weekdays a Lunch Buffet, with a different theme each day (seafood, Italian) is $11.95. Saturday and Sunday from 11:30am to 2pm, the restaurant features an extended buffet (which they prefer not to call brunch) of hot and cold entrees, glorified breakfast dishes, salads, bread, dessert.

Amenities: Room service (6am to midnight), concierge, laundry/valet, newspaper delivery, secretarial services, express check-out, valet parking, free coffee, heated indoor pool, fully equipped health club, Jacuzzi, sauna, workout area, business center, conference rooms.

CHEVY CHASE
INEXPENSIVE

Holiday Inn Chevy Chase

5520 Wisconsin Ave., Chevy Chase, MD 20815. ☎ **800/HOLIDAY** or 301/656-1500. Fax 301/656-5045. 226 units. A/C TV TEL. Weekday from $79 single, from $89 double; weekend $79 single or double. Children 18 and under stay free in parents' room. "Great Rates" and "Best Breaks" packages are available through the toll-free reservation number. AE, CB, DC, MC, V. Free parking. Metro: Friendship Heights. Pets accepted.

This Holiday Inn is ideal for families that want to mix heavy doses of shopping with their sightseeing. Stroll over to Chevy Chase Pavilion, Saks Fifth Avenue, Lord & Taylor, Gucci, Brooks Brothers, Yves St. Laurent, and Mazza Gallerie (with Neiman Marcus and many upscale boutiques and specialty stores). When you run out of money and want to head downtown for some free sightseeing, the Friendship Heights Metro is only a block away.

The third-floor outdoor pool is watched over by a lifeguard from Memorial Day to Labor Day, and guests have use of the on-site fitness center. While you're working out, the younger kids can enjoy an in-room movie on Showtime or watch their favorite sports on ESPN. The family pooch can room here for free.

There's a slew of family restaurants within walking distance, too. Clyde's, the Cheesecake Factory, and Chadwick's all welcome families. Work off the cellulite and cheesecake in the on-site fitness center.

And if you don't want to leave the hotel, you can always try the Avenue Deli, which is open for breakfast and lunch and has a children's menu with plenty of good things to eat for hungry girls and boys, and an adult menu for those footing the bills. At Julian's (an upscale steak, pasta, and seafood restaurant), families can enjoy lunch and dinner specials such as grilled salmon and prime rib in a more formal dining room setting. Older kids are welcome here; preschoolers are not.

LANHAM
INEXPENSIVE

✪ Best Western Capital Beltway

5910 Princess Garden Pkwy., Lanham, MD 20708. ☎ **800/866-4458** or 301/459-1000. Fax 301/459-1526. www.bestwester.com. 169 units. A/C TV TEL. Weekday/weekend

$69–$99. Children 18 and under stay free in parents' room; rollaway $10, crib $10. Ask about spring and summer family specials. AE, DC, DISC, MC, V. Free parking. Metro: New Carrollton.

With such low rates you may want to move here permanently. Located in Prince George's County, near the intersection of Route 450 and the Beltway (495), the Best Western provides complimentary van service every half hour, from 7am until 8pm, to the New Carrollton Metro station, just 1 mile away. There you can board a train and be in the heart of downtown D.C. in 20 minutes. At off-hours, van service is by request.

The spacious two-story lobby is comfortably and attractively furnished, accented with stained-glass panels. A video game room with snack and drink machines is off the lobby, as well as a small gift shop. Adorning a wall near the front desk is a large Metro route map. In my humble opinion, this should be required reading in every D.C.-area hotel/motel.

A lovely indoor pool with a retractable roof is open year-round. The roof is open from Memorial Day weekend to early September. Refurbishment of all guest rooms is slated for completion by early 2000. You'll find ice machines on every floor; laundry facilities on the second floor. Microwaves and refrigerators are available on request. The sixth-floor rooms have king-size beds, hair dryers, microwaves, and refrigerators. The other floors have two doubles each—perfect for a family whose kids have not yet had a growth spurt. Traffic noise from the Beltway is a dull hum. At these prices, it's worth investing in earplugs. The quietest quarters are poolside and odd-numbered rooms.

Neptune's on the lobby level is a comfy, kid-friendly restaurant serving a breakfast buffet and dinner daily. The **Bay Street Nightclub** is a large wood-accented space (kind of clubby in appearance) that caters to those 25 and above. Within a 5-minute drive are oodles of fast-food and sit-down restaurants such as Red Lobster and Sizzler. Less than a mile away in Greenbelt are dozens more. Since this is, for the most part, a nonresidential neighborhood, I don't suggest a walk after dark.

Amenities include room service, shuttle service to Metro, meeting/banquet facilities, gift shop, coin-op laundry facilities, valet services, pool, game room, and free parking.

10 Suburban Virginia

The Virginia suburbs are marked by fine shopping, restaurants, and gridlock. If you travel into the District on Metro—a 10- to 30-minute ride, depending on where you're staying (Rosslyn is closest, Vienna farthest)—you won't have to fight the traffic.

ARLINGTON
EXPENSIVE

Embassy Suites Crystal City

1300 Jefferson Davis Hwy., Arlington, VA 22202. ☎ **800/EMBASSY** (362-2799) or 703/979-9799. Fax 703/920-5947. 267 suites. A/C MINIBAR TV TEL. Weekday $139–$259; weekend $109 and up. Rates include full breakfast and cocktails daily. Children 12 and under stay free in parents' room; crib free. Special weekend packages (from $109). Ask about AAA rates. AE, CB, DC, DISC, JCB, MC, V. Garage self-parking $10. Metro: Crystal City.

Except on weekends and in summer, business types account for most of this hotel's clientele. I'm surprised more families don't stay here year-round. For starters, you can walk or take the hotel's free transportation to the Crystal City or Pentagon City Metro stops. Board a train and be downtown within 10 minutes on the

Yellow or Blue line, depending on the day's agenda. The hotel also provides a free shuttle to National Airport. Relax on the sundeck while the kids play in the indoor pool.

The guest suites are newly refurbished and surround a soaring open atrium. A microwave, coffeemaker, and refrigerator are standard amenities. Suites are distinguished by comfortable and attractive furnishings and a spacious bathroom. Not enough can be said about the merits of having the kids sleep in a separate room with their own TV—worth twice the price in my mind.

If you have the time, snoop around Crystal City Underground, filled with shops and restaurants, or take the complimentary shuttle to the Fashion Centre at Pentagon City, where you won't need security clearance, just lots of moolah. While Macy's and Nordstrom are the anchors here, of greater interest to kids are Record World, the Disney Store, the Nature Company, the Gap, and Gap Kids. There are 13 eateries in the Food Court, a number of "proper" sit-down restaurants, and six movie theaters. The mall is a great escape if you run into foul weather. Nearby is the recently opened Pentagon Centre, a discount mall with upscale flair.

Dining/Diversions: Breakfast and late-afternoon cocktails are complimentary. **Scrimmage's,** a sports-theme restaurant (open daily), has a children's menu for the 12-and-under set.

Amenities: Complimentary breakfast and afternoon cocktail hour, newspaper, transportation to Reagan National Airport and nearby shopping, express checkout, exercise equipment, Jacuzzi, jogging track, indoor pool, gift shop, conference facilities, audiovisual equipment, laundry/valet service.

MODERATE

Days Inn Crystal City
2000 Jefferson Davis Hwy. (U.S. 1), Arlington, VA 22202. ☎ **800/329-7466** or 703/920-8600. Fax 703/920-2840. 250 units. A/C TV TEL. Weekday $119–$149; weekend from $79. Children under 17 stay free in parents' room. Weekend and seasonal packages available. AE, CB, DC, DISC, MC, V. Free parking. Metro: Crystal City.

Price and accessibility to the major sights are the drawing cards at this family pleasing property close to Reagan National Airport. Metrorail is only 1½ blocks away. Complimentary shuttle service is provided daily to and from Reagan National Airport from early morning to 11pm.

Rooms have two phones, TV with CNN, coffeemakers, and hair dryers. Munchie machines are strategically placed in the lobby.

A lifeguard is on duty at the outdoor pool (open Memorial Day to Labor Day). Get your fill of shopping and eating at Crystal City Underground (within walking distance) and the Fashion Centre at Pentagon City (a quick Metro ride). All the downtown sights and Old Town, Alexandria, are 10 to 15 minutes away via the Metro. You can also get off at the Rosslyn stop and walk over the Key Bridge to Georgetown. Numerous restaurants are within walking distance.

Gatwick's Restaurant, with a children's menu at lunch and dinner for those 10 and under, serves reasonably priced fare in casual surroundings; it's open daily for breakfast, lunch, dinner.

Amenities include room service (6am to 10pm), dry cleaning/ laundry service, express checkout, courtesy shuttle, free coffee in lobby, complimentary shuttle service to Reagan National Airport, outdoor pool, sundeck, health club, conference rooms, car-rental desk, tour desk.

VIENNA
EXPENSIVE

Embassy Suites Tysons Corner

8517 Leesburg Pike, Vienna, VA 22182. ☎ **800/EMBASSY** or 703/883-0707. Fax 703/883-0694. www.embassy-suites.com. 234 suites. $189–$199 single or double; weekend $99–$149. Children 12 and under stay free in parents' room; crib free. Extra person $10. Several packages available. AE, CB, DC, DISC, MC, V. Free parking. Metro: Dunn Loring.

By now you know that if you stay at an Embassy Suites, you and your kids won't be tripping over each other. There's a lot to be said for that, especially when you're spending every waking moment in each other's company. All suites and public areas were completely refurbished in 1998. Each suite has a king-size bed in the bedroom and a queen-size sleeper sofa in the living room. The bedroom and living room each have a TV with Spectravision movie channels. Other standard amenities include air conditioning, two telephones, a microwave, wet bar, refrigerator, coffeemaker, hair dryer, iron and ironing board. Every morning your family can look forward to a full American breakfast; evenings, wind down at the 2-hour manager's reception (drinks and munchies). All the extras are included in your room rate. Is this livin', or what?

Several suites are wheelchair-accessible.

Although the Metro is not within walking distance, and you're about 12 miles from the city, the hotel provides free transportation to the Dunn Loring station as well as anywhere within a 5-mile radius of the hotel. Serious shoppers won't want to miss visiting nearby Tysons Corner Center and Tysons II. Drivers will find plenty of on-site complimentary parking.

Dining/Diversions: The Carnevale Cafe serves American fare (crab cakes, steak, and pasta are featured) in a casual setting. Among the items on the kids' menu are a personal pizza for $2.49 and spaghetti and meatballs for $7.95. Swim a few laps in the pool, then come back for more. A full cooked-to-order breakfast and happy-hour drinks are complimentary at Embassy Suites.

Amenities: Room service (11am–10pm), transportation to metro and shopping, dry cleaning and laundry service, newspaper delivery, free coffee in lobby, complimentary cooked-to-order breakfast and evening cocktails, heated indoor pool, sundeck, Jacuzzi, sauna, health club, conference rooms, self-service Laundromat, car-rental desk, game room, gift shop.

Sheraton Premiere at Tysons Corner

8661 Leesburg Pike, Vienna, VA 22182. ☎ **800/325-3535** or 703/448-1234. Fax 703/893-8193. 455 units. A/C MINIBAR TV TEL. Weekday $110–$150 single or double, $250–$400 suite; weekend $81 and up single or double. Children under 12 stay free in parents' room; crib and accompanying stuffed animal free. Extra person $15. Weekly rates; also special promotional packages. AE, CB, DC, DISC, MC, V. Free parking. Metro: Dunn Loring or West Falls Church.

The Sheraton Premiere offers luxury accommodations with all the frills. Our family has attended several functions at the Sheraton, and the facilities, service, and food are first class. The location is convenient to Tysons Corner and Tysons II, Toys "R" Us, 18 movie theaters, and numerous restaurants. Complimentary transportation to the Metro is provided by request.

There are two restaurants and two bars on the premises to serve you, plus great recreational facilities. The weekend package includes free continental breakfast. Be sure to ask!

Dining/Diversions: Ashgrove's is the Sheraton's family-friendly restaurant for informal dining. At the Tuesday night Italian Buffet, kids under 12 (one child per parent) eat free—a bargain any way you slice it. **Baron's** is open for fine dining (main courses $21 to $35). Sandwiches and light fare are available in the lobby, along with piano music starting at 5pm.

Amenities: 24-hour room service, poolside service, laundry/valet, baby-sitting arrangements, complimentary shuttle to Dulles and Reagan National Airport, indoor and outdoor pools with lifeguard, exercise equipment, weights, Jacuzzi, sauna, masseuse, Lifecycles, two racquetball courts, lighted tennis privileges, 18-hole golf privileges (greens fees), hair salon, gift shop.

11 Bed & Breakfasts

Staying in a B&B can enhance your family's visit because you'll receive personalized service and have a chance to meet and greet other visitors in an intimate setting. The downside is that you may not be near a Metro station and will have to rely more on taxis and buses. I personally love B&Bs, but I think families with young children are better served by staying in a hotel. Having said that, rooms in B&Bs run the gamut from pint-size rooms (with the john down the hall) to suites accessorized with antiques in historic buildings.

In addition to my specific B&B recommendation, I've listed two reservations services. Reserve as early as possible to get the best selection of locations and lowest rates, and do specify your needs and preferences: For instance, discuss children, pets, smoking policy, preferred locations (do you require convenient public transportation?), parking, availability of TV and/or phone, preferred breakfast, and choice of payment.

B&B RESERVATION SERVICES

The **Bed and Breakfast League/Sweet Dreams & Toast,** P.O. Box 9490, Washington, DC 20016 (☎ **202/363-7767**), is a reservation service representing over 85 B&B accommodations in the District. Through them, you might find a room in a mid-1800s Federal-style Capitol Hill mansion, a Georgetown home with a lovely garden, or a turn-of-the-century Dupont Circle town house filled with Victorian furnishings. Accommodations are all screened, and guest reports are taken seriously. Hosts are encouraged, though not required, to offer such niceties as fresh-baked muffins at breakfast. All listings are convenient to public transportation. Rates for most range from $48 to $150 single, from $58 to $175 double, and from $10 to $25 per additional person. There's a 2-night minimum-stay requirement and a booking fee of $10 (per reservation, not per night). Most credit cards are accepted.

Bed & Breakfast Accommodations Ltd., P.O. Box 12011, Washington, DC 20005 (☎ **202/328-3510;** fax 202/332-3885; bedandbreakfastdc.com), has about 80 homes, inns, guest houses, and unhosted furnished apartments in its files. Its current roster offers, among many others, a Georgian-style colonial brick home on a tree-lined avenue near the Tenleytown metro, an 1887 restored Victorian home with a fenced-in yard in the heart of downtown, and a charming suburban home in Chevy Chase, Maryland. Rates are from $55 to $110 double in private homes, $15 for an extra person, and from $65 for a full apartment. At guest houses and inns, rates run the gamut from $65 to $265. Ask about off-season or longer-stay discounts. Most major credit cards are accepted.

A DOWNTOWN B&B RECOMMENDATION

✪ **Morrison-Clark Inn**

Massachusetts Ave. NW, at 11th St., Washington, DC 20001. ☎ **800/332-7898** or 202/898-1200. Fax 202/289-8576. www.morrisonclark.com. A/C MINIBAR TV TEL. Weekday

$135–$195 single, $155–$210 double; weekend from $99–$195 single or double. Rates include continental breakfast. Children under 16 stay free in parents' room. Extra person $20. Group rates available. AE, CB, DC, DISC, MC, V. Valet parking $15. Metro: Metro Center, then taxi.

Even if you have no intention of staying here, squeeze in a visit to the Morrison-Clark Inn to your sightseeing list when you visit. It's a feast for the eyes and also the home of one of the city's finest restaurants. The original twin buildings were erected in the 1860s, and it is on the National Register of Historic Places. The interior is worthy of an *Architectural Digest* spread, from the Victorian entry parlor to the beautifully decorated guest rooms, individualized with wicker, antiques, original art, and fresh bouquets. All rooms have air-conditioning, private bathrooms, two phones (bed and bathroom), remote-control color TVs with CNN, VCRs, stocked minibars, hair dryers, and voice mail. A total of 25 Victorian rooms and Parlor Suites have kitchenettes and/or other enhancements, at a higher cost than the standard rooms. Special rooms and other amenities are available for travelers with disabilities. Some accommodations have bougainvillea-draped trellised balconies or private porches surrounding a fountained courtyard garden.

A complimentary continental breakfast of fresh-baked breads, muffins, croissants, brioches, and pastries is served in the delightful Club Room. An attempt at damage control, after the pastries and croissants, can be made in the complimentary on-site Fitness Center. Gratis daily newspapers, twice-a-day maid service with Belgian chocolates at bed turndown, and complimentary overnight shoeshines are but a few of the extras at the Morrison Clark, which raise the B&B concept to new heights of luxury. The management is very gracious about accepting children of all ages, but because there are so many pretty things to break, consider staying here only if your kids are at least 11 or 12.

Dining: The hotel's noted restaurant of the same name is open daily for highly acclaimed regional American cuisine at lunch, dinner, and Sunday brunch. It was named in the October 1998 issue of *Gourmet* magazine as one of the top 20 restaurants in the country, and was also on the list of the 100 best restaurants in the Washington, D.C., area in the January 1999 *Washingtonian* magazine. Reservations are a must. While the management encourages parents to bring their children, I'd think twice before bringing preschoolers into the elegantly appointed Victorian dining room for dinner. Not because they're not welcome, but it's not fair to the other diners if they decide to throw a tantrum or initiate a food fight.

Amenities: Concierge, room service, complimentary continental breakfast, dry cleaning and laundry service, newspaper delivery, twice-daily maid service, babysitting, secretarial services, express check-out, valet parking ($15 overnight), video rentals. Fitness club, business center, and conference rooms.

12 Campgrounds

Maybe you're an outdoorsy family? If so, consider staying in one of Maryland or Virginia's many campgrounds. Here are two of the closest and best equipped.

○ Aquia Pines Camp Resort

3071 Jefferson Davis Hwy., Stafford, VA 22554. ☎ **800/726-1710** or 540/659-3447. www.gocampingamerica.com/aquiapines. E-mail: WashDCCamp@aol.com. $22 per recreational vehicle (including two persons); $3.50 each additional guest (nonfamily); $22.25 no hookup; $24.85 water and electricity; $29.50 water, electricity, sewer; campsites with cable/phone hook-up $33.50; rustic cabin (1–4 persons) $39.75; luxury cabin $95. Washington, D.C., Tour/Shuttle Specials Apr 1–Oct 30. Fall and spring discounts. AE, DISC, MC, V. Pets accepted.

Billed as "The Campground Most Convenient to the White House," Aquia Pines lies 1 mile from Exit 143a off I-95, about 35 miles south of D.C. and 10 miles north of George Washington's boyhood home, Fredericksburg. The campground is heavily treed, and the bathrooms are so clean they were photographed by the National Campground Association for a training film. Now that's clean!

For those who want to rough it less, consider renting one of the 30 deluxe camp-sites with instant phone hookup and cable TV, or a modest cabin, consisting of one room with a double bed, two bunk beds, and a porch. You'll have to use the camp-ground rest rooms, and linen service is strictly BYO, but I dare you to do better within a 35-mile radius of D.C. (unless you stay with relatives). Or you can opt for one of three deluxe cabins with a bathtub in the bathroom and kitchenette.

Amenities include a large heated pool, game room, shopping arcade, self-service Laundromat, car-rental desk, tour desk, minigolf course, basketball court, and play-ground. There are also hot showers, picnic tables, and a general store. Free firewood is provided. Guided tours of Washington pick up passengers at the campground. Shuttle service to the Mall museums and rental cars are available. In season, there are nightly orientation programs on Washington and historic Virginia, as well as special summertime and weekend family activities. A Wal-Mart and two supermar-kets are 1 mile from the campground (a third is 2 miles away). So, if you forgot the marshmallows, your stay won't be spoiled. Pets are welcome, but *not* in the cabins.

○ Cherry Hill Park

9800 Cherry Hill Rd., College Park, MD 20740. ☎ **800/801-6449** or 301/937-7116. Fax 301/937-3110. www.cherryhillpark.com. E-mail: DCCamping@aol.com. $35 per recre-ational vehicle includes 2 persons; or 4 persons in pop-up camper; $3 each additional person age 5 and over; $27 tent camping (2 persons). Ask about discounts. DISC, MC, V. Metrobus No. 83 from park to College Park Metro station.

This 53-acre campground lies just 10 miles from downtown Washington, with easy access via I-95. Despite the addition of more tent sites in a heavily wooded area, staying here will hardly be considered a back-to-nature experience by purists searching for Walden Pond.

In season, April through October, two certified master RV technicians are on site for repairs and advice. During the same period, food service is available at the pool-side cafe if you don't feel like messing with your Coleman. And when was the last time you "roughed it" with a walk-in beach-style pool, separate kids' pool, play areas with age-appropriate equipment, nature trails, Jacuzzi, sauna, sundeck, large-screen TV room and game rooms, fitness classes, 30-plus washers and dryers, and tour options? Hey, there's even a concierge onboard to serve you, and dog walkers available to take Poochy on his midnight bathroom run. The Gurevich family runs the place like a Southern-style Borscht Belt resort. In summer, your children will love the location. A second pool is oriented to kids' activities, and a new bathhouse and basketball court opened in time for the 1999 season. Just 20 minutes away is Six Flags America, which opened to rave reviews and weekend traffic jams in April '99. (More about Six Flags in Chapter 10, "Easy Excursions"). The Gureviches have added more trees and nat-ural floral landscaping in recent years to absorb the traffic drone from the nearby interstate. But if you're light sleepers, it might be a good idea to pack earplugs.

All buildings are wheelchair-accessible, and the level camping sites are without barriers.

Family-Friendly Restaurants

5

With nearly 3,500 restaurants of every ethnic persuasion to choose from, finding a place to eat is never a problem in Washington. The hard part is choosing. Be adventurous; your family's education doesn't end when you leave the Smithsonian. If you're raising your children in a meat-and-potatoes environment, expand their gustatory horizons and try a Thai or an Ethiopian restaurant (check out the "Restaurants by Cuisine" listing in section 2 of this chapter). And if your family has never tasted fresh crabmeat, here's your opportunity to savor this delicious local specialty that is harvested from nearby Chesapeake Bay from late spring into fall.

Since space prohibits listing every family restaurant, consider this chapter a sampling. Unless otherwise noted, the welcome mat is out for families with children of all ages. Well-behaved kids who like to dine rather than eat and run are welcome at any restaurant in the city. Most "grown-up" places require reservations and appreciate a sartorial effort a step or two beyond sweats and athletic shoes.

When deciding where to dine with a very young child, please consider the appropriateness of your choice. Some people persist in taking colicky infants and hyperkinetic toddlers to strictly adult places when everyone would have a much better time at a family style establishment. Nobody wants to dress up and pay a lot of money in a fine restaurant to play peek-a-boo with an antsy, whining tot in the next booth.

The drinking age in D.C. is 21. No exceptions are made for almost-21-year-olds dining with adults, so don't even think of offering your offspring a sip of your cocktail. A single violation could close the restaurant for good.

To save time on days when you want to pack in as much downtown sightseeing as possible, eat in a museum or federal building restaurant or cafeteria; you'll find listings for these in chapter 6. When you want simple, walk-away fare—hot dogs, chips, ice cream, and sodas—look for the pagoda-style roofs of the freestanding food-service kiosks nestled among the elms on the Mall. Another option is to head for a food court in one of D.C.'s enclosed malls. Everyone can exercise his or her freedom of choice at these popular eateries, where the selections are consistent, inexpensive, and served with a smile. Feeling homesick? The nearest fast-food establishment is only a Golden Arch away. When you're rushed, take advantage of the many food vendors and pushcarts stationed strategically throughout the city. On a beautiful day, buy a movable feast at a restaurant or carryout shop and picnic on the grass or on a park bench.

Kids who would rather blow bubbles into their drink than eat a square meal are served better by fast food, takeout, or street food. This may be the nation's capital, but give them a break and don't make a federal case out of mealtime. (They may not be on their best behavior after 14 museums in 2 days.) Of course, it's always a good idea to have crackers or other snacks in your bag to pacify little ones who may grow impatient waiting for the rolls to arrive.

Nothing can ruin an otherwise pleasant day faster than an interminable wait in a mobbed restaurant. Since there's a chance that sometimes service may be less than speedy, especially during peak times, you could bring along some crayons, scrap paper, and a few playthings. If you don't have reservations and you want attentive service, try to get seated before noon or after 2pm for lunch and no later than 6 or 6:30pm for dinner. You don't have to act chic for your kids. They love you just the way you are.

The tax on restaurant meals is 10% in the District. I agree—it's pretty harsh.

ICE CREAM

An ice-cream break can be just what the doctor ordered when spirits and arches are sagging. While nothing I've sampled locally quite equals the ice cream scooped at Gruning's, the temple of my youth, many of the establishments listed in this chapter dish out some reasonable facsimiles. In case you're interested, our family's vote for the best ice cream in D.C. is split—as in banana split—between **Ben & Jerry's,** 3135 M St. NW, Georgetown (☎ **202/965-2222**); 11th Street and Pennsylvania Ave. NW in the Old Post Office Pavilion (☎ **202/842-5882**), 1333 19th Street, NW, next to the Dupont Circle Cineplex (☎ **202/785-4882**), and **Gifford's,** 7720 Wisconsin Ave. (☎ **301/907-3436**). (My daughter, Rachel Lightbourne, and grandson, Joshua Lightbourne, ice-cream lovers extraordinaire, helped with the research for these places.)

COOKIES

Wars have been started over nuttier things than who sells the best cookies in town. For my dough, Baltimore-based **Berger's** wins the prize. Picture a vanilla hockey puck dipped (actually, hand-dipped) in chocolate fudge. I fall in love every time I devour one. In the D.C. area, you'll have to travel to the nearest **High's** convenience store or **BJ's.** Call first, as they are not always in stock. (It's worth a trip to a store that does have them. Trust me.) **Snider's,** 1936 Seminary Rd., Silver Spring, Maryland, and **Magruder's,** 170 Halpine Rd. and 1605 West St. in Rockville, Maryland, also sell these mouthwatering treats. Closer to home, I think **Mrs. Field's,** 3222 M St., in the Georgetown Park Mall, makes chocolate chip cookies as good as they get outside of my own kitchen. But, hey, don't take my word for it. Go out and try 'em all and then decide for yourself.

Factoid ———————————————————————————

In the trendier "in" spots, families can stretch their dining-out dollars by ordering an appetizer or soup and salad and enjoying the (usually) free bread. Try it! If anyone gives you a hard time please let me know.

AFTERNOON TEA

Many downtown hotels have adopted the veddy civilized British custom of serving afternoon tea. Family members can practice their party manners while graciously wolfing down quantities of finger sandwiches, tea breads, scones, fruit tarts, petits fours, pastries, and fresh fruit. With a spread like this, who needs tea?

The price for full tea is around $15 to $20; some hotels also offer a children's tea (substitute milk shake) and light tea with sweet breads and scones for a few dollars less. If you sip your cuppa late enough in the day, you can probably skip dinner altogether. So dust off your white gloves, Vaseline your patent-leather shoes, and do make advance reservations.

I personally recommend the **Four Seasons Hotel Andreas,** 2800 Pennsylvania Ave. NW (☎ 202/342-0444). In the elegant setting of the **Garden Terrace,** tea is served daily from 3 to 5pm. Here the kids can sip their favorite soft drink while you enjoy steaming potfuls of Earl Grey, pretending you're to the manner born.

1 Best Bets

Many of the following restaurants don't pretend to serve haute cuisine, but they do offer families good value, pleasant ambience, and, in most instances, food that is at least on a par with Mom's home cooking.

- **Best Spot for a Celebration: Planet Hollywood,** 1101 Pennsylvania Ave. NW (☎ 202/783-7827), or **Kinkead's,** I Street between 20th and 21st streets NW (☎ 202/296-7700), are festive spots for a special event. Choose the first if you like being in the spotlight, plenty of action, and noise; the second if your family appreciates fine food and prefers to provide its own entertainment.
- **Best Decor: Seasons** restaurant in the Four Seasons Hotel, 2800 Pennsylvania Ave. NW (☎ 202/342-0444), is luxurious but unstuffy. Light-filled and comfortable, Seasons overlooks Rock Creek Park and is like a breath of spring in any season. (see the write up of the Four Seasons Hotel in chapter 4.)
- **Best View: Sky Terrace,** atop the Hotel Washington, 15th Street and Pennsylvania Ave. NW (☎ 202/638-5900), enjoys a primo view of downtown and serves drinks, light fare, and dessert from May through October (weather permitting).

  At the **Chart House Restaurant** in Alexandria, Virginia, at 1 Cameron St. (☎ 703/684-5080), you can drink in the waterfront scene along with your favorite cocktail, roast beef, or coconut shrimp (see its listing in chapter 10).
- **Best American Cuisine/Best Seafood: Kinkead's,** I Street between 20th and 21st streets NW (☎ 202/296-7700), in Foggy Bottom, has an eclectic menu but the kitchen specializes in seafood. Of the light fare choices, the chowder and fried clams would do New England proud. Graze downstairs in the bar area or on the covered terrace, or dine more formally in one of the intimate upstairs nooks.
- **Best Continental Cuisine: Jockey Club,** 2100 Massachusetts Ave. NW (☎ 202/835-2100), in the Westin Fairfax, an in place since it opened on the eve of JFK's inauguration, still pleases; and there's a children's menu.
- **Best French Bistro: Senses,** 3206 Grace St. NW (☎ 202/342-9083), in Georgetown, is open for breakfast, lunch, tea, and dinner every day but Monday. Chef/owners Xavier and Bruno have made Senses a welcome addition to the D.C. dining scene.
- **Best Italian Cuisine: Spaghetti Garden,** 2317 18th St. NW (☎ 202/265-6665), has long been a family favorite known for its uncomplicated, hearty meals and air of good feeling. Bambinos are welcomed with open arms.

- **Best Mexican Cuisine: Rio Grande Café,** 4919 Fairmont Ave., Bethesda, Maryland (☎ **301/656-2981**), serves simply wonderful food—from the freshly made chips and salsa to *sopapillas*—in a south-of-the-border warehouse setting. I hate to sound like a broken record. Go early or late, especially on weekends. You'll find another Rio Grande at 4302 N. Fairfax Dr., Ballston, Virginia (☎ **703/528-3131**).

- **Best Steaks: Morton's of Chicago**—in Georgetown at 3251 Prospect St. NW (☎ **202/342-6258**), downtown at 1050 Connecticut Ave. NW (at L Street) (☎ **202/955-5997**); in Tysons Corner, 8075 Leesburg Pike, Vienna, Virginia (☎ **703/883-0800**); and in the Sheraton Hotel, 300 S. Charles St., Baltimore (☎ **410/547-8255**)—serves the *second* best steak I've ever eaten, but it's a lot easier to get to Morton's than Florence, Italy. The portions are humongous.

- **Best Burgers: Houston's**—with locations in Georgetown at 1065 Wisconsin Ave. NW (☎ **202/338-7760**); in Bethesda, Maryland, at 7715 Woodmont Ave. (☎ **301/656-9755**); and in Rockville, Maryland, at 12256 Rockville Pike (☎ **301/463-3535**)—has the best burgers between D.C. and Kansas City. They are generous, tasty, and cooked to the right degree of doneness. What more is there to say? Oh yes. Go at off times or bring something to amuse the troops while you wait.

- **Best Pizza: Geppetto** (take-out only), 2917 M. St. NW, Georgetown (☎ **202/333-2602**), or 10257 Old Georgetown Rd., in Bethesda, Maryland (☎ **301/493-9230**), draws pizza lovers from far and near. Though the prices are high compared to the nondescript chains, Geppetto doesn't skimp on the cheese and a little goes a long way.

- **Best Desserts: Senses,** 3206 Grace St. NW, Georgetown (☎ **202/342-9083**), is the place to head for exceptional pastries turned out by Bruno (he's the one with the whipped cream on his cheek and funny white hat).

- **Best Ice Cream: Ben & Jerry's,** 3135 M St. NW, Georgetown (☎ **202/965-2222**); Old Post Office Pavilion, 11th Street and Pennsylvania Ave. NW (☎ **202/842-5883**); and 1333 19th St. NW, next to Dupont Circle Cineplex (☎ **202/785-4882**), gets my vote in the District. When in Maryland, make a beeline for a hot fudge sundae at **Gifford's:** 7720 Wisconsin Ave. (☎ **301/907-3436**).

- **Best Late Night Dining: El Tamarindo,** at 4910 Wisconsin Ave. NW (☎ **202/244-8888**), in Upper Northwest; at 1785 Florida Ave. NW, Adams–Morgan (☎ **202/328-3660**); and at 7331 Georgia Ave. NW (☎ **202/291-0525**), is open till the wee small hours for Salvadoran food that is plentiful and reasonable. If you're in your PJs when hunger pangs strike, call **Geppetto** (☎ **202/333-4315**) for delivery.

- **Best Outdoor Dining: Sea Catch Restaurant and Raw Bar,** at Canal Square, 1054 31st St. NW, Georgetown (☎ **202/337-8855**), has seating overlooking the picturesque C&O Canal.

- **Best People Watching: Senators' Dining Room,** at the U.S. Capitol, takes the cake in this category *if* you recognize the pols you'll be rubbing elbows with, and if your youngsters are over 10. (For requirements for lunching at the Senators' Dining Room, see the introductory text to section 3 in this chapter.) Otherwise, head for the **Cheesecake Factory,** 5345 Wisconsin Ave. NW (☎ **202/364-0500**), or at the White Flint Mall, North Bethesda, Maryland (☎ **301/770-0999**). Brown-bagging it on the Mall is another option.

- **Best Afternoon Tea: Four Seasons,** 2800 Pennsylvania Ave. NW (☎ **202/342-0444**), serves tea from 3 to 5pm daily in the elegant **Garden Terrace,** as inviting and gracious a setting as you'll find this side of the Atlantic. Children can order from a special menu that includes peanut butter and jelly finger sandwiches and brownies.

- **Best Brunch: Kinkead's,** I Street, between 20th and 21st streets NW (☎ 202/296-7700), and the **Four Seasons,** 2800 Pennsylvania Ave. NW (☎ 202/342-0444), share top honors in my as yet unpublished brunch book. At Kinkead's the tab is reasonable; at the Four Seasons, it's pricey, but includes music by a jazz trio.
- **Best Picnic Fare:** Head for **Dean & Deluca,** 3276 M St. NW, Georgetown (☎ 202/342-2500). They'll pack a mouthwatering meal for you and yours to tote to your destination of choice (including your hotel room). Or enjoy your picnic "down by the riverside" at Washington Harbour or along the C&O Canal.

2 Restaurants by Cuisine

AFTERNOON TEA

Four Seasons Hotel (Georgetown)
Park Hyatt Hotel (Downtown)
Renaissance Mayflower Hotel
  (Downtown)
The St. Regis Washington, D.C.
  (Downtown)
Washington National Cathedral
  (Upper Northwest)

AMERICAN

America (Capitol Hill, *I*)
Brickskeller (Dupont Circle, *I*)
Bullfeathers (Capitol Hill, *I*)
Capitol City Brewing Co.
  (Convention Center,
  Capitol Hill *I*)
Chadwick's (Upper Northwest, *I*)
Chili's (Vienna, Virginia, *I*)
Cheesecake Factory (N. Bethesda,
  Maryland, Upper Northwest, *I*)
Clyde's (Georgetown, Vienna,
  Virginia, *M*)
Dirksen Senate Office Building South
  Buffet Room (Capitol Hill, *I*)
Fedora Cafe (Vienna, Virginia, *M*)
Fuddrucker's (Rockville, Maryland, *I*)
Garrett's (Georgetown, *M*)
Hamburger Hamlet (Bethesda,
  Maryland, *I*)
Hard Rock Cafe (Convention
  Center, *I*)
Houston's (Bethesda, Maryland,
  Georgetown, Rockville,
  Maryland, *I*)

Kenny's Smoke House
  (Capitol Hill, *I*)
Kinkead's (Foggy Bottom, *E*)
Kramerbooks & Afterwords Cafe
  (Dupont Circle, *I*)
Library of Congress Cafeteria, James
  Madison Memorial Building
  (Capitol Hill, *I*)
Market Lunch (Capitol Hill, *I*)
Morton's (Vienna, Virginia, *E*)
Morton's of Chicago (Downtown,
  Georgetown, *E*)
Old Ebbitt Grill (Downtown, *M*)
Philadelphia Mike's (Bethesda,
  Maryland, *I*)
Planet Hollywood (Convention
  Center, *M*)
Sherrill's (Capitol Hill, *I*)
Sholl's Colonial Cafeteria
  (Downtown, *I*)
Supreme Court Cafeteria
  (Capitol Hill, *I*)
Tastee Diner (Bethesda, Maryland, *I*)
T.G.I. Friday's (Downtown, Foggy
  Bottom, Vienna, Virginia, *I*)
Tunnicliff's Tavern (Capitol Hill, *I*)

CAJUN/CREOLE

Louisiana Express (Bethesda,
  Maryland, *I*)
Tunnicliff's Tavern (Capitol Hill, *I*)

CANDIES

Bread & Chocolate (Downtown)
Chocolate Chocolate (Downtown)

Key to abbreviations: *VE* = Very Expensive, *E* = Expensive, *M* = Moderate, *I* = Inexpensive

Fannie Mae (Downtown)
Kron Chocolatier (Upper Northwest)

CHINESE

China Inn (Convention Center, *M*)
Foong Lin (Bethesda, Maryland, *M*)
Hunan Chinatown (Convention
Center, *M*)

CONTINENTAL

Clyde's (Vienna, Virginia, *M*)
Jockey Club (Dupont Circle, *VE*)

COOKIES

Bread & Chocolate (Downtown)
Larry's Cookies (Capitol Hill,
Dupont Circle)
Mrs. Field's Cookies (Georgetown)

EAST ASIAN

Pan Asian Noodles & Grill
(Downtown, *I*)

ECLECTIC/FOOD COURTS

Food Courts at the Old Post Office
Pavilion (Convention Center, *I*)
Food Hall at the Shops at National
Place (Downtown, *I*)
Market Lunch (Capitol Hill, *I*)
Union Station Food Court (Capitol
Hill, *I*)

ETHIOPIAN

Red Sea (Adams–Morgan, *I*)

FRENCH

Jockey Club (Dupont Circle, *VE*)
Senses (Georgetown, *M*)

GERMAN

Cafe Mozart (Convention Center, *M*)

GREEK

Athenian Plaka (Bethesda,
Maryland, *I*)

ICE CREAM

Baskin-Robbins (Downtown, Upper
Northwest)
Ben & Jerry's (Downtown, Dupont
Circle, Georgetown)
Café Café (Foggy Bottom)

Cone E Island (Foggy Bottom,
Vienna, Virginia)
Gifford's (Bethesda, Maryland)
Häagen-Dazs (Capitol Hill,
Georgetown)
I Can't Believe It's Yogurt (Upper
Northwest)
Le Sorbet (Downtown)
Thomas Sweet (Georgetown)
Uptown Scoop (Upper Northwest)

ITALIAN

A.V. (Convention Center, *I*)
Filomena's (Georgetown, *M*)
I Matti (Adams–Morgan, *M*)
Otello (Dupont Circle, *I*)
Paolo's (Georgetown, *M*)
Spaghetti Garden
(Adams–Morgan, *I*)

LIGHT FARE

Sky Terrace (Downtown, *I*)

MEXICAN

El Tamarindo (Adams–Morgan,
Upper Northwest, *I*)
Enriqueta's (Georgetown, *M*)
Rio Grande Café (Ballston, Virginia,
Bethesda, Maryland, *I*)

MOROCCAN

Marrakesh (Convention Center, *M*)

PIZZA

Generous George's Pizza (Alexandria,
Virginia, *I*)
Geppetto (Bethesda, Maryland,
Georgetown, *I*)
Il Forno (Bethesda, Maryland, *I*)

RIBS/BARBECUE

Houston's (Georgetown, Bethesda,
Maryland, Rockville, Maryland,
I–M)
Kenny's Smoke House
(Capitol Hill, *I*)
O'Brien's Pit Barbecue (Rockville,
Maryland, *I*)
Red, Hot & Blue (Arlington,
Virginia, *I*)

SALVADORAN

El Tamarindo (Adams–Morgan, Upper Northwest, *I*)

SANDWICHES

Roy's Place (Gaithersburg, Maryland, *I*)

SEAFOOD

Crisfield (Silver Spring, Maryland, *M*)

Kinkead's (Foggy Bottom, *E*)Sea Catch Restaurant and Raw Bar (Georgetown, *E*)

SOUTHWESTERN

Chili's (Vienna, Virginia, *I*)

TEX-MEX

Austin Grill (Convention Center, Bethesda, Maryland, Georgetown, *I*)

Cactus Cantina (Upper Northwest, *M*)

THAI

Jandara (Upper Northwest, *M*)

VIENNESE

Cafe Mozart (Convention Center, *M*)

3 Capitol Hill

A host of casual and pleasing dining establishments fills the Hill. Of all of D.C.'s dining neighborhoods, this one seems to be the most family friendly. If your stomach starts growling while you're touring the Capitol, Supreme Court, or Library of Congress, try one of their dining rooms or cafeterias for a quick meal or snack; you'll find listings for these in chapter 6.

For a special treat, your family can slurp Senate bean soup alongside the legislators weekdays between 1:30 and 3pm in the exclusive ✪ **Senators' Dining Room** in the U.S. Capitol. There are two hitches: (1) You must first secure a "request letter," which you can pick up the very day the spirit moves you, from any Senate office; and (2) men are required to wear a jacket and tie (no hair rollers or flip-flops for women). If the rules are too stringent, walk around the corner to the **Family Dining Room,** open from 11:30am to 3:30pm. It's less expensive and kids are welcome (☎ **202/224-3121**).

INEXPENSIVE

America

Union Station, 50 Massachusetts Ave. NE. ☎ **202/682-9555.** www.arkrestaurants.com. Reservations recommended. Main courses $9–$16.95. AE, DC, DISC, MC, V. Sun–Thurs 11:30am–midnight, Fri–Sat 11:30am–1am. Children's Services: High chairs, boosters. Metro: Union Station. AMERICAN.

Try the Navaho fried bread, Kansas City steaks, chicken "lips," or anything else from the ambitious menu in this cavernous, multilevel Union Station restaurant that diligently tries to be all things to all people. Weekly specials focus on different U.S. regional cooking styles. Opt for a balcony table for a view of the spectacular Main Hall.

Bullfeathers

410 1st St. SE. ☎ **202/543-5005.** Reservations recommended. Main courses $8 (sandwiches), $14–$15 dinner; kids' menu $2.95–$3.95. AE, DC, DISC, MC, V. Mon–Thurs 11:15am–10:30pm, bar until about 1am (some food service available); Fri 11:30am–1am, Sat noon–9pm; Sun brunch 10:30am–3pm; lunch and dinner menu until 10:30pm. Bar open until 2am. Children's services: high chairs, booster seats, kids' menu. AMERICAN.

Really good hamburgers, nachos, and a full menu of meat, pasta, and fresh daily seafood specialties make this a popular spot for diners of all ages. The bargain children's menu includes peanut butter and jelly sandwiches, chicken, and a 3½-ounce kiddie burger. Light fare and nightly beer specials are served in the saloon.

Downtown Dining

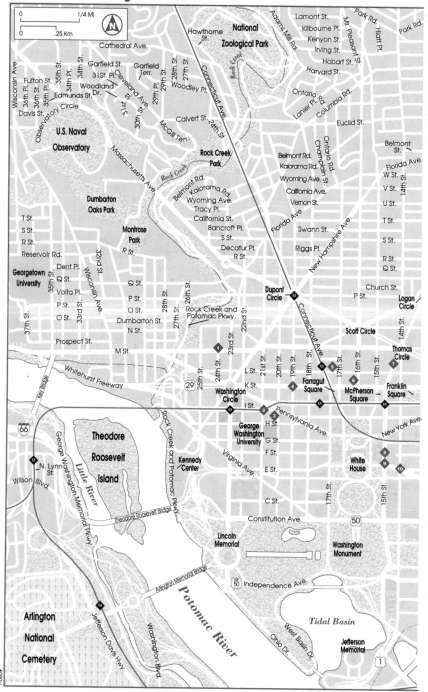

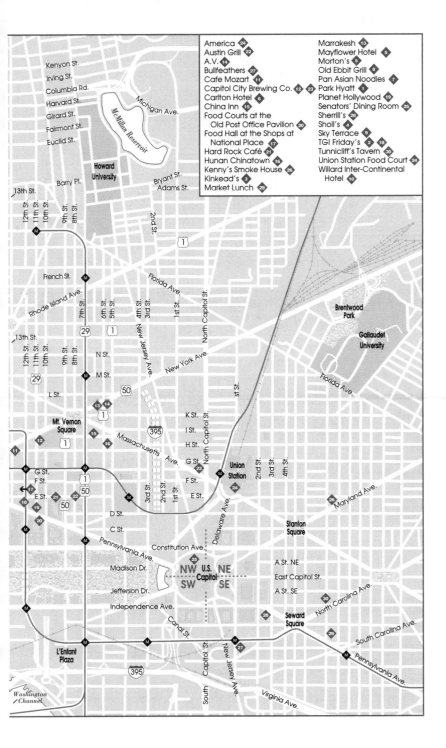

America 24
Austin Grill 22
A.V. 14
Bullfeathers 27
Cafe Mozart 11
Capitol City Brewing Co. 12 23
Carlton Hotel 6
China Inn 15
Food Courts at the
  Old Post Office Pavilion 20
Food Hall at the Shops at
  National Place 17
Hard Rock Café 21
Hunan Chinatown 16
Kenny's Smoke House 26
Kinkead's 3
Market Lunch 29

Marrakesh 13
Mayflower Hotel 5
Morton's 5
Old Ebbit Grill 8
Pan Asian Noodles 7
Park Hyatt 1
Planet Hollywood 19
Senators' Dining Room 25
Sherrill's 28
Sholl's 4
Sky Terrace 9
TGI Friday's 2 18
Tunnicliff's Tavern 30
Union Station Food Court 24
Willard Inter-Continental
  Hotel 10

Kenny's Smoke House

732 Maryland Ave. NE. ☎ **202/547-4553.** Reservations accepted for 10 or more. Lunch and dinner $6.50–$7.50; AE, MC, V. Mon–Sat 11am–10:30pm, closed Sun. Children's services: high chairs, boosters. AMERICAN/RIBS/BARBECUE.

Who needs fancy digs when you're chowing down on yummy slow-cooked ribs and chicken or tangy minced barbecue? Main courses come with a Southern-style side dish. Try the greens or cornbread. You won't leave here hungry. Oink.

Market Lunch

225 7th St. SE. ☎ **202/547-8444.** Reservations not accepted. Breakfast $2–$3.95; lunch $2.95–$12.95. No credit cards. Tues–Sat 7:30am–3pm; Sun 11am–3:30p. (lunch only). Children's services: High chairs. Metro: Eastern Market. ECLECTIC/AMERICAN.

Try the mouthwatering blueberry buckwheat pancakes or French toast at breakfast at this restaurant in the heart of bustling Eastern Market. The soft-shell crab (seasonal) sandwich on homemade bread is a lunchtime specialty, with the crab cake a close second. Weather permitting, there's outdoor seating. Weekends the place jumps with live music and hordes of shoppers hunting for bargains at the nearby flea market.

Sherrill's

233 Pennsylvania Ave. SE. ☎ **202/544-2480.** Breakfast $3.75–$6.95; lunch (sandwiches) $2.50–$3.95; platters $5.50–$6. No credit cards. Mon–Fri 6am–7pm, Sat 7am–6:30pm; Sun and holidays 7am–4:30pm. Children's services: sassy seats, boosters. Metro: Capitol South. AMERICAN.

The subject of a 1989 documentary that was nominated for an Academy Award (it should have won!), Sherrill's has been serving home-cooked meals since 1922. Eggs and omelettes are served all day long, every day. The pastries (éclairs, napoleons, and cream puffs) and soups are made in-house and are quite good. So is breakfast. Everyone gets a kick out of the soda counter serving old-fashioned milk shakes. Take a trip back to the future at this colorful establishment and grab a gingerbread man for snacking on later.

Tunnicliff's Tavern

222 7th St. SE. ☎ **202/546-3663.** Fax 202/544-7479. www.tunnicliffs.com. Reservations strongly recommended. All items $3.50–$17.50; AE, DC, MC, V. Mon–Fri noon–11pm; brunch Sat–Sun 11am–2pm. Children's services: high chairs, boosters, children's coloring book. Metro: Eastern Market. AMERICAN/CAJUN.

Tunnicliff's is your basic friendly neighborhood bar, so even though there's a no-smoking section, if you're troubled by smoke, you may want to go elsewhere. That said, this is a comfy, casual spot, thanks in large part to Lynne Breaux Cooper, who knows a thing or two about making families feel at home. At Tunnicliff's, hamburgers and french fries star, along with engagin' Cajun specialties. Or try a turkey

---

On the Run

In a hurry? For a quick bite when you're on the go, grab a snack from a street vendor. My kids were raised on hot dogs, soft pretzels, and ice cream without ill effect. They even graduated college and are gainfully employed. Some vendors sell upscale treats such as filled croissants and Chipwiches (ice cream sandwiched between two chocolate chip cookies). Many hawk pizza and egg rolls, but these are usually less than satisfactory. My personal favorite—an addiction begun during numerous visits to New York City as a child—is a Sabrett's hot dog with "the works." Look for a pushcart with the blue-and-yellow umbrella bearing the Sabrett's logo. Accept no substitutes!

sandwich on pita or something from the grill. Although there's no kids' menu, the kitchen is flexible when it comes to pleasing smaller appetites.

Drivers can take advantage of metered parking in front of the restaurant.

Union Station Food Court

50 Massachusetts Ave. NE. ☎ **202/371-9441.** Reservations not accepted. Most items $1–$8. No credit cards. Mon–Sat 10am–9pm, Sun noon–6pm. ECLECTIC.

It's fun casing the many stands before making a selection at this bustling and booming food court. Some of the best bets for youngsters include the all-beef European kosher hot dog at Dogs Plus, the deep-dish pizza at Ilardo's, and the charbroiled hamburger at Flamer's. There's a deli, Tex-Mex, and sushi for the more adventurous, or tote your lunch over to the Capital Children's Museum on a nice day and picnic on the grounds. Top off your visit with a double-scooper from Häagen-Dazs.

COOKIES, CANDY & ICE CREAM

Häagen-Dazs

Union Station, 50 Massachusetts Ave. NE. ☎ **202/789-0953.**

Häagen-Dazs certainly rates up there with the best commercially produced ice cream anywhere. If you can't decide, try the cookies-n-cream or mocha chip.

Larry's Cookies

Union Station, 50 Massachusetts Ave. NE ☎ **202/289-7586.**

Many disagree, but my family of cookie monsters thinks these cookies are rather ho-hum. Let me know how you rate them. There's another Larry's at 1633 Connecticut Ave. NW, near Dupont Circle (☎ **202/234-2690**).

4 Convention Center

If you're staying in this area or have tickets to an event at the MCI Center, this is a logical neighborhood in which to dine. The choices are varied, and Chinatown, with the greatest concentration of Asian restaurants in the city, is here. You'll also find many other ethnic restaurants, hotel dining rooms and coffee shops, and two kids' favorites: Planet Hollywood and the Hard Rock Cafe.

MODERATE

✪ Cafe Mozart

1331 H St. NW. ☎ **202/347-5732.** Fax 202/347-4958. Reservations recommended at dinner. Breakfast $3.50–$7.95; lunch $6–$21; dinner $7.50–$21.95. AE, CB, DC, DISC, MC, V. Mon–Fri 7:30am–10pm, Sat 9am–10pm, Sun 11am–10pm. Closed Thanksgiving, Dec 25, Jan 1. Children's services: high chairs, boosters, kids' menu. Metro: Metro Center or McPherson Square. GERMAN/VIENNESE.

You could do a lot "wurst" than to dine at this gemütlich restaurant tucked behind a deli where the sauerbraten and Wiener schnitzel (breaded veal cutlet) are almost as good as my grandmother's. The food is robust and tasty, and the service is warm and friendly. The mood is pure Oktoberfest when there's live music, Friday and Saturday from 6 to 10pm. From noon to 4pm on the second and fourth Saturdays of the month, someone plays the zither (a stringed instrument played with a pick and fingers). Kids of all ages are welcome for breakfast and lunch; older kids only in the evening. Free parking is provided Monday through Friday after 6pm.

Hunan Chinatown

624 H St. NW. ☎ **202/783-5858.** Reservations recommended. Appetizers $1.50–$4.20 lunch, $1.50–$5 dinner; most main courses $7–$12 lunch and dinner. AE, CB, DC, DISC, MC, V. Sun–Thurs 11am–10pm; Fri–Sat 11am–11pm. Closed Thanksgiving and Dec 25. Children's services: high chairs, boosters. Metro: Gallery Place. CHINESE.

What you see is what you get at another of Chinatown's standbys, specializing in Hunan and Szechuan dishes. The food is consistent if uninspired. Many of the dishes are hot, hot, hot—so, depending on your tolerance, ask the kitchen to go easy on the chile peppers and hot oil, especially on your youngsters' orders. Children can make a meal of such appetizers as spring rolls, fried wonton, and meat-filled steamed or panfried dumplings. Waistline watchers can order from the light menu.

✪ Marrakesh

617 New York Ave. NW. ☎ **202/393-9393.** Reservations required. Fixed-price dinner $25 per person; kids under 10 half price Sun–Thurs. No credit cards; checks accepted with 2 phone numbers. Mon–Sat 5:30–11pm, Sun 5–11pm. Closed Mon, Thanksgiving. Metro: Gallery Place. MOROCCAN.

Celebrate a birthday or the summer solstice or whatever at this lively, colorful oasis. Sink into the pillowed banquettes and partake of the multicourse fixed-price dinner built around entrees of lamb and chicken. At Marrakesh eating is strictly a hands-on experience, accompanied by Middle Eastern music and belly dancing. Don't be surprised if someone in your party becomes part of the entertainment. A lot of fun for the money, and reasonable except for the pricey wine. Valet parking is $5, well worth it in this not-so-hot neighborhood.

✪ Planet Hollywood

1101 Pennsylvania Ave. NW. ☎ **202/783-7827.** www.planethollywood.com. Reservations not accepted. Appetizers $3.95–$6.95; main courses $7.50–$18. AE, DC, M, V, DISC, JCB. Daily 11am–midnight. Children's services: High chairs, boosters, kids' menu. Metro: Metro Center. AMERICAN.

Unless you've just landed on Planet Earth, you know that Bruce, Sylvester, and Arnold are laughing all the way to the bank over the success of their Tinseltown-motif restaurants. It's frequently SRO as fans line up to scarf down burgers and better-than-all-right french fries and other standard American "gourmet" fare. The restaurant/sound stage decor includes memorabilia like the Joker's singed dinner jacket and cardboard cutouts of the stars (movie stars, that is). Everywhere you look movie clips play on big screens. Before making your grand exit, audition your sugar tolerance on the Hollywood Mousse Pie (Oreos, mousse filling, ice cream, and whipped cream). Planet Hollywood is not inexpensive—I dropped $50 on lunch for two recently—but it's G-rated family entertainment. Don't forget the souvenir shop on the way out (surely your kids won't).

INEXPENSIVE

Austin Grill

750 E St. NW, between 7th and 8th sts. ☎ **202/393-3776.** www.austingrill.com. Reservations not accepted. Main courses $7–$15. AE, DC, DISC, MC, V. Mon 11am–10pm, Tues–Thurs 11am–11pm, Fri–Sat 11am–midnight, Sun 11am–10pm. Children's services: boosters, high chairs, kids menu, crayons. Metro: Gallery Place or Archives. TEX-MEX.

This place has a partylike atmosphere, with inexpensive Tex-Mex fare served in a totally unpretentious setting. Try the house-braised carnitas ($12.95), hot Texas chili, or fajitas and a margarita.

From the children's menu, kids can order a single taco, enchilada, quesadilla, or burger, which comes with free refills on soda (served in a colorful kids cup) and a scoop of ice cream—all for $3.75.

Things can get lively—some would say boisterous—with the mostly under-30 crowd. While your children will probably love it, you *may* end up with a headache. The restaurant is convenient to the FBI, Ford's Theatre, and the Convention Center. In season, there's outside dining shaded by awnings and trees.

The original Austin Grill is at 2404 Wisconsin Ave. NW, above Georgetown (☎ 202/337-8080). In Alexandria, Virginia, visit the location at 801 King St. (☎ 703/684-8969). In Springfield, Virginia, there's one on 8430-A Old Keene Mill Rd. (☎ 703/644-3111). The Bethesda, Maryland, location is at 7278 Woodmont Ave. (☎ 301/656-1366). In Baltimore, there's one at 2400 Boston St. (Fells Point), ☎ 410/534-0606.

A.V.

607 New York Ave. ☎ **202/737-0550.** Reservations for 10 or more only. Appetizers $4–$8; main courses $7–$18. AE, CB, DC, DISC, MC, V. Mon–Thurs 11:30am–11pm, Fri 11:30am–midnight, Sat 5pm–midnight. Children's services: high chairs, boosters. Metro: Gallery Place. ITALIAN.

Since sliding its first pizza from the oven more than half a century ago, A.V. has spawned numerous spin-offs in the D.C. area. The early grunge decor may not win *Architectural Digest*'s approval, but the ristorante still reigns supreme when it comes to hearty orders of pasta smothered in no-nonsense sauces. Your kids can share a single portion, enough for two adults in many cases. Start with the white pizza (with or without cheese), first introduced to D.C. diners here decades ago. Fresh fish, simply prepared, is always a sure thing (and healthful too!) The thin-crust, New York–style pizza brightens the smiles of die-hard tomato pie lovers. If you skip the specials, you can dine like a don for less than $15 a head. Feed your loose change into the jukebox and enjoy your favorite opera aria.

Capitol City Brewing Co.

1100 New York Ave. NW (corner of H and 11th sts.). ☎ **202/628-2222.** (A second location is at 2 Massachusetts Ave. NE [National Postal Museum]. ☎ 202/842-BEER). www. capcitybrew.com. Reservations for groups of 15 or more. Lunch and dinner $6.95–$18.50 (hamburgers from $6.95). AE, DC, MC, V, DISC. Sun 11am–midnight; Mon–Sat 11am–2am. Children's services: high chairs, boosters, kids' menu. Metro: Metro Center. AMERICAN.

The first brew pub in D.C., Capitol City is noisy, fun, and reasonable—three good reasons to bring your half-pints—but not the spot for an intimate conversation. Beer lovers will want to try one of the microbrews made on the premises (we favor the amber) and take an informal tour of the brewery. Children seem fascinated by the equipment, maybe because it's reminiscent of the illustrations from their favorite Maurice Sendak storybook.

The welcoming basket of pretzels and mustard is a nice touch and—aren't they clever?—makes you *very* thirsty. The generous hamburgers are yummy and served with seasoned french fries. Barbecued ribs are a popular item, and several fish, pasta, and beef items are also listed on the menu. My clan likes the burgers, chili, and crunchy onion rings. A wait is not unusual at dinner (after 6:30 especially) and on weekends. Capitol City has a suburban branch in Arlington, Virginia. When you're in Baltimore, raise a mug at the Inner Harbor (☎ 410/539-7468).

Food Courts at the Old Post Office Pavilion

1100 Pennsylvania Ave. NW. ☎ **202/289-4224.** Most items $1–$7. No credit cards. Summer hours. Mon–Sat 10am–9pm, Sun noon–7pm. Metro: Federal Triangle. ECLECTIC.

If you're sightseeing on the Mall or along Pennsylvania or Constitution avenues, duck in here for a quick meal or a snack in the East and West Atriums. You'll find everything from Indian and Asian fare to burgers and fries. Save room for Ben & Jerry's.

Hard Rock Cafe

999 E St. NW, next to Ford's Theatre. ☎ **202/737-ROCK.** Fax 202/628-6595. www.hardrock.com. Reservations not accepted. Main courses $6.30–$17. AE, DC DISC, MC, V. Sun–Thurs 11am–midnight, Fri–Sat 11am–1am. Bar open until 2am. Children's Services: high chairs, boosters, kids menu. Metro: Metro Center. AMERICAN.

Let the good times roll as you ogle a Michael Jackson costume with rhinestone kneepad, autographed Stones photo, and one of Chuck Berry's guitars. Nobody comes here for the food, so stick to the basics: burger platters, sandwiches, and chicken salads. I think the filling in the "Pig Sandwich" (hickory smoked pulled pork) should have been left on the pig. Don't miss the hot fudge brownie sundae— it'll make you feel like dancin'. So will the 28 video monitors strategically placed throughout the restaurant. Go at off times unless you like lines.

5 Downtown

Visiting the Corcoran or Renwick late in the day? Watching the protestors in Lafayette Park across from the White House? Celebrating a special occasion? With older kids, slip into one of the upscale restaurants on K Street NW, Washington's restaurant row, for a heady (and expensive) dining experience. If you have tickets to a show at the Warner or National, try one of the many restaurants that have sprouted up in recent years on and around Pennsylvania Avenue, between 7th and 14th streets. If you're in a casual frame of mind, a sure bet is the Old Ebbitt Grill for super saloon food.

MODERATE

Old Ebbitt Grill

675 15th St. NW, between F and G sts. ☎ **202/347-4801.** www.clyde's.com. Reservations recommended, especially weekends. Breakfast $1–$9; lunch main courses $7.95–$18.95; dinner $12.95–$18.95; Sun brunch $7.95–$18.95. AE, CB, DC, DISC, MC, V. Mon–Fri 7:30am–1am, Sat 8am–1am, Sun 9:30am–1am; light fare daily until 1am. Closed Dec 25. Children's services: high chairs, boosters, kids' menu. Metro: Metro Center. AMERICAN.

Around the corner from the White House, the Ebbitt is consistently good. I suggest sticking to the beef and pasta dishes at dinner. The staff and kitchen go overboard to please munchkins, so don't hesitate to ask for half portions of whatever tickles their fancy. The hustle-bustle of this large but cozy saloon (part of the Clyde's family) is appealing with its polished wood, brass, and gaslights. It's easy to keep your tab in the budget range with something from the raw bar, a sandwich or hamburger, or a sumptuous dessert—how about a hot-fudge sundae made with home-made vanilla ice cream or a chocolate brioche bread pudding topped with vanilla sauce, fresh whipped cream, and pecan-praline crumble. The new **Ebbitt Express,** a fast-food deli on site, is open Monday through Thursday from 7:30am to 8pm, Friday from 7:30am to 6pm.

INEXPENSIVE

Food Hall at the Shops at National Place

1331 Pennsylvania Ave. NW (enter on Pennsylvania Ave. or F St.). ☎ **202/662-1250.** Most items $2–$6. No credit cards. Mon–Sat 10am–7pm, Sun noon–5pm. Children's services: high chairs. Metro: Federal Triangle or Metro Center. ECLECTIC/FOOD COURTS.

Nibble your way through the 19 stands selling ethnic food, pizza, subs, potatoes, yogurt, hot dogs, deli, cookies, and ice cream. There's plenty of seating, but you'll have to improvise a booster seat. Nobody calls this fine dining, but it's quick and cheap. Groups of 15 or more should call for information on discount group meal programs.

Pan Asian Noodles & Grill

1018 Vermont Ave. NW, 2nd Floor, between 14th and 15th sts. ☎ **202/783-8899.** Reservations for large groups. Main courses $6.95–$8.95. AE, MC, V, DISC. Mon–Fri 11:30am–8pm. Metro: McPherson Square. EAST ASIAN.

Because it's very good and very reasonable, Pan Asian is also very crowded, especially at lunchtime. Go early or late for a quick, inexpensive meal of soup (the wonton is especially worthwhile), noodles, and grilled dishes derived from various Asian cuisines, real and imagined. Fancy it's not, but the service is as crisp as a fried noodle.

There's another branch at 2020 P St. NW (☎ **202/872-8889;** Metro: Dupont Circle).

Sholl's Colonial Cafeteria

1990 K St. NW, in the Esplanade Mall. ☎ **202/296-3065.** www.washingtonpost.com/ yp/sholls. Reservations not accepted. Most appetizers $1; main courses $2–$6. No credit cards. Mon–Sat 7–10:30am, 11am–2:30pm, and 4–8pm. Also open Sun 8am–3pm, Mar–July only. Children's services: boosters. Metro: Farragut West. AMERICAN.

A Washington institution since 1928, Sholl's still dishes out freshly prepared quality vittles at low, low prices. Load your tray with a full breakfast (two eggs, bacon, home fries, juice, coffee or milk, and fresh-baked biscuits) for less than $5. At lunch and dinner, the hot main dishes cost less than $5. How about a dinner of roast beef, mashed potatoes, broccoli, coconut cream pie, and coffee or milk for $4.95? And the homemade pies and cakes are definitely a cut above average. Sholl's motto is "Live well for less money with quality food at reasonable prices." A great motto for families.

✪ Sky Terrace

Hotel Washington, 15th St. and Pennsylvania Ave. NW. ☎ **202/638-5900.** www. hotelwashington.com. Reservations not accepted. All items $7–$12. AE, DC, DISC, MC, V. May–Oct 11:30am–1am. Metro: Metro Center. LIGHT FARE.

Go anytime in good weather to graze on a sandwich, Monument Salad—a mixed-green Caesar with grilled chicken—cheese and fruit plate, or dessert, or to enjoy drinks on this very special rooftop. The extraordinary view of downtown and the environs is feast enough for most souls. You can almost touch the planes landing and taking off from National Airport. See how many buildings you can identify.

COOKIES, CANDY & ICE CREAM

Bread & Chocolate

2301 M St. NW. ☎ **202/833-8360.**

Don't limit yourself to cookies here. Go ahead, sample the just-out-of-the-oven croissants and pastries, or enjoy a salad, sandwich, or hot entree in the dining area. Bread & Chocolate is open for breakfast, lunch, and dinner. Eat in or take out.

There are other branches at 666 Pennsylvania Ave. SE on Capitol Hill (☎ **202/547-2875**); 5542 Connecticut Ave. NW (☎ **202/966-7413**); Bread & Chocolate Express, 801 15th St., NW. (☎ **202/289-0300**); 7704 Woodmont Ave., Bethesda (☎ **301/986-9008**).

Chocolate Chocolate

1050 Connecticut Ave. NW. ☎ **202/466-2190.** Fax 202/466-2190. Mon–Fri 10am–6pm. AE, DISC, MC, V. Metro: Farragut North.

Chocolate Chocolate: my two favorite words in the English language. The shop carries a sweet selection of imported and locally made confections. Special-order gift baskets are available, too. Co-owners Frances and Ginger Park wrote *My Freedom Trip: A Child's Escape from North Korea* in 1998. Autographed copies of the book, which won the 1999 International Reading Association's Children's Book Award, are sold at the store.

Le Sorbet
1776 G St. NW. ☎ **202/789-1313.**

The servings are a mite skimpy, but the ice cream is flavorful and satisfying. Try the fruit-flavored ices, which are especially refreshing on a hot summer's day. Le Sorbet also serves sandwiches and rotisserie chicken.

AFTERNOON TEA

Park Hyatt Hotel
24th and M sts. NW. ☎ **202/789-1234.** www.hyatt.com.

Fill your plate as many times as you like in the elegant lobby lounge from 3 to 5pm Thursday through Sunday. You can also order à la carte. $16.95, Queen's tea $19 (including a glass of champagne).

Renaissance Mayflower Hotel
1127 Connecticut Ave. NW. ☎ **202/347-3000.** www.renaissancehotels.com/wassh.

The soothing setting of the Café Promenade is the scene for tea for two—or three or four or more—Monday through Saturday from 3:30 to 5:30pm. $17.75. No discounts for children.

St. Regis Washington, D.C. Hotel
923 16th St. NW. ☎ **202/638-2626.** www.starwood.com.

Full tea is served in the Elspinasse restaurant Friday, Saturday, and Sunday from 3 to 5:30pm, for $19. No discounts for kids.

6 Foggy Bottom

Row houses fronted by brick sidewalks and postage-size gardens make Foggy Bottom one of the most attractive and charming areas of the city. If you have business at the State Department or are attending a Kennedy Center or Lisner Auditorium performance, you've come to the right place.

EXPENSIVE

✪ Kinkead's
2000 Pennsylvania Ave. NW (entrance on I St. between 20th and 21st sts.). ☎ **202/296-7700.** Fax 202/296-7688. Reservations recommended. Main courses $12–$18 lunch, $22–$26 dinner; Sun brunch $12–$21.95. AE, CB, DC, DISC, MC, V. Lunch Mon–Sat 11:30am–2:30pm, brunch Sun 11:30am–2:30pm, dinner daily 5:30–10pm; raw bar menu 11:30am–11pm. Metro: Foggy Bottom. AMERICAN/SEAFOOD.

In a Foggy Bottom town house where restaurants used to come and go as quickly as call girls on the Hill, Kinkead's, like true love, is here to stay. This is a dining establishment for those who know and enjoy fine food. Kinkead's welcomes children but, frankly I don't think it's appropriate for kids under 8 or 10. And it is pricey. Whether you choose a table in the upstairs dining room—actually several minirooms and alcoves—or the more casual downstairs, you'll enjoy the creations of chef Bob

Kinkead. He's the winner of several awards, among them, the 1995 James Beard Award for best chef in the mid-Atlantic region. Kinkead whips up some mighty tantalizin' regional and international dishes. Everything is made from scratch, with only the freshest ingredients. They even make their own mayonnaise. The menu changes daily, but one mainstay I can personally vouch for is the pepita-crusted grilled salmon with shrimp, crab, and chiles. When featured, the Brazilian pork sampler served with black beans and pureed sweet potatoes is outta sight. For dessert, try the crème brûlée, sometimes a three-pot variation on a theme—caramel, orange, and chocolate. Ask for a few spoons, pass it around the table, and vote for your favorite.

Downstairs, in the cafe/raw bar area, you can show up in shorts if you wish and graze on soups, salads, and appetizer-size portions (most with seafood in one form or another). A tinkling piano adds atmosphere during the evening. Although clearly not for the cholesterol conscious, the New England clam chowder and fried Ipswich clams rival any I've sampled on Cape Cod or in Maine. With young children, I think you'll feel more comfortable (and so will other diners) if you sit in the enclosed courtyard.

The clientele is comprised largely of locals, pols (the White House is 5 blocks away), and business types. Sunday brunch appeals to families trying to capture some quality time before Monday rears its ugly head. Diners can choose from main dishes such as eggs Benedict, french toast, and omelets, served with baskets of tempting sweet rolls and breads.

After 5:30pm there's valet parking.

INEXPENSIVE

T.G.I. Friday's
2100 Pennsylvania Ave. NW (entrance on 21st St. at I St.). ☎ **202/872-4344;** and 1201 Pennsylvania Ave. NW. ☎ **202/628-8443.** www.tgifridays.com. Reservations accepted for 10 or more. Main courses $5.75–$14.95; kids' menu $1.95–$2.75. AE, DC, DISC, MC, V. Sun–Thurs 11am–11pm (till midnight at the 2100 Pennsylvania address); Sat 11am–1am. Children's services: high chairs, boosters, kids' menu, crayons. AMERICAN.

The servers are enthusiastic and young, and the place looks like a before picture of a garage sale with Tiffany lamps, hanging plants, antiques, and photos *everywhere.* Those 12 and under can choose from standbys such as grilled cheese, hamburgers, and hot dogs on the kids' menu. Try any of the chicken dishes and save room for the mocha mud pie (layers of chocolate almond mousse and coffee ice cream in a cookie crust topped with hot fudge and toasted almonds).

Try Friday's any day of the week, including the branches in Maryland and Virginia. Both the 2100 Pennsylvania Ave. NW Friday's, on the campus of George Washington University, and the branch at 1201 Pennsylvania Ave. NW, in the redeveloped Pennsylvania Quarter, enhance their respective neighborhoods.

ICE CREAM

Café Café
2816 Pennsylvania Ave. NW. ☎ **202/338-6778.** Spring and summer: Mon–Fri 11am–midnight, Sat–Sun 11am–1am; fall and winter: daily 11am–10pm. AE, DISC, MC, V. Metro: Foggy Bottom, then any no. 30 bus for Georgetown.

Halfway between the Foggy Bottom Metro station and Georgetown is Café Café, an ideal spot for a quick sandwich, cold drink, fountain specialty, or sundae (in a waffle cone, if you feel like really splurging). The all-natural smoothies are delicious and kinder to the waistline.

Cone E Island
2000 Pennsylvania Ave. NW. ☎ **202/822-8460.** Fax 202/342-0383. Open daily noon–midnight. Metro: Foggy Bottom

Kids of all ages love the waffle cones, loaded with ice cream, hot fudge, and whipped cream. What's not to like? A bit pricey for ice cream, but loyal fans will tell you it's well worth the cost and calories. A second branch is at Tysons Corner, Virginia (☎ **703/442-8502**).

7 Georgetown

Georgetown is one of Washington's most visited tourist areas, so there are quite a few restaurants there. I seriously doubt you'll have trouble finding a restaurant with your favorite ethnic cuisine in Georgetown. The Metro does not run into Georgetown, but you can take Friendship Heights buses (no. 30, 32, 34, and 36) from Pennsylvania Avenue near the Foggy Bottom metro station at 23rd and I streets NW to any point in Georgetown.

EXPENSIVE

✪ Morton's of Chicago
3251 Prospect St. NW, just off Wisconsin Ave. ☎ **202/342-6258.** www.mortons.com. Reservations recommended. Main courses $19–$31. AE, CB, DC, MC, V. Mon–Fri 5:30–11pm, Sat 5–11pm Sun 5–10pm. Closed most major holidays. AMERICAN.

Come here for one of the best steaks in town, maybe in the country. While some Morton's fans prefer the veal chop or oversized lobsters, I'm a sucker for the steak and side orders of hash browns and fresh vegetables-enough for two or three servings. Well-mannered kids over 10 with healthy appetites are welcome. Check out the permanent collection of Leroy Neiman paintings.

There's a downtown Morton's at 1050 Connecticut Ave. NW (at L Street; ☎ **202/955-5997**); branches in Tysons Corner, Virginia (☎ **703/883-0800**) and in the Sheraton Hotel, 300 S. Charles St., Baltimore (☎ **410/547-8255**).

✪ Sea Catch Restaurant and Raw Bar
Canal Square, 1054 31st St. NW, at M St. ☎ **202/337-8855.** www.seacatch.com. Fax 202/337-8855. Reservations recommended. Main courses $14.95–$21.95 lunch, $16.95–$27.95 dinner. AE, CB, DC, MC, V. Mon–Sat noon–3pm and 5:30–10pm. Closed Sun. Children's services: high chairs. Metro: Foggy Bottom, then any no. 30 bus. SEAFOOD.

When you're in the mood to linger over lovingly prepared seafood dishes, reserve a canalside table at this attractive stone-and-brick historic landmark, once a warehouse for goods transported on the C&O Canal. Pop some oysters or clams at the 40-foot marble raw bar to whet your appetite for seasonal specialties such as Dover sole, soft-shell crabs, crab cakes, or lobster. Several meat and chicken entrees are also listed. Key lime pie or cheesecake are fitting finales. Well-behaved kids over 7 are welcome. Free parking (3 hours) with validation in Georgetown Park garage at Wisconsin Avenue and M Street.

MODERATE

Clyde's
3236 M St. NW. ☎ **202/333-9180.** www.clyde's.com. Reservations strongly recommended. Bar food and lunch $6–$10; dinner main courses $11.95–$18.95. AE, CB, DC, DISC, MC, V. Mon–Thurs 11:30am–2am, Fri 11:30am–3am, Sat 10am–3am, Sun 9am–2am. Children's services: high chairs, boosters, kids' menu. AMERICAN/CONTINENTAL.

Georgetown Dining

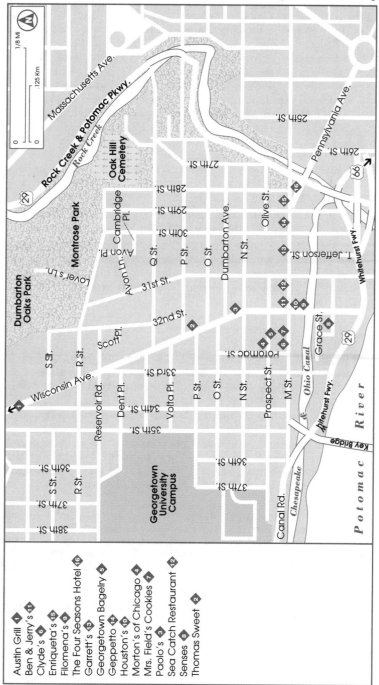

Austin Grill 4
Ben & Jerry's 11
Clyde's 6
Enriqueta's 15
Filomena's 9
The Four Seasons Hotel 16
Garrett's 13
Georgetown Bagelry 5
Geppetto 14
Houston's 10
Morton's of Chicago 4
Mrs. Field's Cookies 7
Paolo's 3
Sea Catch Restaurant 12
Senses 8
Thomas Sweet 2

The granddaddy of Georgetown saloons, Clyde's has been SRO since opening in 1963. Have brunch in the sunny Omelette Room or head for the bright and breezy Patio Room for a burger, sandwich, salad, or something more substantial. Kids can busy themselves with a souvenir Busy Bag, filled with a coloring book, and crayons. Stay out of the bar area if you bring the children—or if you want to retain your hearing and sanity. The 4-to-7pm "Afternoon Delights" snack menu inspired the Starland Vocal Band to write their hit song. Look for the gold record in the Patio Room. Clyde's is making a valiant, and long overdue, effort to lower prices. (Applause.) After visiting the Washington Dolls' House and Toy Museum or shopping at Mazza Gallery, Lord & Taylor or Saks, stop at the Clyde's at 76 Wisconsin Circle, Chevy Chase, Maryland, near the Friendship Heights Metro station (☎ **301/951-9600**). You'll also find Clyde's in Reston and Vienna, Virginia, and Columbia, Maryland.

Enriqueta's

2811 M St. NW. ☎ **202/338-7772.** Reservations for 6 or more. Main courses $6–$15. AE, MC, V. Mon–Sat 11:30am–3pm. Closed Sun. Children's services: boosters. MEXICAN.

This is not the place to come for a quick taco or burrito. The seafood and beef dishes and chicken with mole (a spicy tomato-and-beef-based sauce with onions, chiles, and Mexican chocolate) are noteworthy in the closet-size cantina tucked between Foggy Bottom and Georgetown. The service is quick (some say too quick), but the food is consistent and authentic, and the prices are reasonable. Local families have enjoyed Enriqueta's *con mucho gusto* for years. Stay away if you have a disk problem or if you're sensitive to hard seats—the chairs are unyielding.

Filomena's

1063 Wisconsin Ave. NW, below M St. ☎ **202/338-8800.** Reservations recommended. Main courses $4.50–$11.95 lunch, $11.95–$26.95 dinner; buffet lunch $8.95. AE, DC, DISC, MC, V. Daily 11:30am–11pm. Closed Jan 1, Thanksgiving, Dec 24 (evening) to Dec 25. ITALIAN.

Even with a reservation, on Friday and Saturday nights you may have to wait, so eat early or go on a weeknight. Your teens are welcome here; younger children are not. Filomena's is fun and serves delicious pasta (made daily on the premises) with a variety of interesting sauces. For a real treat, try the pesto or sun-dried tomato bread. Everybody's friendly, and it's not unusual to hear your neighbor's life story before the espresso arrives. Don't miss the home-baked desserts.

Garrett's

3003 M St. NW. ☎ **202/333-1033.** Fax 202/333-8055. E-mail: Rhinorest@aol.com. Reservations accepted. Appetizers $3.50–$4.95; sandwiches $5.75–$7.50; main courses $6–$8 lunch, $8–$12 dinner. AE, CB, DC, DISC, MC, V. Downstairs: Mon–Fri 11:30am–10:30pm; Sat–Sun noon–10:30pm. Terrace: Mon–Fri 11:30am–2:30pm; Sat noon–3pm; Sun (fall and winter) brunch noon–3pm. Children's services: boosters, high chairs, kids' menu, crayons/paper. AMERICAN.

Shhhhhh! If you like Garrett's, please don't tell anyone else. Thomas Sim Lee, the second governor of Maryland, built the tavern in what is now a National Historic Trust building. Locals belly up to the three copper-topped bars and feed one of the hottest juke boxes around. Bypass the noisy bar scene downstairs, decorated with vintage train memorabilia, for a table on the charming glass-enclosed second-floor terrace. Nice, huh? You can't get lunch on the Terrace after 2:30pm weekdays, but the restaurant will be happy to serve you downstairs. Kids can make a meal out of the nachos appetizer, or a quesadilla, or a burger—generous and juicy. Check out the seafood chowder, other seafood dishes, and delectable salads at this casual eatery.

The kitchen is flexible in this neighborhood watering hole and has been a longtime favorite of local families.

Paolo's

1303 Wisconsin Ave. NW, between N and Dumbarton sts. ☎ **202/333-7353.** www. capitalrestaurants.com. Reservations accepted for lunch and brunch. Main courses $6.95–$12.95 lunch/brunch, $8.95–$17.95 dinner. Mon–Sat 11:30am–midnight, Sun 11am–midnight. Children's services: high chairs, boosters, sassy seats, kids' menu, crayons/paper. ITALIAN.

Paolo's is a looker, but we're happy to report its beauty is more than skin deep. Munch the crisp breadsticks while deciding on one of the California-style pastas, pizzas, chicken, or fish dishes, or a salad—all well seasoned and attractively served. A house specialty is the massive shrimp scampi for $18.95. Since Paolo's is a hot spot, especially on weekends, try it at off times. The kitchen will split orders for children.

There are Paolo branches in Reston, Virginia; Baltimore's Inner Harbor; and Towson, Maryland—check them out if you are in the neighborhood.

✪ Senses

3206 Grace St. NW, off Wisconsin Ave. just below M St. ☎ **202/342-9083.** www.senses.com. Reservations accepted. Breakfast items $1.50–$8; main courses $5–$11 lunch, $6–$10 brunch, $12–$18.50 dinner. AE, DC, MC, V. Tues–Sat 8am–11pm, Sat–Sun 9am–3pm, Sun 6–10pm. Closed Mon. FRENCH.

Senses opened in 1999 on the site of the former Patisserie Café Didier. They serve breakfast, lunch, tea (3 to 5pm), and dinner every day but Monday, when business partners/chefs Xavier (cook) and Bruno (pastry) hang up their toques.

The setting could easily be on the Left Bank of the Seine rather than the *rive gauche* of Wisconsin Avenue. Seating for 45 is at tables set with immaculate white tablecloths, sparkling stemware, and fresh flowers. Our informants suggest the omelette with Swiss cheese, mushrooms, asparagus, and country-style potatoes at breakfast (maybe with a croissant on the side!), warm goat cheese salad and seafood risotto at lunch, pan-seared salmon fillet with truffled mashed potatoes, or any other featured seasonal special at dinner. Less adventurous appetites may opt for appetizer-size miniraviolis, a salad, or sautéed chicken breast. For a midafternoon picker-upper, try one or more of the two dozen pastries and cookies. If you're a chocoholic like me, sink your fork and teeth into the raspberry and chocolate mousse cake, chocolate pecan pie, or Black Forest cake.

INEXPENSIVE

Georgetown Bagelry

3245 M St. NW, off Wisconsin Ave. ☎ **202/965-1011.** Bagels plain 60¢ each, dressed $1.50–$5.50. Cash only. Mon–Fri 6am–7pm; Sat 7am–7pm; Sun 7am–5pm. AMERICAN.

Now here's an oxymoron—a truly inexpensive Georgetown restaurant! In 1999, the bagels here won a blind tasting of six bagel shops by unbiased *Washington Post* staff. Near the busy crossroads of Wisconsin Avenue and M Street, Georgetown Bagelry offers counter seating for about 20 bagel noshers. Plagued by so many choices, so little time? Try my favorite, an ET (everything) bagel with Nova Scotia salmon and cream cheese ($5.50), with a fresh squeezed OJ chaser. If you have room, finish with a dish of fresh fruit salad. In nice weather get it and go to the canal or river-front. How many places can you buy lunch and walk away with change from $10? A second location, at 5227 River Rd., Bethesda, Maryland (☎ **301/657-4442**), is open Monday through Friday, 6am to 5pm, Saturday 7am to 4pm, Sunday 7am to 3pm. Tours of the Bethesda branch are by appointment.

✪ Geppetto

2917 M St. NW. ☎ **202/333-2602.** Reservations not accepted. Pies $7.45–$23.25. AE, DC, DISC, MC. Mon–Thurs noon–11pm, Fri–Sat noon–12:30am, Sun noon–10:30pm. PIZZA.

Some pizza lovers grow misty-eyed describing the white pizza, loaded with garlic, onion, and fontina cheese. Others engage in heated discussions over the merits of the deep-dish versus regular crust variety. Life is hard. Since the restaurant is not much larger than a pizza itself, you can't eat here. But you can pick up a pie to go and eat it on the lawn behind the Old Stone House. Or call from your hotel and Geppetto will deliver. You'll find a sit-down Geppetto restaurant in Bethesda, Maryland, at 10257 Old Georgetown Rd. (☎ **301/493-9230**).

✪ Houston's

1065 Wisconsin Ave. NW, below M St. ☎ **202/338-7760.** Reservations not accepted. Appetizers $7–$9; most main courses $7–$15. AE, MC, V. Mon–Thurs 11:30am–11pm, Fri–Sat 11:30am–midnight, Sun noon–10pm. Children's services: high chairs, boosters. AMERICAN.

Absolutely and positively, Houston's serves the best hickory-grilled hamburgers in Washington. Sometimes you could die waiting for a table, but it's worth it. When the line is long (at peak lunch and dinner hours), put your name on the list and take a walk to Kathmandu. Or solve the problem by eating early or late. The barbecued ribs ($18 for a full rack) and salads are outstanding, washed down with a or frosty mug of beer. Portions are large enough for little ones to share. This attractive restaurant is part of a chain extending from Atlanta to Phoenix to Chicago. Its popularity is easily understood: Houston's ambience is welcoming to all ages, and the food is fresh and first quality.

You'll also find Houston's in Maryland at 7715 Woodmont Ave., Bethesda (☎ **301/656-9755**), and 12256 Rockville Pike, Rockville (☎ **301/468-3535**).

COOKIES, CANDY & ICE CREAM

✪ Ben & Jerry's

3135 M St. NW. ☎ **202/965-2222.** www.benjerry.com.

Who'd have thought two young men dishing it out at a stand in Burlington, Vermont, would've created such an empire? Sample this rich environmentally correct product and you'll know why Ben and Jerry are mooing all the way to the bank. (Have you tried the Triple Caramel Chunk yet?) Other locations are at 11th and Pennsylvania Ave. NW in the Old Post Office Pavilion (☎ **202/842-5882**) and 1333 19th St. NW, next to the Dupont Circle Cineplex (☎ **202/785-4881**). Further afield you'll find Ben & Jerry's in Old Town, Alexandria, Virginia, and still another in Gaithersburg, Maryland.

Mrs. Field's Cookies

Georgetown Park Mall, Wisconsin Ave. and M St. NW. ☎ **202/337-5117.**

These soft, chewy, chip-laden cookies are nearly as good as homemade, and the muffins are excellent. They make the perfect bribe when you need one (with kids, that's about every 30 seconds). I only wish they carried my name so I could retire to the Caribbean.

Thomas Sweet

3214 P St. NW (at Wisconsin Ave.). ☎ **202/337-0616.**

This neighborhood ice-cream parlor reminds me of the "malt shoppe" in the Archie comics. The ice-cream-making operation (135 flavors!) is in nearby Silver Spring, Maryland, where it handles the large demand from area restaurants and the Smithsonian. The best-seller here is the "Blend In," a customized mix of up to three toppings (fresh fruit, cookies, and candies) with any flavor of ice cream or yogurt. The bittersweet chocolate is said to be the best in the world. If you're off sweets, try one of the sandwiches or homemade soups while enjoying the passing parade of students, tourists, Brooks Brothers suits, and blue-haired ladies.

AFTERNOON TEA

Four Seasons Hotel Andreas

2800 M St. NW. ☎ **202/342-0444.** www.fourseasons.com.

Enjoy tea in the beautiful Garden Terrace overlooking Rock Creek Park from 3 to 5pm on Monday through Saturday and 4 to 5:30pm on Sunday. A children's tea menu features minipeanut butter and jelly sandwiches, milkshakes, and brownies. Full tea $18; children's tea $9 for those 12 and under.

8 Dupont Circle

VERY EXPENSIVE

Jockey Club

Westin Fairfax, 2100 Massachusetts Ave. NW. ☎ **202/835-2100.** www.westin.com. Reservations required. Main courses $12–$23 lunch, $13.50–$34 dinner. AE, CB, DC, MC, V. Daily 6:30–11am breakfast, noon–2:30pm lunch, 6–10:30pm dinner. Children's services: high chairs, boosters, kids' menu. Metro: Dupont Circle. CONTINENTAL/FRENCH.

An "in" spot with Washington politicos and power brokers since it opened in the former Hotel Fairfax on the eve of John F. Kennedy's inauguration, this elegantly clubby (as in old money) establishment wants the world to know that junior power brokers are welcome, too. A children's menu, in the form of a coloring book, lists hamburgers, chicken, spaghetti, and even peanut butter sandwiches. More highly developed tastes will want to sample one of the fish or veal main courses or outstanding crab cakes. Service is always special at the Jockey Club, even if your family pedigree says you are not. If you're staying at the Westin, there's a room-service menu for kids. Pretty cushy!

INEXPENSIVE

Brickskeller

1523 22nd St. NW. ☎ **202/293-1885.** Reservations accepted for 6 or more. All items $6–$12. AE, DC, DISC, MC, V. Mon–Thurs 11:30am–2am, Fri 11:30am–3am, Sat 6pm–3am, Sun 6pm–2am. Children's services: boosters, high chairs. Metro: Dupont Circle. AMERICAN.

I wish I had a nickel for every visit I made to the Brick in my student days. If you long for a fraternity house setting, head for the corner of 22nd and P streets, where pub fare is served in a tastefully tacky setting accessorized with dart boards and video games. More than 800 kinds of beer and an oldies-filled jukebox will nurture your nostalgia trip while your underagers play electronic games and munch on chicken wings, burgers (regular and buffalo), and other light fare. The Brickskeller has been pleasing patrons for 40 years. Add your name to the list with a visit.

Kramerbooks & Afterwords Café

1517 Connecticut Ave. NW., between Dupont Circle and Q St. ☎ **202/387-1462.** www.kramerbooks.com. Breakfast $1.75–$8.50; appetizers $3.95–$5.75; main courses $8.75–$12.25. AE, MC, V. Mon–Thurs 7:30am–1am; continuously from Fri 8am to Sun 1am. Metro: Dupont Circle. AMERICAN.

After browsing at Kramerbooks, stop for a meal or snack at Afterwords, where the atmosphere is as close to Greenwich Village in its heyday as Washington allows itself to get. The menu changes seasonally. Try the quesadilla or bagels with smoked salmon and cream cheese at breakfast. The OJ is fresh squeezed. At other times you'll find everything from salads, sandwiches, and pasta to calorie-packed desserts such as sour cream blackout cake and banana splits. We're partial to the Fettuccine New Orleans made with shrimp, sausage, onions, and sweet peppers, finished with Cajun spices and cream. Great diet dinner! Wednesday through Saturday evenings there's live music-folk, jazz, or blues. Grown-ups could indulge in margaritas ($17.50 for a huge pitcherful with nachos on the side) while the children enjoy ice-cream treats.

Otello
1329 Connecticut Ave. NW. ☎ **202/429-0209.** Reservations recommended. Main courses $7.75–$9.50 lunch, $9.50–$12.50 dinner. AE, CB, DC. Mon–Fri noon–2:30pm; Mon–Sat 5:30–10:30pm. Metro: Dupont Circle. ITALIAN.

Otello is a friendly, family operated neighborhood trattoria, more typical of those found in New York than D.C. The flavorful sauces pack the right amount of punch, and the seafood and veal dishes are as fine as you'll find south of Little Italy. The osso bucco (veal shanks in a well-seasoned sauce) is a house specialty. Not suitable for bambinos under 8.

9 Adams–Morgan

Note: Parking is next to impossible in the Adams–Morgan area, especially on weekends, and the nearest Metro stop is a hefty walk. Take a taxi, and enjoy the many ethnic eateries.

MODERATE

I Matti
2436 18th St. NW. ☎ **202/462-8844.** Reservations recommended. Main courses $12.95–$16.95. AE, DC, MC, V. Tues–Sat 11:30am–2:30pm (lunch); Tues–Sun 5:30–10:30pm (dinner). Children's services: high chairs; half-order for almost all dishes in the pasta section. Metro: Woodley Park-Zoo (area not safe after dark-I recommend taking a taxi). ITALIAN.

Head for the second, quieter floor at this popular trattoria, where the lines may lead you to believe they're giving the pizza away for free. Best choices are pasta, pizza, and fish. The polenta comes with most main courses but can also be ordered as a side dish. The breads are outstanding, especially the crusty, salt-topped variety. Youngsters can make a meal of the mixed antipasto, and the kitchen is very flexible when it comes to pleasing young diners. If you know what's good for you, stay away on Saturday night. The atmosphere is less frenetic at lunch.

INEXPENSIVE

✪ Spaghetti Garden
2317 18th St. NW, near Columbia Rd. ☎ **202/265-6665.** Reservations for groups of 8 or more. Appetizers $1–$5.45; pasta main courses $4.95–$8.25; meat main courses $8.45–$11.95; children's spaghetti portions $2.95. AE, CB, DC, MC, V. Mon–Thurs noon–midnight, Fri–Sat noon–1am, Sun noon–11pm. Closed Thanksgiving, Dec 25, Jan 1. Children's services: high chairs, boosters, children's portions. Metro: Woodley Park-Zoo. ITALIAN.

The former Adams–Morgan Spaghetti Garden may have dropped the "Adams–Morgan," but it hasn't dropped its family friendly attitude. This may not be gourmet fare, but most of the hearty large-portioned pasta dishes—lasagna, spaghetti, ravioli, and the like—are still priced at $7.95. Chicken, veal, and shrimp (served with a side of spaghetti marinara) go from $7 to $12 (pinch me, I'm

Adams-Morgan & Dupont Circle Dining

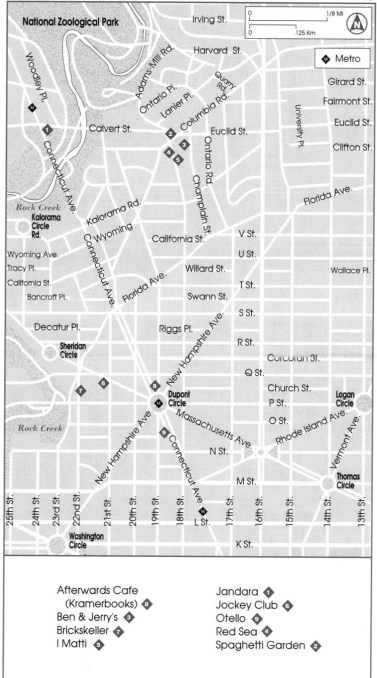

Afterwards Cafe
(Kramerbooks) 8
Ben & Jerry's 3
Brickskeller 7
I Matti 5

Jandara 1
Jockey Club 6
Otello 9
Red Sea 4
Spaghetti Garden 2

dreaming!). Bowing to the Spanish/Mexican craze, the menu offers the Italian version of tapas, *spunerii,* with such appetite whetters as antipasto, grilled Portobello mushrooms, and fried calamari. The pizza puttanesca is adorned with black olives, tomato, capers, and plenty of garlic. Bellisima! This may be the last place in the city where you can get a glass of wine for under $3. The second-floor rooftop affords a view of one of the city's more interesting neighborhoods. It's a hike from the nearest Metro, and parking is scarce, so I'd take a taxi.

Red Sea

2463 18th St. NW, near Columbia Rd. ☎ **202/483-5000.** Reservations recommended. Appetizers $1.95–$4.75; main courses $6.95–$10.95. AE, DC, DISC, MC, V. Open daily 11:30am–11:30pm. Children's services: high chairs, boosters, half portions. Metro: Woodley Park-Zoo. Metrobus no. 42 or L-2. ETHIOPIAN.

Select an Ethiopian tune from the jukebox to get in the proper mood, and roll up your sleeves, as your silverware is dangling at the ends of your arms. You'd probably yell if your children ate like this at home, and that's why they'll love scooping up the stewlike main dishes with pieces of *teff* (spongy pancakelike Ethiopian bread made with wheat, buckwheat, and flour). One of the sampler platters of meat and vegetables steeped in spicy sauces or herbed butter will amply feed two little ones. *A word of caution: Wat* items are hot and spicy; *alecha* dishes are milder. The sometimes spotty service is more bearable when enjoying the passing parade at an outdoor table.

10 Upper Northwest

MODERATE

Cactus Cantina

3300 Wisconsin Ave. NW. ☎ **202/686-7222.** Fax 202/362-5649. Reservations not accepted. Appetizers $3.25–$9.95; main courses $6.50–$17. AE, CB, DC, DISC, MC, V. Sun–Thurs 11:30am–11pm, Fri–Sat 11:30am–midnight. Children's services: high chairs, boosters, kids' menu, crayons/coloring books. Metro: Tenleytown; then take any no. 30 bus. TEX-MEX.

It's hard to believe this cozy cantina, decorated with twinkling lights and other charmingly tacky touches, is on busy Wisconsin Avenue (1 block from the National Cathedral and a short drive from the National Zoo)—not on some dusty plain south of the border. To accommodate adoring fans, a few years back the Cantina doubled its seating capacity to 400. Tex-Mex mavens drool at the mention of mesquite-grilled fajitas and generous combination platters. The kids' menu consists of smaller portions of items on the adult menu. Watch the tortilla chips birthed by a weird contraption similar to a see-through oven. The restaurant is one of the most popular of its ilk in the D.C. area, so show up before 6pm for dinner, especially on weekends.

Jandara

2606 Connecticut Ave. NW, at Calvert St. ☎ **202/387-8876.** Appetizers $3.95–$6.95; main courses $6.95–$24.95. AE, CB, DC, DISC, MC, V. Mon–Thurs 11am–10:30pm, Fri–Sat 11am–11pm, Sun 11am–10:30pm. Children's services: high chairs, boosters. Metro: Woodley Park-Zoo. THAI.

Appetizers such as barbecued chicken in peanut sauce, spring rolls, and coconut chicken soup will keep you busy while deciding among the many fish, chicken, and pork main dishes. If your innards are heat sensitive, ask your server to recommend some of the milder dishes. If you don't mind bus fumes, there's sidewalk dining in nice weather. Jandara is convenient to the National Zoo.

INEXPENSIVE
Chadwick's
5247 Wisconsin Ave. NW, at Jenifer St. ☎ **202/362-8040.** Reservations for 6 or more. Main courses $5.95–$9.95 lunch, $5.95–$17.95 dinner. AE, CB, DC, DISC, MC, V. Mon–Thurs 11:30am–midnight (bar open until 2am), Fri–Sat 11:30am–1am (bar open until 3am), Sun 10am–midnight (bar open until 2am). Children's services: high chairs, boosters, kids' menu, crayons. Metro: Friendship Heights. AMERICAN.

Going to Chadwick's is like visiting an old friend. Children are greeted with balloons, crayons, and their own menu to color. The service is friendly and prompt, the cocktails generous. The hamburgers and sandwiches are ample and tasty, and Sunday brunch is a bargain at $5.95 to $9.95. A shaded outdoor patio is a welcome addition.

I've been receiving good reports on the seafood and pasta, as well as the daily $6.50 super deal lunch that includes a soft drink. If you're visiting Georgetown or Alexandria, Virginia, Chadwick's is there, too, at 3205 K St. NW (☎ **202/333-2565**), and 203 S. Strand St., Old Town (☎ **703/836-4422**), respectively.

✪ Cheesecake Factory
5345 Wisconsin Ave. NW. ☎ **202/364-0500.** Main courses $5.95–$18.95. AE, DISC, MC, V. Mon–Thurs 11:30am–11:30pm, Fri–Sat 11:30am–12:30am, Sun 10am–11pm. Children's services: high chairs, boosters. Metro: Friendship Heights. AMERICAN.

The California-based Cheesecake Factory blew in like a Santa Ana, but judging by the lines this is no ill wind. The first-class french fries are crunchy and greaseless, the salads and chicken dishes tasty though humongous (two could easily share one portion). The leftovers make a fine late-night snack. The extensive menu is worthy of framing. Many complain about the noise and the wait. I'll keep saying it until I'm blue in the face: Go early, especially with easily tired young'uns. Don't forget the real reason you came: to try at least one of the 35 kinds of cheesecake. When in Montgomery County, try the Cheesecake Factory at White Flint Mall in North Bethesda, Maryland (☎ **301/770-0999**), and at the Inner Harbor in Baltimore (☎ **410/234-3990**).

✪ El Tamarindo
4910 Wisconsin Ave. NW, at 42nd St. ☎ **202/244-8888.** Main courses $5.95–$10.95. AE, CB, DC, MC, V. Mon–Thurs 11am–10pm, Fri 11am–midnight, Sat 11am–2am, Sun 11am–1am. Children's services: high chairs, boosters. Metro: Tenleytown or Friendship Heights. MEXICAN/SALVADORAN.

Weather permitting, eat on the patio at this friendly neighborhood spot whose specialty is chicken, beef, or shrimp fajitas. Kids can order à la carte items such as burritos and tacos. Those in the know say the dishes are authentically prepared. All I know is the food is tasty, families are treated well, and the prices are ridiculously low. The congenial atmosphere is gratis.

El Tamarindo is also a good choice when you wake up starving at 1am. Other branches are at 1785 Florida Ave. NW, in Adams–Morgan (☎ **202/328-3660**), and 7331 Georgia Ave. NW, Upper Northwest (☎ **202/291-0525**).

ICE CREAM & CANDY
Baskin-Robbins
2604 Connecticut Ave. ☎ **202/483-4820.**

They must be doing something right. They sell more ice cream than any other retail dealer in the country. The franchises are institutional, but, like an old friend, they're there when you need them.

I Can't Believe It's Yogurt
4000 Wisconsin Ave. NW. ☎ **202/363-8933.**

The answer to a weight-watcher's prayer, each creamy ounce has only 27 calories; the nonfat, 20 calories. If you keep the ounces in the single digits and refrain from loading up on the candy toppings, you and yours will stay out of fat city. But what fun is that?

Kron Chocolatier
Mazza Galleria, 5300 Wisconsin Ave. NW. ☎ **202/966-4946.** Fax 202/244-5148. E-mail: kronchocolatier@juno.com.

In a recurring dream, I fall into a vat of Kron's melted bittersweet chocolate and live happily ever after. Try the Budapest cream truffles and chocolate-dipped strawberries, and you too will have sweet dreams. Kids will find their own favorites. Underground parking is free with ticket validation. Open Monday through Friday 10am to 8pm, Saturday 10am to 6pm, Sunday noon to 5pm.

Uptown Scoop
3510 Connecticut Ave. NW ☎ **202/244-4465.**

Stop before or after a visit to the zoo for a double scooper or sundae with all the trimmings at this sweet neighborhood spot.

AFTERNOON TEA
Washington National Cathedral
Massachusetts and Wisconsin aves. NW. ☎ **202/537-8993.**

What a lovely setting in which to enjoy tea every Tuesday and Wednesday afternoon after the special 1:30pm cathedral tour. Teatime is 2:30pm and it costs $5. Reservations are required a week in advance.

11 Suburban Maryland

Years ago, if you lived in or visited the suburbs and wanted a decent meal, you had to venture downtown. Now there are so many good restaurants ringing the Beltway that most diners are content to stay put—as well they should be. Here are a few (my editor will holler if I list too many) of Maryland's many family friendly restaurants.

BETHESDA
MODERATE

✪ Foong Lin
7710 Norfolk Ave., Bethesda, Maryland ☎ **301/656-3427.** Reservations accepted. Main courses $4.50–$7.50 lunch, $7.50–$17.95 dinner. AE, MC, V. Mon–Thurs 11am–10:30pm, Fri–Sat 11am–11pm, Sun noon–10pm. Closed Thanksgiving. Children's services: high chairs, boosters. Metro: Bethesda. CHINESE.

This neighborhood restaurant has a friendly wait staff, which is especially kind and considerate to families with young children. Foong Lin turns out a host of above-average Cantonese, Hunan, and Szechuan favorites, and the menu features seasonal specialties. The crispy whole fish is exceptional (see if you can talk the kids into trying it). What more do you want? Guaranteed good news in your fortune cookie?

INEXPENSIVE

Athenian Plaka
7833 Woodmont Ave., Bethesda, Maryland ☎ **301/986-1337.** Reservations accepted. Main courses $4.95–$7.95 lunch, $6.95–$17.95 dinner. AE, CB, DC, DISC, MC, V. Mon–Thurs

11am–10pm, Fri–Sat 11am–11pm, Sun 10am–11pm. Children's services: high chairs, boosters, kids' menu. Metro: Bethesda. GREEK.

Consistency is what you'll get at this pleasant suburban restaurant, where the portions are generous and well prepared. Daily specials at lunch and dinner are a good value. Try any of the authentically prepared lamb dishes. If they're not up to a full meal, younger kids can order a bowl of egg-lemon soup and/or an appetizer portion of stuffed grape leaves, hot or cold. If your kids make faces tell them the *dolmas* are Greek egg rolls. It's easy to make a button-popping meal of the *melitzanosalata* (I can't pronounce it either; ask for eggplant dip flavored with garlic and lemon juice) and a large Greek salad. Or get creative and build a meal around Athenian Plaka's *oretikia*. The Greek version of tapas includes small portions of tasty morsels such as *thalasini pikilia* (fried mixed seafood), shrimp and feta, and fried zucchini and eggplant, priced at $5 (appetizers).

Opt for a table on the patio in the summer. The decor and service are old world—gracious but not stuffy—and the rice pudding is better than my grandmother's, may her soul rest in peace.

Hamburger Hamlet

10400 Old Georgetown Rd., Bethesda, Maryland ☎ **301/897-5350.** Reservations accepted for 8 or more. Main courses $5.95–$14.95. AE, CB, DC, DISC, MC, V. Daily 11am–10:30pm. Children's services: high chairs, boosters, kids' menu, crayons. AMERICAN.

It's kind of expensive for glorified fast food, the kitchen can be erratic, hamburgers don't always come out to the requested degree of doneness, and the service is far from brisk in many instances. So why does everyone keep coming back for more? Beats me, but it's been a family favorite since opening here in 1979. Who am I to argue with success? Children can amuse themselves with the restaurant-supplied crayons until the grub comes. Stick to the burgers, Zucchini Zircles, chicken wings, fries, and shakes. Be prepared to wait 15 minutes or longer at prime time. In Gaithersburg there's a branch at 9811 Washington Blvd. (☎ **301/417-0773**). In Virginia, you'll find one at Crystal City Underground (☎ **703/413-0422**).

Il Forno

4926 Cordell Ave., Bethesda, Maryland ☎ **301/652-7757.** Reservations not accepted. Pies $5.75–$16.95. MC, V. Mon–Thurs 11am–10pm, Fri–Sat 11:30am–1am, live music from 9pm–1am Fri–Sat. Children's services: high chairs, boosters. Metro: Bethesda. PIZZA.

You can't get pizzas like these delivered. No cardboard residue here! They're baked in huge wood-burning ovens so that the thin New York–style crust has just the right amount of bite and doesn't collapse under the weight of the very fresh toppings. The garlic bread and calzone are worth trying, too. Space is tight indoors, so opt for a seat outside in favorable weather.

Il Forno is also at 8941 N. Westland Dr., Gaithersburg.

Louisiana Express

4921 Bethesda Ave., Bethesda, Maryland ☎ **301/652-6945.** Fax 301/652-6945. Reservations not accepted. Appetizers $3–$4; most main courses $6–$11; soups, salads, sandwiches, and omelettes $3–$7. MC, V. Mon–Thurs 7:30am–10pm, Fri–Sat 7:30am–11pm, Sun 9am–9pm (brunch 9am–2:30pm). Children's services: high chairs, boosters. Metro: Bethesda. CAJUN/CREOLE.

Cajun, casual, and cheap, Louisiana Express excels at New Orleans–style po'boys (aka subs, hoagies, grinders), fish fritters, and gumbos. For the kiddies' more sensitive palates there's unspicy chicken and french fries. Any of the "small portions" would be suitable for your young ones. Try one of the breakfast sandwiches or omelettes served from 7:30 to 11am daily. The Sunday brunch features pastries and pancakes, along with traditional Nawlins egg dishes. You can stuff your craws with some mighty good eats for less than $10. Dining here is the next best thing to Felix's Oyster Bar in the French Quarter. Seating is limited, as is street parking, but there's a garage a block away.

Philadelphia Mike's

7732 Wisconsin Ave., Bethesda, Maryland ☎ **301/656-0103.** All items under $7. DISC, MC, V. Mon–Fri 8am–9pm, Sat 9am–9pm, Sun 9am–4pm. Children's services: high chairs, boosters. Metro: Bethesda. AMERICAN.

You'll have to order at the counter and share an oil-cloth–covered table with strangers—a small price to pay for the best cheese steak sandwich, on still-warm, baked-on-the premises bread, this side of South Philly (where it's pronounced *cheesteak*). Try one of the variations of grilled paper-thin steak slices and melted cheese with lettuce, tomato, fried onions, hot peppers, and oil dressing, but please don't taint it with mayonnaise. In Philadelphia that's a capital offense. If you crave something sweet afterward, slip into Gifford's, in the same building, for an ice-cream treat.

✪ Rio Grande Café

4919 Fairmont Ave., Bethesda, Maryland ☎ **301/656-2981.** Reservations not accepted. Appetizers $3.25–$9.95; main courses $6.25–$10.95 lunch, $6.75–$17.25 dinner. AE, CB, DC, DISC, MC, V. Sun–Thurs 11:30am–10:30pm, Fri–Sat 11:30am–11:30pm. Children's services: high chairs, boosters, kids' menu. Metro: Bethesda. MEXICAN.

Build a better burrito and the world will beat a path to your door. Just ask the owner of Rio Grande. Dig into the warm tortilla chips and chunky salsa while the kids watch the weird Rube Goldberg contraption that produces around 400 tortillas an hour. The "Fajitas Al Carbon" are *numero uno* for big appetites, while an appetizer or an à la carte taco or burrito will most likely fill *los niños*. Finish with honey-drenched sopapillas. *Que bueno!* Go at off-times, especially on weekends or holidays. Don't say I didn't warn you.

There's a branch in Ballston, Virginia (☎ **703/528-3131**), and Reston (☎ **703/904-0703**). For complete details, see the entry in the "Suburban Virginia" section, later in this chapter.

Tastee Diner

7731 Woodmont Ave., Bethesda, Maryland ☎ **301/652-3970.** Reservations not accepted. Breakfast $1.75–$3.50 (kiddie breakfast $1.65); lunch and dinner $2.95–$9. MC, V. Daily, 24 hours. Closed Dec 25. Children's services: High chairs, boosters, crayons, coloring books. Metro: Bethesda. AMERICAN.

Round the clock, 7 days a week, 364 days a year, 365 days in leap years (closed Christmas) are the hours of the Tastee Diner. None of the new neon-and-chrome-plated establishments calling themselves diners holds a candle to the Tastee, which served its first creamed chipped beef on toast in 1942. Come here for the hearty breakfasts, homemade chili and soups, sandwiches, and desserts. At breakfast the Kiddie Special consists of one large pancake or one egg with a strip of bacon for $1.65. The tired leatherette booths, individual jukeboxes, colorful regulars, chatty short-order cooks, and beehived waitresses spell *Happy Days*.

Elsewhere in Maryland there are Tastee Diners in Silver Spring, at 8516 Georgia Ave. (at Wayne; ☎ **301/589-8171**), and Laurel, at 118 Washington Blvd. (U.S. 1; ☎ **301/725-1503**).

Ice Cream

Gifford's

7720 Wisconsin Ave., Bethesda, Maryland ☎ **301/907-3436.**

The family owned Gifford's chain had a corner on the market before dying out in the 1970s and 1980s. Many of us went into prolonged mourning. Then along came

Dolly Hunt. Bearing the original recipes, she reopened Gifford's on July 4, 1989. Hello, Dolly! The Swiss chocolate and hot fudge sundaes are worth the trip (a short walk from the Bethesda Metro station) from wherever you are. If you're tired of cups and regulation-size sugar cones, try the generous waffle cone.

GAITHERSBURG
INEXPENSIVE

✪ Roy's Place

2 E. Diamond Ave., Gaithersburg, Maryland ☎ **301/948-5548**. Reservations accepted. 62¢ (ice-cube sandwich) to $18 (largest multilayer sandwiches). AE, CB, DC, DISC, MC, V. Mon–Sat 11am–11pm, Sun 11:30am–10:30pm. Children's services: high chairs, boosters. SANDWICHES.

Granted it's a trip from downtown D.C., but it's worth it. Allow extra time to digest the 18-page menu of sandwich combinations, variations, and permutations. We bought a menu over 25 years ago so we could study the choices in the car. That menu survived wars, braces, broken bones, and hearts, puberty, and numerous pets. So has Roy's. Several imported beers are offered on tap. *Directions:* Route 355 north (the extension of Wisconsin Avenue and Rockville Pike) into Gaithersburg. Cross the bridge, then left at Chestnut, left on East Diamond to Roy's on left. Plenty of free parking on Roy's lot.

ROCKVILLE
INEXPENSIVE

Fuddrucker's

1300 Rockville Pike, Rockville, Maryland ☎ **301/468-3501**. Reservations not accepted. Main courses $3.95–$6.95. AE, DC, DISC, MC, V. Sun–Thurs 11am–10pm, Fri–Sat 11am–11pm. Children's services: high chairs, boosters. Metro: Twinbrook. AMERICAN.

It's strictly self-service, appropriately noisy, and almost always crowded, but the burgers are yummy and actually grilled to the degree you desire; the lines move quickly, and kids 12 and under eat free from 4 to 10pm. Can you beat that? Step up to the side bar and drown your burgers with all the toppings. The taco salad is tasty and filling (and calorie laden!); hot dogs, french fries, and desserts are only so-so. A second Fuddrucker's is at 2111 Darnestown Rd., Gaithersburg (☎ **301/869-6010**).

✪ Houston's

12256 Rockville Pike, Rockville, Maryland ☎ **301/468-3535**. Reservations not accepted. Appetizers $7–$9; most main courses $7–$15. AE, MC, V. Sun–Mon 11am–10pm, Tues–Thurs 11am–11pm, Fri–Sat 11am–midnight. Children's services: high chairs, boosters. Metro: Twinbrook (1 mile south). AMERICAN.

Plan on arriving by 11:45am for lunch or 5:30pm for dinner, or bring a book, like *War and Peace.*

O'Brien's Pit Barbecue

387 E. Gude Dr., Rockville, Maryland ☎ **301/340-8596**. Fax 301/762-9455. Reservations not accepted. Most items $5–$10. AE, DISC, MC, V. Sun–Thurs 11am–9pm, Fri–Sat 11am–9:30pm. Closed Thanksgiving, Christmas, Easter. Children's services: high chairs. RIBS/BARBECUE.

Texas ribs and barbecued beef brisket are top draws in this award-winning Western-style cafeteria and carryout, family owned for nearly 30 years. In my opinion, O'Brien's very best offering is the chopped pork sandwich with plenty of barbecue sauce and side dishes of smoky baked beans and coleslaw. If I tie the knot again, bare feet will be mandatory and O'Brien's will cater. Personal checks are accepted.

If you're not into pork, try the smoked turkey or chicken breast. Junior cowpokes are made to feel right at home by the friendly wait staff. There's plenty of free on-site parking. Another branch is at 46005 Regal Plaza, Sterling, Virginia (☎ **703/ 450-8490**).

SILVER SPRING
MODERATE

Crisfield
8012 Georgia Ave., Silver Spring, Maryland ☎ **301/589-1306.** Reservations not accepted. Main courses $5–$12 lunch, $12–$39 dinner; kids' (under 12) platters $8. AE, MC, V. Tues–Thurs 11am–9:45pm, Fri–Sat 11am–10:45pm, Sun noon–9:15pm. Children's services: high chairs, boosters, kids' menu. Metro: Silver Spring. SEAFOOD.

The decor may be early rest room, but don't let the cinder block turn you off. Crisfield's serves some of the freshest seafood west of the Chesapeake Bay. The crab imperial, crab cakes, and baked stuffed fish and shrimp have been pleasing patrons for more than 50 years. The sinfully rich and delicious seafood bisque of shrimp, lobster, and crabmeat in a tomato-cream base is a steal at $5.50. Kids under 12 can order a crab cake, fried shrimp, or fried fish platter for $8. Avoid dinnertime on weekends or go early.

12 Suburban Virginia

With so many restaurants in northern Virginia, you well may wonder where all the patrons come from. The area near and beyond the Beltway, which a generation ago was considered the "boonies," continues adding to an ever-growing list of restaurants. With an overabundance of fast food, pizza, pub, ethnic, and fine dining establishments, you won't have to search for your next meal.

ALEXANDRIA
INEXPENSIVE

✪ **Generous George's Pizza**
3006 Duke St., Alexandria, Virginia ☎ **703/370-4303.** Reservations accepted. Most items $14.95–$16.95. MC. V. Sun–Thurs 11am–10pm, Fri–Sat 11am–midnight. Children's services: high chairs, boosters. PIZZA/PASTA.

George's has been doing right by families for more than 20 years. No wonder it is consistently voted one of the best family restaurants in the metropolitan area. A foursome can enjoy superior pizza in a supercasual, funky 1950s setting and escape for $25. And you won't have to "shush" your little pepperonis. Try George's ingenious creation, a Positive Pasta Pie: linguine, fettuccine, seafood, or chicken served on a pizza crust. The Georgie combo (large) is $20.85 and the European Combo (pesto, pizza sauce, onions, peppers, mushrooms, tomatoes, black olives, imported ham, and extra cheese) is $17.95. Either feeds a family of four.

There are two more George's in Virginia, at 6131 Backlick Rd., Springfield (☎ **703/ 451-7111**), and 7031 Little River Turnpike, Annandale (☎ **703/ 941-9600**).

ARLINGTON
INEXPENSIVE

✪ **Red, Hot & Blue**
1600 Wilson Blvd., Arlington, Virginia ☎ **703/276-7427.** Reservations not accepted. Main courses $6.50–$17.50. AE, DISC, MC, V. Sun–Thurs 11am–10pm, Fri–Sat 11am–11pm. Closed

Thanksgiving, Dec 25. Children's services: high chairs, boosters, kids' menu, crayons, coloring book. Metro: Rosslyn or Court House. RIBS/BARBECUE.

Some think it's easier to get into heaven than to snare a table at Red, Hot & Blue. The Memphis ribs, pulled-pig sandwiches, and onion loaf are fast becoming a legend in these parts. From the children's menu, those 12 and under can order a hamburger, cheeseburger, hot dog, grilled cheese, small rib, chicken nuggets, barbecued beef, pork or chicken sandwich, from $2.50 to $4.95. All are served with french fries. The place is nothing to look at, but if you want beauty go to the National Gallery. If you want great ribs, wet (with sauce) or dry, come here. Take home a souvenir bottle of the tangy barbecue sauce. Avoid a wait by arriving before 6pm.

There is an RH&B Express at 3014 Wilson Blvd., Arlington, Virginia (☎ **703/ 243-1510**), and branch restaurants in Laurel (☎ **301/953-1943**), Annapolis, and Baltimore, Maryland.

BALLSTON
INEXPENSIVE

✪ Rio Grande Café

4301 N. Fairfax Dr., Ballston, Virginia ☎ **703/528-3131**. Reservations not accepted. Main courses $6.25–$10.95 lunch, $6.75–$17.25 dinner. AE, CB, DC, DISC, MC. V. Sun–Thurs 11:30am–10:30pm, Fri–Sat 11:30am–11:30pm. Children's services: high chairs, boosters. Metro: Ballston. MEXICAN.

Warm tortilla chips and chunky, fresh-daily salsa are served as soon as you sit down. While you adults contemplate fajitas al carbon, suggest to your youngest niños a quesadilla appetizer, or taco, or burrito for their smaller appetite. Finish with honey-drenched sopapillas. *Muy deliciosa!*

Rio Grande has one other Virginia location: 1827 Library St., Reston (☎ **703/ 904-0703**), beside the flagship restaurant in Bethesda, Maryland.

VIENNA
EXPENSIVE

✪ Morton's

Fairfax Square at Tysons Corner, 8075 Leesburg Pike, Vienna, Virginia ☎ **703/883-0800**. www.mortons.com. Reservations recommended. Main courses $6.95–$18.95 lunch, $19–$29 dinner. AE, CB, DC, MC, V. Mon–Fri 11:30am–2:30pm; Mon–Sat 5:30–11pm, Sun 5–10pm. AMERICAN.

Most steak lovers concur that Morton's serves some of the area's best aged prime beef. This congenial steak house is tastefully decorated and invites leisurely dining. Certainly not your typical kids' restaurant, this Morton's has a more relaxed policy than its Georgetown progenitor and welcomes all ages, though parental discretion is advised and there are no high chairs. Stick to the broiled-to-perfection steaks and chops, and expect to pay $40 to $50 for dinner, without wine. What do you expect of a restaurant whose neighbors are Gucci, Hermès, and Tiffany?

MODERATE

Clyde's

8332 Leesburg Pike, Vienna, Virginia ☎ **703/734-1901**. www.clydes.com. Reservations recommended. Main courses $6–$10 lunch, $11.95–$18.95 dinner. AE, CB, DC, DISC, MC, V. Sun–Thurs 11am–midnight, Fri–Sat 11am–12:30am. Children's services: high chairs, boosters, kids' menu, crayons, coloring books. AMERICAN/CONTINENTAL.

The burgers (especially the blue-cheese-and-bacon variety), ribs, pasta dishes, and salads are delish and kids can order from the children's menu. There's a full range of chicken, burger, pizza, and pasta items, as well as seasonal specialties such as crab cakes. The biggest seller is the grilled chicken salad. A visual stunner, Clyde's merits a look around on your way in or out. Kids dig the giant palms and the naked ladies (don't worry, they're just paintings) in the main dining room.

Fedora Café

8521 Leesburg Pike, Vienna, Virginia ☎ **703/556-0100.** Fax 703/556-0105. Reservations recommended. Main courses $7.95–$10.95 lunch, $15.75–$19.95 dinner. AE, CB, DC, DISC, MC, V. Mon–Thurs 11:30am–3pm and 5:30–10:30pm, Fri 11:30am–3pm and 5:30–11pm, Sat noon–3pm and 5:30–11pm, Sun 10:30am–2:30pm (brunch and dinner menu) and 4:30–9:30pm. Children's services: high chairs, boosters, kids' portions. AMERICAN.

Fedora is a good choice for families staying in the Tysons Corner area. Like the Tower of Pisa, the trendy menu leans toward Italy. For openers, try one of the specialty pizzas. The varied menu changes seasonally, and children can enjoy half portions of anything on the menu. You can't go wrong with the rotisserie chicken or one of the fish specials in this attractive spot frequented by local yuppies. We tip our hats (and forks) to Fedora's homemade pastries and desserts. Free parking in the garage at the rear of the building.

INEXPENSIVE

✪ Chili's

8051 Leesburg Pike, Vienna, Virginia ☎ **703/734-9512.** Reservations not accepted. Main courses $4.25–$9.95. AE, DISC, MC, V. Mon–Thurs 11am–11pm, Fri–Sat 11am–midnight, Sun 11am–10pm. Children's services: high chairs, boosters, kids' menu. SOUTHWESTERN/ AMERICAN.

Elegant it ain't, but Chili's serves good food and loves families, which is probably why so many families love Chili's. It's the kind of place where you don't have to keep reminding your kids to keep their voices down. Many fajitas freaks, young and old, say these are the best in town. The burgers, well-seasoned french fries, and salads are all tasty and generous, and the barbecued ribs score a 10. When you're in Maryland, try the Chili's in Rockville.

T.G.I. Friday's

2070 Chain Bridge Rd., Tysons Corner, Vienna, Virginia ☎ **703/556-6173.** www. tgifridays.com. Reservations not accepted. Main courses $5.75–$13.95; kids' menu $1.95–$2.75. AE, CB, DC, DISC, MC, V. Daily 11am–2am. Children's services: high chairs, boosters, kids' menu. AMERICAN.

T.G.I. Friday's is a family friendly link in the popular national chain. The servers are enthusiastic and young. Children under 12 can choose from such standbys as grilled cheese sandwiches, hamburgers, and hot dogs on the kids' menu. The grown-ups' menu is filled with possibilities, but save room for one of the yummy desserts.

What Kids Like to See & Do

You could spend an entire lifetime discovering the wonders of Washington. But you probably have other things to do as well, so be realistic and scale down your expectations. It's better to spend quality time on a few attractions than to dash through a multitude.

Look to your children when planning your itinerary. Be sure to factor in time for relaxing. Visit a few well-chosen sites and then let off steam in one of the city's many parks and recreational areas. Dunk in the hotel pool, or if shopping is your favorite sport, browse in one of the glitzy indoor malls. Remember, this is a vacation, not an endurance contest!

The night before a museum visit, some parents read their kids a relevant story. Others buy postcards on entering a museum or gallery and accompany their youngsters on a scavenger hunt to find the pictured object or work of art. You probably have your own preferred ways of getting your youngsters psyched for sightseeing. If you're new at this, the best advice I can offer is don't overschedule. Young children have short attention spans. Catch a movie, puppet show, or theater presentation for a change of pace. Preschoolers often get antsy after 20 minutes in a museum. When they do, it's fruitless to push them further. Stop for a snack, rest, or get some fresh air. Then try again. You'll know when they've had it!

Here's a tip from a savvy friend of mine. When you're visiting a museum with a gift shop, let the kids stop to look around and buy a souvenir first. If logic prevails, you'll avoid the unpleasantness of having them bug you while you're viewing the exhibits.

When you're on a tight schedule, concentrate your sightseeing in and around the downtown area known as the National Mall (see map later in this chapter). Here you will find the presidential monuments, most of the Smithsonian museums, the U.S. Capitol, White House, and numerous other attractions—all free, and within walking distance of each other.

Suggested Itineraries

For Toddlers

Day 1   Run, don't walk, to the zoo. Go early, especially in the summer and on weekends. There's plenty to keep everyone occupied for several hours. Pack a picnic or buy lunch at one of the snack bars or the cafeteria/restaurant on the premises.

Day 2   Visit the animal exhibits and O. Orkin Insect Zoo in the National Museum of Natural History. Cross the Mall to the Smithsonian Castle. Ride the carousel. Then grab lunch in one of the museum cafeterias or from a street vendor. Eat outside, weather permitting. A pleasant dining alternative is the Food Court at the Old Post Office Pavilion, where there's often family entertainment, or The Shops at National Place. In the afternoon, visit the Aquarium in the Commerce Department. If you're not too tired, cross the street to the National Museum of American History and single out one or two exhibits.

Day 3   Start out at the Capital Children's Museum with its many interactive exhibits especially geared to preschoolers. In fair weather pack a picnic (or pick up something yummy in the Food Hall at Union Station on your way) and eat lunch on the museum's grounds. Tuck in a siesta after lunch, then visit one of the Smithsonian museums you've missed. Mature 4- and 5-year-olds and older siblings will enjoy seeing a movie in the Air and Space Museum, but don't sit too close to the screen. The larger-than-life images and booming soundtrack may frighten younger kids. If time permits, spend a half hour or so looking around; that's about all kids this age can take. Have dinner near your hotel (or spring for room service) and turn in early.

For 6- to 8-Year-Olds

Day 1   Hop on a Tourmobile tram, and after you've completed the loop and listened to the narrator's spiel, spend the afternoon visiting one or two sights that interested you most on the tour.

Day 2   Visit the Air and Space Museum in the morning, then have lunch at one of the museum eateries on the Mall. In the afternoon, tour the Hirshhorn, especially the outdoor sculpture garden, then ride the carousel nearby. Cross the Mall to the Museum of Natural History and/or the Museum of American History, or cast an eye (but not a fishing line) into the tanks of the Commerce Department's Aquarium. Have dessert at The Shops at National Place or the Old Post Office Pavilion, or go back to your room and rest. You deserve it.

Day 3   At the Bureau of Engraving and Printing see how money is made—literally. Pool your pennies for lunch, then visit the past at the DAR Museum's Children's Attic. If you're still rarin' to go, visit any or all of the presidential memorials: the Washington Monument, Lincoln, Jefferson, and Roosevelt Memorials. You may want to include, or substitute, the Vietnam and Korean War Veterans Memorials. In the warm-weather months, rent a boat or bicycle and paddle or pedal away the afternoon. In winter, ice skate at the National Sculpture Garden or Pershing Park rink, or warm up in the U.S. Botanic Garden (due to reopen late in 2000). After dark take a taxi tour to see the illuminated monuments.

For 8- to 10-Year-Olds

Day 1   Start early and spend the morning at the FBI, one of the most popular tours in all D.C. Splurge on lunch at the Hard Rock Café or Planet Hollywood or grab a hot dog or slice of pizza from a street vendor. Visit Ford's Theatre and the Petersen House across the street, where Lincoln died. Go back to your hotel for a swim or hop on Metro and choose one of the following: Interact with the displays at the National Geographic Society's Explorers Hall or U.S. Postal Museum, or stroll through Georgetown, stopping for dessert along the way.

Day 2   Divide the day into thirds for a Mall crawl. Start at the Air and Space Museum (be sure to buy movie tickets first). Have lunch on the Mall, then hit the Natural History and American History Museums. Pick up a map at each information desk and concentrate on a few exhibits. Between thirds, take pictures on the Mall

Highlights for Kids:
The Top 10 Attractions by Age Group

Picking Washington's top 10 attractions for kids of different ages is like trying to name the top 10 restaurants in New York City—next to impossible. Depending on your kids' ages and interests, your family's top 10 will probably include a mix of some of the following along with selections listed in this chapter under "For Kids with Special Interests." When all is said and done, you know your kids best.

2 to 4   National Zoo, Capital Children's Museum, National Museum of Natural History (native culture and animal exhibits, Discovery Room, O. Orkin Insect Zoo), National Aquarium, DAR Museum, National Museum of American History (first-floor transportation exhibit), National Air and Space Museum (planes suspended from ceiling and DC-7 fuselage), Hains Point playground (East Potomac Park), carousel on the Mall, Dolls' House and Toy Museum.

4 to 6   National Zoo, American Museum of Natural History, Capital Children's Museum, DAR Museum, National Air and Space Museum, National Museum of American History, Bureau of Engraving and Printing, Hirshhorn Sculpture Garden, Oxon Hill Farm (Maryland), Dolls' House and Toy Museum.

6 to 8   National Zoo, Capital Children's Museum, American Museum of Natural History, National Air and Space Museum, National Museum of American History, Presidential Monuments (Washington Monument, Lincoln, Jefferson, and Franklin Delano Roosevelt Memorials), Bureau of Engraving and Printing, DAR Museum.

8 to 10   National Zoo, American Museum of Natural History, National Air and Space Museum, National Museum of American History, Presidential Monuments, the FBI Building, the Capitol, National Geographic Society, Bureau of Engraving and Printing, Capital Children's Museum.

10 to 14   National Zoo, National Museum of American History, American Museum of Natural History, National Air and Space Museum, Presidential Monuments, the FBI Building, the White House, the Capitol, National Geographic Society, Bureau of Engraving and Printing.

Over 14   Lend them your plastic and point them toward Georgetown, Old Town, Alexandria, or the nearest shopping mall.

or fly a kite (you can buy one in the Air and Space Museum's gift shop). Still standing after dinner? Take an after-dark tour via bus or taxi.

Day 3   Spend the day on "the Hill." Tour the Capitol, then say hello to your senator or representative. Eat at one of the many family friendly places on the Hill or at Union Station (see chapter 5). If time allows, see the Capital Children's Museum and one or more of the following: Supreme Court, Library of Congress, Folger Theatre, Eastern Market, or Union Station. Wind down with a visit to the exotic world of the U.S. Botanic Garden at the foot of Capitol Hill (closed until late in 2000).

For Preteens

Day 1   Same as Day 1 for 8- to 10-year-olds. Stroll around Georgetown or Union Station after dinner, see a movie and indulge in a yummy dessert, or catch a theater performance.

Washington, D.C. Attractions

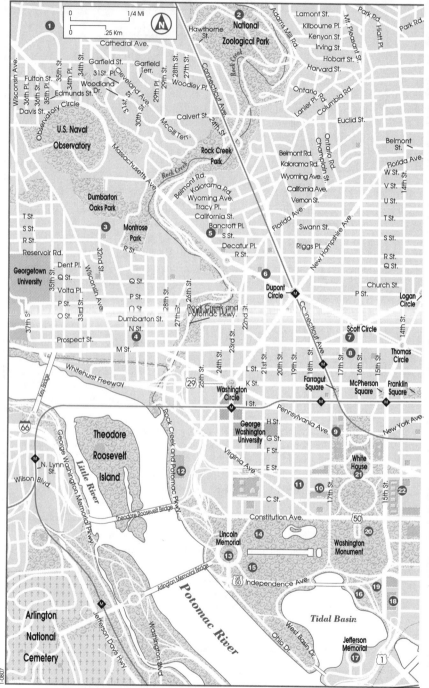

National Zoological Park

Hawthorne St.
Cathedral Ave.

0   1/4 Mi
0   .25 Km

Lamont St.
Kilbourne Pl.
Kenyon St.
Irving St.
Hobart St.
Harvard St.

Adams Mill Rd.
Park Rd.
Hiatt Pl.
Park Rd.
Mt. Pleasant St.

Garfield St.
31st Pl.
Garfield Terr.
Woodland Dr.
Edmunds St.
Davis St.
Fulton St.
36th Pl.
35th Pl.
34th Pl.
34th St.
35th St.
35th St.
36th St.
Cleveland Ave.
29th Pl.
29th St.
28th St.
27th St.
31st St.
30th St.
Woodley Pl.

Ontario Pl.
Lanier Pl.
Columbia Rd.
Ontario Rd.
Champlain St.

Euclid St.

Belmont St.

Wisconsin Ave.

Observatory Circle

U.S. Naval Observatory

Calvert St.
24th St.
McGill Terr.

Rock Creek Park

Belmont Rd.
Kalorama Rd.
Wyoming Ave.
California Ave.
Vernon St.

Belmont St.
Florida Ave.
W St.
V St.
U St.
14th St.

Massachusetts Ave.

Rock Creek

Dumbarton Oaks Park

Belmont Rd.
Kalorama Rd.
Wyoming Ave.
Tracy Pl.
California St.
Bancroft Pl.
S St.
Decatur Pl.
R St.

Swann St.
Riggs Pl.

New Hampshire Ave.

Florida Ave.

T St.
S St.
S St.
R St.
Q St.

T St.
S St.
R St.
Reservoir Rd.

Montrose Park

Dent Pl.
Q St.
Volta Pl.
P St.
O St.

32nd St.
Wisconsin Ave.

Georgetown University

35th St.
37th St.
33rd St.

Q St.
P St.
O St.
Dumbarton St.
N St.
M St.

28th St.
27th St.
26th St.

Rock Creek and Potomac Pkwy.

Prospect St.

Dupont Circle

Connecticut Ave.

Church St.
P St.

Logan Circle

Scott Circle

Thomas Circle

14th St.
15th St.
16th St.
17th St.
18th St.
19th St.
20th St.
21st St.
23rd St.
24th St.
25th St.

L St.
K St.
I St.

Washington Circle

Farragut Square
McPherson Square
Franklin Square

Whitehurst Freeway

Key Bridge

66

N. Lynn St.
Wilson Blvd.

George Washington Memorial Pkwy.

Theodore Roosevelt Island

Little River

Rock Creek and Potomac Pkwy.

Theodore Roosevelt Bridge

George Washington University

H St.
G St.
F St.
E St.

Virginia Ave.

Pennsylvania Ave.

New York Ave.

White House

C St.

Constitution Ave.

17th St.

Arlington National Cemetery

Jefferson Davis Hwy.

Washington Blvd.

Arlington Memorial Bridge

Potomac River

Lincoln Memorial

Independence Ave.

Washington Monument

Tidal Basin

West Basin Dr.
Ohio Dr.

Jefferson Memorial

1

124

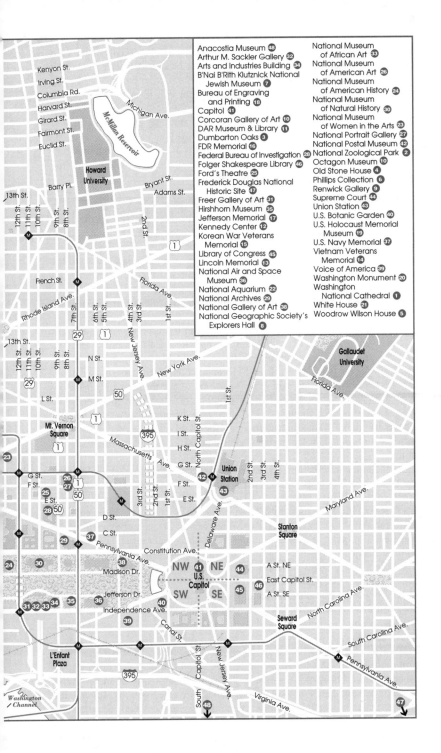

Day 2   Same as Day 2 for 8- to 10-year-olds. You may want to skip a museum or two and substitute the U.S. Archives or Arlington National Cemetery. Or maybe your crew's idea of a good time is cruisin' Georgetown or an indoor mall for souvenirs. Take a nighttime tour of the major sights or visit the Washington Monument or Lincoln Memorial on your own.

Day 3   Same as Day 3 for 8- to 10-year-olds, omitting the Capital Children's Museum. Ride a bike, take a hike, or pick out something else you like. A visit to Arlington National Cemetery, Mount Vernon (by boat in nice weather), or Alexandria's Old Town is in order. In the evening, see a show, sporting event, or concert— or snuggle in bed with pizza and a cable movie.

1 The Smithsonian Institution

According to the Greater Washington Board of Trade, "If all the treasures of the Smithsonian Institution were lined up in one long exhibit, and you spent one second looking at each item, it would take you more than 2½ years of around-the-clock touring to see them all." I haven't double-checked their computations, but you have to admit, the statistics are impressive. According to one poll, 40% of all Americans have visited the Smithsonian, the largest museum/research complex in the world.

Like other cultural institutions adversely affected by cutbacks, the Smithsonian has, in recent years, sought funding from corporations and individuals, hence the O. Orkin Insect Zoo and Janet Annenberg Hooker GGM (geology, gems, and minerals) Hall at the Museum of Natural History. Currently, the federal government supplies about 75% of the Smithsonian's revenues. While the need for fund-raising is an unarguable necessity, one hopes the Smithsonian need not compromise the integrity of its mission through their alliance with the private sector. The board of regents has thus far voted down an across-the-board admission fee. However, it won't be surprising if, in coming days, admission to special exhibits will become the norm.

A little inside information: Washingtonians chuckle when tourists ask for directions to the Smithsonian, which actually comprises 16 museums (the two newest are the National Postal Museum near Union Station and the National Museum of the American Indian, temporarily housed in the Arts and Industries Building on the Mall) and the National Zoological Park. When asking directions, be specific or you could end up staring at wings in Air and Space when you want dinosaur bones in Natural History.

In 1846, when English scientist James Smithson willed funds to the United States (105 bags of gold sovereigns equal to about $500,000) to establish an institution "for the increase and diffusion of knowledge among men," he probably never imagined that today the Smithsonian conglomerate would house some 13 million artifacts, encompass numerous buildings, and become one of the world's major tourist attractions.

For a full page of Smithsonian special events for the coming month, residents can turn to the "Smithsonian Sampler" in the *Washington Post Weekend* magazine, published the third Friday of every month. The Smithsonian museums are open from 10am to 5:30pm daily except December 25. The "Castle," with its Visitor Information Center, is open from 9am to 5:30pm. Every year Congress votes whether to extend hours in spring and summer. Usually the vote is affirmative, and the museums remain open an extra half hour or more (occasionally until 9pm!). Be good to yourself and call ahead to avoid disappointment (☎ 202/357-2700).

The Mall

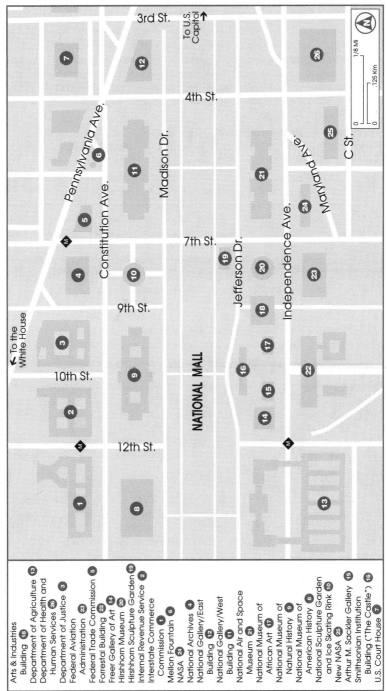

Arts & Industries
  Building 18
Department of Agriculture 13
Department of Health and
  Human Services 3
Department of Justice 3
Federal Aviation
  Administration 23
Federal Trade Commission 5
Forrestal Building 22
Freer Gallery of Art 14
Hirshhorn Museum 20
Hirshhorn Sculpture Garden 19
Internal Revenue Service 2
Interstate Commerce
  Commission 1
Mellon Fountain 6
NASA 24
National Archives 4
National Gallery/East
  Building 12
National Gallery/West
  Building 11
National Air and Space
  Museum 21
National Museum of
  African Art 17
National Museum of
  Natural History 9
National Museum of
  American History 8
National Sculpture Garden
  and Ice Skating Rink 10
New NASA 25
Arthur M. Sackler Gallery 15
Smithsonian Institution
  Building ("The Castle") 16
U.S. Court House 7

Because one third of the approximately 15 million people who visit the Smithsonian annually do so in June, July, and August, you may want to schedule your visit for any other month. Or arrive when the doors open. Bear in mind that Mondays are the quietest, Saturdays and Sundays the busiest; early morning and late afternoon are the least crowded. Tuck these Smithsonian phone numbers in your wallet or commit them to memory: Information (☎ 202/357-2700), Dial-A-Museum (☎ 202/357-2020), and TDD (☎ 202/357-1729). You may also visit the Web site at www.si.edu.

Smithsonian Institution Building ("The Castle")

1000 Jefferson Dr. SW. ☎ **202/357-2700.** www.si.edu. Free admission. Daily 9am–5:30pm. Closed Dec 25. Metro: Smithsonian. Ages 4 and up.

As I mentioned earlier, the Information Center in the flagship of the Smithsonian Institution is a good place to begin your tour of D.C. Press a button on one of the 13 video-display monitors to get information on the Smithsonian and more than 100 other attractions. Eleven pages on the computer screen are devoted to kid-pleasing things to see and do. You may have trouble prying your progeny away from the monitors' highly imaginative and colorful graphics.

Also check the video screens mounted on the information desk where "Today at the Smithsonian" lists events and exhibits, and ask for **"10 Tips for Visiting the Smithsonian with Children,"** which includes a map, family highlights, and a quiz for kids—all free. In the gift shop you can purchase a "Guide to the Nation's Capital," a detailed map with brief descriptions of the major museums and attractions. Not only is the map immensely helpful, it makes a nice souvenir.

A 20-minute video is shown throughout the day giving a Smithsonian overview, and electronic wall maps put you in touch with all the popular attractions. Knowledgeable staff are on hand to give directions and answer questions, and guides printed in seven languages are available for foreign visitors. While you're at the Castle, you may want to inquire about the Smithsonian Young Associate Program, which offers workshops, films, and live performances for children throughout the year (☎ 202/357-3030).

If you enter the Castle from Jefferson Drive (on the Mall), you'll find, on the left, the crypt bearing the remains of James Smithson. Although he died in Genoa, Italy, on June 26, 1829, he was brought to this spot—ironically his first time on U.S. soil and his final resting place—in 1904.

P.S.: Before you leave the Castle, make a quick sweep of the Children's Room, open daily from 10am to 5:30pm. The original trompe l'oeil fantasy garden and skylights have been restored to their original state in the cozy, light-filled space. From here you can exit to the Mall's enchanting Enid A. Haupt Victorian Garden.

Anacostia Museum and Center for African-American History and Culture

1901 Fort Place SE. ☎ **202/357-1300.** www.si.edu/anacostia. Free admission. Daily 10am–5pm. Closed Dec 25. Metro: Anacostia, then W-1 or W-2 bus. By car, take 395 north to 295 south to Martin Luther King Ave. Left on Morris Ave., which becomes Erie St. then Fort Place. Ages 4 and up.

You have to cross Washington's lesser-known river, the Anacostia, to get to this recently renovated Smithsonian facility that focuses on African American art, culture, and history. The museum devoted to increasing public understanding and knowledge of the African American experience operates on this site and also in the Arts and Industries Building on the National Mall.

Augmenting its permanent collection and changing exhibits, the Anacostia offers free family workshops and shows throughout the year. Call the museum's education department (☎ **202/287-3369** or 202/357-4500) to find out about upcoming family activities and guided tours offered Monday through Friday.

Visitors with reservations can take a guided walk along the George Washington Carver nature trail on the museum grounds. It's less than a third of a mile long, so even the youngest scouts in your party should be able to keep up the pace. You may want to tote snacks or lunch to eat in the picnic area, since there's no on-site restaurant and the neighborhood surrounding the museum is not recommended for casual strolling.

Arts and Industries Building

900 Jefferson Dr. SW, on the south side of the Mall. ☎ **202/357-2700.** www.si.edu/ai. Free admission. Daily 10am–5:30pm. Closed Dec 25. Metro: Smithsonian (Mall exit). Ages 2 and up.

The building is recognizable by the carousel outside the Mall entrance. Rides are $1.25, year round from 10am to dusk, weather permitting. The contents of this brick-and-sandstone edifice, the first national museum, constitute a time capsule of Victoriana. The 1876 Philadelphia International Exposition was re-created here for the nation's 1976 bicentennial and celebrates the first 100 years of American technology. Have a look at everyday objects found in a Victorian home, samples of 19th-century clothing, and copies of Uncle Tom's Cabin and cookbooks of the day in the North Hall. Older kids will enjoy wandering through the West Hall exhibits of items from a bygone era—an ice-cream machine, telegraph, and printing press.

A 45-foot model of the cruiser USS *Antietam* and the restored 1876 Santa Cruz Railroad locomotive engine are kid-pleasers too, as are actual pieces of Plymouth Rock and Lincoln memorabilia. Stop at the **Experimental Gallery** in the south wing (around the corner from Discovery Theater) to see the current traveling exhibit. Actors, dancers, mimes, musicians, and puppeteers grace the **Discovery Theater** stage in performances for children during the school year. Tickets are $5 (☎ **202/357-1500**). See chapter 9 for details.

Freer Gallery of Art

Jefferson Dr. at 12th St. SW, on the south side of the Mall. ☎ **202/357-2104.** www.si.edu/asia. Free admission. Daily 10am–5:30pm. Closed Dec 25. Metro: Smithsonian (Mall or Independence Ave. exit). Ages 10 and up.

It is nearly impossible to visit the Freer and not be taken with the beauty of the museum itself as well as its contents. As you emerge from the Mall exit of the Smithsonian Metro station, the stunning Renaissance-style facade and colorful banners of the Freer will greet you. In a concerted effort to draw young people, the museum has added a number of colorful workbooks that challenge youngsters to examine what they see and to *think* critically and creatively.

The museum is named for Detroit industrialist and art connoisseur Charles Lang Freer, who made a bundle from manufacturing the first railroad cars in the Midwest and became James McNeill Whistler's chief patron; this is where you'll find the world's largest Whistler collection—more than 1,200 pieces. The museum is also recognized internationally for its collection of Asian art spanning 6,000 years. To give you an idea of the breadth of the Freer, at any given time, 10% or less of the museum's permanent collection is on view.

Among these riches, the hands-down favorite is Whistler's *Harmony in Blue and Gold: The Peacock Room.* The actual dining room you see before you was painted by

Activities That Don't Cost a Penny

Watch the sun set behind the Lincoln Memorial.

Ride to the top of the Washington Monument at night.

Warm up in the National Zoo's Amazonia rain forest exhibit.

Attend a summertime concert on the Ellipse (behind the White House), at the Capitol (West Lawn), or Navy Memorial Plaza (Pennsylvania Avenue between 7th and 9th streets.)

Redesign the FBI Building.

See who, or what, is buried in the crypt under the Capitol.

Guess the weight of the globe in the National Geographic Society's Explorers Hall.

Imagine how you'd spend the money printed in 1 day at the Bureau of Engraving and Printing.

Find world heavyweight champion Joe Louis's grave at Arlington National Cemetery.

Discover your favorite work of art in the Corcoran Gallery.

Ask a Native American docent at the Department of Interior Museum about his or her ancestry.

Lie down next to the bed where Lincoln died in the Petersen House.

Rename the works in the Hirshhorn Museum's Sculpture Garden.

Count the crystals in the Kennedy Center Opera House chandelier.

Visit Bert and Ernie in the Madison Building of the Library of Congress.

Trace the origins of your family tree at the National Archives.

In-line skate in front of the White House.

Measure the interior perimeter of the National Building Museum.

Make up a story about Fragonard's *Young Girl Reading* in the National Gallery's West Building.

Skip rocks in the Tidal Basin.

Whistler between 1876 and 1877 for the British businessman Frederick Leyland, who engaged Whistler to redecorate his dining room around the artist's painting, *The Princess from the Land of the Porcelain,* and a large collection of blue-and-white Oriental porcelain. Whistler's feelings about Leyland's failure to pay what he felt the job was worth are reflected in the mural of two peacocks over the sideboard.

The Princess and the Peacocks, a charmingly illustrated book for children telling the story of the room from the point of view of the princess in Whistler's painting, is sold in the museum shop. Young art-historians will also appreciate "Peacocks, Patterns, and Paint," a 10-page workbook for young people 6 to 12 to enhance their visit of the Peacock Room and other collections in the Freer. Children over 10 are usually intrigued to learn the story behind this extraordinary dining room, which has been moved, piece by piece, from London to Detroit to Washington, D.C. See if your children can find Whistler's trademark butterfly signature. (He left his imprint in four places in the room!)

Two other thematic family guides are available free at the information desk. "Ganesha's Guide to the Galleries" features the elephant-headed Hindu god offering

Find out what Star Route means in the National Postal Museum.

Picnic behind the Old Stone House in Georgetown.

See how long it takes to walk the length of the National Mall (Lincoln Memorial to the Capitol, or vice-versa).

Talk about how Renoir's *The Luncheon of the Boating Party* in the Phillips Collection makes you feel.

Feed the ducks in Constitution Gardens.

Journal your impressions of Washington.

Hear a case before the Supreme Court (October through April).

Enjoy the vista from the Washington National Cathedral's Pilgrim Observatory Gallery.

Fly a kite on the Mall.

Write a letter to the president.

View downtown from the tower in the Old Post Office.

Sit in Albert Einstein's lap (2101 Constitution Ave. NW).

Wish on a star at the Naval Observatory.

Wet your feet in the Reflecting Pool (but please, no swimming allowed!).

Explore the 2-mile nature trail in Glover Archbold Park.

Test your fitness on the 1.5-mile exercise course in Rock Creek Park.

Identify the birds, and planes, over Theodore Roosevelt Island.

Stroll along the Maine Avenue/Water Street SW waterfront and choose your dream boat.

Watch a polo match in West Potomac Park (Sunday afternoon, late April through October, excluding August).

Plan a return visit.

insights on museum work behind the scenes. "Arts of China" helps visitors understand and appreciate art created thousands of years ago.

Of particular note is **ImaginAsia,** a free program for children 6 to 12 and their parents (or other adult companions). After touring the collections with a guide, participants translate their impressions into their own work of art to take home. ImaginAsia is held on Saturday from March through October and on Monday and Wednesday in July and August. Call to verify times (☎ **202/357-2700**). Reservations are required for the 1:30pm Saturday sessions for groups of 8 to 20 children (☎ **202/357-4880,** ext. 245).

Docent-led tours are offered daily. Call for a current schedule (☎ **202/ 357-2700**). Reservations for group tours must be made in writing at least 4 weeks in advance. The Freer is joined by an exhibition gallery to the adjacent Arthur M. Sackler Gallery.

✪ Hirshhorn Museum and Sculpture Garden

Independence Ave. and 7th St. SW, on the south side of the Mall. ☎ **202/357-2700.** www.si.edu/hirshhorn. Free admission. Daily 10am–5:30pm; sculpture garden daily dawn–dusk; plaza daily 7:30am–5:30pm. Closed Dec 25. Metro: L'Enfant Plaza (Smithsonian exit) or Smithsonian. Ages 2 and up.

While other teenage boys were hanging out on the front stoop or getting into mischief, a young Latvian immigrant, Joseph Hirshhorn (1899–1981), was buying etchings in New York. The rest, as they say, is history. The museum bearing the mining magnate and art collector's name opened in 1974 with his little "gift" of mostly 20th-century art—2,000 pieces of sculpture and 4,000 paintings and drawings. When Hirshhorn died at the age of 82, additional works were bequeathed from his estate. The collection continues to receive gifts from other donors and is the fifth most visited art museum in the United States.

Even kids who gag at the mention of going to an art museum find something to like at the Hirshhorn. Since preschoolers relate best to large three-dimensional objects, take them outside to the sculpture garden. The plaza provides an inviting and soft-edged setting for more than a dozen works, including Calder's *black stabile, Two Discs,* and Claes Oldenberg's *Geometric Mouse.* Your children should have something interesting to say about Lucio Fontana's billiard ball–like spheres. Lie on the grass or rest on one of the benches amid the greenery and contemplate the scene. It's always the right time to ride the carousel next to the garden.

Kindergartners on up will be intrigued by the museum's doughnutlike inner space. It's easy to become disoriented while traversing the concentric rings, but that's part of the fun. Paintings hang in the galleries of the outer circle, while sculptures and plenty of comfortable seating fill the inner circle (known as an ambulatory) where light pours in through floor-to-ceiling windows. There is a museum shop and an auditorium on the first floor (lower level). On the second floor, look for *Guardian Angel* and works by Rodin and Degas. Ask your kids which of Matisse's *Heads of Jeanette* looks like you in the morning. Upstairs, introduce them to Henry Moore's work.

Kids 10 and older can explore on their own (if it's okay with you) after viewing a short orientation film in the lower-level theater. They may like the portraits by Eakins and Sargent on the third floor, before moving on to works by Bellows, Sloane, O'Keeffe, de Kooning, Dias, Pollock, and others. Many young people find the more abstract works appealing, even though "they don't look like anything." For a sweeping panorama of the Mall area, peer out the windows of the Abram Lerner Room, and don't miss Calder's *Fish mobile.* It used to dangle in the Hirshhorns' Connecticut hallway.

At the information desk, pick up a free family guide highlighting works in the collection that are favorites with children and a calendar of events. Ask about films for families, too. Children's workshops on select Saturdays feature hands-on activities

Break Time

At the Hirshhorn's **Full Circle Café,** located on the south side of the Mall at Independence Avenue and 8th Street SW, you'll find a self-service outdoor cafe open in season, Memorial Day to Labor Day. Featured are hot and cold sandwiches, pizza, salads such as Thai noodles and chicken in a spicy peanut sauce, fountain beverages, bottled drinks (including beer and wine), and espresso and cappuccino. Desserts include an almond amaretto bar and jumbo chocolate chip cookie. Hot dogs, sandwiches, and pint-size cheese pizzas are always on hand for small fry. Main courses range from $5.95 to $8.95. Reservations and credit cards are not accepted. It's open daily from late May to early September from 11am to 3pm, weather permitting.

in conjunction with exhibitions. Reservations are required (☎ **202/ 357-3235**). Tours are given Monday through Friday at 10:30am and noon; Sunday at noon and 2pm. In the museum shop you'll find posters, art books, and prints.

⊙ National Air and Space Museum
7th St. and Independence Ave. SW (enter at Independence Ave. or Jefferson Dr.). ☎ **202/ 357-2700.** www.nasm.edu. Free admission. Daily 10am–5:30pm; ask about extended summer hours. Closed Dec 25. Metro: L'Enfant Plaza (Smithsonian Museums exit). Ages 2 and up.

Note: Renovations to Air and Space are ongoing until sometime in 2002. During this period, the museum will remain open, but some of the exhibits described below may be under wraps.

Longer than two football fields, the most visited museum in the world is a huge pinkish marble monolith that opened July 1, 1976, in time for the U.S. Bicentennial. Not much to look at from the outside, the magic begins when you enter. Inside, major historical and technological feats of air and space flight are documented in 23 exhibit areas.

Almost every specimen in the Air and Space Museum was flown or used to back up a craft, and this triggers excitement and a sense of immediacy in kids of all ages. The planes suspended from the ceiling appear to be in flight, and younger kids (young enough not to be embarrassed) may want to lie down and look straight up for the maximum effect. Before your family flies off in different directions, line up at the **Langley Theater** and buy tickets ($5.50 adults, $4.25 youths 2 to 21 and seniors 55 and over) for one or more of the special flight-related movies shown several times a day on the five-story IMAX screen. If you have time for only one, make it *To Fly,* the museum's inaugural film. I've seen it more times than I have fingers, and I think it's safe to say that you won't ever forget it. *Cosmic Voyage,* featured since 1996, combines live-action footage with animation to explore the universe. *Mission to Mir* takes audiences through the Russian space station, manned by international teams of scientists since 1986. You may recall that Mir made headlines in 1997 after colliding with a satellite. Live-action shots blend with historical footage for a breathtaking adventure. Another film or two may alternate with the above-mentioned films when you visit. (See the "Cinema" section in chapter 9 for details.) *A tip:* The first morning show almost never sells out. Go early and avoid disappointment.

Next, if you're interested in catching a heavenly show, take an out-of-this-world journey at the **Albert Einstein Planetarium.** *Sky Quest* is geared to families with children between the ages of 4 and 8, while *And a Star to Steer Her By* explores nothing less than the history of navigation, with narration by Sir Alec Guinness. I suggest buying your tickets for the planetarium shows ($3.75 regardless of age) before you begin circling the exhibits. Don't let your little jet-setters slip into different orbits on the way to the ticket booth. And here's something that's free! *The Stars Tonight,* shown at 3pm daily, takes a look at the sky over Washington through the planetarium's fancy-schmancy microscope.

Now, let's get down to the nitty-gritty. Stop at the information desk for a floor plan and list of events. To avoid wasting time and energy—this place is huge—note the exhibits that interest your crew most. If you have kids over 8 or 10, decide if you want to take the 1½-hour free guided tour (daily at 10:15am and 1pm) or rent an audio tour ($4.75 for individuals; $4 for students, seniors, and Smithsonian associates). Call ahead for information on group tours. With kids under 6, it's best to see the highlights on your own. Tell 2- to 4-year-olds to "look up," as the overhead sights appeal to this age group the most.

Fasten your seatbelts—we're ready to blast off. Start on the first floor with **Milestones of Flight,** in the two-level gallery at the museum's entrance. If you view nothing else in this museum, make sure to see this permanent exhibition. There's a good reason why it occupies the museum's center stage. Highlights include the Wright brothers' *1903 Flyer,* Charles Lindbergh's *Spirit of St. Louis,* John Glenn's *Friendship 7, Gemini 4,* the Apollo 11 command module *Columbia, Pioneer 10,* and Chuck (*The Right Stuff*) Yeager's *Bell X-1.* Don't leave without touching the moon rock (excuse me, "Lunar Sample"). *Note:* Until sometime in 2002, when the museum's renovation is completed, one or more of these milestones may be encased in protective material.

When the line isn't too long, school-age kids love to walk through the **Skylab Orbital Workshop,** a backup for America's first space station. Check out the Apollo lunar module on the first floor's east end.

The *Surveyor, Lunar Orbiter,* and *Ranger* are hangared in the hall devoted to Lunar Exploration Vehicles. In **Rocketry and Space Flight,** the evolution of the spacesuit is traced. Those interested in aviation history will want to see the *Vega,* flown by Amelia Earhart on the first transatlantic flight by a woman, and the *Chicago,* which took nearly 6 months (with no in-flight movie) to complete the first around-the-world flight.

Tomorrow's astronauts will learn more about the early years of manned space flight in **Apollo to the Moon.** In 1999, the 30th anniversary of Apollo 11 was widely celebrated, and who knows, the party may be ongoing. Check out the Soviet SS-20 that came to the NASM in 1990 in exchange for a Pershing II on display in St. Petersburg.

Younger children enjoy peering up at the mildly menacing Curtiss P40E Warhawk with the shark smile and boarding a replica of an airplane carrier hangar deck in **Sea-Air Operations.** And even children who have flown enjoy boarding the nose section of an American Airlines DC-7.

Computer whizzes will appreciate **Beyond the Limits: Flight Enters the Computer Age.** This second floor exhibit shows, with the aid of interactive computers, how computer technology is applied to aerospace in such areas as aerodynamics, design, flight testing, and flight simulation. The model of the X-29 aircraft, Cray-1 supercomputer, and the radio-controlled HIMAT aircraft are but a few of the must-sees for those smart enough to understand the right stuff.

Also on the second floor, **Where Next, Columbus?** investigates space as the next frontier for a new generation of explorers. This major exhibition opened at the end of 1992 and is slated to run for at least a decade. Through interactive displays and exhibits, you'll be exposed to weightlessness, robotics, the Mars landscape, and a hydroponic garden. Catch one or more of the three short films that are ongoing throughout the day. If your time is limited, see the one on Einstein.

In what may be the museum's most successful educational project to date, **How Things Fly** is a largely interactive exhibit that makes principles of aerodynamics accessible to school-agers on up. The internal workings of a piston engine are revealed in the Continental cutaway. Aspects of lift and drag are provided by wind tunnels and computer activities. Climb into a full-size Cessna 150 and handle the controls regulating the wings and tail; learn about orbits and trajectories via computer. As part of its Explainers program, local students are on hand to demystify concepts for younger visitors.

For visitors interested in the rocketry and space flight milestones and missions touched off by the Soviet Union's launching of *Sputnik,* October 4, 1957, **Space Race** has your name on it. The exhibition in the renovated Space Hall focuses on the many firsts—satellite, man in space, space walk—spawned by the Cold War contest between the United States and the former Soviet Union. An impressive historical collection of space-related memorabilia—rockets, spacecraft, and artifacts—is displayed in this major retrospective encompassing 50 years of aerospace right (and sometimes wrong) stuff.

Reservations for school group tours can be made through the tour office (☎ **202/357-1400**).

Be sure to touch down in the Shuttle Shop and Museum Gift Shop to pick up some freeze-dried ice-cream sandwiches for snackin'. The selection of books, kites, models, souvenir posters, and T-shirts is one of the best in the city.

Currently, the NASM overflow is housed in the **Paul E. Garber** facility in Suitland, Maryland (☎ **202/357-1400**). Free tours for kids over 14 of the unheated, nonair-conditioned warehouses are by reservation only. Call Monday through Friday between 9am and 5pm to make reservations, or write to Tour Scheduler, National Air and Space Museum, Smithsonian Institution, Washington, DC 20560. The facility *usually* holds an open house every other April. *Note:* The tour lasts 3 hours and is not especially kid friendly at this time. For a free calendar of events write to Calendar, National Air and Space Museum, Room 3733 MRC 321, Washington, DC 20560.

Parents of babies will appreciate the clean and well-equipped unisex Baby Service Station across from the gift shop.

National Museum of African Art

950 Independence Ave. SW. ☎ **202/357-2700** or 202/357-4600. Fax 202/357-4879. www.si.edu/nmafa. Free admission. Daily 10am–5:30pm. Closed Dec 25. Metro: Smithsonian (Mall or Independence Ave. exit). Ages 4 and up.

Most kids over 5 will find the carved wooden masks, fertility dolls, and somewhat menacing Cameroon court figure of particular interest here, the only museum in the United States dedicated solely to African art. The bovine gong on the first-floor

Break Time

The **National Air and Space Museum Flight Line Cafeteria** is a stunning, futuristic dining complex, worth a visit, even if you're not hungry. Talk about letting the sunshine in! The 800-seat cafeteria, with its eye-catching tubular construction and expansive windows overlooking the Mall, National Gallery, and Capitol, is a knockout. Help yourself from several buffet stations where salads, sandwiches, hot main courses, soups, pizza, and dessert are appealingly displayed. Breads and pastries are baked fresh daily. The more-than-adequate fare and bright, airy setting combine to make this an ideal refueling spot. Sandwiches and main courses range from about $4 to $10. Reservations are not taken. AE, DISC, MC, and V are accepted. It's open daily from 10am to 5:30pm. High chairs and boosters are available.

Also in the National Air and Space Museum is the **Wright Place** restaurant (☎ 202/371-8777). Above the Flight Line is an attractive table service continental cafe decorated with greenery and aviation photographs. The ambience outflies the trendy food and the views are somewhat obstructed, but the hamburger and children's menu (with such items as grilled cheese, hamburger, fried chicken fingers plus potatoes, vegetable, milk or soda, and a chocolate sundae) make up for the deficiencies. Prices range from $8 to $10, with the kids' menu hovering in the $3 to $4 range. Due to its popularity, reservations are recommended. AE, DISC, MC, and V are accepted. It's open daily from 11:30am to 3pm; extended hours in summer. High chairs and booster seats are available.

Sad to say, the Old Patent Office Building, which houses the **National Museum of American Art** and the **National Portrait Gallery**, is closed for renovation until sometime in 2003. (Hey, this is Washington, D.C.; be patient!) The renovation will include updating the antiquated fire, electrical, and communications systems and improving access for the handicapped. Some exhibitions and programs of the National Museum of American Art will continue at the Renwick Gallery at 17th Street and Pennsylvania Ave. NW. Some of the exhibitions of the National Portrait Gallery will hit the road, traveling to other institutions in the United States and abroad.

landing is a hit with youngsters, especially after they discover what happens when they push the button next to it. The collection of mostly 19th- and 20th-century traditional arts and artifacts, formerly housed in cramped Capitol Hill quarters, was relocated here in 1987. The tomblike setting is shared with the Arthur M. Sackler Gallery of Asian and Near Eastern art. More than 6,000 objects in the permanent collection are displayed in rotating exhibits. One or two weekends a month (more often in summer) there's storytelling for kids, focused on an individual country or special subject. Inquire at the information desk about the free gallery guide and other children's activities. Parents are invited to call ahead for a schedule of family workshops, films, and storytelling (☎ 202/357-4860). The **Warren M. Robbins Library** is open to researchers by appointment Monday through Friday from 10am to 5pm (☎ 202/357-4875). The museum shop, with crafts, artifacts, clothing, and jewelry, is open from 10am to 5:30pm daily (☎) **202/786-2147**).

✪ National Museum of American History

14th St. and Constitution Ave. NW, entrances on Constitution Ave. and Madison Dr. ☎ **202/357-2700**. www.si.edu/nmah. Free admission. Daily 10am–5:30pm. Closed Dec 25. Metro: Smithsonian (Mall exit) or Federal Triangle. Ages 4 and up.

Major aspects of America's cultural, scientific, and technological life come alive here, intriguing kids of all ages. Three floors, packed with exhibits that bridge 200 years—from the country's early days (the original Star-Spangled Banner that inspired our national anthem) to the present (Archie and Edith Bunker's well-worn chairs and Dorothy's ruby slippers)—provide a comprehensive overview of American social history. Don't try to cover it all in one visit.

First, pick up "Hunt for History," a self-guided tour brochure for two age groups (6 to 9 and 10 to 13) in English and Spanish. "Let's Take a Trip" (¡Vamos de Paseo!) is a workbook for 3 to 5 year-olds. "Who Lives in the White House?" ("¿Quien Vive en la Casa Blanca?") is geared to 5- to 7-year-olds.

I think the first-floor of this museum is hot (or "cool" if you prefer), and so do most kids. Over the years I've found that, for the most part, things are less interesting on the second and third floors. Maybe it's just too difficult to breathe life into sweeping sociological generalizations. Just my opinion—I'd like to know what you think.

With preschoolers, I recommend heading to the first-floor exhibits devoted to farm and power machinery and transportation. If it's big and it moves, they like it.

Railroad Hall, with its electric streetcar and huge steam locomotives, which chugged through the late 19th and early 20th centuries, is a good place to start. Next door at Road Transportation are a Conestoga wagon, stagecoach, and vintage steam- and gas-powered automobiles. (Wouldn't mind parking the 1913 Model-T

Ford in my driveway.) Understandably, both galleries are favorites of the 2-to-5 set. Elsewhere, the **Information Age** demonstrates the many ways technology has affected the gathering and dissemination of information, drawing kids 8 and up with its touch-screen interactive stations.

Also on the first floor, the **Hands-On Science Center,** part of the Science in American Life exhibition, simplifies concepts for kids (according to the entrance sign) from "5 to 105." Don't drop off your kids and disappear. Kids 5 through 12 must be accompanied by an adult. Under the supervision of docents, children are invited to don neon safety goggles and take part in various experiments involving dry ice, DNA profiling, and pH levels of liquids—to name a few. (*Note:* Participants must be at least 5 years old, and those 12 and under must be accompanied by an adult. Free tickets are available at the door of the center.)

A Material World salutes many of the brand-name household products that helped shape this country. This exhibit is fun, a real nostalgia trip for those of us over 30. It's like the museum's version of a garage sale, with items such as a G.E. toaster, Eames chair, and Electrolux vacuum cleaner acting as barometers of our changing cultural values. Younger kids may not get the message, but they'll definitely go for the '86 Swamp Rat XXX, the first top-fuel dragster to cruise at 270 m.p.h. Awesome!

The museum's second floor is devoted to social and cultural history. There, until sometime in 2001 or 2002, visitors can peer into a lab where highly skilled weavers are preserving the original **Star-Spangled Banner.** It will take about 3 years and $18 million to patch up Old Glory, which survived the 1814 British attack on Fort McHenry in Baltimore but succumbed to the ravages of light, air pollution and 185 years. Free same-day entry passes are available at the kiosk on the second floor near the Mall entrance at 10am (for entrance between 10:30am and 1pm) and at 1pm (for entrance between 1:30 and 5:30pm). Advance passes may be ordered through TicketMaster for $2.50 per pass (*ouch!*) and $1 per order (up to 6 passes) at ☎ **800/ 551-SEAT** or 202/432-SEAT.

In these enlightened times, peek at the exhibit **First Ladies: Political Role and Public Image.** Besides the gowns worn by presidential wives, plenty of First Lady memorabilia—photographs, jewelry, personal effects, and campaign mementos— are displayed, and the exhibit points up the women's public and political roles. Adjacent to the first ladies is **From Parlor to Politics,** examining women's changing roles and contributions during the early decades of the 20th century, the so-called Progressive Era.

After the Revolution is an exhibit of late 18th-century Americana, where kids can peer into a log house and typical New England and Southern interiors to see what family and community life was like for America's first generation. **Field to Factory** is dedicated to the effects of African American migration (south to north) in the first half of the 20th century. The re-created Maryland tenant farmer's house makes a poignant statement.

Don't miss the related **Hands-On History Room,** also on the second floor, where more than 30 activities relate to everyday American life between 1780 and 1850. Kids can ride a high-wheeler bike (in place), harness a fiberglass mule, gin raw cotton on a reproduction of Eli Whitney's hand cotton gin, or poke through the contents of a peddler's pack to gain insight into the life of an immigrant peddler who traveled through upstate New York in the mid-1800s. Most activities are geared to kids 5 and older. The room is open from noon to 3pm Tuesday through Sunday (summer hours may be extended). Pick up free tickets as you enter.

Break Time

Rest your weary feet and grab a snack at the **National Museum of American History, Palm Court (Victorian Ice Cream Parlor, ☎ 202/357-2700)**. Once you've admired the etched-glass mirrors, potted palms, and wicker, you can get down to the business at hand in this authentically rendered turn-of-the-century ice-cream parlor on the museum's first floor. You could start with something healthful from the brief menu, such as a sandwich or soup, but why bother? Dig right into the Double Devil (brownies, ice cream, fudge sauce, whipped cream, and sprinkles), a too-thick-to-sip-through-a-straw malt, or pie à la mode. Kids can order a junior-size sundae. Most items are in the $3 to $5 range. It's open daily from 11am to 4pm. High chairs and boosters are available.

Growling stomachs and cranky tots can also be appeased in the **Museum of American History Main Street Cafes (☎ 202/357-2700)**. At the cafeteria, located on the lower level across from the museum shop and bookstore, you can satisfy your hunger with a large selection of hot and cold items—made-to-order sandwiches, pizza, hot dogs and hamburgers, desserts, or comfort food (meat, potatoes, veggies). Hey, this is far from gourmet fare, but it's convenient. The spacious refueling spot is open for breakfast, lunch, and snacks. Plenty of high chairs and seating are here, and most major credit cards are accepted. The lunch lines, even when long, move pretty quickly. Most items are from $2 to $6. Hours are from 10am to 5pm; extended hours in summer are possible.

Take a peek at the colossal Horatio Greenough statue of **George Washington** out of uniform. The public was outraged when toga-clad George was first placed in the Capitol rotunda in 1841. The 20-ton statue was moved a couple of times before finding a permanent home at this museum. From the looks of things, he's not budging.

Swing by the **Foucault Pendulum,** your golden opportunity to witness Earth's rotation. It's easy to fall into a hypnotic trance as the pendulum swings slowly back and forth, knocking down the encircling pegs one by one. Tell your kids that the pendulum's arc remains the same, but Earth is moving underneath it. When you're done explaining it to them, please come explain it to me.

The third floor is of special interest to those whose hobbies include music, the graphic arts, medals, photography, ship models, textiles and, last but not least, money—an interest all ages seem to share. Here you'll find the flag known as Old Glory and the *Philadelphia,* a gunboat built and sunk in 1776 that was raised in 1935. A small exhibit showcases the musical talents of native son Duke Ellington.

Tours of the museum's highlights are at 10am and 1pm daily. The museum hosts *Our Story,* a family series for 6- to 12-year-olds and their adult companions that explores history through children's literature. The workshops begin in September and are held the third Saturday of the month from 10:30am to 1pm. Advance reservations are recommended at least 1 month in advance by calling ☎ 202/633-6752.

✪ National Museum of Natural History

10th St. and Constitution Ave. NW (second entrance on Madison Dr.). ☎ **202/357-2700.** www.nmnh.si.edu. Free admission. Daily 10am–5:30pm. Closed Dec 25. Metro: Smithsonian or Federal Triangle. Ages 2 and up.

I've always been partial to this museum, and so are most kids. Before you enter, I suggest walking around to the 9th Street side of the museum to see the outdoor

Butterfly Garden. The living exhibition simulates four environments: wetlands, wood's edge, wilderness, and urban garden.

Begin your tour at the ground-floor display of about 300 birds that are native to the eastern United States. Next, go to the four-story, marble-pillared rotunda on the first floor and pick up a floor plan at the information desk. The child hasn't been born who won't ooh and aah over the 8-ton **African Bush Elephant,** which is over 13 feet tall!

Why save the best until last? Make like a fly and buzz upstairs to the **O. Orkin Insect Zoo,** a living museum exhibit and a favorite with young and old alike. Leave your arachnophobia at the door before meeting the tarantulas. Here you can inspect cockroaches, get a close-up view of bees swarming around their hive, watch ants building a colony, observe millipedes as long as stretch limos, and marvel at the amazing Amazon walking stick (a dead ringer for Tommy Tune).

The insect zoo, with many clever and colorful visual aids, crawls with more than one million visitors annually. On one display, kids can test their knowledge of insect camouflages. The youngest members of your colony are invited to crawl through a replica of an African termites' mound (in the wild, these mounds grow to 25 feet!). You may go bug-eyed peering inside a model home for common household insects that most likely cohabitate with your family. Touch models of four insect heads in the **Adaptation Section,** and increase your knowledge of spider strategies and ants' sociability. The **Rain Forest Exhibit** features giant cockroaches, leaf-cutter ants, and tropical plants to demonstrate the insects' role in balancing the rain forest's ecosystem.

Pay your respects to Big Bob, one of the largest species of tarantulas. She (honest!) is the size of a dinner plate and modeled for the film *Arachnophobia.* Not to worry, Big Bob's web-weaving days are ancient history.

If you're interested in observing a tarantula's table manners, be here for chow call, weekdays at 10:30 and 11:30am and 1:30pm. Weekend meals are served at 12:30 and 1:30pm (they like to sleep late). Docents circulate to answer questions and dispel myths.

You haven't forgotten *Jurassic Park* already, have you? In **Dinosaur Hall** get up close and personal with skeletons of the stegosaurus and triceratops, among others, and rare bones of juvenile dinosaurs. If you want to go eyeball to eyeball with quetzalcoatlus, the largest flying reptile (here suspended from the ceiling), climb the stairs where you can also examine several oldies but goodies mounted on the wall. In the **Fossil Collection,** you'll find specimens of creatures that swam in the seas 600 million years ago and a 70-million-year-old dinosaur egg. Skeletons of dinosaurs that lived more than 100 million years ago are always big hits.

Wait till your kids get their first glimpse of the 92-foot blue whale suspended from the ceiling and the giant squid model in the **Sea Life Hall.** And yes, those **Giant Squids** (here preserved) are real—the world's largest invertebrates. Watch the

Break Time

The new Atrium Café (so-called for its six-story soaring space) is a glorified food court/cafeteria with several food stations. Not tempted? For a sandwich or dessert, take your hungry brood to the **Palm Court** or the **Cafeteria** in the **National Museum of American History,** a few blocks away at 14th Street and Constitution Avenue. About the same distance away is the **Food Court** in the **Old Post Office Pavilion,** 11th Street and Pennsylvania Avenue NW. Of course, there are always the food vendors parked end to end outside the museums.

A Gem of a Story

Talk about romancing the stone. The legendary Hope Diamond was once the eye of a Hindu Idol in India when it was stolen in the 17th century, and as the story goes, the gods put a curse on all future wearers.

The stone was named for British gem collector Henry Philip Hope, who listed the gem in his 1839 catalog. The rock first caught socialite Evalyn Walsh McLean's eye in 1908 when she noticed it in the Constantinople harem of the sultan of the Ottoman Empire. McLean was on a 3-month honeymoon trip with her husband, Ned, whose family owned the *Washington Post*. Before McLean purchased the stone from jeweler Pierre Cartier for $184,000 in 1911, previous owners included Louis XIV, Louis XVI, and Marie Antoinette, who learned the hard way that diamonds aren't necessarily a girl's best friend.

McLean, the last person to wear the celebrated 45½-carat blue diamond, was born in 1886 and spent her early years in Colorado mining camps. When her father struck gold, he moved the family to Washington, where he invested heavily, and successfully, in real estate. Her family, the Walshes, called the Beaux Arts mansion at 2020 Massachusetts Avenue home; it is now home of the Indonesian Embassy. McLean counted presidents and monarchs among her friends, owned several homes, and, on the surface, led a charmed life, once spending $48,000 for a dinner party in 1912. But it was a life marred by tragedy (or perhaps the curse of the Hope Diamond). Her husband went insane, the marriage dissolved, and then her eldest son was killed in an accident. Still, she continued to wear the diamond. In the wake of the Great Depression, financial ruin followed. In 1933, the *Post* was sold at auction to Eugene Meyer. The curse continued—in 1946, McLean's only daughter died of a drug overdose at the age of 24.

When McLean died in 1947, friends put the diamond in a cigar box. When no bank would accept it, it found a temporary haven in an FBI vault before being sold to jeweler Harry Winston in 1949 to pay McLean's estate taxes. Nine years later, Winston donated the gem to the Smithsonian. It is said that the mailman who delivered the gem to the Smithsonian had his leg crushed in a truck accident. Soon thereafter his wife and dog died and his house burned to the ground.

5-minute video, which runs continuously, for a handle on these intimidating but fascinating creatures.

In the hall off the rotunda featuring **Native Cultures of the Americas,** younger children usually enjoy the diorama of an Eskimo boy fishing. Preschoolers also feel at home in the **Discovery Room,** where they can touch everything except for a few very fragile items. Among the room's treasures are large labeled boxes of bones, reptile skins, and sea urchins. There's even a preserved rattlesnake in a jar. The Discovery Room is open September through May, Monday through Thursday from noon to 2:30pm, and Friday through Sunday from 10:30am to 3:30pm. From Memorial Day to Labor Day the hours are 10:30am to 3:30pm. Free passes are given out at the door. Sometime in 2002 an expanded Discovery Room is due to open on the top floor of the Discovery Center.

Mammals, especially those shown in their natural habitats, engross young and old visitors. And unlike zoo animals, these are always awake (in a manner of speaking) and visible. Pres. Theodore Roosevelt, the old Rough Rider himself, shot many of the big game animals displayed in the dioramas during an African safari. ("Walk softly, but carry a big gun.") The penguins in the **Birds of the World** exhibit are particularly appealing to youngsters.

The **Janet Annenberg Hooker Hall of Geology, Gems and Minerals** opened in 1997 after a $13 million, 2-year renovation. It's dazzling, and sure to intrigue young and old alike. Divided into seven areas, the hall is designed to accommodate visitors in a hurry as well as those interested in lingering to digest the in-depth exhibits and explanations.

The centerpiece is the 45½-carat **Hope Diamond** in the **Harry Winston Gallery** (named for the esteemed jeweler who purchased the diamond from McLean's estate and donated it to the museum in 1958), valued at $100 million. Many visitors are surprised by its color—and size. And that's no rhinestone setting! The most visited object in all the Smithsonian museums was once owned by Washington socialite Evalyn Walsh McLean, who wore the stone frequently, despite its supposed curse. (We should all be so cursed.) Walsh is reported to have said, "I always thought it was garish—until I owned it." Touché!

The rock revolves in a freestanding glass case and is lit dramatically from above.

Among the other glittering treasures are diamond earrings supposedly worn by Marie Antoinette on her final ride—to the guillotine—and a necklace comprised of 374 diamonds and 15 emeralds. In accompanying displays, the minerals and gems in their natural state nearly upstage the polished gems with their striking resemblance to contemporary sculpture.

The most comprehensive exhibit of its kind in the world, the Janet Annenberg Hooker Hall of Geology, Gems and Minerals (named for the philanthropist who donated $5 million and a collection of rare yellow diamonds) is also enhanced by scores of interactive stations and monitors. How refreshing after the old hall's strictly hands-off policy.

In another section of the hall a world map records the activity of every volcano and earthquake in the last 40 years, accompanied by sound effects. Kids (and you too!) can pound the granite mounting of a seismograph that demonstrates the sensitivity of the instrument. You'll encounter a video of how gems and minerals are shaped, formed, and mined in the dimly lit hall where four mines are realistically re-created. After exiting this area be sure to peek through the window to catch a glimpse of another jewel: the National Mall.

Moon rocks brought back by the Apollo astronauts and a 1,371-pound meteorite are on display in the space devoted to Earth and the solar system. If your kids are into rocks, they can access a computer linking various meteorites and craters.

Elsewhere in the museum, **in Western Civilization: Origins and Traditions,** school-age visitors can look at murals, dioramas, and films that help to explain the origins and legacies of ancient civilizations.

The **Discovery Center** (as in Discovery Channel) encompasses the recently expanded restaurant, museum shop, and 500-seat **Samuel C. Johnson Theater**. Here you can view large-scale movies about the natural world. The opening film, *Africa's Elephant Kingdom,* was shot in Kenya and Zimbabwe. If at all possible, see it, even if the elephant is not your political symbol of choice. The stunning 40-minute film is shown eight times a day between 10am and 5pm. Buy tickets ($5.50 adults, $4.50 kids 2 to 17 and seniors 55 and older) as soon as you arrive, preferably in the morning when the museum opens. Locals can purchase tickets 2 weeks ahead. Sorry, no phone orders at this time.

The **Naturalist Center,** a research library/lab for those 10 and older, is located at 741 Miller Dr. SE, Suite G2, Leesburg, VA (☎ **800/729-7725** or 703/779-9712).

The center is open Tuesday through Saturday from 10:30am to 4pm; closed Sunday, Monday, and federal holidays.

Tours of the museum's highlights are offered Monday through Thursday at 10:30am and 1:30pm, Friday at 10:30pm. Meet at the Yap stone on the ground floor. While admission is free to the museum, the museum shops and restaurants accept Discover, Visa, MasterCard, American Express, and JCB cards.

Sometime during your visit, do stop at the museum shops on the ground floor, open from 10am to 5:30pm. Look no further for a wide selection of crafts, jewelry, books, science kits, toys, posters and T-shirts, and more.

National Postal Museum

2 Massachusetts Ave. NE (Washington City Post Office Building next to Union Station). ☎ **202/357-2700,** or 202/357-2991 to schedule group tours. www.si.edu/postal. Free admission. Daily 10am–5:30pm. Closed Dec 25. Metro: Union Station (1st St. exit). Ages 6 and up.

A joint project of the Postal Service and the Smithsonian Institution, the National Postal Museum opened July 30, 1993. The largest and most comprehensive collection of its kind in the world, it is a must stop for philatelists and anyone interested in postal service history. A 1924 DeHavilland airmail plane suspended, along with others, from the ceiling of the 90-foot-high atrium, greets visitors descending the escalators from the very ornate lobby entrance. At the information desk, pick up copies of "A Self-Guided Tour for Very Young Visitors" and "Check It Out!"

Binding the Nation, one of the museum's permanent exhibitions, covers early postal history from pre-Revolutionary days to the late 19th century. Did you know, for example, that Benjamin Franklin served as postmaster for the colonies? Or that he was fired? Find out why and lots more during your visit.

Moving the Mail explores the ways the postal service moves 600 million pieces per day. The amazing thing is that most of it is delivered (eventually). Aside from displays of stamps and postal documents, you'll see an 1850s stagecoach and replica of a Southern Railway mail car, complete with mailbags and sorting table. At one time 95% of the U.S. mail was delivered via rail by 32,000 railway mail clerks, considered the elite of the postal service. Usually seven or eight men worked in a car, but at holidays the number swelled to 18 or 19! I learned all of this and much more from a retired railway clerk who is one of the museum guides leading the informative 11am, 1pm, and 2pm walk-in tours. Groups must call ahead.

If you've ever wondered what the heck "Star Route" means, it is explained here. In the **History of Stamps Exhibit,** find out the different sources of stamp gum (corn, sweet potatoes, and cassavas are among them). Kids zip over to the 30-plus interactive areas, especially the video games inviting them to choose the fastest intercity mail routes, and the profiles of different ZIP code residents. For a small sum, you can send a special souvenir postcard.

Junk (as in junk mail) is a four-letter word at the Postal Museum, which is why **What's in the Mail for You!** resonates. It is dedicated to "direct mail," a cleaned-up term for junk. You know, all those irritating circulars, inserts, and postcards that jam your mailbox at home. Direct mail accounts for nearly 85% of what arrives in America's mailboxes (as if you needed to be reminded). In the **Customers and Consumers Gallery** of the museum, floating laser images, holograms, and 3-D motion pictures flood the space—as well as one's senses. Visitors are invited to photograph themselves with a digital camera. The photo is stored as you proceed through the exhibition, then returned with a surprise at the end. An actor, portraying merchants such as Aaron Montgomery Ward and L. L. Bean, talks to "customers" in period dress about the advantages of ordering goods through the mail.

There's also a museum shop and philatelic sales center worth perusing. As a souvenir you may wish to purchase a bank made from an old mailbox, stamp jewelry, assorted writing paper, or postcards. You'll also find books and workbooks on stamps and postal history. Self-directed projects and monthly family activities take place in the museum's Discovery Center, the third Saturday of most months from 1 to 3pm. When you're in the Union Station/Capitol Hill area, squeeze in this museum, posthaste. It has my stamp of approval!

✪ National Zoological Park

3001 Connecticut Ave. NW. ☎ **202/673-4800** or 202/673-4717. www.si.edu/natzoo. Free admission. AE, DISC, MC, V (bookstore). Buildings: May 1–Sept 15, 10am–6pm; Sept 16–Apr 30, 10am–4:30pm. Grounds: May 1–Sept 15, 6am–8pm; Sept 16–Apr 30, 6am–6pm. Closed Dec 25. The ZOOlab and Bird Resource Center are open Sat-Sun 10am–2pm. Zoo bookstore open daily 9am–5pm. Closed Dec 25. Fee for parking based on length of visit. Free parking for FONZ members, disabled visitor parking in Lots A, B, and D; some street parking. Strollers rent for $2 and $3 for FONZ members, $7 and $10 for nonmembers plus a paid deposit, driver's license, or military ID. Pets are not allowed in the park. Metro: Cleveland Park (an easier walk) or Woodley Park-Zoo, then northbound L-2 or L-4 bus, or walk ³⁄₁₀ mile (*warning:* It's an uphill climb). Ages 2 and up.

Before we go any further, please memorize the following tips. There may be a test later.

1. Go early, especially if you drive. The parking lots often fill by 10am weekends, holidays, school vacations, and May through September.
2. Wear comfy, nonskid shoes.

More than 5,000 animals call the National Zoo home, and your children will probably want to see each and every one of them. Occupying 163 acres a few Metro stops from the White House, the zoo boasts many rare and endangered species. It has long been a front-runner in the breeding, care, and exhibition of its nonhuman residents. Part of the Smithsonian Institution, the zoo is perennially a premier attraction for local and out-of-town families. On weekends, during school vacations, and in the summer, go early in the morning, not only because it's less crowded, but because the animals are spunkier. Typically they nap in the middle of the day (sounds good to me). In May and June when the zoo residents become parents, it's an especially appealing time to bring *your* little ones. You may be lucky enough to see some newborns. Speaking of newborns, Kerinci, a Sumatran tiger, gave birth to three live cubs June 23, 1999. They'll be about ready for preschool when you visit. And the zoo begat a new **American Prairie** exhibit in 1999 that'll have you humming "Home on the Range" in no time flat. Prairie dogs (actually rodents, but cute rodents) prowl the prairie grasses of their new home when they're not burrowing to escape the stares of funny-looking tourists. Roaming the range are two American Bison, Ten Bears (a boy) and Kicking Bird (a girl), which weigh in at close to 2,000 pounds each.

Olmsted Walk is the zoo's main drag, and more than 3 miles of trails crisscross the park. If you follow the helpful signs along the way, you won't get lost. The terrain is hilly, so leave your flip-flops under the bed and wear your most comfortable nonskid shoes. Be sure to lift up your kids in strollers so that they can see everything. If they don't get cranky along the way, you could easily spend half a day or longer here. Older kids, of course, can go on forever, and you'll probably be the one shouting "Uncle."

Stop first at the **Visitor Center** near the zoo's Connecticut Avenue entrance to pick up a map and check on any special programs or movies on the schedule. In the **ZOOlab,** youngsters from ages 3 to 7 are encouraged to handle animal bones and skins, nests, and feathers. Volunteers are on hand to answer questions. Listen to the tape recordings of animal sounds. How many can your kids identify?

Nearby are the large land mammals—rhinos, hippos, giraffes, and elephants. The elephants delight audiences with demonstrations at 10:30 and 11:30am. **Uncle Beazley,** a replica of a 25-foot-long triceratops that for many years was a fixture on the Mall, then a homeless dinosaur, found a home at the zoo. You'll find it outside the Elephant House, next to the rhinos. A funny thing happened shortly after Beazley's arrival early in 1995. Mistaking Beazley for a rival, one of the rhinoceroses broke through a fence and pushed Beazley into the moat, where it was rescued and reinstated on terra firma by zoo workers! From the Elephant House, follow Olmsted Walk to the large and small cats, apes, orangutans, gibbons, and reptiles.

Kids are always entertained by the otters, seals, and sea lions, so childlike in their playfulness and spontaneity. Try to catch the **Sea Lions' Training Demonstration** at 11:30am (check first at the information desk), and stop to peek through the window in the otter pool for a close-up of these endearing animals' high jinks.

The **Invertebrate Exhibit** features tanks of starfish, sponges, and crabs, as well as spiders—all displayed very much out in the open. While grown-ups are occasionally turned off, children usually want to inspect the dirt-filled sandbox inhabited by a bunch of creepy-crawlers. Last time we checked, this exhibit was open Wednesday through Sunday only.

You won't find bipeds in pinstripe suits or pantyhose in the **Think Tank** here. Instead, in an awesome spectacle, you can watch orangutans ("orangs" to those in the know) swingin' overhead between the Great Ape House and Think Tank. They navigate along cables 45 feet above the main path, simulating their movements in the wild. Daily demonstrations engage the public in three areas—language, tool use, and sociability. Along with macaques (a genus of chiefly Asian monkeys, including the rhesus), the orangutans demonstrate their problem-solving skills, while scientists explain their behavioral research findings to onlookers. As visitors, you are invited to participate in a variety of activities here. If you've ever longed to examine elephants' brains, fish for termites chimpanzee style, and decipher animal communications (to better understand how and what animals think), this one's for you! Part of the zoo's **BioPark** concept is to inform and instill in visitors a healthy respect for nature conservation. Think Tank is aimed primarily at older children and adults.

Ever wonder why flowers are colorful? Or what butterflies eat? Find out the answers to these questions and many more in the **Pollinarium,** also part of the zoo's BioPark exhibit. The focus here is on the biological process, which affords visitors a window on the fascinating relationships between plants and animals in pollination. Hummingbirds, bees, and butterflies pollinate flowers before your eyes and a model demonstrating the mechanics of pollination invites visitors to maneuver a huge bee into a gigantic flower.

The **Great Outdoor Flight Cage,** which is 130 feet in diameter, is a sky-high, mesh-enclosed hemisphere that your little chickadees can enjoy. Older kids and adults may carry their featherweight concerns to the **Bird Resource Center** at the rear of the Bird House and take a guided tour of a room in which eggs incubate and zoo workers examine some of our ailing fine-feathered friends.

Don't miss **Amazonia,** still being greeted with great fanfare since opening nearly a decade ago. An ideal cool-day escape—it's plenty steamy inside—the re-created rain forest at the edge of Rock Creek Park lies at the foot of Valley Trail. The exhibit supports a broad array of plants and animals. Enjoy an underwater view of the freshwater fish of the Amazon, some of which are 7 feet long.

The National Zoological Park

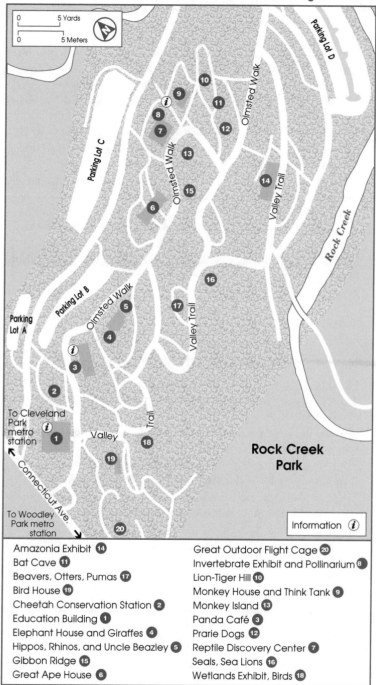

Amazonia Exhibit 14	Great Outdoor Flight Cage 20
Bat Cave 11	Invertebrate Exhibit and Pollinarium 8
Beavers, Otters, Pumas 17	Lion-Tiger Hill 10
Bird House 19	Monkey House and Think Tank 9
Cheetah Conservation Station 2	Monkey Island 13
Education Building 1	Panda Café 3
Elephant House and Giraffes 4	Prarie Dogs 12
Hippos, Rhinos, and Uncle Beazley 5	Reptile Discovery Center 7
Gibbon Ridge 15	Seals, Sea Lions 16
Great Ape House 6	Wetlands Exhibit, Birds 18

Where Children Can:

Crawl through a replica of an African termites' mound—the O. Orkin Insect Zoo in the **National Museum of Natural History.**

Produce their own TV show—the **Capital Children's Museum.**

Gin raw cotton—the Hands-On History Room in the **National Museum of American History.**

Whisper and be heard clear across the room—the **U.S. Capitol's Statuary Hall.**

Watch millions of dollars being printed—the **Bureau of Engraving and Printing.**

Descend 897 steps to ground level—the **Washington Monument.**

Take a simulated orbital flight—Earth Station One in the **National Geographic Society's Explorers Hall.**

See a statue of the father of our country half naked—Horatio Greenough's toga-clad George Washington in the **National Museum of American History.**

View 5,000 confiscated firearms—the **FBI Building.**

Enter an underground museum dedicated to a U.S. president—**beneath the Lincoln Memorial.**

Be dazzled by a 45½-carat diamond—the **National Museum of Natural History.**

Sink their teeth into a freeze-dried ice-cream sandwich—the **National Air and Space Museum's gift shop.**

Pedal a boat next to a presidential monument—the **Tidal Basin next to the Jefferson Memorial.**

Touch a moon rock—the **National Air and Space Museum.**

Dress in colonial clothing—the **DAR Museum.**

Watch a clock that always reads 7:22am—the **Petersen House,** where Lincoln died on April 15, 1865, at 7:22am.

Ride a carousel in the heart of the city—outside the **Smithsonian's Arts and Industries Building.**

Peer up at a 15-story ceiling—the **National Building Museum.**

Pet a horseshoe crab—**in the National Aquarium's "touch tank."**

Explore the oldest house in Washington—the **Old Stone House in Georgetown.**

Dine with U.S. senators—the **Senate Dining Room in the Capitol.**

Tour a building with 17½ miles of corridors—the **Pentagon.**

Find the grave of the founder of the Smithsonian Institution—the **Smithsonian "Castle."**

For a behind-the-scenes view of Smithsonian research as it happens, step into the **Amazonia Science Gallery,** adjacent to the Rainforest Exhibit, where the biodiversity of the Amazon is re-created. The concept of a cutting-edge working research institute allows visitors to analyze their own voices and compare them to animal vocalizations. Scientists and education specialists are on hand to explain what they do and how they do it. In the **GeoSphere,** projectors, satellite imagery, and computer-generated information provide visual images that illustrate the earth's geophysical process.

Almost faster than a speeding bullet are the cheetah brothers, Lars and Vince, and Jomu, which moved here from Texas in 1995. They occasionally race (weather permitting) in the zoo's **Cheetah Conservation Station** next to the Visitor Center. The station comes mighty close to mirroring the cheetahs' African savanna home. *Kids:* Cheetahs in the wild have been clocked doing 70 m.p.h., and these three are training hard to improve their personal best. Keeping the boys company nearby when they're not racing are blesboks (can you say it quickly five times?), gazelles, and Grévy's zebras.

"What if Adam and Eve were tempted by a fuzzy-tailed squirrel rather than a snake?" This is one of the questions posed in the **Reptile Discovery Center.** You have to admit it's a step up from "snake house." The center, with its many hands-on exhibits, is attempting to raise the biological literacy of zoo visitors and modify negative notions about reptiles and amphibians. The desired effect is nearly achieved by having the reptile keepers and docents who are on hand to answer questions.

Note: Due to the popularity of Amazonia and the Reptile Discovery Center, lines sometimes form early, so make these your first two stops at the zoo and go early in the day—especially weekends, holidays, and during the summer.

Snack bars and ice-cream stands are scattered throughout the park. At the **Panda Cafe,** enjoy a fast-food break at tables with umbrellas. The **Panda Express Grill,** across from the Panda House, serves sandwiches, salads, cotton candy, and ice cream from 10am to 4pm and accepts most credit cards.

The **Mane Restaurant** is at the bottom of the hill if you started at Connecticut Avenue. Hot dogs, hamburgers, and fresh salads are available. But many visitors prefer to bring sandwiches, buy drinks and ice cream, and dine alfresco at one of the zoo's grassy picnic areas.

(*Note:* Across the street from the main entrance is the Zoo Bar, at 3000 Connecticut Ave. Cross the street for quesadillas, barbecue, sandwiches, and burgers. The Zoo Bar is filled with families at noon, but at night the local animals take over.)

The gift shop in the Visitor Center is open daily and carries a wonderful selection of zoo-related books on several reading levels, stuffed (excuse me, "plush" is the politically correct term) animals, and animal puzzles.

Renwick Gallery

Pennsylvania Ave. at 17th St. NW. ☎ **202/357-2700.** www.nmaa.si.edu. Free admission. AE, CB, DISC, MC, V (in museum shop). Daily 10am–5:30pm. Closed Dec 25. Metro: Farragut North (K St. exit) or Farragut West (17th St. exit). Ages 6 and up.

Washington's first private art museum was the original home of the Corcoran collection. The Renwick, a department of the National Museum of American Art, celebrated its 25th anniversary in 1997. The gallery, in a stunning 19th-century French Second Empire-style building, is a personal favorite of mine. While some of the exhibits showcasing contemporary crafts and decorative arts in the recently renovated galleries appeal to kids, some don't. Most kids over 6 have at least a fleeting appreciation of the interior space. Especially impressive are the puffy circular couches in the 90-foot Victorian Grand Salon, with its wainscoted plum walls and 38-foot skylight ceiling, reached by a broad, carpeted staircase. You almost expect the trumpets to announce your arrival.

Without a doubt, the most popular work in this museum for young people is Larry Fuente's whimsical *Game Fish,* an eye-catching sailfish trophy whose scales glitter with a colorful array of toys and game pieces. If you can lure them away, show them Patti Warashina's *Convertible Car Kiln.*

The Octagon Gallery was designed for Hiram Powers's nude, *The Greek Slave* (now in the Corcoran). Because of its prurient nature (for the Victorian era), viewing times were once different for men and women. The Octagon Gallery is the new home of a remarkable example of trompe l'oeil imagery. Wendell Castle's *Ghost Clock* is actually a solid piece of carved mahogany. Honest!

Walk-in tours are weekdays at noon; Saturday and Sunday at 2pm. Prearranged tours are at 10 and 11am and 1pm (☎ 202/357-2532). The merchandise in the intimate museum shop—crafts, books, clothing—is well chosen and unique, a favorite of mine for gift buying.

✪ Arthur M. Sackler Gallery (of Asian and Near Eastern art)

1050 Independence Ave. SW. ☎ 202/357-2700. www.si.edu/asia. Free admission. Daily 10am–5:30pm. Tours Mon–Fri 11:30am and 2:30pm, Sun 11:30am. Tours daily; call for times. Closed Dec 25. Metro: Smithsonian. Ages 6 and up.

The Sackler shares a 4.2-acre underground museum complex with the National Museum of African Art, the International Gallery, and several Smithsonian classrooms and services. If you're claustrophobic, the plants, skylights, and fountains will remind you that you haven't been buried alive. While Chinese bronzes, Southeast Asian sculpture, and Persian manuscripts may not appeal to your kids on entering, they're sure to have a change of heart during their visit.

Children with an interest in archaeology can pursue exhibitions of some of the oldest art ever made. Even the youngest visitors enjoy counting the fanciful animal forms among the intricate designs on 4,500-year-old bronze vessels in **Arts of China.** In **Puja: Expressions of Hindu Devotion,** children can learn more about one of the world's major religions through videos, touchable sculptures, and a reading area. Displays such as sandals of the gods and the colorfully robed bronze statues of deities capture their attention and imagination, too. What will your youngsters think of the two-headed 9,000-year-old statue, excavated in hundreds of pieces near Amman, Jordan, then reconstructed (over a decade!) in the Smithsonian's Conservation Analytical Laboratory? A free family guide, *Getting to Know the Hindu Gods,* is available at the information desk.

You can pick up two other free family guides at the information desk. *Ganesha's Guide to the Galleries* has insights on behind-the-scenes museum work served up by the elephant-headed Hindu god. "Arts of China" is an aid for understanding and appreciating art made thousands of years ago.

ImaginAsia is the highly successful program cosponsored by the Sackler and Freer galleries aimed at children from 6 to 13 and their companions. Participants tour with a special activity guide and then create their own works of art based on their impressions of what they've seen. ImaginAsia is held on Saturday from March through October and on Monday and Wednesday in July and August. Sessions for groups of 8 to 20 children may be reserved 3 weeks in advance for Saturdays at 1:30pm (☎ 202/357-4880, ext. 422). Call for the current schedule of docent-led tours offered daily (☎ 202/357-2700). Reservations for group tours must be made in writing at least 4 weeks in advance (☎ 202/357-4880, ext. 245).

After a visit, families come away with a better understanding of the cultures represented at the Sackler. For information about museum programs and temporary exhibits, call ☎ 202/357-3200, or inquire at the information desk.

On the way out, visit the Victorian-style **Enid A. Haupt Garden** (see also the description in section 1 of chapter 7), with its geometric parterre. On one side of the garden you can enter a moon gate to an Asian garden; on the other, a waterfall cascades into a small pond. The garden is open Memorial Day to Labor Day from 7am to 8pm; the rest of the year from 7am to 5:45pm.

2 Monuments, Memorials & the National Cathedral

PRESIDENTIAL MONUMENTS

Four U.S. presidents have been honored with monuments in the nation's capital: George Washington, Abraham Lincoln, Thomas Jefferson, and Franklin Delano Roosevelt. Try to see them all. I could wax poetic on the feelings elicited by each, but you should find out for yourself.

Franklin Delano Roosevelt Memorial

900 Ohio Dr. SW (western shore of the Tidal Basin, West Potomac Park). ☎ **202/426-6841** (Monument no. 4). www.nps.gov. Free admission. Daily 8am–midnight. Closed Dec 25. Metro: Smithsonian. Ages 6 and up.

The newest of the presidential monuments was dedicated in May 1997. The length of three football fields, it lies on the western shore of the Tidal Basin, near the Jefferson Memorial. Entrances are at several points from the pathway along the Tidal Basin. It's about a 10-minute walk from the Smithsonian Metro station, longer from the Foggy Bottom and Arlington Cemetery stations. The Tourmobile trams also stop here. I hesitate to recommend this, but *limited* street parking is available in front of the memorial.

The site was selected nearly 100 years ago as part of the overall plan to erect presidential monuments within a kite-shaped grid. In 1955 Congress authorized construction, but it wasn't until 1958 that the design was approved. Groundbreaking began in 1991. You need look no further for a prime example of government bureaucracy in action.

Anchored by rest rooms at both ends, the FDR monument is marked by imposing granite walls, fountains, meditative areas, and bunkerlike areas evoking Roosevelt's first inauguration, the Great Depression, World War II, postwar optimism, and FDR's accomplishments.

Of interest to younger children, beside the awesome fountains, is the sculpture of FDR's beloved Fala (here 3 feet high) at his feet. A 39-ton statue of Eleanor Roosevelt stands at the entrance of Room Four. (Hey, she was a big woman, but not that big!) Mrs. Roosevelt is the *first* First Lady to be honored in a presidential memorial. Can Hillary be far behind?

One obvious boo-boo, which was readily apparent to the visually impaired soon after the monument's unveiling: The raised Braille dots on the bronze wall, "Social Programs," are unreadable. The initials of so-called alphabet agencies, such as the WPA and CCC, are too big and too spread out to be read by mortal fingertips.

Perhaps the most inspiring aspect of this latest stone homage to U.S. presidents is the view across the Tidal Basin to D.C.

You'll find an Information Center and bookshop (open 9am to 9pm) at the main entrance (south end). On display in the Information Center, among the Roosevelt memorabilia, is a replica of FDR's wheelchair, which he designed. A pamphlet containing the quotes etched in the granite walls of the memorial is a meaningful souvenir.

✪ Thomas Jefferson Memorial

Tidal Basin, south end of 15th St. SW, in West Potomac Park. ☎ **202/426-6821**. www.nps. (Monument no. 3). Free admission. Daily 8am–midnight. Closed Dec 25. Transportation: Accessible by car, cab, or Tourmobile; Metro (Smithsonian) is a hike. Ages 8 and up.

Some students of history think Jefferson was the Rodney Dangerfield of his time, that he "got no respect." While the memorials to Washington and Lincoln enjoyed prestigious downtown addresses for quite a spell in accordance with L'Enfant's plan, Mr. Jefferson wasn't appropriately honored until April 13 (his birthday) in 1943, when the Jefferson Memorial was dedicated.

Well, good things come to those who wait. On a parcel reclaimed from the Potomac, on line with the south axis of the White House, a memorial was erected similar to Rome's Pantheon. This architectural model was so favored by Jefferson that he used its columned rotunda design at the Virginia State Capitol, the University of Virginia, and Monticello, his home in Charlottesville.

Above the entrance, he is seen standing before Benjamin Franklin, John Adams, Roger Sherman, and Robert Livingston, members of the committee appointed to write the Declaration of Independence. Engraved on the interior walls are inscriptions from Jefferson's writings that sum up his philosophies on freedom and government. History buffs may note that certain "liberties" were taken with the Declaration of Independence. There are 11 mistakes that can't be blamed on the typing pool. Can your family find them?

The Capitol, White House, Washington Monument, and Lincoln Memorial are visible from the steps, and it's a front-row seat for the Cherry Blossom Festival. Ask your kids if they can connect the Jefferson and Lincoln Memorials and Washington Monument to form a triangle. After a visit to the memorial, you'll probably agree that Jefferson finally received the respect that he so richly deserved. For high drama, come at night. If your kids don't think it's awesome, leave them home next time.

✪ Lincoln Memorial

West of the Mall at 23rd St. NW, between Constitution and Independence aves. NW. ☎ **202/ 426-6895.** www.nps. (Monument no. 2). Free admission. Daily 24 hours. Park staff on duty 8am–midnight. Metro: Foggy Bottom. Ages 4 and up.

I had an English professor who said if you weren't moved by the Lincoln Memorial, your heart had probably stopped.

If the only image you hold of the 16th U.S. president is on a penny, toss it aside and come see this one. The 19-by-19-foot statue of a seated, contemplative Abraham Lincoln was designed by Daniel French. It took 28 blocks of marble and 4 years of carving to complete and is the focal point in the classically inspired monument by Henry Bacon.

A gleam in some politician's eye shortly after Lincoln's death in 1865, this Parthenon look-alike was not completed until 1922. The Doric columns number 36, one for each state in the Union at the time of Lincoln's death. The names are inscribed on the frieze over the colonnade. The names of the 48 states at the time of the memorial's dedication appear near the top of the monument, and a plaque for Alaska and Hawaii was added later.

The stirring words of Lincoln's Gettysburg Address and Second Inaugural Address are carved into the limestone walls, and above them allegorical murals by Jules Guérin represent North-South unity and the freeing of the slaves.

If you can come here at night, when the crowds thin out, I urge you to do so. From the rear of the memorial, gaze across the Potomac to Arlington National Cemetery and the eternal flame at John F. Kennedy's grave. From the steps, take in the **Reflecting Pool,** a nighttime mirror of the memorial, and past it to the Washington Monument, Mall, and Capitol. If the sight doesn't grab you, well, my English professor spoke the truth.

As the result of a project conceived by a group of high school students visiting from Scottsdale, Arizona, a visitor center opened in the once-gloomy basement of the memorial late in 1994. Most striking in the minimuseum are photographs and film clips of history-making protests and civil rights events that took place at the

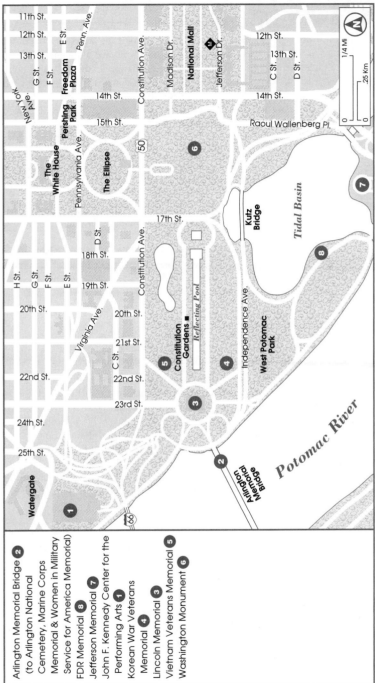

11th St.
12th St.
13th St.

Penn. Ave.
E St.
G St.
F St.

New York Ave.

Pennsylvania Ave.

Freedom Plaza

Pershing Park

The White House

The Ellipse

14th St.
15th St.

50

Constitution Ave.

Madison Dr.

National Mall

Jefferson Dr.

12th St.
13th St.

C St.
D St.

14th St.

Raoul Wallenberg Pl.

6

Kutz Bridge

Tidal Basin

7

8

17th St.

Constitution Ave.

D St.

18th St.

H St.
G St.
F St.
E St.

19th St.

20th St.

Virginia Ave.

20th St.

21st St.

C St.

22nd St.

22nd St.

23rd St.

24th St.

25th St.

Watergate

1

Reflecting Pool

Constitution Gardens

5

4

3

Independence Ave.

West Potomac Park

2

Arlington Memorial Bridge

66

Potomac River

1/4 MI
25 Km

A Little Piece of History

The little stone house on the southwest corner of 17th Street and Constitution Avenue was the lock keeper's house for L'Enfant's "Canal Through Tiber Creek" plan. L'Enfant envisioned a canal meandering along Constitution Avenue from the Potomac River in Georgetown, through the Ellipse and east through the District, before dipping south to the Anacostia River. Believe it or not, the canal was built and used until the coming of the railroads made it obsolete in the 1870s. The lock keeper's house is the only remnant of this piece of D.C. history.

site, such as Marian Anderson's Easter 1939 concert after she, as an African American woman, was barred from singing at DAR Constitution Hall, and Martin Luther King Jr.'s 1963 "I Have a Dream" speech. Also on display are 13 marble tablets carved with Lincoln quotations and exhibits detailing the memorial's design and construction. The **Lincoln Legacy** is a permanent exhibition, open from 8am to midnight daily.

The scaffolding and fencing you may see around the Lincoln Memorial until sometime in 2000 are not part of the original designs, but part of a "monumental" (couldn't resist) effort by the National Park Service to inspect and repair the edifice. *Don't worry:* You'll still have access to the memorial's interior and will be able to take pictures.

✪ Washington Monument

15th St. and Constitution Ave. NW. ☎ **202/426-6841** www.nps. (Monument no. 1). Free admission. First Sun in Apr to Labor Day, daily 8am–midnight; rest of the year, daily 9am–5pm. Closed July 4 and Dec 25. Metro: Smithsonian. Ages 6 and up.

Please note: The monument will be under wraps, encased in scaffolding and blue transparent fabric, while repairs are made. Visitors will be able to watch the work through the fabric cloak designed by postmodern architect Michael Graves. Renovations, inside and out, will be ongoing until sometime in 2000. During this time, you still may visit. If possible, come at night and take a photo. Many think the monument is at its most dramatic after dark, with or without the see-through dress.

If you fly into National Airport, you will be treated to the supreme view of the monument. Standing 555 feet, 5 inches tall in its stockinged feet, the marble-and-granite obelisk is an engineering marvel with walls that taper from 15 feet at the base to 18 inches at the top.

Nearly half a century passed from its conception to the actual construction between 1848 and 1884—a story and a half if you have the time and interest to research it. During the Civil War the unfinished structure was known as Beef Depot Monument because cattle grazed the grounds before they were slaughtered. Another sidelight: The monument is not positioned exactly according to L'Enfant's plan. It had to be shifted eastward a tad because the original site was too marshy. That's a polite way of saying that D.C. was a varmint- and mosquito-infested swamp.

To avoid very long lines, come on a weekday if at all possible. Arrive before 8am or after 8pm during extended summer hours. *Note:* Timed-admission tickets are issued for this popular attraction. To avoid waiting in long lines, I suggest taking this route, especially in spring and summer. Tickets (free at the monument) can be ordered in advance from TicketMaster for $1.50 (☎ **800/505-5040**).

Since visitors are no longer allowed to climb the 897 steps, you'll have to take the elevator—faster than in most apartment buildings—and you'll be at the top in a little over a minute. The view is spectacular, especially after dark. If you're fortunate enough to be on the Mall for the Fourth of July festivities, the sight of the fireworks over the monument is thrilling.

Designed by Robert Mills, architect of the Treasury and Old Patent Office buildings, the monument is two-tone, but not by original design. Notice how the stones darken about 150 feet from the base. During the construction of the monument, the Civil War as well as other matters put the building process on hold. When the government resumed the project in the 1870s, the "new" marble, mined from another part of the quarry, was darker. If you've ever tried to match paint, you'll understand the problem.

When enough Park Service staff are on hand, you may take a **Down the Steps** tour to see the carved stones incorporated in the interior (one is from the Parthenon) and learn more about the monument's construction. *Be forewarned:* Once you begin your descent down the 897 stairs, you can't change your mind. This is no place for the claustrophobic, because there are no windows and space is tight near the top. The tour is usually given year-round at 10am and 2pm and is limited to the first 25 who show up. To be on the safe side, the Park Service suggests calling ahead, especially in winter.

The monument grounds are sometimes the site of concerts and other special events in summer.

WAR MEMORIALS

✪ Arlington National Cemetery

Arlington, Va. (west side of Memorial Bridge). ☎ **703/697-2131.** www.geocities.com. Free admission. Apr–Sept daily 8am–7pm, until 5pm the rest of year. Metro: Arlington Cemetery. You can also walk across Arlington Memorial Bridge (from near the Lincoln Memorial), or board a Tourmobile downtown or at the cemetery's Visitor Center. Ages 6 and up.

More than 216,000 American war dead are buried in the 612 acres of hallowed hills overlooking the nation's capital from the Virginia side of the Potomac River. Try to include this in your itinerary, especially if you have school-age children in tow—there is much to feed the mind and the spirit.

Four million visitors enter Arlington National Cemetery annually to watch specially trained members of the 3rd Infantry Regiment from the adjacent Fort Myer guard stand sentinel day and night over the simple but inspiring white marble **Tomb of the Unknowns.** Four unidentified bodies from this century's four wars are interred here. The soldiers who stand guard are part of the nation's oldest military unit known as the Old Guard, which dates from colonial times. If you're close enough, you may notice that the soldier's white gloves are wet. In a final gesture before standing guard, they soak their gloves to better grip the wood handle of the bayonet-tipped M-14. The changing of the guard takes place every half hour from April through September and every hour on the hour from October through March.

The **Memorial Amphitheatre** is the setting for Memorial Day and Veterans' Day services. Junior historians interested in the Spanish-American War will want to see the mast from the USS *Maine* ("Remember the Maine") on the other side of Memorial Drive.

The imposing Greek Revival building at the top of the hill, **Arlington House,** once belonged to Gen. Robert E. Lee and Mary Randolph Curtis, who just happened to be Martha Washington's great-granddaughter. Lee was married here and lived in the neoclassical mansion until 1861 when he resigned from the U.S. Army to command the Northern Virginia Rebel Army. Four weeks later the house was

Arlington National Cemetery

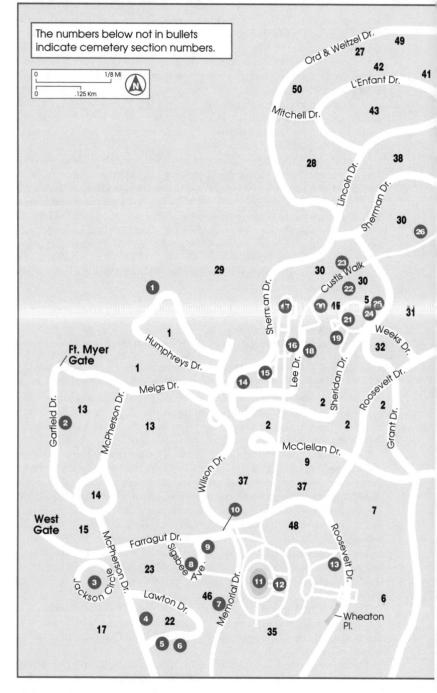

The numbers below not in bullets indicate cemetery section numbers.

0 — 1/8 Mi
0 — .125 Km

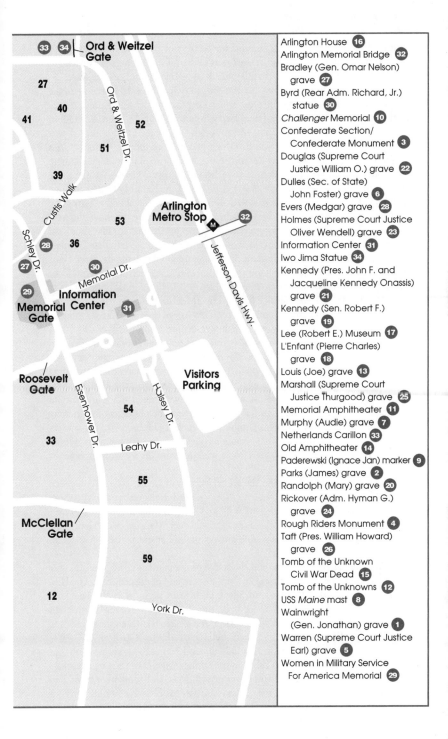

Arlington House **16**
Arlington Memorial Bridge **32**
Bradley (Gen. Omar Nelson)
  grave **27**
Byrd (Rear Adm. Richard, Jr.)
  statue **30**
Challenger Memorial **10**
Confederate Section/
  Confederate Monument **3**
Douglas (Supreme Court
  Justice William O.) grave **22**
Dulles (Sec. of State)
  John Foster) grave **6**
Evers (Medgar) grave **28**
Holmes (Supreme Court Justice
  Oliver Wendell) grave **23**
Information Center **31**
Iwo Jima Statue **34**
Kennedy (Pres. John F. and
  Jacqueline Kennedy Onassis)
  grave **21**
Kennedy (Sen. Robert F.)
  grave **19**
Lee (Robert E.) Museum **17**
L'Enfant (Pierre Charles)
  grave **18**
Louis (Joe) grave **13**
Marshall (Supreme Court
  Justice Thurgood) grave **25**
Memorial Amphitheater **11**
Murphy (Audie) grave **7**
Netherlands Carillon **33**
Old Amphitheater **14**
Paderewski (Ignace Jan) marker **9**
Parks (James) grave **2**
Randolph (Mary) grave **20**
Rickover (Adm. Hyman G.)
  grave **24**
Rough Riders Monument **4**
Taft (Pres. William Howard)
  grave **26**
Tomb of the Unknown
  Civil War Dead **15**
Tomb of the Unknowns **12**
USS *Maine* mast **8**
Wainwright
  (Gen. Jonathan) grave **1**
Warren (Supreme Court Justice
  Earl) grave **5**
Women in Military Service
  For America Memorial **29**

seized by Union troops, which remained for the rest of the Civil War. When the Union Army was looking for a burial site for its soldiers, Gen. Montgomery Meigs—no great fan of Lee's—suggested that the war dead be buried "in Lee's backyard."

The government ultimately bought the property, and since 1933 the National Park Service has been cutting the grass and taking care of the furnishings. Check out the servants' quarters during the free self-guided tour (9:30am to 4:30pm October through March; until 6pm April through September).

The marble, slate, and Cape Cod fieldstone grave site of John F. Kennedy, 35th U.S. president, his wife, Jacqueline Kennedy Onassis, and two of their infant children, lies off Sheridan Drive on the sloping lawn below Arlington House. At night, the Eternal Flame can be seen from the Rooftop Terrace of the Kennedy Center and several other D.C. vantage points. Sen. Robert Kennedy's grave lies close by, marked by a simple cross. The site is best visited early in the morning before the masses arrive.

Pierre L'Enfant was moved from a pauper's grave to his final resting place near Arlington House when it finally dawned on those in power that, despite his supposedly cantankerous disposition, L'Enfant did a bang-up job designing the capital city. Many newcomers (and old-timers too) have trouble finding their way around D.C. and think L'Enfant should have been left undisturbed in his original burial site.

The **Women in Military Service for America Memorial** honors the 1.8 million American women who have served in the military—from the American Revolution to the present. This new memorial, which was dedicated on October 18, 1997, incorporates the spruced up neoclassical granite retaining/entrance wall designed in the 1920s by McKim, Mead & White. An imposing plaza fountain that flows in a black granite trough to a reflecting pool greets visitors to the memorial. According to the husband and wife architects who designed the memorial, the fountain symbolizes the pooling of women's voices over time. Stairwells lead from four niches in the exterior wall to the terrace, signifying the barriers women have had to penetrate in the military. Visitors can access a computerized registry of 250,000 U.S. servicewomen who have submitted their personal recollections and photographs. Eleven glass panels on the terrace roof are etched with inscriptions by women veterans about their military experiences.

Carved from the hillside behind the semicircular wall are the computer registry, a Hall of Honor, theater, conference center, 14 exhibit alcoves, and a gift shop. Kudos to retired Air Force Brig. Gen. Wilma L. Vaught, who oversaw the project for more than a decade, and on-site project manager Margaret Van Voast. The memorial is a fitting and long overdue answer to "What did you do in the war, Mom?"

The **Marine Corps Memorial** and the statue of the marines raising the flag over Iwo Jima are near the Orde-Weitzel Gate at the north end of the cemetery. The U.S. Marine Drum and Bugle Corps and Silent Drill team perform at the Iwo Jima Memorial on Tuesday evenings at 7pm in the summertime (late May through August). Free shuttle buses whisk visitors from the Visitor Center to the parade site (☎ 202/433-4173). Nearby is the **49-bell Netherlands Carillon** (☎ 703/285-2598). You can climb the tower (kids under 12 must be with an adult), or tiptoe through 15,000 blooming tulips in the spring. Enjoy a concert by guest carillonneurs on Saturday and holidays during April, May, and September from 2 to 4pm. In June, July, and August, the concerts are Saturday from 6:30 to 8:30pm.

Just north of Arlington Cemetery at Fort Myer, visit the caisson platoon stables of the Old Guard, which counted George Washington as one of its members. The horses, used in processions and presidential funerals, can be viewed Monday through Friday from noon to 4pm. Drive here or take a taxi from the Arlington

Cemetery Metro or Visitor Center. Nearby, the **Old Guard Museum** contains displays dating from the Revolutionary War era. The museum is open Monday through Saturday from 9am to 4pm, Sunday from 1 to 4pm.

Korean War Veterans Memorial

Southeast of Lincoln Memorial, French Dr., and Independence Ave. ☎ **202/632-1001.** www.nps. Free admission. Daily, 24 hours. Park staff on duty 8am–midnight. Metro: Smithsonian (Independence Ave. exit) or Foggy Bottom, then walk. Ages 2 and up.

After years of squabbling and disagreement over its design, the Korean War Veterans Memorial was unveiled in July 1995. On a 4-acre parcel southeast of the Lincoln Memorial and across from the Vietnam War Veterans Memorial (with your back to Lincoln, it is to the right of the Reflecting Pool), the stainless-steel statues of 19 poncho-draped soldiers on the march make a powerful statement, drawing the viewer into the action. In the background is a black granite mural wall with the etched faces of support troops. The faces were culled from actual photos of Korean War veterans.

Vietnam Veterans Memorial

Northeast of the Lincoln Memorial near 21st St. and Constitution Ave. NW. ☎ **202/ 634-1568.** www.nps. Free admission. Daily, 24 hours, with rangers on duty 8am–midnight. Metro: Foggy Bottom (walk east on H or I St., turn right at 21st St., and walk for 6 or 7 blocks). Ages 10 and up.

The Wall, 140 panels of polished black granite stretching almost 500 feet, honors the nearly 60,000 men and women who died or remain missing as a result of the Vietnam War. The wall's two segments meet at an angle; one end takes aim at the Washington Monument; the other, the Lincoln Memorial. Names are listed chronologically, from the first casualty in 1959 to the last in 1975. Although many leave the site misty-eyed, children too young to know anything of the Vietnam War will probably be bored. Vietnam veteran Jan Scruggs initiated the project in 1979, and since opening on November 13, 1982, the memorial has been one of the most visited sites in Washington. Nearby is the Vietnam Women's Memorial, a bronze sculpture of three women and a wounded soldier, which was dedicated in November 1993.

NATIONAL CATHEDRAL

✪ Washington National Cathedral

(Cathedral Church of St. Peter and St. Paul) Massachusetts and Wisconsin aves. NW. ☎ **202/ 537-6200.** Fax 202/364-6611. www.cathedral.org. Requested donation $3 adults, $1 children. Worship free. Mon–Sat 10am–4:30pm, Sun 12:30–4:30pm; extended summer hours. Metro: Tenleytown, then no. 32, 34, or 36 bus south on Wisconsin Ave. Bus: N up Massachusetts Ave. from Dupont Circle, or take Old Town Trolley. Ages 4 and up.

Because the cathedral is one of the few sights in Washington not close to a Metro station, I suggest taking a taxi, Metrobus, or the Old Town Trolley. The sixth largest religious structure in the world perches on a parcel known as "the close" on Mount St. Alban. The cathedral is visible from several vantage points inside and outside the city. The top of the tower is 676 feet above sea level—that's mighty high, given Washington's zero elevation. Construction began in 1907 on the Gothic-inspired cathedral, but not until 1990, with the completion of the twin west towers, was the cathedral officially consecrated. Pick up an illustrated guide in the Cathedral Museum Shop detailing the history and architecture before exploring on your own, or take the 45-minute guided tour, Monday through Saturday between 10am and 3:15pm, Sunday from 12:30 to 2:45pm. Tours begin every 15 to 20 minutes. No tours Thanksgiving, Christmas, Palm Sunday, and Easter (☎ **202/537-6207**).

The **Space Window,** one of more than 200 stained-glass windows in the cathedral, is dedicated to the Apollo 11 mission. Can your kids, or you with your bifocals, pick out the moon rock? Viewing the **Rose Window** in the North Transept at dusk is a religious experience in itself. The vaulted ceiling above the 518-foot-long nave is 102 feet high. But everything is scaled down to their size in the charming **Children's Chapel,** with its tiny chairs and pint-size pipe organ.

The **Pilgrim Observation Gallery** has a fantastic view of Washington beyond the flying buttresses and gargoyles. The gallery is open Monday through Saturday from 10am to 4pm, Sunday from noon to 4pm.

Let your youngsters loose to run around, or meander with them, through nearly 60 magnificent acres of treed and beautifully landscaped prime real estate. Enjoy a family picnic, perhaps, then stop in at the Bishop's Garden (open daily during daylight hours), south of the cathedral. It's modeled on a medieval walled garden. Dried herbs, teas, gifts, and books are sold in the Herb Cottage. At the **Greenhouse,** on South Road, you can purchase growing herbs and plants. The Museum Shop, Herb Cottage, and Greenhouse are open daily, except December 25 and January 1, from 9:30am to 5pm (☎ 202/537-6267).

The **Flower Mart,** held the first Friday and Saturday in May, features rides, puppet shows, and other activities for kids. **Family Saturday** is a series of workshops linking stories with various aspects of the cathedral. Geared to kids 4 to 8, it is held several spring and summer Saturdays from 10 to 11:30am and noon to 1:30pm. The cost is $5 per child. Call ☎ 202/537-2184 for reservations. In the **Medieval Workshop for Families,** kids get a taste of medieval life through arts-and-crafts projects overseen by docents. They'll learn the purpose of gargoyles (to carry rainwater) while modeling their own out of clay, and they can also try their hand at carving Indiana limestone, or, perhaps, make a ministained-glass window. The workshop (☎ 202/537-2934) is held Saturday from 10am to 2pm on a first-come, first-served basis and costs $4.

The Cathedral Choir sings Monday, Tuesday, and Wednesday at 4pm during the school year. Demonstrations of the cathedral's 10,650-pipe organ are Wednesday at 12:45pm, and anyone can attend. Special gargoyle tours ($5) follow a slide presentation of these weird-looking critters adorning the cathedral. For reservations, call ☎ 202/537-2934. A Summer Festival Concert series and holiday "Messiah" and Joy of Christmas concerts are annual happenings. The cathedral also hosts special concerts, such as Robert Shaw conducting Beethoven's "Missa Solemniss" and a Duke Ellington Celebration in 1999. At the cathedral's annual open house in September, visitors may tour the bell tower.

3 The White House & Branches of the Government

White House

1600 Pennsylvania Ave. NW (visitor entrance at East Gate on E. Executive Ave.). ☎ **800/717-1450.** www.whitehouse.gov. Free admission. Self-guided tours Tues–Sat 10am–noon. Closed during presidential functions. Metro: McPherson Square, Farragut North, or Farragut West. Ages 10 and up.

Don't show up at the White House on a spring or summer morning and expect to get in. Roughly from mid-March to September, you have to stop first at the **White House Visitor Center** (☎ 202/208-1631). The Visitor Center is in the Department of Commerce's Herbert Hoover Building at 1450 Pennsylvania Ave. (near the Federal Triangle Metro stop), and just a stone's throw from the White House. During peak season, from mid-March to Labor Day, tickets for same-day White

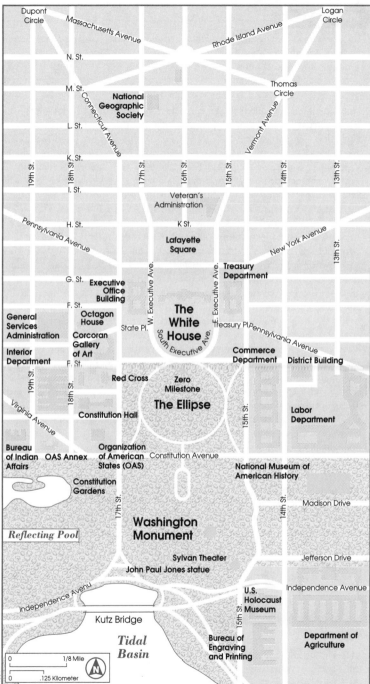

The White House Area

- Dupont Circle
- Logan Circle
- Massachusetts Avenue
- Rhode Island Avenue
- N. St.
- M. St.
- National Geographic Society
- Thomas Circle
- Connecticut Avenue
- L. St.
- Vermont Avenue
- K. St.
- I. St.
- 19th St.
- 18th St.
- 17th St.
- 16th St.
- 15th St.
- 14th St.
- 13th St.
- Pennsylvania Avenue
- H. St.
- Veteran's Administration
- K St.
- Lafayette Square
- New York Avenue
- 13th St.
- Treasury Department
- G. St.
- Executive Office Building
- W. Executive Ave.
- E. Executive Ave.
- F. St.
- Octagon House
- State Pl.
- The White House
- Treasury Pl.
- Pennsylvania Avenue
- General Services Administration
- Corcoran Gallery of Art
- South Executive Ave.
- Interior Department
- F. St.
- Commerce Department
- District Building
- 19th St.
- 18th St.
- Red Cross
- Zero Milestone
- The Ellipse
- 15th St.
- Labor Department
- Virginia Avenue
- Constitution Hall
- Bureau of Indian Affairs
- OAS Annex
- Organization of American States (OAS)
- Constitution Avenue
- National Museum of American History
- Constitution Gardens
- 17th St.
- 14th St.
- Madison Drive
- Reflecting Pool
- Washington Monument
- Jefferson Drive
- Sylvan Theater
- John Paul Jones statue
- Independence Avenue
- Independence Avenue
- U.S. Holocaust Museum
- 15th St.
- Kutz Bridge
- Tidal Basin
- Bureau of Engraving and Printing
- Department of Agriculture

0 — 1/8 Mile
0 — .125 Kilometer

House tours are available at the Visitor Center for the 10am and noon tours, which are conducted Tuesday through Saturday *only.* To avoid disappointment, arrive at the Visitor Center by 8am when it opens. From Labor Day until mid-March, however, advance tickets are usually not necessary, and visitors may line up at the East Visitors Gate on East Executive Avenue, alongside the presidential mansion. The Visitor Center is open daily from 8am to 5pm, with extended summer hours which tend to change from year to year (to keep us all on our toes!). The Visitor Center also distributes information published by the D.C. Convention and Visitors Association. For **advance VIP tickets,** write to your senator or representative at least 1 month in advance (6 months would be better) and request tickets for the special early morning guided VIP tour, which takes about 45 minutes. A White House spokesperson says the tour is appropriate for kids 12 and over. (I think mature 10- and 11-year-olds will get something out of it too.) Bear in mind that the tour is heavy on history, and sure to bore the pants off small fry. Tickets are limited, so don't expect miracles.

The 20- to 35-minute **self-guided tour** closely resembles a cattle round-up and takes in the ground and main public floors, including the East, Green, Blue, and Red Rooms, the State Dining Room, Cross Hall, North Entrance Hall, and Oval Room where Franklin Roosevelt gave his fireside chats. On display, besides presidential portraits and memorabilia, are period furnishings (for the most part reflecting the Greek Revival and Victorian styles), portraits of the First Ladies, and exhibits on the day-to-day operation of the White House and its role as a national symbol.

If you can't get a tour and you have tots in tow, visit this magnificent residence/museum (209 years old in 2000!) another time. Little kids don't give a hoot about watered-silk walls, Turkish Herede carpets, or Bellange chairs, anyway.

Young children do enjoy the annual Easter egg roll and the spring and fall garden tours (see "Kids' Favorite Events" in chapter 1 for details). The Easter egg roll was held at the Capitol until Pres. Rutherford B. Hayes moved it to the White House in 1879. On the west side of the South Lawn lies the Children's Garden with bronze imprints of the hands and feet of White House children and grandchildren. *A word of caution:* Waits of more than 2 hours in line for the Easter egg roll are not unusual. *My advice:* Take plenty of snacks.

❂ U.S. Capitol

East end of the Mall, entrance on E. Capitol St. and 1st St. NE. ☎ **202/225-6827.** www.senate.gov. Free admission. Sept–Feb daily 9am–4:30pm; Mar–Aug daily 9am–8pm. (Call ahead, as extended hours change from year to year). Tours Sept–Feb every 15–30 min from 9am–3:30pm, Mon–Sat; Mar–Aug every 10–15 min from 9am–7:30pm, Mon–Sat. Closed Thanksgiving, Christmas, and Jan 1. Metro: Capitol South or Union Station. Ages 6 and up.

Even if your home is outside the United States, the Capitol will give you a sense, more than any other federal building, of what this country is all about. As you face the Capitol's East Front, the Senate side is north (right) and the House side is south. Flags fly over the respective sides when either is in session, and night sessions are indicated by a light burning in the dome. Information on committee meetings is

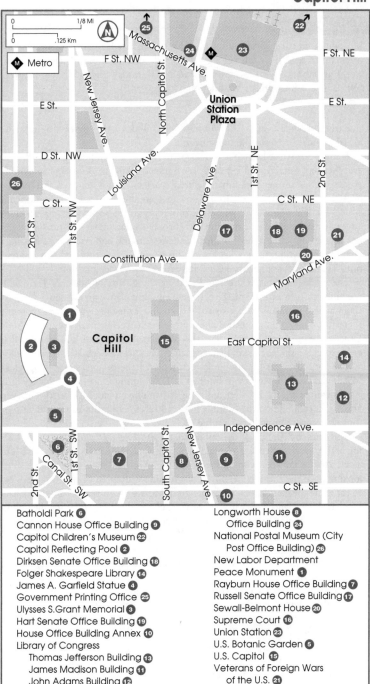

Batholdi Park **6**
Cannon House Office Building **9**
Capitol Children's Museum **22**
Capitol Reflecting Pool **2**
Dirksen Senate Office Building **18**
Folger Shakespeare Library **14**
James A. Garfield Statue **4**
Government Printing Office **25**
Ulysses S.Grant Memorial **3**
Hart Senate Office Building **19**
House Office Building Annex **10**
Library of Congress
    Thomas Jefferson Building **13**
    James Madison Building **11**
    John Adams Building **12**

Longworth House
    Office Building **24**
National Postal Museum (City
    Post Office Building) **26**
New Labor Department
Peace Monument **1**
Rayburn House Office Building **7**
Russell Senate Office Building **17**
Sewall-Belmont House **20**
Supreme Court **16**
Union Station **23**
U.S. Botanic Garden **5**
U.S. Capitol **15**
Veterans of Foreign Wars
    of the U.S. **21**

Factoid

If a family member is celebrating an 80th (or higher) birthday and you'd like the president to send the celebrant a greeting card, send a written request—at least six weeks in advance—with Gram's or Gramp's birthday and address to: Greeting Office, The White House, Washington, D.C. 20500.

published weekdays in the *Washington Post's* "Today in Congress" column. Call ahead if you're interested in a specific bill.

A short-but-sweet half-hour tour departs every few minutes from the Rotunda every day but Sunday, and I strongly recommend taking it. *A word to the wise:* The guides say that during peak times (Saturdays, around major holidays, and March to September) it is best to visit from noon to 1pm and after 5:30 (during extended spring/summer hours). The guides are so well scrubbed, so smooth, and so knowledgeable that they must be running for office. Encourage older kids to ask questions during the tour, then allow time for wandering around and attending a hearing or committee meeting, usually held in the morning or other times when Congress is not in session. If you have toddlers, quit after the introductory tour.

The guides do a marvelous job describing the history of **Statuary Hall,** where the House met from 1807 to 1857. Note the bronze plaque on the floor where John Quincy Adams collapsed on February 21, 1848. He died in an adjoining room soon thereafter. Due to an acoustical anomaly, whispers can be heard across the room. Usually, the guide will demonstrate this phenomenon, to your kids' delight. If the guide forgets, ask. It's the kind of experience that sticks in a child's memory forever.

The rotunda's cast-iron dome (which replaced the original one of copper and wood) was begun in 1855 and finished in 1863 during Lincoln's presidency. It has a diameter of nearly 100 feet and weighs 9 million pounds. Don't get nervous: You're safe standing on the rotunda floor, 180 feet beneath it, as more than 5,000 tons of ironwork provide the girding.

Constantino Brumidi's allegorical fresco, the *Apotheosis of Washington,* lines the very top of the dome and depicts Washington accompanied by Liberty, Victory, and Fame. The 13 figures crowned with stars represent the 13 original states. If your neck stiffens looking up at the masterpiece, pity poor Brumidi, who spent 11 months on his back to complete the glorification of Washington. More than 25 years of Brumidi's handiwork is also evidenced elsewhere in the Capitol—in the frieze encircling the rotunda, the Senate reception room, the President's Room, and the first-floor Senate corridors.

The **Crypt** was originally intended as Washington's final resting place, but his relatives insisted on Mount Vernon. (You know how family can be.) So, instead of Washington, the Crypt holds changing exhibits that tell about the history and construction of the Capitol.

If you visit the **House Gallery,** the Democrats will be seated to the right of the presiding officer and Republicans to the left. Senators have assigned seats, according to seniority, but representatives do not, and a system of bells informs those not in attendance what is going on. Wouldn't the kids love this when they're absent from school?

The Supreme Court met in the **Old Supreme Court Chamber** from 1800 to 1860. Thomas Jefferson was sworn in as president here in 1801, and in 1844 Samuel F. B. Morse sent the first telegraph message, "What hath God wrought," to Baltimore from here.

If you visit the handsome **Old Senate Chamber,** built between 1793 and 1800 and in use until 1859, imagine for a moment the highly charged pre–Civil War

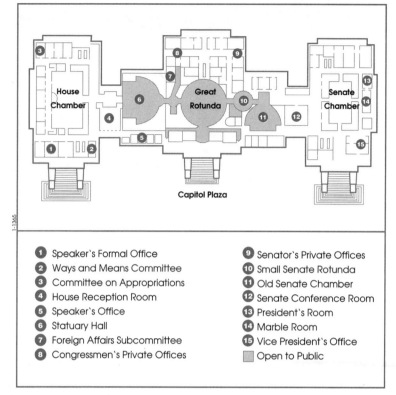

Capitol Plaza

1-1365

1. Speaker's Formal Office
2. Ways and Means Committee
3. Committee on Appropriations
4. House Reception Room
5. Speaker's Office
6. Statuary Hall
7. Foreign Affairs Subcommittee
8. Congressmen's Private Offices

9. Senator's Private Offices
10. Small Senate Rotunda
11. Old Senate Chamber
12. Senate Conference Room
13. President's Room
14. Marble Room
15. Vice President's Office
▨ Open to Public

atmosphere as rich oratory and heated debate filled the air. Note the mahogany desks with inkwells and sand shakers for blotting the ink and handsome red carpet with gold stars. No wonder this was considered the hottest show in town for many years. When crowds overflowed the galleries, it is said some senators politely gave their seats to ladies. In the new Senate Chamber, they now lose their seats to ladies.

Led by Sen. Jefferson Davis (later president of the Confederacy), Congress appropriated $100,000 in 1850 for building a Capitol extension to include new House and Senate wings. The Senate moved into its new quarters on January 4, 1859. The House convened for the first time in the new south building on December 16, 1857. Originally the House met in what is now Statuary Hall.

Before you leave here, do two things:

1. Take your kids down to the basement for a ride on the subway, run by electromagnets, between the Capitol and Dirksen and Hart Senate office buildings. Until the new subway began running in 1994, our representatives rode an antiquated open-air tram. Think, as you're riding, about the cost: a trifling $18 million of our tax dollars.

2. Stroll around to the West Front for an unbroken view of the Mall, Washington Monument, and Lincoln Memorial.

Morning VIP tours, appropriate for kids 10 and up, include admission to the House and Senate galleries. Usually, the House and Senate convene from noon until late afternoon, but exceptions are almost a rule. Whether you want the special tour,

● **Did You Know?**

- The Capitol cornerstone, misplaced during work on the East Front in the 1950s, is still missing.
- Dan Quayle and Al Gore are the only vice presidents missing a bust in the Senate wing (no jokes, please).
- Several years ago a women's rest room was created closer to the Senate side of the Capitol to accommodate the growing number of women in the Senate (nine at press time). It has two stalls, two sinks, and no glass ceiling.
- The 19½-foot statue of Freedom, perched atop the dome since 1863, was supposed to be nude. You can imagine what a furor that caused in the mid-1800s, so sculptor Thomas Crawford draped the figure in a flowing robe. Despite the feathers flowing from the eagle-topped helmet, Freedom is not a Native American. All seven tons of Freedom were lowered from the dome by helicopter on May 9, 1993, for cleaning and restoration, which took several months. (You have to admit—130 years is a long time to go without a bath.)

or just passes to the galleries, you must write your representative or senator far in advance (see "Visitor Information" in chapter 1 or check the Web site: www. capweb.net). Last-minute passes are usually available if you stop at your senator's office. Call if you don't know the location (☎ **202/224-3121**). Passes are given to noncitizens who show their passports to the appointment desk on the Senate side, first floor, or the Doorkeeper of the House. In the summer, or any other time when Congress is not in session, visitors can enter the Senate and House galleries without a special pass. Groups of more than 15 may schedule a tour up to 6 months in advance (☎ **202/224-4910**).

○ Federal Bureau of Investigation (FBI)

J. Edgar Hoover FBI Building, Pennsylvania Ave. and 10th St. NW (tour entrance, E St. between 9th and 10th sts.). ☎ **202/324-3447.** www.fbi.gov. Free admission. Mon–Fri 8:45am–4:15pm. Closed weekends and federal holidays. Metro: Archives/Navy Memorial, Metro Center, or Gallery Place. Ages 8 and up.

Everyone is fascinated with the evil that men do, and for many this is the best tour in Washington. If you haven't written to your senator or representative for VIP tickets, arrive by 8:30am, especially in spring and summer, for the hour-long tour conducted every 15 minutes, Monday through Friday from 8:45am to 4:15pm.

Don't let your first impression of the hideous $126 million concrete bunker— dubbed "Fort Hoover" by locals—put you off. Once inside, well-versed FBI guides will take you past a series of exhibits detailing past and current bureau work. Try to stand close to the guide so you don't miss anything.

Also at the Capitol is the **Refectory** (☎ **202/224-4140**) on the first floor, Senate side. There's seating for 75 in this appealing eatery with vaulted ceilings and wainscoted walls. Prices for main courses range from $3 to $9. Reservations are not taken. MasterCard and Visa are accepted. It's open Monday through Friday from 8am to 4pm (later when the Senate is in session). High chairs and boosters are available.

A brief introductory film gives a historical overview of the bureau's activities. With any luck your kids won't recognize a relative among the **Ten Most Wanted,** the famous list begun in 1950. According to FBI legend, two fugitives whose pictures were recognized here by tourists were later apprehended. The late yippie/radical Abbie Hoffman claimed he took the FBI tour several times while on the lam.

Although they may not recognize Al Capone or Ma Barker in the rogues' gallery, your kids will snap to attention when they see the gangsters' weapons, the U.S. Crime Clock as it ticks off the numbers and frequency of violent crimes in this country, devices used by spies for transporting microfilm, and an actual surveillance tape.

A whopping 187 million fingerprints are on file, and they're retained for 83 years before being discarded. Along the way, you'll be shown more than 5,000 confiscated firearms (no two exactly alike!), as well as a room full of furs, jewelry, silverware, and art objects seized in narcotics and tax evasion cases. Sorry, no souvenirs.

If you happen to see a white-coated technician examining a bloody fabric sample in the **Serology Lab,** be assured, it's the real thing. They don't use props here. Drug samples and related paraphernalia are part of the Drug Enforcement Agency's (DEA) exhibit; a world map shows the routes taken by carriers of illicit substances into this country. You'll also learn how the bureau is waging the battle against illegal drugs.

Older children will particularly enjoy visiting the **Instrumental Analysis Unit,** where a car's make and model can be determined from a paint chip (20,000 samples are on hand from foreign and domestic models), **the Firearms Identification Unit,** and the **Hairs and Fibers Lab.**

What leaves kids gasping, however, is the tour's bang-up finish. In a small auditorium facing a firing range, you'll hear and see a sharp-eyed agent pump several rounds from a 9mm automatic pistol and submachine gun (successor to the notorious Tommy Gun) into several defenseless paper targets, which end up like so many slices of Swiss cheese. What a show!

✪ Bureau of Engraving and Printing

14th and C sts. SW (enter on 14th St.). ☎ **202/622-2000.** www.bep.treas.gov. Free admission. Mon–Fri 9am–2pm. Closed federal holidays and Dec 25–Jan 1. Metro: Smithsonian. Ages 4 and up.

You can bet your bottom dollar that the buck starts here. Kids old enough to appreciate money will go gaga over the green stuff. My son has never recovered from being denied a souvenir $5 bill after touring the bureau for the first time when he was 6. That was big bucks in the 1970s. He still can't understand why, with all that moolah, the bureau couldn't spare a bill.

This guided tour is so popular, especially in the summer, that you need tickets during the months of June, July, and August. Same-day free tickets are available at

Break Time

The **South Buffet Room** in the Dirksen Senate Office Building is a convenient refueling spot when exploring Capitol Hill (☎ **202/224-7196**). Getting here is half the fun. Take the free subway that runs under the Capitol to this all-you-can-eat buffet. There's a carvery station featuring ham, roast beef, or turkey, plus several steamer trays with additional hot main courses, side dishes, a full salad and fruit bar, a wide choice of desserts, and beverages included in the price of admission. Finish the feast at the make-your-own sundae bar. The lunch buffet is $9.50 for adults and $6.50 for children under 12. Reservations are taken for large groups. MasterCard and Visa are accepted. It's open Monday through Friday from 11:30am to 2:30pm. High chairs and boosters are available.

the kiosk on 15th Street SW beginning at 8:30am. They're usually gone by 11am, so get up and at 'em extra early!

The bureau also prints Treasury bonds and White House invitations. Workers in round-the-clock shifts print about 22 million notes per day; that's about $77 billion annually.

Intaglio is not some new pasta shape but the process by which the bills are printed. Each sheet (plain old paper at the start) picks up color from ink-filled lines engraved in the heavy steel plates. The backs are printed first; the faces the next day. At the FBI, you'll learn that counterfeiting at this level is very difficult.

If you think pieces of eight were coined by Robert Louis Stevenson for *Treasure Island,* stop between 8:30am and 3:30pm at the Visitor Center, where you'll find the real thing as well as electronic games and video displays related to the "root of all evil." You may also purchase a souvenir bag of shredded green. The bureau is redesigning currency as protection against sophisticated counterfeiting technology. Next time you get a "new" $20 note (issued since late 1998), notice the 20 in the lower right front corner; green when viewed straight on, it's black at an angle. Cool! (Incidentally, the life expectancy of a $1 bill is 18 months. Easy come, easy go.)

Department of Interior Museum

1849 C St. NW. ☎ **202/208-4743.** www.doi.gov. Fax 202/208-1535. Free admission. Mon–Fri 8:30am–4:30pm; third Sat. of month, 1–4pm. Photo ID (driver's license, student ID, employment card). Closed federal holidays. Metro: Farragut West. Limited metered street parking. Ages 6 and up.

If you thought the Department of the Interior was a government decorating firm, do pay a visit here to see what the National Park Service, Fish and Wildlife Service, Geological Survey, Office of Territorial and International Affairs, and Bureaus of Land Management, Reclamation, Mines, and Indian Affairs are all about. Happy belated birthday to the department, which celebrated its 150th in 1999. Many aspects of their activities are effectively displayed in the museum's exhibits of Native American artifacts and crafts, mapping techniques, mineral specimens, and early land bounties (grants of land given in lieu of monetary payment for military service).

Children are drawn to the imposing buffalo head, sand paintings, wood carving, birch-bark canoe, baskets, pottery, and beadwork. They also enjoy viewing the 1930s-era dioramas, like the depiction of an Alaskan gold mine. Can they identify the tribes in the silhouetted scenes of Native American life? Special tours for kids 5 and older, in groups of three or more, must be made at least a month in advance. Across the hall in Room 1023, the Indian Craft Shop sells quality Indian pottery, jewelry, and other crafts Monday through Friday from 8:30am to 4:30pm.

Department of State Diplomatic Reception Rooms

23rd and C sts. NW. ☎ **202/647-3241.** Fax 202/736-4232. Free admission. Tours Mon–Fri 9:30am, 10:30am, 2:45pm, by reservation only. Strollers not permitted; leave them and kids under 12 at home. Closed major holidays. Metro: Foggy Bottom. Ages 12 and up.

Kids over the age of 12 who are interested in seeing a $30 million showcase of 18th-century and early 19th-century American furniture and decorative arts can take a fine arts tour of the diplomatic reception rooms on the eighth floor of the State Department. If you want to throw a fancy shindig, this is the place to do it. Secretaries of state, veeps, and cabinet members have all hosted bashes here. But no keg parties. Renovation has been ongoing since 1961, and the results are impressive. The terrace views of the Lincoln Memorial and Potomac River aren't bad, either.

Library of Congress

Capitol Hill, 1st St. SE between Independence Ave. and East Capitol St. ☎ **202/707-8000.** www.lcweb.loc.gov. Free admission. Mon–Sat 10am–5pm. Closed Dec 25 and other major holidays. Metro: Capitol South. Ages 10 and up.

The nation's library is also the world's largest. Established as a research center for Congress in 1800, the library's first collection, then housed in the Capitol, was burned during the War of 1812. The cornerstone for the Thomas Jefferson Building section, a formidable example of Italian Renaissance architecture, was laid in 1890, and construction lasted 11 years until it was complete. (When you're on the Hill, stop to see the exterior and Great Hall of the Thomas Jefferson Building, and enjoy the view of the Capitol from the west steps.)

Anyone over high-school age may do research or browse here, but unlike your public library at home you may not borrow the books. More than 500 miles of shelves fill the Thomas Jefferson, James Madison, and John Adams Buildings.

To get to the library's new visitor center, enter from First Street SE at Independence Avenue (sidewalk level).

The **Main Reading Room,** located in the Jefferson Building, underwent a 3-year, $81.5 million restoration about a decade ago. I think you'll agree that the **Great Hall** is a sight to behold, with its soaring arches, ceilings decorated with mosaics, and marble stairways cleaned to a spit-and-polish shine. In the Southwest Gallery and Pavilion on the second floor, you'll find **American Treasures of the Library of Congress,** a permanent exhibition of maps, rare books, and photographs. Among the treasures is L'Enfant's blueprint for Washington. Direct your youngsters to the contents of Lincoln's pockets the night he was assassinated.

The only way for nonresearchers to gain entry into the Main Reading Room is during the hour-long guided tour. But first, catch the video in the new theater. Tours are Monday through Friday at 10am, 1 and 3pm. Most kids 10 and older should find it interesting; anyone younger (unless they're especially precocious or bookish), *bor*-ing. Among the special collections housed in 20 reading rooms are children's literature and genealogy. The recently expanded gift shop invites browsers and souvenir collectors.

The **Gutenberg Bible** and **Giant Bible of Mainz** are displayed on the main floor, along with rotating exhibits of photographs, music manuscripts, prints, and posters. With very young children, skip the Jefferson Building tour and head for the Madison Building next door on 1st Street, between Independence Avenue and

Break Time

At the **Library of Congress Cafeteria** (☎ 202/554-4114 or 202/707-8300), located on the sixth floor of the Madison Building, you can relax and grab a quick bite to eat at this handsome cafeteria, which has a wall of windows overlooking the city. There's always a salad bar at lunch, as well as hot main dishes, carved meats, health food, pizza, fast food (fried chicken, burgers), deli sandwiches, and desserts— pies, cakes, and puddings. Prices for main courses range from $2.50 to $6.25. Reservations and credit cards are not accepted. It's open Monday through Friday from 9:30 to 10:30am and from 12:30 to 3:30pm.

The more formal **Montpelier Room** adjoining the cafeteria serves a marvelous $8.50 buffet lunch Monday through Friday between 11:30am and 2pm. Prime rib is featured on Friday. Reservations are required for four or more. MasterCard and Visa are accepted here. This place is definitely not for very young kids.

C Street SE. The **Copyright Office,** one of the library's departments, is located here. On the fourth floor, the copyright exhibit features one of the original Maltese falcons, masks from *Star Wars,* Bert and Ernie puppets, Barbie dolls, posters, and more! Visit anytime between 8:30am and 5pm.

The Pentagon

Arlington, Va. (across the 14th St. Bridge). ☎ **703/695-1776.** www.defenselink.mil. Free admission. Mon–Fri 9am–3pm every hour on the hour. Times may change, so call first. Enter at the tour window, next to the entrance to the Metro station. Those 16 and older must have a photo ID. Groups of 9 or more must reserve 2 weeks ahead. Metro: Pentagon. Ages 8 and up.

To avoid disappointment, get here by 8:45am in summer as the tours are usually full by 10 or 10:30am. The world's largest office building (3.7 million square feet) is the headquarters for the Department of Defense—that's the army, navy, air force, and Joint Chiefs of Staff. Any school kid can tell you it was named for its five-sided construction. About 22,000 people work here daily, occupying offices along 17.5 miles of corridors. Those who drive to work park in 8,770 spaces on the nearly 600-acre site.

If your kids are interested in the service branches' large art collection or portraits of Medal of Honor recipients, by all means bring them. Personally, I think it's rather dry stuff, and rest assured there's no way you or your kids will be admitted to the War Room or anywhere else that demonstrates what really goes on here. The decor is also less than inspiring; downright depressing, I'd say. If you still want to see it, despite my caveat, tours are available and may interest kids over the age of 8. If your kids are still talking to you afterward, take 'em to Pentagon City to shop and eat.

Now for the good news. Move over Michael Jackson; you have no monopoly on reconstructive surgery. The Pentagon is undergoing a $1.1 *billion* face-lift. Hey, Uncle Sam always has deep pockets for his pet projects. Section by section, the toxic lead paint and asbestos, decaying pipes, and inefficient heating system are submitting to a 14-year, stem-to-stern renovation. And the basement rat population is receiving a one-way ticket to oblivion. Let's see, according to my calculations the Pentagon should be shipshape by 2007. If they spruce up the tour in the process, it'll be well worth the bucks.

✪ Supreme Court

1st St. and Maryland Ave. NE, opposite the U.S. Capitol. ☎ **202/479-3000.** Free admission. Mon–Fri 9am–4:30pm. Closed holidays. Metro: Capitol South or Union Station. Ages 10 and up.

About 150 cases are heard annually by the highest court in the nation, empowered by Article III of the Constitution to ensure that congressional, presidential, and state actions comply with the Constitution.

In the imposing structure of classic Greek design, once thought too grandiose for its intention, the Supreme Court hears cases during about half the weeks from the first Monday in October through April. Only about 100 seats are open to the public, so arrive by 9am. Cases are heard Monday through Wednesday from 10am to 3pm, with a lunch-hour recess from noon to 1pm. While children are welcome in the courtroom, no disruptions are tolerated. This is serious stuff! Phone the information office (☎ **202/479-3211**) or consult the *Washington Post's* "Supreme Court Calendar" for the schedule.

From mid-May to early July, you may attend half-hour sessions on Monday at 10am, when the justices release orders and opinions. Older children will be fascinated by the many rituals attendant with the justices' entrance. You can tell them that "oyez! Oyez!" is French legalese for "Hear ye, hear ye."

Break Time

Hear ye, hear ye. The decision is out on the food in the **Supreme Court Cafeteria** (☎ **202/479-3246**): It may not be supreme, but it's appealing. Fresh-baked muffins are featured at breakfast; soup, sandwiches, main courses, salad bar, ice cream and desserts at lunch. There's also a carryout snack bar with homemade cakes and pies selling for under $2 per slice. Each Wednesday a different ethnic cuisine is featured. Main courses range from $2.40 to $4.95. Reservations and credit cards are not accepted. It's open Monday through Friday from 7:30 to 10:30am and 11:30am to 2pm. The snack bar is open Monday through Friday from 10:30am to 3:30pm when the court is in session.

When the court is not in session, you may attend a free lecture (9:30am to 3:30pm, every hour on the half hour) about Court procedure and the building's architecture. Follow up the lecture with a walk through the Great Hall and see the 20-minute film on the workings of the Court (☎ **202/479-3211**).

On the ground floor, take a look at the imposing spiral staircases and Court-related exhibits. There's also a gift shop on this level. From the top of the entrance steps, there's a wonderful view of the Capitol.

4 Other Museums & Archives

ARCHITECTURE

National Building Museum

401 F St. NW, at Judiciary Square, between 4th and 5th sts. NW. ☎ **202/272-2448**. www.nbm.org. Free admission. Mon–Sat 10am–4pm, Sun noon–4pm. Closed major holidays. Metro: Judiciary Square. Ages 10 and up.

Once you visit the former Pension Building, which somewhat resembles Rahway Prison on the outside, Roman bath and Renaissance palace on the inside, you'll know why this museum is dedicated to the building arts. It is the only U.S. institution dedicated solely to architecture, urban planning, design, engineering, and construction.

Statistics to stick in your suitcase: The exterior measures 400 feet by 200 feet. It took 15,500 bricks for the facade. (No, I didn't count them. I have my own Deep Throat.) The interior Corinthian columns are 75 feet high, 8 feet in diameter, and 25 feet in circumference.

The magnificence of the setting far surpassed the entertainment and starring players at an inaugural ball I attended here some years ago. In 1885, Grover Cleveland was the first president to hold an inaugural ball here. In case you're planning a future event and your family room doesn't cut it, the Great Hall is available for other than presidential social functions.

Several government agencies occupied the space between 1926, when the Pension Bureau vacated, and 1981, when Congress appropriated funds for restoration. The **Great Hall** measures 316 feet by 116 feet, and the ceiling is 159 feet high. That's about 15 stories. Take your kids without any fanfare; perhaps blindfold them first. If they're not impressed, bring 'em back when they're 18.

A permanent exhibition, **An Architectural Wonder: The U.S. Pension Building,** details the building's history and construction. **Washington: Symbol and City,** also a permanent fixture here, provides a comprehensive overview of the growth and development of the nation's capital. If your children are over 10 or have an interest in architecture and urban development, this is an excellent introduction to D.C.

More than 50 temporary exhibitions have been mounted since the museum opened in 1985.

Tours are conducted Monday through Friday at 12:30pm, Saturday and Sunday at 12:30 and 1:30pm. The Museum Shop, on the ground floor, has a broad selection of books on architecture along with gifts reflecting the theme of the building.

The Octagon (the museum of The American Architectural Foundation)
1799 New York Ave. NW. ☎ **202/638-3105.** Fax 202/879-7764. www.aafpages.org. Admission $3 adults, $1.50 students and seniors, free for children under 5. AE, MC, V. Tues–Sun 10am–4pm. Closed major holidays. Metro: Farragut West or Farragut North. Ages 10 and up.

Built in 1800 as a summer retreat for a family of wealthy Virginia planters, the Federal-style town house (not really a perfect octagon) was a temporary home for President Madison and the missus after the British burned the White House during the War of 1812. Madison signed the Treaty of Ghent here in 1815. Today, it's the headquarters of the American Institute of Architects, which built offices behind the house. The building is undergoing a major restoration that includes archaeological examination, and finds from the dig are on display. Walk-in tours of interest to kids 12 and older are continuous. Story times for kindergartners to third-graders are free with museum admission at 10:30am.

ARCHIVES & LIBRARIES

See also the entry for the Library of Congress in section 3 of this chapter.

Folger Shakespeare Library
201 E. Capitol St. SE. ☎ **202/544-7077.** www.folger.edu. Free admission. Mon–Sat 10am–4pm. Metro: Capitol South or Union Station. Ages 10 and up.

The 19th-century oil magnate Henry Clay Folger built this library for his vast collection of original First Folios and other rare books and manuscripts. Since opening in 1932, the Folger, whose neoclassical white marble facade is decorated with sculpted scenes from Shakespeare's plays, has been recognized as one of the world's most esteemed research libraries on Will (as he was known to his Elizabethan friends) and the Renaissance.

Anyone wishing to do research on 16th- or 17th-century European life—social history, geography, science, and law—need look no further. To become a "reader" (researcher) you must first call the registrar before gaining access to the library's materials (☎ **202/675-0306**).

The library is home to a gem—an authentic Elizabethan theater that is open to visitors when not in use for rehearsals or performances. The highly regarded **Folger Consort** performs here regularly, and Shakespeare's birthday (April 23) is celebrated with an open house every year on the closest Saturday. Free guided tours are given Monday and Wednesday through Saturday at 11am; Tuesday at 10 and 11am. Family performance workshops (like "Hamming it up with Hamlet") feature drama and improvisation for kids 8 to 14, some Saturdays from 10:30am to 12:30pm. Shakespeare-related activities for families take place Saturdays at 12:30 and 2:30pm. The charge is $10 per person. For information, call ☎ **202/544-7077.**

National Archives
Constitution Ave. and 8th St. NW. ☎ **202/501-5000** for information on exhibits and films, or 202/501-5402 for research information. www.nara.gov. Free admission. Day after Labor Day to Mar 31 daily 10am–5:30pm; Apr to Labor Day daily 10am–9pm. Closed Dec 25. Metro: Archives. Ages 6 and up.

If you have any doubts about the inscription on the statue out front—"What is past is prologue"—step inside the rotunda. The building is a classical structure with 72— count 'em—Corinthian columns designed by John Russell Pope, architect of the National Gallery and Jefferson Memorial. Each of the bronze doors weighs 6.5 tons, so don't slam 'em! Trivia fact no. 479: Because the building was built on Tiber Creek, which ran through the city, more than 8,500 pilings had to be driven into the ground before construction could begin. Take a gander first at the 1297 version of the Magna Carta, then at the Declaration of Independence, two pages of the Constitution, and the Bill of Rights. Every night our country's three "Charters of Freedom," already sealed in helium-filled bronze-and-glass cases, are lowered into a bomb- and fireproof 55-ton steel-and-concrete vault. During the day armed guards keep an eye on things, so kids will have to look elsewhere for show-and-tell souvenirs.

The National Archives is also the storehouse for five million photos (including Mathew Brady's Civil War snapshots), nearly 12 million maps, charts, and aerial photographs, and 91 million feet of motion-picture film. And talk about odd couples, the Archives has a photo of Elvis Presley and Richard Nixon at the White House in 1970.

Thousands of old newsreels can be screened in the motion picture, sound, and video branch on the ground floor, but you have to make an appointment first. Be sure to pick up an events schedule listing films, lectures, and workshops. I strongly recommend the free behind-the-scenes docent tours, appropriate for older school-age kids and adults, weekdays at 10:15am and 1:15pm. Tours last about 1½ hours. Call the tour office between 9am and 4pm and reserve well in advance (☎ **202/501-5205**).

Alex Haley began searching for his *Roots* here. So can you! Researchers must be 14, have a valid photo ID, and be accompanied by an adult. Call first for details and hours. Research and microfilm rooms are open Monday through Saturday, except for federal holidays. Use the Pennsylvania Avenue entrance and stop in Room 400 for advice before you begin your quest. Books and souvenirs are sold in the lobby museum shop.

You'll find **Archives II,** built to house the overflow from the main building, in College Park, Maryland. Aimed primarily at researchers (you must be 16 or older to enter), the new facility occupies a 33-acre site near the University of Maryland. Hours are Monday and Wednesday from 8:45am to 5pm; Tuesday, Thursday, and Friday from 8:45am to 9pm; and Saturday from 8:45am to 4:45pm (☎ **301/713-6800**).

ART

See also section 1 of this chapter for listings of the following art museums: the Freer Gallery of Art, the Hirshhorn Museum and Sculpture Garden, the National Museum of African Art, the Renwick Gallery, and the Arthur M. Sackler Gallery of Asian and Near Eastern Art.

Corcoran Gallery of Art

500 17th St. NW, at New York Ave. ☎ **202/639-1700.** www.corcoran.org. Suggested donations of $3 adults, $1 students and seniors, $5 families. Fri–Mon and Wed 10am–5pm, Thurs 10am–9pm. Closed Thurs, Dec 25, and Jan 1. Metro: Farragut West or Farragut North. Ages 8 and up.

Although Washington's oldest private museum is best known for its permanent collections of American 19th-century landscapes and impressionist art, and special exhibitions of contemporary art and photography, the first-floor double atrium and imposing marble staircase may impress your little ones more than what's hanging on the walls. When you enter, ask at the information desk for a brochure aimed at 6- to 12-year-olds intended to arouse their interest in specific artworks.

The free **Sunday Traditions Workshops** (☎ 202/638-3211, ext. 321), from 3 to 4:30pm (not every Sunday), introduce children from 4 to 12 years old to various aspects of the museum's architecture and contents. A typical program sends participants searching for different styles of columns and other distinguishing features of the museum's Beaux Arts facade. The budding Frank Lloyd Wrights then return to the classroom to create and embellish their own building out of cardboard and glue.

Tours are conducted daily except Tuesday at 12:30pm and Thursday at 7:30pm. The Corcoran School of Art offers a 4-year program to students of the fine arts and photography and offers studio classes for children of all ages. Inquire at the information desk or call for a catalog about the Children's Workshops and Young People's Program (☎ **202/628-9484**).

In the gift shop, you'll find children's books and educational trinkets as well as art books for all. For information on special and family events and group tours, call the education department (☎ **202/638-3211**, ext. 321, or 202/638-1439).

✪ National Gallery of Art and Sculpture Garden

On the north side of the Mall between 3rd and 7th sts. NW (entrances at 6th St. and Constitution Ave. or Madison Dr.). ☎ **202/737-4215**. Free admission. Mon–Sat 10am–5pm, Sun 11am–6pm. Closed Dec 25 and Jan 1. Metro: Archives or Judiciary Square. Ages 4 and up.

Those of you old enough to remember Ed Sullivan will recall his fondness for telling audiences, "This is a really big show." Well, the National Gallery is a really big show. Let's dispense with the details first. The East and West Buildings are connected by an underground concourse with a moving walkway. You can enter the West Building from the Mall (Madison Drive) or Constitution Avenue at 6th Street; also at 4th or 7th streets between Constitution Avenue and Madison Drive. The only aboveground entrance to the East Building is on 4th Street.

Baby strollers are available at each entrance. Information on special exhibitions, tours, lectures, films, and concerts are available at the art information desks in the West Building and the ground floor of the East Building. When there's a "really big show," go on a weekday before noon. Family guides and programs complement the special exhibitions (☎ **202/842-6249**).

If you're reading this and have just entered the museum, turn around and go outside again. By far the nicest thing to happen in Washington in 1999 (aside from the end of the Starr investigation) was the opening of the museum's Sculpture Garden. As my young niece says, "it's way cool." Most kids will find this a helluva lot more

---

Break Time

Café des Artistes (☎ 202/639-1786), at the Corcoran Gallery of Art, is a delightful addition to the downtown light-dining scene. In a gardenlike setting, choose from several cold main dishes, sandwiches, soups, and salads. The menu changes frequently, and the emphasis is always on fresh ingredients. You'd have to travel far to find a key lime pie as delectable. The kids (and you) will flip over the refreshing fruit slushes, especially on a hot summer's day. Main courses range from $6.95 to $10. Reservations are recommended on weekdays. Credit cards accepted include American Express, Carte Blanche, Diners Club, Discover, MasterCard, and Visa. It's open Monday, Wednesday, and Friday from 11am to 3pm, Thursday from 11am to 8:30pm, and Sunday from 11am to 2pm.

A Sunday Gospel Brunch, $18.95 for adults, $8.95 for kids 12 and under, is served from 11am to 2pm.

interesting than what's indoors. Amid indigenous plantings and trees, and a fountain that, we are told, will become an ice rink, a score of 20th-century sculptures have found a new home. And they should spark some interesting comments from your offspring. Wait till they see the giant *Typewriter Eraser,* headless figures by Polish-born Magdalena Bakanowicz, whimsical *Thinker on a Rock,* and concrete block *Four-Sided Pyramid.* Your kids may not "get" the inscrutable Noguchi work, *Great Rock of Inner Seeking,* but they're sure to flip over *Six-Part Seating.* Could I go on? Oh my, yes. But I'll leave further joys of discovery to you and yours. Let me know what you think.

When you're done perusing the Sculpture Garden, pick up a copy of "West Building Highlights" in the museum shops. It will help your family zero in on the galleries that will interest you the most.

The National Gallery consistently tops the list of the 10 most popular art museums in the United States, attracting more than six million visitors annually. The classically inspired **West Building,** another John Russell Pope creation, houses 12th- to 20th-century sculpture and paintings within its 500,000-square-foot interior. Industrialist Andrew Mellon's collection formed the nucleus, augmented by the sizable collections of Samuel H. Kress, Joseph Widener, Chester Dale, and numerous individual donors.

Bulletin! Bulletin! How would you like to focus on a favorite work of art from the comfort of a plush chair? Well, you can do just that in the museum's **Micro Gallery** by touching one of the 13 computer screens. Visitors are invited to focus on their favorite artist or a particular painting from the gallery's vast collection—even if it's on loan elsewhere. Zoom in, if you like, for a close-up of a minute detail or the artist's brush strokes. Best of all, you can enhance your family's visit and save time by charting your own course through the gallery with a computer-generated printout. You'll find the Micro Gallery near the Mall entrance of the West Building.

Here are a few suggestions in the West Building that may appeal to your children: the *Byzantine Madonna and Child,* Giotto's *Madonna and Child,* Filippino Lippi's or Botticelli's *Portrait of a Youth,* Raphael's *St. George and the Dragon,* anything by El Greco (kids think he's "weird"), Holbein's portrait of *Edward VI as a Child,* Fragonard's *Young Girl Reading,* Renoir's *A Girl with a Watering Can,* Copley's *Watson and the Shark,* and the Degas sculptures. They may like Winslow Homer, too, but you can definitely skip the Renaissance tapestries and furniture.

Do show them the bronze statue of Mercury on top of the fountain in the rotunda, then head for either of the lovely colonnaded garden courts. Under arched skylights, with comfortable upholstered chairs overlooking putti fountains, these courts provide sublime settings for resting museum-weary feet (and children).

Given its size and the breadth of its exhibitions, the West Building can be overpowering and bewildering to an adult. It'd be better to show the kids a few things here and then hightail it over to the less intimidating East Building.

The **East Building** is like a breath of fresh air, and if your kids see nothing more than the soaring ground-level central court with its three-story-high Calder mobile and vibrant (much-too-large-for-the-living-room) Miró tapestry, *Woman,* you will have accomplished something. Ask them if they recognize the shape of the building. It's a trapezoid, which architect I. M. Pei ingeniously divided into two interconnected triangles.

If you're traveling with kids between ages 4 and 8, pick up the colorful *Shapes + Patterns* booklet, a self-guided tour for children and their families. It's very well

Break Time

If you are trying see everything in the National Gallery of Art, you'll definitely need a break. And you won't have to leave the building to get it. Please note that in summer hours are usually extended. The National Gallery eateries accept American Express, Diners Club, Discover, MasterCard, and Visa. Anytime is a good time to head for the **Cascade Buffet,** open from 10am to 4pm Monday through Saturday and 11am to 3pm Sunday. The line moves quickly in this bright and cheery space, with seating for 450. It's located on the Concourse level between the museum's two wings. If you overslept you can grab a continental breakfast before beginning your tour. Breakfast is available Monday through Saturday from 10am to 11am. At lunch, create your own salad, choose a premade sandwich or one with hand-sliced deli meats from the carvery, or a hot main dish. There are passable hot dogs, burgers, and fries that pose no threat to Mickey D's, and a wide selection of desserts. Kids can make their own sundaes from frozen yogurt and varied toppings. Try to snag a table near the ersatz waterfall. The **Cascade Cafe** has a full espresso bar and also offers sandwiches, salads, and homemade gelato. Most prices are in the $2 to $6 range. Reservations are not accepted. The cafe is open Monday through Saturday from 10am to 4pm, Sunday from 11am to 5pm, extended hours in summer. High chairs are available.

The **Garden Cafe** (☎ 202/216-2494) is located on the ground floor of the museum's West Building. Come here to reflect, cool your heels, and have dessert or sample one of the chef's seasonal offerings amid the ferns. Eating is incidental to the pleasant surroundings. Most main courses range from $5 to $8. Reservations are accepted. It's open Monday through Saturday from 11am to 3pm, Sunday from noon to 4pm. High chairs are available.

The **Coffee Bar** (☎ 202/789-3201) is found on the upper level of the museum's East Building overlooking Calder's mobile and the Mall. Stop for a cold drink, espresso, and cookies before pressing on to another gallery. Belly up to this bar Monday through Saturday from 10am to 3pm, Sunday from noon to 4pm. High chairs and boosters are available.

---

done, and your little ones will sharpen their visual skills and learn a bit of geometry and spatial relations before they know what hit them.

Usually, kids are drawn to either the neatness of Mondrian's grids or the sloppiness of Motherwell's *splotches.* See what they make of the latter's inkblot, *Reconciliation Elegy.* Their answers should make for interesting conversation. Roy Lichtenstein's *Look Mickey* will strike a familiar chord, while Matisse's *Large Composition with Masks* enchants all ages.

From the upper level, climb the spiral staircase (it's only 25 steps!) to the **Tower level,** where special works are hung. Getting there is half the fun and kids enjoy discovering this "secret" place.

Don't leave without inspecting the **Concourse level.** Kids usually enjoy the moving walkway and the waterfall (really the overflow from aboveground fountains) next to the Concourse Buffet, good for a snack or meal Monday through Friday from 10am to 3pm, Saturday from 10am to 4pm, and Sunday from 11am to 4:30pm.

National Museum of Women in the Arts

1250 New York Ave. ☎ **202/783-5000.** Fax 202/393-3234. www.nmwa.org. Suggested donation $3 adults, $2 seniors and children. AE, MC, V. Mon–Sat 10am–5pm, Sun noon–5pm. Closed Thanksgiving Day, Christmas, Jan 1. Metro: Metro Center. Ages 8 and up.

Opened in 1987 after $8 million worth of restoration to the former Masonic Grand Lodge, this museum has more than 1,200 paintings, prints, and sculpture by 400 women spanning five centuries. In 1982 the museum's founders, Wallace and Wilhelmina Holladay, donated their collection and library—a cornucopia of art works by women spanning five centuries. Come for the permanent collection featuring artists such as Mary Cassatt, Georgia O'Keeffe, Helen Frankenthaler, Elaine de Kooning, Käthe Kollwitz, and Judy Chicago, as well as special exhibits and programs, and kids' events requiring reservations (☎ 202/783-7370).

Works with special appeal for young people include Noah's Ark in the mezzanine members' lounge and the story quilts by Faith Ringgold. A snappy self-guided tour workbook for 7- to 12-year-olds, "Artventure," is free at the information desk. Kids are invited to find decorative elements on the mezzanine, distinguish faux marble from the real thing, and examine portraits for the sitter's mood and occupation. At the information desk unearth the latest museum doings: storytellers, hands-on activities, and folksingers. Some Sundays during the school year, the museum hosts family programs. The museum's Elizabeth A. Kasser Wing, just east of the preexisting museum, has an expanded gift shop and two upstairs galleries, one dedicated to female artists displaying their works for the first time and the other devoted to sculpture. The Mezzanine Café is open for light fare Monday through Saturday from 11:30am to 2:30pm. Or grab a bite at nearby A.V. or Capitol City Brewing Company (see chapter 5).

○ Phillips Collection

1600 21st St. NW, at Q St. ☎ **202/387-2151.** Fax 202/387-2436. www.phillipscollection.org. Free admission weekdays, but contributions are suggested. Weekends $6.50 adults, $3.25 full-time students and seniors over 62, free for age 18 and under; additional charge for some exhibitions. Tues–Wed 10am–5pm, Thurs 10am–8:30pm, Fri–Sat 10am–5pm, Sun noon–7pm (summer noon–5pm). Free tours Wed and Sat at 2pm. Closed July 4, Thanksgiving, Christmas, and Jan 1. Metro: Dupont Circle, Q St. exit. Ages 6 and up.

The Phillips is a rich repository of impressionist, postimpressionist, and contemporary American paintings. Kids take to the intimate museum off Dupont Circle because it is homey (maybe not like your home, but homey nonetheless), with elegant furniture, polished floors, and Asian rugs. Most kids react favorably to the playfulness of Klee's works, the sunny colors and good feeling of Renoir's *The Luncheon of the Boating Party,* and the large color canvases of Mark Rothko. When you enter, pick up "A Child's Adventure into the Artist's World of Color," a guide for adults and kids 6 to 12 to use together.

The museum's education department offers two activities for families with kids between the ages of 6 and 12 to ignite their interest in art. **Art at Home** is designed to enhance a child's reaction to a work of art by, for example, writing a story or poem about a particular painting. In **Observation and Imagination,** children are encouraged to express themselves through various media. The programs are offered Tuesday through Sunday for groups of 5 to 20 and must be pre-arranged. If your family is small, hook up with another to meet the quota (☎ 202/387-2151). The Phillips also sponsors family workshops throughout the year. Call to be put on a mailing list (☎ **202/387-2151,** ext. 247). Although inappropriate for younger children, every Thursday from 5 to 8:30pm the **Artful Evenings** program includes a musical performance or gallery talk ($5). Grab a light bite in the cafe Tuesday through Saturday from 10:45am to 4:30pm and Sunday from noon to 4:30pm. The museum shop carries posters, postcards, and art books.

HISTORY

See also: section 1 for individual listings on the Smithsonian Building, the National Museum of American History, and the Anacostia Museum and Center for African-American History and Culture; all of section 2; all of section 3; the Octagon in "Architecture," above in this section; and the Folger Shakespeare Library and the National Archives in "Archives & Libraries," above in this section.

B'nai B'rith Klutznick National Jewish Museum

1640 Rhode Island Ave. NW. ☎ **202/857-6583.** www.bnai/brith.org. Free admission, but donations appreciated. Sun–Fri 10am–5pm. Closed Jewish and legal holidays. Metro: Farragut North. Ages 8 and up.

More than 20 centuries of Jewish history and culture are documented in the first-floor museum of B'nai B'rith national headquarters. Supplementing the permanent collection of religious books, Torahs, Judaic art, and ceremonial objects are special exhibits focusing on immigration, the Holocaust, and other aspects of Jewish history and cultural life. Visit the sculpture garden and the museum shop for books, ceremonial items, and crafts. It's open from 10am to 4:30pm. A family Hanukkah celebration is held every December, as well as a Family Fun Day on December 25. Family events take place throughout the year; call for information on specific events (☎ **202/857-6583**).

Frederick Douglass National Historic Site

1411 W St. SE. ☎ **202/426-5961.** www.nps.gov. Admission $3 for ages 7–61, $1.50 for age 62 and over, free for children 6 and under. Reservations required (☎ **800/365-2267** for families, or 800/401-4775 for school groups). Mid-Apr to mid-Oct daily 9am–5pm, mid-Oct to mid-Apr daily 9am–4pm. Closed Thanksgiving, Christmas, and Jan 1. Metro: Anacostia, then B-2/Mt. Rainier bus (8 blocks).

Abolitionist and orator Frederick Douglass purchased Cedar Hill, the 20-room Victorian home on the Anacostia, in 1877 after living on Capitol Hill for 5 years. Nearly all the original furnishings are on display. Among them are the rolltop desk in the study, where Douglass composed many of his speeches, and a picture of Abraham Lincoln over the parlor mantle. The dining room table is set with Douglass's china and sterling. In the upstairs bedrooms you'll find personal memorabilia—barbells, a typewriter, sewing machine, and the like—belonging to Douglass and his wife, Charlotte.

From the hill leading to Cedar Hill one can enjoy a sweeping panorama of the Anacostia River, Washington Navy Yard, Washington Monument, and Capitol.

A short film detailing Douglass's early years as a slave, his subsequent escape to the North, and lifetime achievements is shown in the visitor center. Self-educated, this civic leader, writer, publisher, and orator carved a significant niche in American history as a spokesman for the downtrodden and oppressed.

During February, which is Black History Month, films and special programs honor this unique individual. February 14, Douglass's birthday, is marked by a wreath-laying ceremony.

✪ Ford's Theatre and Lincoln Museum

511 10th St. NW, between E and F sts. ☎ **202/426-6924** for historic site, or 202/347-4833 for box-office information. Fax 202/426-1845. www.nps.gov. E-mail: Ford's-Theatre@nps.gov. Free admission. Museum daily 9am–5pm; box office daily 10am–6pm. Closed Dec 25. Metro: Metro Center. Ages 6 and up.

On April 14, 1865, Pres. Abraham Lincoln was shot by John Wilkes Booth while attending a performance of *Our American Cousin* at Ford's. Lincoln was carried to the house of William Petersen across the street, and the president died there the next morning. The incident was anything but good for business, and Ford's was not used again as a theater until 1968. In the interim, it was a records-processing site and Army Medical Museum before Congress coughed up the funds to fully restore the theater to its 1865 appearance.

A 15-minute presentation is given hourly in the theater. Then visitors are free to tour on their own.

Among the Lincoln memorabilia in the basement museum are the clothes Lincoln wore the night he was assassinated and the Derringer pistol used by Booth. Two of the more eerie items in the exhibit are the Lincoln life mask and plaster casts of his hands. Audiovisual displays describe Lincoln's early life, political experiences, and presidential years.

Several shows have gone on to Broadway after premiering at Ford's, and every December Dickens's *A Christmas Carol* is revived. Catch a performance at this historic theater if time permits. Sometimes, students with an ID get reduced-price tickets half an hour before curtain time. The theater is occasionally closed to visitors due to a performance.

To round out your picture of the events surrounding Lincoln's assassination, visit the **Petersen House** ("The House Where Lincoln Died") at 526 10th St. (☎ **202/ 426-6924**). It gives me the willies, but kids love it. Because the bed in the ground-floor bedroom was too short for his lanky frame, Lincoln was laid diagonally across it. The original blood-stained pillow makes a powerful impression on kids (and adults, too). In the front parlor, the clock is stopped at 7:22am, the time of Lincoln's death. In 1896, the government bought the house for $30,000, and now it is maintained by the National Park Service.

Old Stone House

3051 M St. NW. ☎ **202/426-6851.** Free admission. Wed–Sun 10am–4pm, with extended summer hours. House closed Thanksgiving, Dec 25, Jan 1, and other federal holidays. Gardens open daily. Metro: Foggy Bottom, then a 15-minute walk or take no. 30 bus from Pennsylvania Ave. Ages 4 and up.

Stop here when you're in Georgetown. Kids feel comfortable in this modest prerevolutionary house, probably because it's small like they are. Sometimes in summer, concerts are held in the garden, where you may picnic (as long as you clean up when you're through). A candlelight tour is held around Christmas. See "Kid's Favorite Events" in chapter 1 for more information.

U.S. Holocaust Memorial Museum

100 Raoul Wallenberg Place (15th St. SW). ☎ **202/488-0400.** www.ushmm.org. Free same-day tickets (usually gone by 10:30am) at museum box office for permanent exhibits. For advance tickets, call TicketMaster (☎ **202/432-7328**). Daily 10am–5:30pm. Closed major holidays. Metro: Smithsonian (Independence Ave. exit). Ages 10 and up.

When this museum opened in April 1993, I was among the skeptics who was certain it could not possibly measure up to the nearly suffocating advance media hype. I was wrong. The subject matter, architecture, and contents conspire to evoke a visceral reaction among visitors, regardless of religious or ethnic background. In fact, officials who track such things say that 80% of the museum's visitors are non-Jews. It would be easy to spend the better part of a day here. My personal limit is 2½ hours before I crave a brisk walk outdoors.

Public response has been overwhelming since the museum opened. Nearly two million visitors per year—inner-city children, Holocaust survivors, Iowa farmers, heads of state, bikers, and even an Indian chief among them—cross the cobblestones once part of the Warsaw Ghetto to gaze at the photographs of those who perished. The museum planners' intended purpose has been masterfully and pow-erfully realized. I strongly recommend a visit here, but with some reservations.

Do not bring very young children. Discuss the Holocaust with older kids before visiting. Suggested answers to typically asked questions are available at the infor-mation desk or by writing to U.S. Holocaust Museum, Communications Depart-ment, 100 Raoul Wallenberg Place SW, Washington, DC 20024-2150.

Mature 8 year-olds on up can, and should, see the first-floor exhibit **Daniel's Story: Remember the Children** and the **Children's Wall** in the lower-level educa-tion center. No passes are required to view these. Daniel's Story details a fictional but historically accurate German youth's odyssey from a comfortable and secure home in 1930s Frankfurt, to a 1941 ghetto, to the gates of Auschwitz. Visitors walk Daniel's path, literally and emotionally. While the experience is sobering and unset-tling, it stops well short of horrific. At the end, a short film reinforces the tragic message of a family's demise due to genocide. Young visitors are encouraged to express their reactions by writing down their thoughts with the markers and paper provided and posting their notes in a museum mailbox. *Note:* Although tickets are still required (as we go to press) to view the permanent exhibits, none are required for Daniel's Story or the Children's Wall.

The **Children's Wall,** opposite the Resource Center, consists of 3,300 tiles painted by American schoolchildren as a memorial to the more than one million children who died in the Holocaust. Taken as a whole, it is decorative and lovely in its simplicity. On closer inspection it elicits some of the most poignant feelings one experiences in this museum.

The **Permanent Exhibition** is housed on the fourth, third, and a portion of the second floors. The museum's planners, with input from educators and child psy-chologists, think youngsters 10 or 11 can handle the experience. I agree, but you know best what may or may not upset your kids. Along the way, 4-foot 10-inch walls shield young visitors from the most "difficult" exhibitions. Visitors entering the permanent collection receive an identity card with the name and family history of a Holocaust victim, whose fate can be traced during the tour.

After entering the Hall of Witness, visitors ride to the fourth floor to begin the tour. (The fifth floor, with its library and archives, is devoted to scholarly pursuits. High-school students are welcome to do research here between 10am and 5:30pm. Help is provided by library staff.) The fourth tower deals with the rise of Nazism from 1933 to 1939; the third tower with the persecution of minorities, ghetto life, and the death camps from 1940 to 1944. Part of the second tower details the lib-eration of the camps and refugees' resettling efforts. Young people take note: Also in the second tower space is the **Wexner Language Center** where you can learn about the Holocaust at your own pace through the user-friendly—if I can do it, so can you—interactive computer system, which uses photographs, videos, and oral histories.

After several visits, I still find the most powerful exhibits to be the huge photo-graph of American soldiers liberating a camp; the *Nazi Rise to Power* and other his-torical films; the Tower of Faces, photos of more than 100 shtetl families taken between 1890 and 1941 near Vilna (now Lithuania); the Anne Frank exhibit; a railcar that once stood on the tracks near Treblinka; Voices from Auschwitz (mem-ories of survivors); thousands of shoes from death camp victims; and artwork by children in Auschwitz. Whenever I visit it is solemnly, yet appropriately, quiet in the Holocaust Museum.

The Museum Shop contains books on the Holocaust, personal narratives, CDs, audio- and videotapes, and several shelves of titles for young readers.

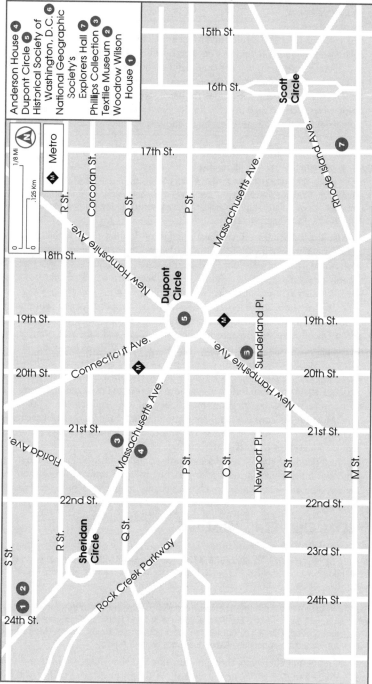

Anderson House ❹
Dupont Circle ❺
Historical Society of
Washington, D.C. ❻
National Geographic
Society's
Explorers Hall ❼
Phillips Collection ❸
Textile Museum ❷
Woodrow Wilson
House ❶

◆ Metro

1/8 MI
.125 Km

15th St.
16th St.
Scott Circle
17th St.
Corcoran St.
Q St.
P St.
Massachusetts Ave.
Rhode Island Ave.
R St.
18th St.
New Hampshire Ave.
Dupont Circle
19th St.
19th St.
Connecticut Ave.
Sunderland Pl.
New Hampshire Ave.
20th St.
20th St.
21st St.
Massachusetts Ave.
21st St.
P St.
O St.
Newport Pl.
N St.
M St.
Florida Ave.
22nd St.
22nd St.
Q St.
23rd St.
R St.
Sheridan Circle
Rock Creek Parkway
24th St.
S St.
24th St.

Break Time

The cafeteria-style **U.S. Holocaust Museum Café** is located in a light-filled annex adjacent to the museum and was once occupied by the Department of Agriculture, and (if you're interested) before that, the Bureau of Engraving and Printing. The limited menu is not kosher and includes sandwiches, fruit, desserts, and drinks—ideal for a between-meal pick-me-up or light lunch. Seating is available at several nondescript tables. Prices range from $2 to $8. Reservations are not accepted. It's open daily from 9am to 4:30pm. High chairs and boosters are available.

Woodrow Wilson House Museum

2340 S St. NW. ☎ **202/387-4062.** Fax 202/483-1466. Admission $5 adults, $2.50 students and senior citizens, free for children under 7. AE, MC, V. Tues–Sun 10am–4pm. Closed Mon and major holidays. Metro: Dupont Circle, then walk north on Massachusetts Ave. for 6 blocks to right at S St. Ages 4 and up.

The handsome Georgian Revival mansion just off Embassy Row in Kalorama is the only former president's residence in the District open to the public (the White House doesn't count). Wilson lived in this stately residence for 3 years after his second term, and his widow, Edith, resided here until her death in 1961. Since then, it's been maintained by the National Trust.

Visitors are surprised to learn that despite his stern appearance and demeanor, the former scholar and university president was just a regular guy—a movie buff who was a fan of Tom Mix, an early cowboy movie star, and subscribed to *Photoplay* movie magazine. On a more sublime level, you can see Wilson's inaugural Bible, the casing of the first shell fired in World War I, a White House Cabinet chair, and a vintage 1915 elevator. The 45-minute guided tour, Tuesday through Sunday between 10am and 4pm, offers insight into the private life of the man behind the wire-rimmed spectacles. Programs for school groups are available during the school year. **Meet the Wilsons** is a family program in which children 8 to 12 have tea and cookies after a scaled-down tour of the house, while younger siblings (4 to 8) are sent on a scavenger hunt. (Good planning!)

The Friends of the Wilson House sponsor the popular Kalorama House and Embassy Tour, which includes a stop at one or more ambassadors' private residences. The annual event is usually the second Sunday of September. For more information and to make reservations, call ☎ **202/387-4062,** ext. 18.

SPECIAL CHILDREN'S MUSEUMS

✪ Capital Children's Museum

800 3rd St. NE (at H St.). ☎ **202/675-4120.** Fax 202/675-4140. www.ccm.org. Admission $6 adults and age 3 and older, $4 seniors, free for children 2 and under. AE, DISC, MC, V. Daily Easter to Labor Day 10am–6pm, Labor Day to Easter 10am–5pm. Closed Easter, Thanksgiving, Christmas, and Jan 1. Metro: Union Station, then up the escalator at the rear of the station (parking garage), exit right onto H Street, follow hopscotch figures to bottom of bridge, go left at light, and cross H to the big brick building at 3rd and H sts. NE. Or, since this is not the best neighborhood, take a taxi outside the main entrance of Union Station (Massachusetts Ave.). On-site and street parking at the museum is limited. Ages 2–10.

How refreshing after filing through museums and shops filled with signs warning PLEASE DO NOT TOUCH, or YOU BREAK, YOU PAY, to visit this facility where you can tell your kids, "Go ahead, touch!" Yep, learning is strictly a hands-on affair for toddlers to preteens at the Capital Children's Museum.

In the **International Hall,** kids experience the culture of Mexico as they head south of the border and don Mexican clothes, make tortillas, grind Mexican chocolate beans, or do the Mexican hat dance. How adventurous they feel climbing the Mayan-style pyramid that grazes the ceiling. After their descent they can take off their shoes and socks to wiggle their toes in the sand of a Mexican beach.

In **Japan,** the newest permanent exhibit in the International Hall, children are invited to take a simulated ride on a Bullet train and explore a traditional Japanese home, removing their shoes before entering a Tatami Room for a tea ceremony. In the re-created school room they can try on a backpack worn by Japanese schoolchildren and dig their chopsticks into morsels more exotic than peanut butter and jelly. Taking their place behind the lunch counter of a Bento (food) shop favored by Japanese businesspeople, kids serve customers from a large selection of plastic foods. When the lunch traffic ends, the "help" can spend their earnings in the kimono or electronics store down the street.

What distinguishes this museum is that children learn by doing, experiencing things well outside their reach in the real world. In **Changing Environments,** for example, preschoolers can explore the underside of a city street, drive a bus, visit an automated factory, and navigate a maze.

Little hands can hunt and peck on a Braille typewriter, tap a communiqué in Morse code, slide down a fire pole, or send a message on a ship's blinker. A highlight tracks the history of communication, from Ice Age cave drawing to satellite-delivered data. The highly interactive **U-TV studio,** where aspiring anchors and producers can use the same state-of-the-art special-effects equipment used by the pros, is part of the exhibit on animation. After learning some behind-the-scenes secrets, kids will have fewer illusions about what they see on the tube. For this contribution alone, CCM deserves an award.

Lovers of animated cartoons won't want to miss **Chuck Jones: An Animated Life,** which features celluloids, animations, and original drawings of Bugs Bunny, Road Runner, and other Jones creations. Kids are encouraged to try the many interactive displays, among which are monitors for creating their own animated work. If you've ever wondered about the process from first sketch to finished animation, you've come to the right place.

A nursing and diaper-changing room is located on the first floor. Special weekend activities are open to all, and performances (frequently with audience participation) in the Storyteller Theater are ongoing throughout the year. Workshops and classes on animation, computers, and media arts are held in the MediaWorks center. If you visit spring through fall you may want to pick up sandwiches at Union Station and enjoy the museum's picnic area.

✪ Dar Museum

1776 D St. NW. ☎ **202/879-3241.** Fax 202/628-0820. www.dar.org/museum. E-mail: museum@dar.org. Free admission. Mon–Fri 8:30am–4pm, Sun 1–5pm. Closed Sat., national holidays, during DAR's annual meeting in Apr. Metro: Farragut West or Farragut North; walk south 7 blocks on 17th St. Ages 4–10.

Do not pass go, do not collect $200, just make a beeline for the New Hampshire Toy Attic on the third floor to see (but not touch!) 18th- and 19th-century children's furniture, toys, and dolls. Dollhouse aficionados will delight in the miniature furniture and accessories. To introduce young ones to early American history, 1-hour Colonial Adventure tours for 5- to 7-year-olds are held the first and third Sundays of most months from 1:30 to 2:30pm and 3 to 4pm. Groups of 2 to 15 are welcome, as long as they've made reservations well in advance (☎ **202/**

879-3239). Kids don colonial-style garb and visit a reproduction of a one-room house while imagining what it would be like to sleep in a trundle bed right beside their parents.

The **Touch of Independence** area is filled with touchable kid-size period furniture and old-style toys and dolls. A rectangular piece of wood that looks like a cutting board bears the alphabet and Lord's Prayer on a small piece of paper. This horn book, so named because a thin sheet of animal horn protected the paper from the elements, was once a child's introduction to reading. Guided tours of furnished period rooms are offered Monday through Friday from 10am to 2:30pm and Sunday from 1 to 4 or 5pm. Tours are self-guided before 10am and after 2:30pm. Call for special exhibition information (☎ 202/879-3241).

Discovery Creek Children's Museum

7300 MacArthur Blvd., Glen Echo. NW. ☎ 202/364-3111. www.discoverycreek.org. Admission $8 children, free adults. Family memberships are $50 a year. Sat 10am–3pm, Sun noon–3pm, by reservation. No drop-ins. Closed to general public (open to groups) Mon–Fri. No metro nearby. From D.C. take MacArthur Blvd. to Glen Echo Park and follow signs. Ages 6–12.

This nature-oriented museum geared to children between ages 3 and 12 occupies a former stable. The original museum—still open but to groups only—welcomed its first visitors in 1994 in a Civil War–era one-room school down the road. Since then Discovery Creek has garnered wide attention for its hands-on programs where kids can get down and dirty, for real.

Past activities have included "Wild Wonders of the Wetlands" (3 tons of dirt were dumped on the former horse paddock) and "Preposterous Plants" family workshops, nature stories for 3- to 5-year-olds; "Bone Voyage," where 7- to 12-year-olds examined fossils and assembled a skeleton; and "Earth Art," a 6-week course exploring design elements in nature.

The museum's family programs stress conservation and an appreciation of the natural world. To find out about upcoming events or for a copy of the museum's newsletter, call or write.

✪ Washington Dolls' House & Toy Museum

5236 44th St. NW. ☎ 202/244-0024. Fax 202/237-1659. Admission $4 adults, $3 seniors, $2 children under 12. AE, DISC, MC, V. Tues–Sat 10am–5pm, Sun noon–5pm. Closed Thanksgiving, Dec 25, and Jan 1. Metro: Friendship Heights. Ages 2 and up.

What a treasure house this is! I can't imagine any youngster from 18 months to 80 years not finding pleasure in this wonderland of exquisite dollhouses and antique toys and games. Founded by writer and avid dollhouse and toy collector Flora Gill Jacobs in 1975 with half of her personal collection, the museum has acquired additional space and numerous gifts from Jacobs and other donors over the years. Happy 25th birthday, doll-ing!

If learning were this much fun in school, all kids would bring home A's. The Dibb House is pure Victorian fantasy. The 1920s mansion by Tynietoy (the Rolls of dollhouses) sports an old radio and female figure with a "bob"; (notice how the playing cards are fanned out just-so on the parlor table). The Schoenut circus has nearly as many animals as the National Zoo. Viewing "A Shop Windowful of Shops" is like walking down a 19th-century Main Street. Lest boys think this is sissy stuff, show them the early Lionel electric train, shoebox-size dentist's office, Humpty Dumpty circus, and "The Ultimate Ark." They may not admit it, but they'll like the dollhouses, too.

In the second-floor shops, collectors will find books and magazines on dolls and dollhouses, furniture and accessories—even miniature quilt kits—and cases full of consignment dolls and toys.

A small Edwardian tearoom with potted palms, glass-topped tables, and an old scale that promises to deliver "honest weight one cent" is available for birthday parties by reservation for groups of 12 or more. The staff, in period dress, serve the young lady and gentleman guests sandwiches and sweets.

5 For Kids with Special Interests

AIRPORTS

Dulles Airport
Chantilly, Va. ☎ **703/572-2700.** Daily, 24 hours. Directions: Constitution Ave. to Theodore Roosevelt Bridge, Route 66 west, bear left and follow signs to Dulles Airport only. From Key Bridge, take Route 29 to Route 66 and follow the signs. Ages 6–10.

Visitors are welcome to tour Eero Saarinen's soaring masterpiece (recently renovated to twice its original size) and ride on a mobile lounge to the airfield. Pick up info for a self-guided tour at the information desk inside the main terminal. The drive alone is worthwhile, especially at dawn or dusk, but never during rush hour, to view this stunning example of avian architecture.

College Park Airport
1909 Cpl. Frank Scott Dr., College Park, Md. ☎ **301/864-5844.** Free admission. Daily 7am–10pm. Call at least 1 week ahead to schedule a tour. Metro: College Park, then walk 2 blocks. Ages 6–10.

The world's oldest continuously operating airport opened its doors—make that field—in 1909. Remember Wilbur and Orville? Well, they taught the first two army officers to fly here the year the field opened. Other firsts include the first testing of a bomb dropped from a plane (1911) and the first U.S. Air Mail service (1918). Wing it on your own and visit the recently upgraded museum (☎ **301/864-3029**), then get something to eat in the 94th Aerosquadron (☎ **301/699-9400**). Kids love this restaurant. It's decorated like a World War I squadron and faces the runway! They may be too excited to eat. Every September, the airport hosts a weekend Air Fair with airplane, helicopter, and hot-air balloon rides, displays, and children's entertainment.

FACTORIES

General Motors Baltimore Assembly Plant
2122 Broening Hwy. Baltimore, Md. ☎ **410/631-2112.** Free admission. Tours Mon and Thurs 9am and 6:30pm, except for several weeks in midsummer. Call and reserve 3–4 weeks ahead. Directions: Take I-95 north to 695 (Baltimore Beltway) east over Key Bridge. Go through the extreme right-hand toll booth lane (an automatic exit). Left at Stop sign (Broening Hwy.) to plant. Ages 10 and up.

If your kids are over 10 (or at least in fifth grade) and they can stand the grinding noise and smell of burning steel that's worse than anything in an orthodontist's office, press the pedal to the metal and hightail it up to "Bawlmer" (the local pronunciation) to witness the birth of a Chevy Astro or GMC Safari.

Visitors walk right through the 3-*million*-square-foot, unair-conditioned work area, amid the auto workers and heavy power equipment. On this 2-hour tour, be prepared for 2½ miles of walking! If you have trouble walking, call to make special arrangements. No canes, crutches, or wheelchairs are allowed. Neither are open-toed shoes or sandals. This isn't discriminatory; it's done for safety's sake. While we're on the subject of no-no's, no cameras or tape recorders are permitted. Foreign nationals must be preapproved.

On a good day, nearly 3,000 United Auto Workers at this GM plant play mid-wife to seemingly unrelated stacks of parts that exit the assembly line with frightening rapidity as living, breathing vans—about 47 an hour. Since tours are given only to groups of 10 to 25, carpool with another family or two, or ask GM if they can place you with a larger group.

THE MILITARY

See also section 2 in this chapter for individual listings on Arlington National Cemetery, the Korean War Veterans Memorial, and the Vietnam Veterans Memorial.

Marine Corps Museum

Washington Navy Yard, Building 58, 9th and M sts. SE. ☎ **202/433-3840.** Fax 202/433-7265. www.usmc.milhistorical.nsf. Free admission. Mon–Sat 10am–4pm, Sun noon–5pm. Closed major holidays. Metro: Eastern Market. Ages 4 and up.

With the exception of former marines, many visitors don't know this museum exists. The history of the corps is traced, from the John Hancock–signed commissioning papers of the first officer in 1775 to a skull-and-crossbones Sandinista flag from Nicaragua. The actual flag the marines raised on Iwo Jima (immortalized in the monument in Arlington, Virginia), is in Building 58. Kids gravitate to the Vietnam exhibit, which evokes images of Vietcong guerrillas and steamy rice paddies. Not just a repository for battle memorabilia, the small museum provides an overview of American history from our country's earliest days to the present.

Navy Museum

Building 76, Washington Navy Yard, 9th and M sts. SE. ☎ **202/433-6897.** Fax 202/433-8200. www.history.navy.mil. Free admission. Mon–Fri 9am–4pm, Sat–Sun 10am–5pm. Closed major holidays. Metro: Eastern Market, then a 15-minute walk—I'd take a taxi. Plenty of free parking on weekends. (During the week it's taken by the people who work here.) Ages 6 and up.

The history of the U.S. Navy is chronicled from the Revolutionary War to the present. New exhibits include "200 Years of the Washington Navy Yard" and "The Navy in the Korean War." Kids gravitate to the model ships and weaponry. They can turn a sub periscope, climb on cannons, and work the barrels of antiaircraft weapons. When they tire of war games, they can board the destroyer USS *Barry* berthed outside.

U.S. Navy Memorial & Visitor Center

701 Pennsylvania Ave. NW, between 7th and 9th sts. ☎ **202/737-2300.** Fax 202/737-2308. Free admission. AE, MC, V (in Ship's Store). Apr–Oct Mon–Sat 9:30am–5pm; Nov–Mar Tues–Sat 9:30am–5pm. Closed major holidays. Metro: Archives. Ages 6 and up.

There's more here than first meets the eye. After taking a family picture with Stanley Bleifeld's statue *The Lone Sailor* on the plaza, enter the below-ground visitor center, which is unmistakably shiplike. *The Homecoming,* another work by Bleifeld, welcomes visitors at the entrance. Throughout the Gallery Deck are interactive video kiosks. Push a button and learn about Navy history, or retrieve information on naval ships and aircraft. If you have friends or relatives who've served in the navy, see if they're registered in the Navy Memorial Log. If they're not, pick up an enrollment form.

At Sea, a lively, moving, action-packed movie, is shown Monday through Saturday at 10am, noon, 2, and 4pm; Sunday and holidays at 1 and 3pm. It's a winner! Admission is $3.75 for adults, $3 for age 18 and under and seniors.

Check out the **Wave Wall,** where 200 years of naval history are depicted in 13 panels, before picking up souvenirs in the Ship's Store, full of nautical gifts and memorabilia.

From Memorial Day to Labor Day, you may want to take in at least one of the armed forces' 8pm concerts in the outdoor amphitheater (weather permitting). Tickets are not required. Call ☎ **202/737-2300,** ext. 768, for dates.

MODEL TRAINS

All aboard! As you probably know, model trains are not just for Christmas anymore. Model railroading is a hotly pursued hobby, and several stations in the suburbs and farther afield enchant visitors with their minichoo-choo displays.

With your little cabooses in tow, try train spotting at the following locations.

B&O Railroad Museum

901 W. Pratt St., Baltimore, Md. ☎ **410/752-2490.** Admission $6.50 adults, $4 ages 3–12, free for children 2 and under. Open daily 10am–5pm.

Drive an hour, or get in the spirit and take a Marc or Amtrak train from Union Station or New Carrollton, Md., to Baltimore's Penn Station and this two-story kid-friendly museum of trains large and small. Button pushers of all ages are invited to start several of the model trains, then climb aboard a real locomotive in the 1886 roundhouse.

Ellicott City B&O Railroad Station Museum

Main St. and Maryland Ave., Ellicott City, Md. ☎ **410/461 1944.** Admission $4 adults, $3 seniors and students, $2 children. DISC, MC, V. Call for current hours. Take Colesville Rd. (Rte. 29/Old Columbia Pike) north from 495 to Rte 144 East (Old Frederick Road–Main Street). Follow signs to Historic District and museum. Short-term parking available on the street.

About an hour's drive from downtown D.C., the museum is housed in an old railroad station. Catch a glimpse of life in the 19th century at several seasonal exhibits: May to October (early railroad history), December to January (holiday model train display), and February to April (Civil War history in Maryland). My money is on the annual holiday event. On permanent display is an HO-scale model replica of the first 13 miles of the Baltimore and Ohio Railroad, the nation's first. When it opened in 1827 it ran from Baltimore to Ellicott City (then Ellicott Mills). You'll need a car to get here. If you wish to stay longer to explore more of quaint Ellicott City, park in one of the several metered lots within walking distance.

Fairfax Station Railroad Museum

11200 Fairfax Station Rd., Fairfax Station, Va. ☎ **703/425-9225.** www.fairfax-station.org. Suggested donation $2 adults, $1 children. Sun 1–4pm (permanent exhibit in caboose); model trains third Sun of every month. Directions: Rte. 123 South of George Mason University to Fairfax Station Rd., ¼ mile to museum. Free parking.

Visitors lay tracks for the N-gauge model train displays the third Sunday of every month. But *every* Sunday, the public is invited to check out the quaint train depot filled with Civil War and Red Cross memorabilia (Clara Barton nursed wounded soldiers at the original site after the Second Battle of Manassas). The caboose houses a permanent model train exhibit. The museum serves as a staging area for lectures, workshops, and craft shows. With a little advance planning, children can celebrate their birthday with a caboose party. A small gift shop features railroad and Civil War souvenirs.

Vienna Railroad Station
231 Dominion Rd., Vienna, Va. ☎ **703/938-5157.** Call for open house dates and times.

On the old site of the W&OD Railroad, members of the Northern Virginia Model Railroaders have set up a section of the Western North Carolina Railroad with HO-scale trains. Across the bike path is an old caboose that's ripe for climbing.

PHOTOGRAPHY

Kids who tire of posing in front of a camera from the time they're 20 seconds old until they hit puberty enjoy switching rolls, er, roles from takee to taker. Professional photographer Karen Keating, who teaches at Glen Echo Park's Photoworks and the Field School, says any inexpensive, lightweight point-and-shoot camera (even the preloaded throwaway kind) is sufficient for youngsters starting out. Most photography teachers concur that kids over the age of 6 find picture-taking a snap. The following children's workshops have exposed numerous budding artists. Maybe yours will be among them.

Fillmore Arts Workshop and Arts Camp at Fillmore Arts Center
35th and T sts. NW. ☎ **202/333-8340.** Fax 202/625-1543. Ages 6 and up.

This D.C. public schools' affiliate offers after-school photography classes, as part of a broad arts enrichment program, for ages 6 to 14. To reach the center in upper Georgetown, take any northbound No. 30 bus up Wisconsin Avenue from downtown. Hop off at T street. It's a short walk to 35th Street.

Photoworks at Glen Echo Park
7300 MacArthur Blvd., Glen Echo, Md. ☎ **301/229-7930.** Ages 10 and up.

Introductory classes are offered in picture taking and darkroom instruction for kids 10 and older.

THE POSTAL SERVICE

See also the National Postal Museum in section 1 of this chapter.

✪ Old Post Office Pavilion
1100 Pennsylvania Ave. NW, between 10th and 12th sts. ☎ **202/289-4224.** Free admission. Stores: Mon–Sat 10am–8pm, Sun noon–6pm. Restaurants: Mon–Sat 10am–9pm, Sun noon–8pm. Closed major holidays. Metro: Federal Triangle. Ages 6 and up.

While this is no longer a working post office, families love to come here to eat, shop, and enjoy the family entertainment. Do take a few minutes from your chicken wings and peanut butter fudge to inspect the impressive architecture. Built in 1899 as quarters for the federal postal department, it suffered years of neglect. The three-level renovated complex reopened in May 1984, thanks largely to the efforts of Nancy Hanks, a former head of the National Endowment for the Arts in the 1970s. Hanks spearheaded a campaign with the preservationist group, Don't Tear It Down, that lobbied Congress to curtail demolition plans and restore the building. Renovation began in 1978 and took 6 years to complete. The stage was once a dirt basement. You may get dizzy if you look up it's 196 feet to the skylight roof. Not bad, huh?

Please, if you do nothing else, tour the clock tower. The vista, from the equivalent of a high-rise's 12th floor, is astounding. On your way to the tower, stop on the 10th floor and check out the **10 Congress Bells,** replicas of those at Westminster Abbey. They range from 600 to 3,000 pounds, and each one is about 5 feet in diameter. In change ringing, the order in which the bells are struck changes continuously, and it takes nearly 4 hours to go through all the permutations. A full peal honors the opening and closing of Congress, state occasions, and national holidays. You may attend a practice session Thursday between 7 and 9pm, but I suggest calling first. Tours of the tower are conducted by the National Park Service (☎ **202/ 606-8691;** www.nps.gov) from 8am to 11pm in April through August and 10am to 5:45pm in September through March. Meet your guide in the lower lobby near the 12th Street entrance for a ride up, up, and away in the glass elevator. The windows on the 12th floor are covered with thin wires, so you don't have to be nervous about your little ones.

○ Washington, D.C., Processing and Distribution Center

900 Brentwood Rd. NE, between Rhode Island and New York aves. ☎ **202/636-2148.** Free admission. Tours daily (with at least 1 week's advance reservation) 9:30am–6pm. Metro: Rhode Island Ave. Ages 6 and up.

Kids who are at least 6 years old or in kindergarten are encouraged to put their stamp of approval on the facility where up to seven million pieces of mail are processed every day and 30,000 letters are postmarked per hour. They'll be dazzled by the OCRs (optical character readers) that scan nine addresses per second to make sure the ZIP codes and cities match. Call at least 1 week in advance to schedule a tour.

Most local post offices welcome visitors and provide a fitting introduction for preschoolers to the workings of the postal service. But be sure to call ahead (check the listing in the Blue Pages under U.S. Government, Postal Service). Of course, there's a lot more action at the major area processing centers (especially late in the day Thursday and Friday), where tours last about an hour. Besides the Brentwood Road facility, you might try the following processing and distribution centers: Dulles International (☎ 703/406-6600), Merrifield (☎ 703/698-6519), both in Virginia; Suburban Maryland (☎ 301/670-6000) in Gaithersburg; and Southern Maryland in Capital Heights (☎ 301/499-7600).

POTTERY DECORATING

Made by You

1826 Wisconsin Ave. NW. ☎ **202/363-9590** (3413 Connecticut Ave. NW. ☎ 202/ 363-9590). Mon–Sat 10am–9pm, Sun 10am–6pm.

I've actually observed kids sitting quietly, with smiles on their faces, for hours while decorating pottery in one of these storefront studios that have sprung up recently. What a great idea! Children can choose from more than 150 ready-made pieces (mugs, dishes, animals, and the like), then express themselves by painting designs on their selection. The studio provides the glazing and firing. The Kids Club has fixed-price projects Monday through Friday between 4 and 5pm. Other specials are in place weekdays. On a nasty afternoon, when they're bored out of their minds, this activity provides a welcome and worthwhile reprieve from listening to, "What are we going to do today? We're bored."

The studio fee is $7 per person for the first hour. Call about discounts and other specials. Made by You is also in Bethesda, Maryland (☎ **301/654-3206**), and Arlington, Virginia (☎ **703/841-3533**).

Also try:

- **Kiln Time,** 111 S. Alfred St., Alexandria, Va. (☎ **703/299-8989**)
- **Mud Factory,** 2772 S. Arlington Mill Dr. (The Village at Shirlington), Arlington, Va. (☎ **703/998-6880**)
- **Paint Your Own Pottery,** 10417 Main St., Fairfax, Va. (☎ **703/218-2881**)
- **Paint 'N Place,** Springfield Mall (upper level), Springfield, Va. (☎ **703/ 719-9732**)

SCIENCE & NATURE

See also section 1 in this chapter for listings on the following science museums: the National Museum of Natural History, the National Zoological Park, and the National Air and Space Museum.

Albert Einstein Planetarium

National Air and Space Museum, 7th St. and Independence Ave. SW. ☎ **202/357-2700.** www.nasm.edu. Admission $3.75. Daily 10am–5:30pm. Call for extended summer hours and show times. Closed Dec 25. Metro: L'Enfant Plaza. Ages 4 and up.

Three exciting out-of-this-world experiences await you in the first-floor planetarium of the Air and Space Museum. *Sky Quest,* geared to families with children between the ages of 4 and 8, takes youngsters on a voyage to the stars. It usually plays daily at 11am and 1pm. Children over 8 and/or with longer attention spans will enjoy the breathtaking photography of *And a Star to Steer Her By,* which surveys the history of navigation. The show runs every 40 minutes from 11:40am to 5pm (no show at 1 and 3pm). A free presentation, *The Stars Tonight,* airs at 3pm daily and shows what the night sky looks like during the season of your visit. If you want more, listen to a brief taped message about current stargazing conditions (☎ **202/357-2000**).

✪ Goddard Space Flight Center

Greenbelt, Md. ☎ **301/286-8981.** Free admission. Daily 9am–4pm. Closed major holidays. Directions: Take New York Ave. to I-295 North (Baltimore-Washington Parkway), turn left on Greenbelt Rd. (Route 193), turn left at Soil Conservation Rd., then left at the first gate. Ages 6 and up.

About a half hour from downtown, you can reach the stars in beautiful downtown Greenbelt. Kids over 4 are fascinated by the hands-on interactive displays. On the first and third Sunday of every month, bring your own or be an observer at the model rocket launch, an activity suitable for all ages.

General public tours, suitable for kids in fourth grade and above, are held Monday through Saturday at 11:30am and 2:30pm. A longer tour is conducted the second and fourth Sundays of the month at 11am and 2pm. The longer Sunday tour includes stops at the testing and evaluation center, where they check and double-check satellites and payloads. On Goddard Community Day, usually held in the fall, visitors are allowed to tour NASA facilities normally closed to the public. Bring lunch to enjoy in the picnic area, and pick up space-age souvenirs in the gift shop.

National Aquarium

Department of Commerce (lower level), 14th St. between Pennsylvania Ave. and Constitution Ave. NW. ☎ **202/482-2825.** Admission $3 adults, 75¢ ages 2–10 and seniors, free for children 1 and under. Daily 9am–5pm. Closed Dec 25. Metro: Federal Triangle. Ages 2 and up.

More than 1,000 specimens are contained in 50 tanks at the oldest public aquarium in the nation. Assorted salt- and freshwater fish, including sharks, eels, alligators, and Japanese carp, get along swimmingly. The piranhas—you'll be happy to learn—have their own tank. The sharks are fed Monday, Wednesday, and Saturday at 2pm; the piranhas are fed Tuesday, Thursday, and Sunday at 2pm. In the **touch tank,** kids can get their hands wet examining horseshoe crabs and other noncarnivorous beach-dwellers.

If you're in town on the designated Saturday in late July or early August, you won't want to miss **Shark Day.** A special shark feeding, exhibits, films, and face painting are part of the festivities.

Note: A large multilevel aquarium in Baltimore is also known as the National Aquarium, but the two are oceans apart in content and scope. See the Baltimore entry in chapter 10.

❂ National Geographic Society's Explorers Hall

17th St. and M St. NW. ☎ **202/857-7588.** www.nationalgeographic.com. Free admission. Mon–Sat and holidays 9am–5pm, Sun 10am–5pm. Closed Dec 25. Metro: Farragut North (Connecticut Ave. and L St. exit) or Farragut West. Ages 8 and up.

Before entering Explorers Hall, watch the short introductory videotape on the 16-panel screen to familiarize young trailblazers with the National Geographic Society's mission of "increasing and diffusing geographic knowledge." Permanent and temporary exhibits focus on ancient civilizations, human evolution, and global and space expeditions. Most exhibits are too sophisticated for kids under 8, but older children enjoy Explorers Hall for its relatively intimate size. Here, complex geographic information is explained at a level they can readily understand and appreciate by using the many interactive exhibits and videos, such as "Where did we come from?" (evolution) and "What's shaky and quaky?" (volcanoes). The fascinating geochron—world time map to the uninitiated—is shaded to show daylight and night.

Of special interest to toddlers is a replica of the late Jacques Cousteau's undersea diving bell, a huge globe with a waistline bigger than Daddy's (this equator measures a whopping 34 feet around!), and the suspended model of a pterandon, a nasty-looking flying reptile that lived 190 million years ago.

At the **Mammals Kiosk,** the touch screen reveals pictures of 700 animals and 155 vocalizations. Visitors are encouraged to "touch, play, and learn" while testing their trivial pursuit of geophysical knowledge in **Geographica,** where you can also feel a tornado and walk beneath a flying dinosaur. Experience orbital flight with loved ones in **Earth Station One,** an amphitheater that several times an hour simulates an orbital flight 23,000 miles above Earth's surface. *Note:* Large groups are advised to call ahead (☎ **202/857-7689**).

Your kids may have to drag you away from **Global Access,** an educational, fun-to-play video game. After picking a country you'd like to know more about, choose specific topics (history, culture, flora and fauna) from the menu. Voilà! Press a button and the living atlas knows all, sees all, and tells all.

In the **Television Room,** you can watch scenes from the society's enormously popular and instructive TV series.

Wouldn't your kids like to be on the cover of *National Geographic* magazine? Sure they would! Outside the TV Room are two photo booths where they can choose to have their face plastered on a postcard-size cover. This is one souvenir that won't soon be forgotten.

Gaze at the Washington sky overhead in the small planetarium, then take a gander at a nearly 4-billion-year-old moon rock. Pick up past and current copies of *National Geographic* magazine, a wide and interesting selection of beautifully photographed books for the whole family, intricately detailed maps, globes, and souvenirs in the society's book and gift shop.

Special exhibits usually change every few months.

National Museum of Health and Medicine

Walter Reed Army Medical Center, Building 54, 6900 Georgia Ave. at Elder St. NW. ☎ **202/782-2200.** www.natmedmuse.afip.org. Free admission. Daily 10am–5:30pm. Closed Dec 25. Metro: Takoma Park. Take a taxi 1½ miles to the museum or park for free in the lot. Ages 10 and up.

Former Surgeon General C. Everett Koop has spearheaded an effort to move this hard-to-find museum back to the Mall, its original site before moving uptown in 1972. With a little luck and a lot of money the concept should become a reality before our grandchildren are in college.

Meanwhile, older kids with a strong stomach and interest in medicine and/or pathology won't want to miss this. The museum has numerous exhibits of diseased, injured, and defective body parts, which I prefer not to go into. Of particular interest are Lincoln's skull bone and President Garfield's spine. Don't bring young children. They won't sleep a wink. Future physicians will appreciate "The Patient Is Abraham Lincoln," a computer program that allows them to administer treatment to the critically wounded 16th president. Information on drugs and AIDS is also exhibited. Call about group tours (☎ 202/782-2201).

National Weather Service

Sterling, Va. (near Dulles Airport). ☎ **703/260-0107.** Free admission. Tours Mon at noon, by appointment only. Directions: Theodore Roosevelt Bridge to Route 66 west to Dulles Toll Rd. to Route 28 north to Route 606 west 3½ miles. 7th grade and up.

Willard Scott wannabes who are at least in the seventh grade can tour this facility by appointment. Reservations several weeks in advance are suggested. Groups of two or more are welcome. It may not be around the corner, but it's surely worth the ride to find out why they have so much trouble forecasting the D.C. weather.

✪ Naval Observatory

Massachusetts Ave. at 34th St. NW (enter the South Gate). ☎ **202/762-1467.** www.usno.navy.mil. Free admission. Mon 8:30pm. Closed federal holidays. Ages 8 and up.

On a clear night, you can see forever at the Naval Observatory. You'll have stars in your eyes after peering through the huge telescope at celestial bodies 25,000 light-years away, weather permitting. Line up at least 1 hour before tour time. Only the first 90 people are admitted. The 1½-hour tour is first-come, first-served on Monday evening. Call before 5:30pm to see if it will be a "star-light, star-bright" night. On-street parking is limited and the closest Metro (Dupont Circle) is not so close. The N2 and N4 Metrobus pass by, but you might miss the show, as the buses are less than punctual after 7pm. I'd take a taxi.

✪ Rock Creek Nature Center

5200 Glover Rd. NW. ☎ **202/426-6829.** Free admission. Wed–Sun 9am–5pm. Directions: North on Connecticut Ave., turn right onto Military Rd., then turn right onto Glover Rd. Ages 12 and up.

Free planetarium shows are given weekend afternoons for kids 4 and older. A show for kids and adults that changes monthly is given weekends and Wednesday after-noon at 3:45pm. **Exploring the Sky,** cosponsored by the National Park Service and the National Capital Astronomers, is held one evening a month from April through November at Picnic Grove No. 13, Military and Glover roads NW. Since the time varies from month to month, call ahead.

Plenty of self-guided nature trails and hands-on activities distinguish this facility in the District's largest park. Guided nature walks, films, planetarium shows, and live animal presentations are scheduled throughout the year. Call ahead for specifics, and see the section on "Gardens & Parks" in chapter 7.

MEDIA

Newseum

1101 Wilson Blvd., Arlington, Va. ☎ **888-Newseum.** www.newseum.org. Free admission by timed-entry passes; distribution begins at 9:45am. Wed–Sun 10am–5pm. Metro: Rosslyn.

One of the more exciting blooms on the D.C. area landscape flowered in April 1997. Dedicated to journalism—what, where, when, and why—the Newseum cel-ebrates the press in 72,000 square feet of glass, chrome, and interactive displays. The compelling block-long **Newswall** is a nine-panel barrage of talking heads.

Underneath it, front pages of the world's leading newspapers shout at onlookers in black and white. Headline stories break on electronic bulletin boards in the lobby and on the Newswall. You can run, but you can't hide.

A 10-minute film, *What is News?,* assaults viewers with audiovisual vignettes of news-making triumphs and tragedies, expressing the museum's mission "to show the public how the press works, warts and all."

Visitors can mimic their favorite anchor in a broadcast booth and take home a souvenir videotape for $10. In the video booth, preserve your family's likeness on the cover of a national magazine ($5). You can also sit in on a news broadcast or participate in a talk show in the state-of-the-art studio.

Slip into the gift shop for a souvenir or stop by **News-Byte Cafe** off the lobby, where you'll share a snack counter with computers hooked up to the Internet. When the news gets to be too much, escape to the uncomputerized outdoor **Freedom Park** where a memorial honors journalists who were killed while on assignment.

For an overview of the museum, pick up one of the audio guides, available for $4. A family tour is one of the 48 permutations available.

The *Washington Post*

1150 15th St. NW. ☎ **202/334-7969.** Fax 202/334-4963. www.washingtonpost.com. Free admission, but reservations required. Tours Mon at 10 and 11am, 1, 2, and 3pm. Metro: Farragut North or McPherson Square. Ages 11 and older.

Aspiring journalists who are at least 11 years old or in fifth grade can tour the newsroom, composing room, and pressroom of this Washington daily. Walking tours are given on Monday by reservation. Don't expect to see the presses running. Because the *Post* is a morning paper, the action takes place while you're fast asleep.

Voice of America

330 Independence Ave. SW (enter on C St. only). ☎ **202/619-3919.** Free admission. Tours Mon–Fri 10:30am, 1:30, and 2:30pm. Call for reservations. Metro: Federal Center. Ages 12 and up.

Not far from the Air and Space Museum, the world's largest radio station welcomes those in the eighth grade or above to visit the downtown facility, where programs are broadcast worldwide on 26 channels in 42 languages! During the 45-minute tour you will see the control room, hear part of a feature show, view a short film, and perhaps catch the evening news in Russian. Foreign visitors, who outnumber Americans by a wide margin, are excited when they recognize broadcasters they listen to at home. Windows to studios are high, so don't bring kids under 10. (They'll be bored anyway.)

6 Organized Tours

For an easy way to see D.C.'s major attractions or when you're looking for something to do without wearing out the troops, take a guided tour. Ride one of the National Park Service's **Tourmobile trams** (☎ **202/554-5100;** www.tourmobile.com) and get off as often as you like—or not at all! This is the area's largest sightseeing operation and the only one licensed to make stops at attractions on the Mall. See "Getting Around" in chapter 2 for more information.

The **Washington/Arlington Cemetery tour,** which makes 25 stops, including 15 downtown attractions and the Kennedy grave sites, the Tomb of the Unknowns, and Arlington House at Arlington Cemetery, is $16 for adults, $7 for ages 3 to 11, and free for children 2 and under. In past years, between mid-June and Labor Day, a ticket purchased after 2pm could be used the rest of the day and the following day. (After 1pm the rest of the year.) Call to see if this special is being offered. The combined tour can make for a grueling day, and I wouldn't recommend it for kids under 10. Opt instead for the Washington *or* the Arlington Cemetery tour, and, perhaps, do Mount Vernon another day.

A **Twilight Tour** operates March through December. It leaves Union Station at 7:30pm June 15 through Labor Day, 6:30pm the rest of the year. It's $16 for adults and $7 kids ages 3 to 11.

You can also make tracks for an **Old Town Trolley Tour** (☎ **301/985-3020**), which has the advantage of pickup and drop-off service at many D.C. hotels, but the disadvantage of not stopping along the Mall. The 2¼-hour tour stops at or near 19 major attractions, and, like the Tourmobile, you may get on and off the trolley as many times as you like. The cost is $24 for adults, $12 for ages 5 to 11, and free for children 4 and under. The first tour is at 9am; the last reboard varies with the season.

Gray Line Sightseeing Tours (☎ **202/289-1995**) offers several tours—from 3 hours to 2 days—in and around D.C. and to destinations as far as Williamsburg and Charlottesville, Virginia. **Gray Line** departs from convenient Union Station and picks up passengers at some hotels. My kids—youngsters no more—still get nauseated or fall asleep after 20 minutes on a bus. I hope yours are different. I wouldn't try an all-day trip with preschoolers, who may view the confinement as an invitation to riot. The **Washington After Dark tour,** for my money, is the best of all. Lap-sitters will probably go to sleep, which is fine, while older kids will enjoy seeing the nightlit monuments, federal buildings, and Georgetown. Gray Line also offers a multilingual tour of Washington, departing from the tour company's Union Station terminal. Advance reservations are required (☎ **202/289-1995**).

On **The Tour** (☎ **202/639-0908;** www.flagship.discovery.com), small groups depart the Discovery Channel Store in the MCI Center, 601 F St. NW, daily at 10:30am and 1pm, to discover some of the wonders of the Gallery Place/Chinatown neighborhood. Along the way visitors meet history face to face at the H Street Chinese restaurant that was once Mary Suratt's boarding house. (If the name doesn't ring a bell, she was hanged for her part in Lincoln's assassination.) Other stops along the 90-minute tour route include the old Patent Office building, Treasury Department, and National Building Museum. Kids 10 and older with any interest in history might enjoy this. The tour is $7.50 for adults, $5 for kids 5 and under and seniors 55 and older. Call to reserve tickets.

Tour de Force (☎ **703/525-2948**) creates motor coach and walking tours mainly for incoming groups, but also arranges individual guides for families who prefer a private tour. Call for rates.

Independent guide Anita Allingham (☎ **301/493-8568**) leads a walking **Illuminated Night Tour** that includes stops at the Lincoln Memorial with its unobstructed view of the eternal flame marking John F. Kennedy's grave, the steps of the Jefferson Memorial to ogle the White House and Washington Monument, and the Kennedy Center rooftop for an unequaled panorama of downtown and beyond. The going rate is between $20 and $24 per person and is suitable for families with older children who are less likely to grow bored and restless. Anita is a pro, a D.C. native who's been guiding tourists around the nation's capital since 1976. She'll modify the evening tour to suit you and is also available for tailor-made walking tours (using Metro) and as a guide to Baltimore, Annapolis, and beyond.

A word of caution: If you're considering a small, lesser-known tour company, make sure the tour guides are licensed. A friend once signed up for a Monday tour of the White House with a fly-by-night operation. The White House is closed on

Monday. Let the buyer beware! You don't want to hear about Washington from someone recently arrived from Minnesota who makes up commentary along the way. (Also see "Getting Around" in chapter 2.)

And if you don't know which way to turn, the **Guild of Professional Tour Guides** (☎ 202/298-1474), an association of more than 200 licensed guides with 10 or more years' experience, will steer you toward a guide or company meeting your specific needs.

7 Exploring Georgetown

Walking is the best way to see Washington, which was carefully planned and laid out on a grid. It's easy to find your way around (see chapter 2), and once you get the hang of subdividing the District you'll blaze your own trails. Although the shortest distance between two points may be a Metrorail ride, you'll shortchange your kids and yourselves, missing some of D.C.'s charm and beauty, if you fail to explore what can only be discovered on foot.

Georgetown is the ideal neighborhood for strolling. Kids of all ages take to the unique hodgepodge of old and new. Visions of the past remain and invite exploration—the C&O Canal, historic buildings and homes, and lush parks. On the flip side, scores of up-to-date shops and restaurants line Wisconsin Avenue and M Street and fill Georgetown Park, a three-tiered enclosed mall.

Wisconsin Avenue and M Street is Washington's oldest intersection. Pierre L'Enfant and George Washington set out from this crossroad one frosty October morning in 1791 and traveled east to establish the boundaries of the future District of Columbia. During the 1870s, more than 500 canal boats brought limestone, coal, flour, and other raw goods to the mills, factories, and blacksmiths headquartered along the waterfront of the Port of Georgetown.

On weekends from spring through fall, Georgetown's permanent population of 11,000 (an interesting mix of government bureaucrats, students, merchants, and bluebloods) swells two- or threefold, making it a primo spot for people-watching—and a good reason to arrive aboveground. Given that the 272-block parcel in the city's West End boasts nearly 100 restaurants and bars, you'll never be more than a hop, skip, or a jump away from sustenance, everything from a humble burger to the haughtiest haute cuisine.

Copies of the **Georgetown Visitors Guide and Map** are free at the White House Visitor Center, 1450 Pennsylvania Ave. NW, or call the Georgetown Business and Professional Association (☎ **202/944-5295**).

Walking & Shopping Tour: Georgetown

Take a map and wear comfortable shoes; the area is hilly and some sections are paved with brick or cobblestone. Your kids will be so tired at the end of the walk, they'll sleep for 48 hours.

Start: Old Stone House.

Finish: Foggy Bottom Metro.

Time: 2 to 5 hours (2 hours if you don't eat or shop, up to 5 hours if you want to shop, eat, ride the canal boat, or take a cruise to Arlington).

Best Times: Weekdays.

Worst Times: Weekends, especially April through October—very crowded. If you go on a weekend, start before noon.

If you begin at the Foggy Bottom Metro station at 23rd and I streets NW, it's about a 15-minute stroll to the heart of Georgetown. Walk north on 23rd Street to Washington Circle and go left around the circle to Pennsylvania Avenue. Continue on Pennsylvania to the end and bear left at M Street. The Old Stone House is at 3051 M St. Or if you prefer, take any No. 30 bus on Pennsylvania Avenue (near Foggy Bottom Metro) to Georgetown.

1. **Old Stone House,** 3051 M St., the only prerevolutionary building still standing in D.C., was built in 1765, and the five rooms are furnished with items typical of the late 18th and early 19th centuries. It is open Wednesday through Sunday from 10am to 4pm (usually with extended summer hours). The real treasure on this site is the typical cottage garden behind the house. The garden is open daily, but the house is closed on Thanksgiving, Christmas, and January 1. Kids can run up and down the hilly lawn (no pesticides are used on the grass), and everyone can enjoy the magnificent flowers that bloom from early spring into October. The garden spills over with picnickers in warm weather.

   When you leave, cross M Street (watch the traffic!) to Thomas Jefferson Street, where film buffs will enjoy browsing for posters and other memorabilia at **Movie Madness** (1083 Thomas Jefferson). Then head down the hill toward the river. You'll see:

2. **The Georgetown,** a working canal boat, on your left. One-hour cruises depart several times a day between mid-April and late October. Stop at the National Park Service office in the Foundry Mall, 1055 Thomas Jefferson St., for tickets and information. You may prefer to detour along the canal towpath, a lovely place to stroll. The water's odor can get a mite strong in summer, but most of the time it's tolerable.

   When you reach the end of Thomas Jefferson Street, you've arrived at:

3. **Washington Harbour,** a large complex of offices, private residences, restaurants, and shops fronting the Potomac River. Don't trip over the two painters slapping blue paint on the pale brick (sculptor J. Seward Johnson strikes again!). At the bottom of the stairs is Johnson's Lunchbreak.

   ☕ **TAKE A BREAK**   Speaking of lunch, you could do worse than to fall into the splashy Sequoia Restaurant at 3000 K St. (☎ **202/944-4200**). Reservations are advised, as it's a top draw (and also top drawer!).

4. Walk along the promenade and, facing the water, you'll see **Theodore Roosevelt Island** straight ahead. The infamous **Watergate** and the **Kennedy Center** are to the left. The planes in and out of National need no introduction. **Key Bridge,** to the right, connects Arlington, Virginia, and Georgetown. At the far right of the promenade is Washington Harbour Park. Cruises to Old Town Alexandria aboard the *Matthew Hayes* leave the Washington Harbour dock, at the end of 31st St. NW, several times a day in season (see chapter 7).

   Exit the area onto K Street (under the Whitehurst Freeway) and walk west to 31st Street. Make a right at 31st and go 1 short block and left at South Street. Measure your fitness level as you climb the steep hill with attached homes banked on the right. Turn right at Wisconsin Avenue, the southern end of Georgetown's:

5. **Shopping district.** A few doors below M Street at 1075 Wisconsin is **Georgetown Tees,** selling souvenir shirts. Next door is **Peace Frogs** (1071 Wisconsin) with frog-festooned clothing and accessories. Ribbit. **Banana Republic** (3200 M St.) sells stylish and pricey casual wear in adult sizes. For your listening needs

Walking & Shopping Tour: Georgetown

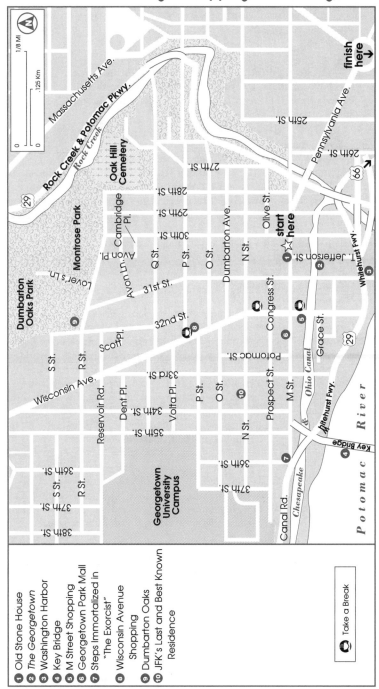

N

1/8 Mi
.125 Km

Rock Creek & Potomac Pkwy.
Rock Creek
Massachusetts Ave.
29
Oak Hill Cemetery
Dumbarton Oaks Park
Montrose Park
Lover's Ln.
Avon Pl.
Cambridge Pl.
Avon Ln.
27th St.
28th St.
29th St.
30th St.
Q St.
P St.
O St.
N St.
Dumbarton Ave.
Olive St.
31st St.
32nd St.
Scott Pl.
S St.
R St.
Wisconsin Ave.
Reservoir Rd.
Dent Pl.
34th St.
35th St.
Volta Pl.
33rd St.
P St.
O St.
N St.
36th St.
37th St.
Georgetown University Campus
Potomac St.
Prospect St.
M St.
Congress St.
Grace St.
Jefferson St.
Olive St.
start here
25th St.
26th St.
24th St.
Pennsylvania Ave.
66
Whitehurst Fwy.
29
Canal Rd.
Chesapeake & Ohio Canal
Key Bridge
Potomac River
finish here
Take a Break

① Old Stone House
② *The Georgetown*
③ Washington Harbor
④ Key Bridge
⑤ M Street Shopping
⑥ Georgetown Park Mall
⑦ Steps Immortalized in "The Exorcist"
⑧ Wisconsin Avenue Shopping
⑨ Dumbarton Oaks
⑩ JFK's Last and Best Known Residence

195

head to **Music Now Records** at 3209 M St. **Benetton's** two-story shop at 1200 Wisconsin Ave. (and M Street) devotes a portion of one floor to trendy fashions in kids' sizes.

☕ **TAKE A BREAK** Houston's (1065 Wisconsin Ave.), **Il Radicchio** (1211 Wisconsin Ave.), **Clyde's** (3236 M St.), **Burrito Bros.** (3273 M St.), and **Pizzeria Uno** (3211 M St.) are all within 2 blocks of Wisconsin Avenue and M Street.

Serious shoppers will want to inspect:
6. **Georgetown Park Mall** at Wisconsin Avenue and M Street. Among the 100 shops in the multilevel mall are **Fit to a Tee,** with the zaniest collection of shirts ever assembled in one place; **FAO Schwarz** for toys; **Benetton 0-12** for stylish kids' togs; **Record Town; Waldenbooks;** and good old **Mrs. Field's.** If it's been more than 20 minutes since you've eaten, there are a number of restaurants and cafes.

If you detour a few blocks and continue walking west on M Street to 36th Street, to your right you'll see the:
7. **Steps immortalized in both the film and book versions of *The Exorcist*.** Get back on track and continue your uphill exploration of:
8. **Wisconsin Avenue** along the west (left) side of the street. The **Original Levi's Store** at 1220 Wisconsin has jeans for big kids and adults. The inimitable **Commander Salamander** has leatherware, way-out fashions, T-shirts, and jewelry. If you're feeling adventurous, they'll spray a colored streak in your hair or make you up for free. At P Street and Wisconsin Avenue, **Another World** sells comic books and sports trading cards. On cobblestoned P Street, west of Wisconsin Avenue, remnants of the city's 1890 electric streetcar lines are visible.

See what the stars have in store or have your palm read by **Mrs. Natalie** before crossing at Volta Place for the downhill walk on Wisconsin Avenue's east side.
9. **Detour:** If you have the time and strength, continue up Wisconsin Avenue to R Street, and go right to **Dumbarton Oaks (museum and gardens)** between 31st and 32nd streets. Dumbarton Oaks was the site of the 1944 Peace Conferences. The small museum of pre-Colombian art and magnificent grounds never disappoint. Robert Woods Bliss and his wife, Mildred, avid collectors of pre-Colombian and Byzantine art, used Dumbarton Oaks as a country retreat between 1920 and 1940. They donated their collection and the property to Harvard University, which housed the art in eight glass pavilions designed by Philip Johnson.

All ages enjoy the formal gardens and grassy expanses on the 10-acre site. It's especially beautiful spring through fall when a riot of seasonal flowers blooms behind rows of boxwood hedges. There are 10 reflecting pools, nine fountains, a Roman-style amphitheater, and an orangery among the broad terraces and twisting paths to captivate the youngest in your entourage. (See "Gardens & Parks," in chapter 7, for more information.)

At 1319, **Betsey Johnson** draws well-heeled teens and their fashion-conscious moms for au courant duds. Farther on Wisconsin, you'll come across **Gap Kids** and **Baby Gap** (1267), **Olsson's Books and Records** (1239), **Hats in the Belfry** (1237), the two-story **HMV** record store (1229), and **Britches Great Outdoors** (1225), with good-looking garb for teenage boys and men (a lot of women shop here, too!).

☕ **TAKE A BREAK**   Anchoring the southeast corner at Wisconsin Avenue and P Street is **Thomas Sweet,** an ideal spot to take a break at an institution that's on the endangered species list (an old-fashioned ice-cream parlor).

Thank heavens for **Little Caledonia** at 1419 Wisconsin Ave. between O and P streets. With so many Georgetown businesses changing hands faster than the weather, this mainstay is still doing things right after more than 50 years. The shop's intimate toy nook specializes in stuffed animals and miniatures. A little farther down Wisconsin Avenue, stop and smell the flowers at **Peter's Flower Stand** (1365).

10. John F. Kennedy's last and best-known residence, 3307 N St. NW, was home to the Kennedys from shortly after Caroline's birth in 1957 until JFK's inauguration and move into the White House on January 20, 1961. JFK resided at seven Georgetown addresses between 1947 and his presidency. Take a slight detour onto N Street if you wish.

☕ **TAKE A BREAK**   Ready to take another break? Stop for a plate of pasta or pizza at the trendy **Il Radicchio,** 1211 Wisconsin Ave., where you pay a base price for each plate, unadorned, and extra for the accessories.

If the sun is shining and it's between 60° and 80°, why not dine alfresco? Pick up a sandwich or snack at one of the numerous carryouts—you can't beat **Dean & Deluca** for gourmet takeout at 3276 M St.—and picnic by (not in) the canal or in the garden behind the Old Stone House.

When you've had enough, you can catch any no. 30 bus (Shipley Terrace or Congress Heights) along Wisconsin Avenue or M Street back to Foggy Bottom Metro. Or, retrace your steps east across M Street—check out **Ben & Jerry's** ice cream (3135) and **Urban Outfitters** (3111) for on-the-fringe and off-the-walls clothing and home furnishings. For all the jocks on your team, the **Downtown Locker Room** stands at 3101. A few doors down at 3005 is **Déjà Blue,** with thousands of pairs of broken-in (okay, they're secondhand) jeans. On the south side of M Street, between 31st and Thomas Jefferson streets, you'll find a large **Barnes & Noble** booksellers at 3040 M. The megastore has a large children's section. At the same address is **Eddie Bauer** for sportswear and outdoor wear. **Animal Sensations,** at 2914, is a gallery with cartoon art and whimsical prints. Satisfy your sweet tooth cravings with a take-out sundae in a cone at **Café Café** at 2816 Pennsylvania Ave. Continue to Washington Circle, and bear right around the circle to 23rd Street and the Metro. Enjoy your nap!

7

Nature, Sports & Other Outdoor Activities

Museums are marvelous mind-expanders, but little people (and big people, too) grow restless after too much hard-core enrichment. To avoid fatigue and brain strain, temper periods of sightseeing with visits to places where kids can romp, roam, and let off steam. (We all know what happens to steam when it isn't allowed to escape.) You won't have far to look for a patch of park or grassy green because downtown and the environs are chock-full of open space, playgrounds, and recreational areas. And the largest front lawn in the neighborhood—the National Mall—is a Frisbee toss away from many downtown attractions.

1 Parks, Gardens & Other Wide-Open Spaces

GARDENS & PARKS

Aztec Garden

OAS Building, 17th St. and Constitution Ave. NW. ☎ **202/458-3000.** Free admission. Mon–Fri 9:30am–5pm. Metro: Farragut West.

Introduce your kids to the exotic banana, coffee, palm, and rubber trees growing on the Tropical Patio at the headquarters of the world's oldest organization of nations. Epitomizing the mission of the OAS is the Peace Tree, planted by President William Howard Taft in 1910. Walk to the back of the building for a display of seasonal plants around the dazzling blue-tiled pool. The fellow overseeing this lush scene is the Aztec god of flowers, Xochipilli.

Battery-Kemble Park

Chain Bridge Rd., between Nebraska Ave. and MacArthur Blvd. NW. ☎ **202/282-1063.** Free admission. Daily, dawn–dusk. Directions: Take Canal Rd., turn right onto MacArthur Blvd., then turn right onto Chain Bridge Rd. The entrance and small parking area are about midway between MacArthur Blvd. and Nebraska Ave.

In a residential area not far from the C&O Canal, this mile-long park boasts flowering dogwood trees in spring, a beautiful fall display of autumn leaves, and good sledding and cross-country skiing in winter. You can fly a kite, picnic, play football, baseball, or soccer on one of the fields, and take a nature walk.

✪ Brookside Gardens

1500 Glenallan Ave., Wheaton, Md. ☎ **301/949-8230.** Fax 301/949-0571. www.clark.net/pub/mncppc. Free admission. Daily sunrise–sunset. Conservatories open daily 10am–5pm; Visitors Center 9am–5pm; Gift Shop open daily 10am–4pm. Closed Dec 25. Metro: Glenmont then taxi. Directions: Take Georgia Ave. north from the Beltway, turn right on Randolph Rd.; after 2 blocks, turn right at Glenallan Ave. On-site parking.

A visit here is like a month in the country. Besides formal and natural-style landscaping on 50 acres (part of Maryland's park system), Brookside is known for its 11 types of gardens, azaleas, roses, and other seasonal displays. The theme for the Children's Garden changes periodically. In the past, children's programs for kids 3 and up have included Weekend Story Time in the Visitors Center, Saturday and Sunday from 2 to 3pm. As part of the Weekend Discoveries, youngsters are invited to take part in projects rooted around various plants and flowers. Call for information on these and other special events (☎ **301/962-1451**).

Take your kids into the Japanese Tea House and through the Mosaic Dragon Garden and Conservatories, filled with exotic plants, a wooden bridge, and waterfall ending in a tiny stream they can tiptoe across. Pick up the coloring book/brochure with games and information for the youngsters. Many of the 2,000 volumes in the horticultural library are geared to young people, but these must be used on-site.

The Visitors Center has classrooms, a library, workshops for schoolchildren and adults, and a 125-seat theater. The light sandstone building was made possible through a bequest from Elizabeth Turner, a Silver Spring secretary who loved to visit Brookside Gardens. The site, which received 30,000 visitors when it opened in 1969, now welcomes more than 300,000 a year. MasterCard, Visa, and personal checks are accepted in the Garden Gift Shop, Marylandica. Do visit, if time permits, but leave pets, food, and drinks behind.

C&O Canal National Historic Park

MacArthur Blvd. and Falls Rd., Potomac, Md. ☎ **301/299-3613.** Admission $4 per car; $2 walk-ins and bikers. Daily, sunrise–sunset. Directions: Take MacArthur Blvd. into Maryland and continue 4 miles beyond the Beltway. Park entrance is at intersection of MacArthur Blvd. and Falls Rd.

Okay, so it isn't in Washington, but if you have a car it's well worth the half-hour drive from most downtown locales. Go during the week or early on weekends, bring a brown-bag lunch, and plan to spend the better part of a day. Orient yourselves at the **Great Falls Tavern Museum,** a short walk from the entrance. Join a nature walk with a park ranger, take a **canal boat ride** (see "Rides for Children" later in this chapter) for an old-fashioned experience. The Park Service also conducts special programs, including hiking and bird watching.

Enjoy mother nature along the towpaths where you can jog or meander on your own. Be sure to cross the footbridges that lead to the **Olmsted Island overlook.** After Hurricane Agnes wiped out the area in 1972, the footbridges were restored and reopened, but not until 1992. The view is spectacular, and it's a great photo-op, but be forewarned: no pets, bikes, or picnics on the bridges. The cliffs attract rock climbers, and the river is favored for kayaking and fishing.

Don't even think of wading in the water, which is frequently rocky and turbulent below the surface. Every year several people drown needlessly because they ignore warning signs. Please, please watch your little ones near the canal locks. This is a good time to practice hand-holding with your junior trailblazers. Leashed dogs are permitted in the park (but not on the bridges), and there's a refreshment stand.

Washington, D.C. Gardens & Parks

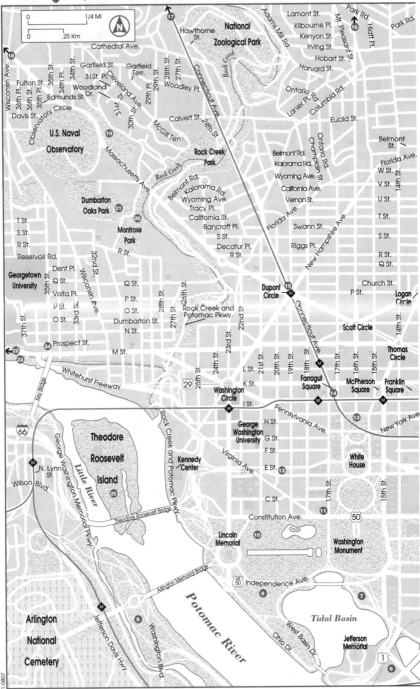

0   1/4 Mi
0   .25 Km

Cathedral Ave.

National Zoological Park

Hawthorne St.

Lamont St.
Kilbourne Pl.
Kenyon St.
Irving St.
Hobart St.
Harvard St.

Park Rd.
Mt. Pleasant St.
Hiatt Pl.
Park Rd.

Adams Mill Rd.
Connecticut Ave.
Rock Creek

Garfield St.
Garfield Terr.
Cleveland Ave.
Woodland Dr.
Woodley Pl.

35th St.
34th St.
34th Pl.
31st Pl.
28th St.
27th St.
29th St.

Fulton St.
36th Pl.
36th St.
35th St.
Edmunds St.
Davis St.
Observatory Circle

Wisconsin Ave.

U.S. Naval Observatory

Massachusetts Ave.

Calvert St.
McGill Terr.
24th St.

Ontario Rd.
Lanier Pl.
Columbia Rd.

Euclid St.

Belmont St.

Belmont Rd.
Kalorama Rd.
Wyoming Ave.
California Ave.
Vernon St.

Ontario Rd.
Champlain St.

Florida Ave.
W St.
V St.
U St.

14th St.

Rock Creek Park

Dumbarton Oaks Park

Montrose Park

Belmont Rd.
Kalorama Rd.
Wyoming Ave.
Tracy Pl.
California St.
Bancroft Pl.
S St.
Decatur Pl.
R St.

Swann St.

Riggs Pl.

T St.
S St.
R St.
Q St.

New Hampshire Ave.

Rock Creek

T St.
S St.
R St.
Reservoir Rd.
R St.

32nd St.

Georgetown University

Dent Pl.
Q St.
Volta Pl.
P St.
O St.

35th St.
33rd St.
Wisconsin Ave.

Q St.
P St.
O St.
Dumbarton St.
N St.

28th St.
26th St.

Rock Creek and Potomac Pkwy.

Dupont Circle

Church St.
P St.

Logan Circle

Scott Circle

Connecticut Ave.

37th St.

Prospect St.

M St.

27th St.

25th St.

24th St.
23rd St.

22nd St.

L St.
K St.
I St.

21st St.
20th St.
19th St.
18th St.
17th St.
16th St.
15th St.

Thomas Circle

Farragut Square

McPherson Square

Franklin Square

14th St.

Whitehurst Freeway

Washington Circle

Pennsylvania Ave.

New York Ave.

Key Bridge

66

Theodore Roosevelt Island

George Washington University

H St.
G St.
F St.
E St.

Virginia Ave.

Kennedy Center

White House

N. Lynn St.
Wilson Blvd

Little River

George Washington Memorial Pkwy.

Theodore Roosevelt Bridge

Rock Creek and Potomac Pkwy.

C St.

17th St.
15th St.

Constitution Ave.

50

Lincoln Memorial

Washington Monument

Arlington National Cemetery

Jefferson Davis Hwy.

Washington Blvd.

Arlington Memorial Bridge

Potomac River

Independence Ave.

West Basin Dr.

Ohio Dr.

Tidal Basin

Jefferson Memorial

1

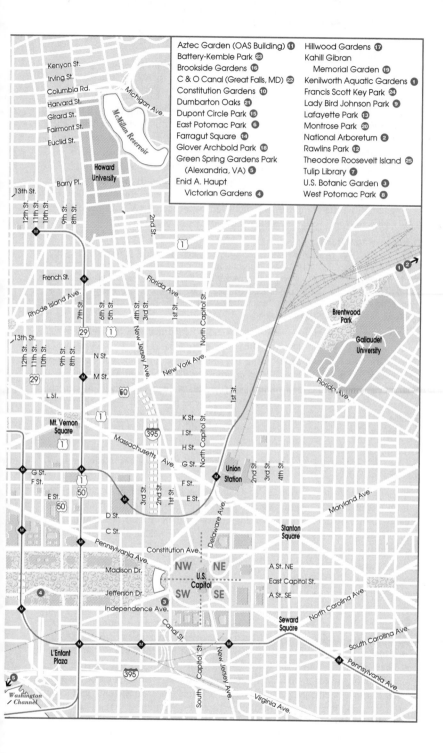

Aztec Garden (OAS Building) ⑪
Battery-Kemble Park ㉓
Brookside Gardens ⑯
C & O Canal (Great Falls, MD) ㉒
Constitution Gardens ⑩
Dumbarton Oaks ㉑
Dupont Circle Park ⑮
East Potomac Park ⑥
Farragut Square ⑭
Glover Archbold Park ⑱
Green Spring Gardens Park
   (Alexandria, VA) ⑤
Enid A. Haupt
   Victorian Gardens ④

Hillwood Gardens ⑰
Kahill Gibran
   Memorial Garden ⑲
Kenilworth Aquatic Gardens ①
Francis Scott Key Park ㉔
Lady Bird Johnson Park ⑨
Lafayette Park ⑬
Montrose Park ⑳
National Arboretum ②
Rawlins Park ⑫
Theodore Roosevelt Island ㉕
Tulip Library ⑦
U.S. Botanic Garden ③
West Potomac Park ⑧

✪ Constitution Gardens

West Potomac Park, Constitution Ave., between the Washington Monument and Lincoln Memorial. ☎ **202/485-9880**. Free admission. Daily, dawn–dark. Metro: Smithsonian.

Close to 100 baby ducks hatch here annually between late March and June, but very few live more than a day. Concerned citizens are lobbying the National Park Service to move the eggs to the safer, fish-free waters of the Reflecting Pool, where the babies have a fighting chance for survival. Your little ducklings are invited to feed the ducks, turtles, fish, and an occasional frog in the small lake of this park, which has walks, bike paths, and a landscaped island reached by a footbridge. Kids can sail small boats near the water's edge, but no swimming is allowed. Have a picnic—there's plenty of room on the 14 acres—and see the monument memorializing the 56 signers of the Declaration of Independence. The Vietnam and Korean War Veterans Memorials are in the western corner of the park.

✪ Dumbarton Oaks

1703 32nd St. NW (garden entrance on R St. between 31st and 32nd sts.). ☎ **202/339-6400**. Fax 202/339-6419. www.doaks.org. Admission $4 adults, $3 seniors and age 12 and under. Apr–Oct daily 2–6pm, Nov–Mar daily 2–5pm. Museum shop (☎ **202/339-6425**) open Tues–Sun 2–5pm. Directions: Take a taxi, or walk from anywhere in Georgetown; Foggy Bottom Metro is more than a mile away. Limited 2-hour on-street parking on R, S, and 32nd sts. *Very* limited on weekends.

Restless feet love to explore every inch of the 16-acre formally designed gardens that lie in the center of Georgetown. The winding brick paths lend themselves to spirited games of hide-and-seek. Spring is glorious when forsythia, narcissus, tulips, daffodils, and flowering trees bloom in profusion. The roses and wisteria flower in late spring and summer, and fall brings forth a showy display of foliage and chrysanthemums. Strollers are allowed but may be more of a hindrance because of the gardens' many steps and levels. No visitor to Washington should leave the city without stopping here.

Dupont Circle Park

Dupont Circle (intersection of Connecticut, Massachusetts, and New Hampshire aves. NW). Free admission. Daily, dawn–dark. Metro: Dupont Circle.

Sit, sun, or stalk the pigeons at Washington's largest circle park, or pick up food from one of the many nearby carry-outs and picnic on a bench. There's plenty of entertainment—intended and unintended—particularly on weekends. Some mighty serious chess games are played here, and you're welcome to watch as long as you don't kibitz.

✪ East Potomac Park

Ohio Dr. SW, south of Independence Ave. and south of the Tidal Basin. ☎ **202/426-6765**. Free admission. Daily, dawn–dark.

A one-way road outlines the 300-plus acres of man-made peninsula between the Potomac River and Washington Channel. Depending on who's counting, 1,200 to 1,300 cherry trees bloom in late March or early April. Today, fewer than 200 of the **original** trees survive. They are marked by bronze plaques. Most of the trees you see have been added over the years. The blossoms usually last 7 to 12 days; less if it's windy or there is a freeze. (See the West Potomac Park entry.) You can stroll, bike, or fish. A well-equipped playground at Hains Point attracts kids with its colorful climbing apparatus. Most are fascinated by the imposing statue of a half-buried figure known as *The Awakening*. The park has picnic grounds, a public swimming pool (☎ **202/727-6523**), 24 tennis courts (☎ **202/554-5962**), and one 18-hole and two 9-hole golf courses (☎ **202/554-7660**). Call for information on the permit you'll need to use the tennis courts.

Farragut Square

Connecticut Ave. and K St. NW. Free admission. Daily, dawn–dusk. Metro: Farragut West or Farragut North.

Noontime concerts are held some summer weekdays in this pretty park in the heart of D.C.'s business district. Brown-bag it on a nice day and watch the power bunch lunch.

✪ Glover Archbold Park

MacArthur Blvd. and Canal Rd. to Van Ness St. and Wisconsin Ave. ☎ **202/282-1063.** Free admission. Daily, dawn–dusk. Directions: Take Wisconsin Ave. north, turn left on Cathedral Ave., then left on New Mexico Ave. Park on New Mexico (with luck!).

The mix of towering trees, a bird sanctuary, and colorful wildflowers make this long and slender 100-acre park, which stretches south from Massachusetts Avenue to Canal Road, a popular destination for families. A 2-mile nature trail begins at 44th Street and Reservoir Road. There are plenty of picnic areas, too.

Green Spring Gardens Park

4603 Green Spring Rd., Alexandria, Va. ☎ **703/642-5173.** Free admission, but reservations and fees required for classes. Park: Daily, dawn–dusk. Horticulture Center: Mon–Sat 9am–4:30pm, Sun noon–4:30pm. Directions: From D.C., take 395 south to Duke St. west. Go about 1 mile to right at Green Spring (between Jerry's Ford and Salvation Army Thrift Shop), then 2 blocks into parking lot.

A new children's garden has a bathtub filled with a water garden. A pumpkin-shaped form supports vines with turtle-shaped rocks in the center. Check out the enchanting *flower* bed frame. (Get it? Flower bed?) Elsewhere on the grounds are two ponds with frogs and fish and an occasional blue heron. Canadian geese and ducks visit frequently. Budding horticulturists can learn the basics of gardening in classes geared to two age groups—Garden Sprouts (3 to 5) and Explorers (6 to 9). Adults can sign up for classes too. The 27-acre public park is filled with native plants, vegetable and herb gardens, and blooming and fruit-bearing trees. Adult classes too. Permanent plant displays are housed in the greenhouse in the Horticulture Center. Generous parents take note: You can rent the gazebo outside the 1760 manor house for your child's next birthday party.

Enid A. Haupt Victorian Garden

Between the Freer Gallery and Arts and Industries Building, 1000 Independence Ave. SW (also accessible from the Sackler Gallery). ☎ **202/357-2700.** Free admission. Memorial Day to Labor Day 7am–8pm; the rest of the year, 7am–5:45pm. Metro: Smithsonian (Mall or Independence Ave. exit).

Named for its philanthropic donor, this 4-acre minipark covers the underground complex housing the Sackler Gallery and Museum of African Art. In summer, the tea roses and saucer magnolias are spectacular.

An ideal rest stop when your family is museumed out, the Haupt Garden is for admiring, not stomping on. I found out the hard way when ordered by a uniformed gent to "Kindly get off the grass." Maybe your kids will be so impressed by the neatness of the 19th-century embroidery parterre, they'll take the concept home and apply it to their rooms. Seasonal flowers brighten the beds and spill from baskets hanging from the iron lampposts.

A handmade brass sundial was built by David Shayt and David Todd, two National Museum of American History staffers. At the dial's corners the four seasons appear as weather symbols. Can your offspring identify summer? (It's the Smithsonian sunburst logo.) If you're smart enough to read a sundial, whip out your protractor and make sure the gnomon is set at approximately 40°, Washington, D.C.'s latitude.

Kahlil Gibran Memorial Garden

3100 Massachusetts Ave. NW, opposite the British embassy. Free admission. Daily, dawn–dusk. Metro: Dupont Circle, then bus north on Massachusetts Ave. Directions: Drive north on Massachusetts Ave. about 1 mile past Dupont Circle. If you reach Wisconsin, you've gone too far. (Note: parking is scarce.)

This quiet, reflective garden is steps away from busy Massachusetts Avenue. It honors the Lebanese-born mystical poet who spent much of his life in the United States. Here he wrote thoughtful phrases that have been devoured for decades by college kids in search of the truth and themselves. Some of Gibran's pithier musings are inscribed in the benches near the main fountain. The bronze bust of Gibran is by Washington sculptor Gordon Kray. Make your pilgrimage on foot or by taxi; neighborhood parking is sparse and there's no Metro close by.

Kenilworth Aquatic Gardens

Kenilworth Ave. and Douglas St. NE. ☎ **202/426-6905.** Free admission. Daily 7am–dusk (park); visitor center closes at 4pm. Metro: Minnesota Ave. or Deanwood. Take the V2 bus to Kenilworth Ave. and Polk St. and walk 1 block to gardens. (This is not a good neighborhood to walk through, so you may want to take a taxi.)

When was the last time you saw an Egyptian lotus (said to be Cleopatra's favorite flower) Well, it is just one of the more than 100,000 water plants growing on 11 acres of ponds in this sanctuary. About 70 varieties of water lilies bloom in May and June. Except in the dead of winter, kids will see turtles, frogs, and small fish. Bring binoculars in spring; migrating waterfowl and songbirds are frequent visitors. If you come in the morning, you won't miss the night-blooming tropicals, which usually close by 10am. There are picnic tables and a playground, and tours are conducted Saturday and Sunday at 9 and 11am and 1pm.

Francis Scott Key Park

34th and M sts. NW, Georgetown. Free admission. Daily, dawn–dusk. Metro: Rosslyn, then cross Key Bridge on foot. Directions: Drive to Georgetown, park on street (good luck!) or in garage at Georgetown Park Mall (Wisconsin Ave. and M St. NW), and walk west on M St. to 34th St.

Key Park fills a once-vacant eyesore of a lot just east of the Georgetown side of Key Bridge, which connects D.C. and Rosslyn (Arlington), Virginia. Featuring a wisteria-covered pergola and bronze bust of Key by sculptor Betty Dunston, it is capped by a flag with 15 stars and stripes similar to the one that inspired Key in 1814 to write "The Star Spangled Banner" at Fort McHenry. A walkway and bike path from the C&O Canal are carefully integrated into the hilltop setting, which has a commanding view of the Potomac River.

Lady Bird Johnson Park

Adjacent to G.W. Memorial Parkway, Va. Free admission. Daily, dawn–dusk. Directions: From D.C., drive over the Arlington Memorial Bridge, take the G.W. Memorial Pkwy. south to and through National Airport, continue north on the pkwy. to Memorial Bridge and D.C.

Although considered part of D.C., the former Columbia Island is accessible only by footbridge from the Virginia side of the Potomac River. I don't suggest it. The best way to enjoy the sight—a must in spring—is to drive or be driven. The park was dedicated to Mrs. Johnson in 1968 to recognize her efforts at beautifying the city and the nation. More than 2,500 dogwoods and *one million* daffodils (I did not make this up) create a gorgeous blanket of gold in the spring. At the south end is a 15-acre grove of white pines, azaleas, and rhododendrons, designated as the Lyndon Baines Johnson Memorial Grove.

Lafayette Park

Between Pennsylvania Ave. and H St. NW, across from the White House. Free admission. Daily, dawn–dusk. Metro: McPherson Square.

Check out the statues of Andrew Jackson and Lafayette, whose heads are favorite roosting spots. Protesters, pigeon lovers and haters, bureaucrats, and people-watchers fill the benches and sprawl on the grass at all hours of the day and night. Depending on their ages, your kids might enjoy talking to the protesters or feeding some of the tamest squirrels in the area.

Montrose Park

R St. at Avon Place NW, Georgetown. ☎ 202/282-1063. Free admission. Daily, dawn–dusk. Directions: From M St., go north on 29th St., and turn left on R St.

What a honey of a spot this is! Come here to picnic, commune with nature, or ramble through the heavily wooded terrain. **Lover's Lane** (off R Street), which forms the western boundary, is a cobblestoned path that led to Baltimore in the 18th century. I don't recommend your trying to reach Charm City in this manner. Next door is Dumbarton Oaks.

✪ National Arboretum

3501 New York Ave. NE. ☎ 202/245-2726. Fax 202/245-4575. www.ars-grin.gov/na. Free admission. Open daily 8am–5pm; bonsai collection and Japanese garden daily 10am–3:30pm; gift shop Mon–Fri 10am–3:30pm; Sat–Sun 10am–5pm. Closed Dec 25. Metro: Union Station, then taxi; or Stadium-Armory; then take a B2, B4, or B5 bus to Bladensburg Rd. and R St. Walk east 300 yards to the R St. gate. Directions: New York Ave. (east) and enter the service road immediately after crossing Bladensburg Rd. Plenty of free parking.

Visitors are *tree*-ted to one breathtaking sensory experience after another at this 444-acre haven in northeast D.C., established by an act of Congress in 1927 to educate the public and do research on trees and shrubs. The arboretum is a special place and the staff is excellent, so most children, regardless of age, will enjoy a visit here. The **koi** (Japanese carp) outside the Information Center approach Brobdingnagian proportions, reaching nearly 3 feet in length and weighing in at 30 pounds. For 25¢ a handful, visitors can feed the fish. The lily pads are said to be sturdy enough to support a small child, but please don't try it—those koi have big appetites.

Worth a visit any time of the year, the arboretum is most popular from late March through October. In late April and May, the **azalea display** (about 70,000 at last count) draws large crowds. Kids can sniff the contents of the **Herb Garden** or become intoxicated in June and July when 100 fragrant varieties of roses perfume the air. The medicinal, dye, Native American, beverage, and fragrance gardens are of special interest to young people, as well as the knot garden with its dwarf evergreens. Some of the specimens in the **National Bonsai Collection**—a gift from Japan to mark our bicentennial—are over 300 years old! Don't leave without seeing the national Capitol columns, the only things salvaged from the Capitol's original facade after renovation of the central portion in 1959. You'll think you've wandered onto Washington, D.C.'s version of Stonehenge.

Note: This place is huge, so if you didn't drive (and this is one of the *few* places in D.C. where a car comes in handy) you should seriously consider the 40-minute guided tram tour, with several departures daily Spring through Fall. Buy same-day tickets at the tram kiosk. The fare is $3 adults, $2 seniors, $1 kids 4 to 16, and free 3 and under.

Rawlins Park

E St., between 18th and 19th sts. NW. Free admission. Daily, dawn–dusk. Metro: McPherson Square or Farragut North or West.

This urban park near the Corcoran Gallery gets passing grades most of the year, but when the magnolias bloom, it rates an A-plus. The statue is of Civil War general John A. Rawlins.

✪ Rock Creek Park

5000 Glover Rd. NW (Visitor Information Center). ☎ **202/282-1063.** Free admission. Open to vehicular traffic around the clock; on foot, dawn–dusk. Directions: Connecticut Ave. north to right on Nebraska Ave. Go 6 blocks into park's entrance and right at Glover Rd. (traffic light).

The leader of Washington parks celebrated its centennial in 1990, making it a full 9 years older than the Queen Mum. The 4-mile-long, 1,800-acre parcel fills the center of northwest D.C. longitudinally like cream cheese in a bagel. About 85% of Rock Creek, as it is informally known, is natural. And it is nothing short of fantastic. If you have the time I urge you to introduce your kids to some of its many wonders during your stay. But not after dark.

Nature Center and Planetarium   If time allows only one stop at Rock Creek Park, make it this one, at 5200 Glover Rd. NW (☎ **202/426-6829**), where kids will find exhibits pertaining to the park's natural history and wildlife, and meet a few of the latter. **Guided nature walks** and **self-guided trails** begin and end here. The center is open year-round, Wednesday through Sunday, from 9am to 5pm; closed holidays. Special **hikes, activities,** and **talks** geared to young trailblazers take place every month.

Stargazing   This dazzling activity is held once a month from April through November (April and May at 8:30pm, June through August at 9pm, September at 8:30pm, October at 8pm, November at 7:30pm), cosponsored by the National Park Service and the National Capital Astronomers. Meet at Picnic Grove No. 13, at Military and Glover roads NW. To receive the upcoming month's activity calendar, "Kiosk," call ☎ **202/426-6829.** The Park Service does a dynamite job with this program.

Pierce Mill   At this mill, near the intersection of Beach Drive and Tilden Street NW (☎ **202/426-6908**), kids over 6 can get a taste of early 19th-century life and watch millstones (powered by a waterwheel) grind corn and wheat into flour. Although the mill is open from 8am to 4:30pm on Wednesday through Sunday, most of the action takes place on weekends from noon to 2pm. You can buy the stone-ground flour/meal after your free tour. The corn makes wonderful bread! Weekday group tours are given by reservation. A short walk from the mill is the Art Barn, where local artists display their works.

Thompson's Boat House   Across from the Kennedy Center and Watergate, you can rent a boat here and paddle or row along the Potomac. Or hop on a bike, also available at Thompson's, and explore nearby Theodore Roosevelt Island (see the listing below).

Candy Cane City (Meadowbrook Recreation Center)   Located at Beach Drive and Leland Street, this recreation center lies across the border in Chevy Chase, Maryland, and is maintained by the Maryland National-Capital Park and Planning Commission. It's a favorite family destination and ideal picnic spot. Little ones can climb, swing, and slide on the playground equipment while older kids and parents play softball, tennis, or basketball (☎ **301/650-2600**).

Other Attractions   Here are a handful of the park's other attractions (call or write for more information and an indispensable map). A **1½-mile exercise course** for fitness freaks and joggers begins near Calvert Street and Connecticut Avenue NW. You can rent a horse or take riding lessons at the **Rock Creek Horse Center** (☎ **202/362-0117**) or blaze 11 miles of bridle trails. There is even a golf course off Rittenhouse Street (☎ **202/882-7332**). Fulfill your day's exercise quota and **hike** or **bike** your way through the park. Much of the signposted bike route running from the Lincoln Memorial through the park and into Maryland is paved and separate from traffic. On Saturday, Sunday, and holidays, Beach Drive is closed to traffic between Joyce and Broad Branch roads and Sherrill and West Beach drives. **Picnic** areas abound—some can be reserved; all require permits (☎ **202/ 673-7646**). **Tennis courts** at 16th and Kennedy streets NW must be reserved from April to November (☎ **202/722-5949**). Take kids into war games to see **Fort deRussey, Fort Reno,** or **Fort Bayard,** among the 68 forts built to protect Washington during the Civil War.

Theodore Roosevelt Island
Off G.W. Memorial Parkway, between Key and Roosevelt bridges on the Virginia side of the Potomac River. ☎ **703/285-2598**. Free admission. Daily 9:30am–dusk. Metro: Rosslyn (Va.), walk 2 blocks to the footbridge at Rosslyn Circle or take the Theodore Roosevelt Bridge to the George Washington Memorial Pkwy. north, park on the right, and walk over the footbridge. Or arrive by rented canoe or rowboat from Thompson's Boat Center (see "Boating" later in this chapter).

Except for the incessant roar of jets overhead, these 88 acres of forest, swamp, and marsh outlined by a rocky shore are pristine and Waldenlike. Hike along the 2½ miles of nature trails of this preserve, which was once inhabited by Native Americans and now memorializes the conservation efforts of Pres. Theodore Roosevelt. A bronze statue of the 26th U.S. president by Paul Manship and Roosevelt's prophetic words inscribed on granite stones can be found in the north-central portion of the island. Rabbits, foxes, muskrats, and groundhogs live in the woods, and you may spot a raccoon or two in the swamp. Bird-watchers have a field day, and so do the mosquitoes in summer—so bring plenty of insect repellent. You can also fish, but you can't picnic on the island, only on the grounds nearby. Depending on staff availability, there are guided tours on weekends, by appointment.

A handicapped-accessible fishing area is located near the island's entrance.

Tulip Library
Near the Tidal Basin between the Washington Monument and the Jefferson Memorial. Free admission. Daily during daylight hours. Metro: Smithsonian.

If you're in town in April and you like tulips, don't miss this dazzling springtime display. It's more colorful than the Fourth of July fireworks and doesn't make any noise. What beauty! Park Service gardeners *hand* plant 10,000 tulip bulbs from Holland every fall. Pick up a brochure from the wooden stand near the beds to help in your identification (about 100 cultivars annually) so you can add your favorites to your home garden. When the tulips fade, the beds are planted with annuals, making this an enjoyable spot year-round.

✪ U.S. Botanic Garden
1st St. and Maryland Ave. SW (foot of Capitol Hill). ☎ **202/225-8333**. Fax 202/225-1561. www.aoc.gov. Free admission. Daily 9am–5pm. Metro: Federal Center SW, and walk 3 blocks; also near the U.S. Capitol Tourmobile stop.

The U.S. Botanic Garden Conservatory is slated to reopen in late 2000 (betcha a Metrorail ride it'll be 2001) after a 3-year renovation, the first major facelift since the Conservatory opened in 1933. The changes include modernizing the electrical and plumbing systems, adding an Independence Avenue entrance, new interior and courtyard plant exhibits, expanding the gift shop, and (drum roll, please) air-conditioning.

No matter the season, I always find a visit here as refreshing as lemonade on a hot summer day. Tropical and subtropical plants, orchids, and seasonal displays—flowering bulbs, azaleas, and Easter lilies in spring; chrysanthemums in fall; peppermint-striped poinsettias around Christmas—dazzle the eye and lift the spirits. The Rose Garden, with more than 200 varieties in octagonal parterres, and Showcase Garden of indigenous mid-Atlantic flora, should be a spectacular addition. An Environmental Learning Center will feature plenty of interactive displays for the entire family, as well as a library, classroom, and outdoor amphitheater. The 80-foot-high Palm House, the former centerpiece of the Conservatory, was dismantled nearly 10 years ago for safety reasons. When it reopens it will be reincarnated as a tropical rain forest. I can't wait to see it. When you're done, be sure to cross the street to Bartholdi Park with its many theme gardens. Rest on the bench, close your eyes, and inhale the rose fragrance. The fountain was designed by Frederic Auguste Bartholdi, better known for sculpting the Statue of Liberty.

West Potomac Park

Approximate boundaries: Constitution Ave. to the north, Jefferson Memorial to the south, Potomac River to the west, Washington Monument to the east. ☎ **202/619-7222.** Free admission. Daily, dawn–dusk.

I'll bet if you ask 10 natives where West Potomac Park is, at least 9 won't know, even though the park takes in the Lincoln, Korean War, and Vietnam War Veterans Memorials, Jefferson Memorial, Constitution Gardens, and the Tidal Basin. The park's main claim to fame is its cherry trees, especially during the 2-week National Cherry Blossom Festival that runs from late March into April. You can write ahead for a schedule of events: National Cherry Blossom Festival, P.O. Box 33224, Washington, DC 20033-0224, or call the hot line (☎ **202/547-1500;** www.nps.gov).

Of the original 3,000 Yoshino trees, a gift from Japan in 1912, only about 200 survive. You'll find them on the north side of the Tidal Basin near the 300-year-old Japanese stone lantern. More of the delicate white- and pale pink–blossomed Yoshinos have been added over the years, and they still predominate, but they now mingle with Akebonos (single pale pink flowers) and the Kwanzan variety (double pompomlike blossoms of deeper pink). Blossoms last up to 2 weeks if Mother Nature has been kind. A total of about 3,300 trees bloom in East and West Potomac Parks, 1,300 Yoshino around the Tidal Basin alone. Start counting!

NATURE CENTERS

See also the Discovery Creek Children's Museum in "Other Museums & Archives," in chapter 6.

✪ Audubon Naturalist Society (Woodend)

8940 Jones Mill Rd., Chevy Chase, Md. ☎ **301/652-9188.** Fax 301/951-7179. www.audubonnaturalist.org. E-mail: HQ@AudubonNaturalist.org. Free admission. 40-acre nature sanctuary open daily dawn–dusk; building Mon–Fri 9am–5pm; bookstore/gift shop open Mon–Wed and Fri 10am–5pm, Thurs 10am–8pm, Sat 9am–5pm, Sun noon–5pm. Closed holidays. Directions: Drive north on Connecticut Ave., turn right onto Jones Bridge Rd., then left at Jones Mill Rd.

Kids can explore self-guided nature trails in this 40-acre wildlife sanctuary and learn about conservation and the environment in special programs. Activities are geared to children 4 and up, with day and weekend family programs, classes, and field

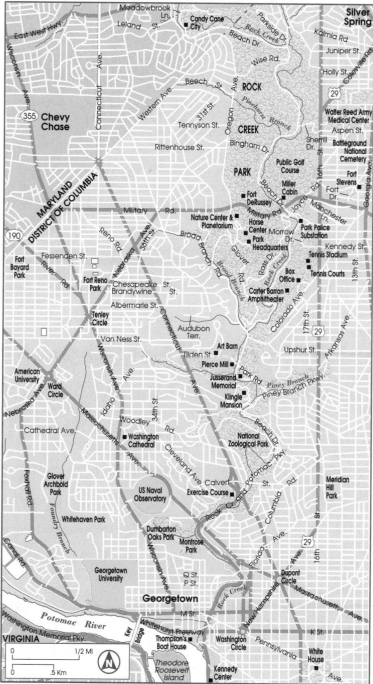

Silver Spring

East West Hwy.

Meadowbrook Ln.

Leland St.

Candy Cane City

Parkside Dr.

Rock Creek

Beach Dr.

Kalmia Rd

Juniper St.

Wise Rd.

Holly St.

Colesville Rd.

Wisconsin Ave.

Connecticut Ave.

Beech St.

Western Ave.

31st St.

Oregon Ave.

Pinehurst Branch

ROCK

29

Walter Reed Army Medical Center

Aspen St.

Sherrill Dr.

Battleground National Cemetery

355 Chevy Chase

Tennyson St.

Rittenhouse St.

Bingham Dr.

CREEK

MARYLAND

DISTRICT OF COLUMBIA

Military Rd.

PARK

Public Golf Course

Miller Cabin

16th Rd.

Fort Stevens

Fort Dr.

Georgia Ave.

190

Fort Bayard Park

Fessenden St.

Reno Rd.

Nebraska Ave.

36th St.

Broad Branch

Beach Dr.

Fort DeRussey

Nature Center & Planetarium

Horse Center

Military Rd.

Morrow Dr.

Park Headquarters

Joyce Rd.

Manchester Ln.

Park Police Substation

Kennedy St.

Fort Reno Park

Chesapeake St.

Brandywine St.

Albermarle St.

River Rd.

Glover Rd.

Ross Dr.

Rock Creek

Box Office

Tennis Stadium

Tennis Courts

13th St.

Tenley Circle

Van Ness St.

Connecticut Ave.

Audubon Terr.

Broad Branch

Carter Barron Amphitheater

Colorado Ave.

17th St.

29

Arkansas Ave.

American University

Ward Circle

Wisconsin Ave.

Idaho Ave.

34th St.

Woodley Rd.

Art Barn

Tilden St

Pierce Mill

Jusserand Memorial

Klingle Mansion

Park Rd.

Upshur St.

Piney Branch

Piney Branch Pkwy.

Nebraska Ave.

Massachusetts Ave.

Cathedral Ave.

Washington Cathedral

Cleveland Ave.

National Zoological Park

Beach Dr.

Glover Archbold Park

Foxhall Rd.

Foundry Branch

Whitehaven Park

US Naval Observatory

Calvert St.

Exercise Course

Rock Creek and Potomac Pkwy.

Columbia Rd.

Meridian Hill Park

Canal Rd.

Dumbarton Oaks Park

Montrose Park

Wisconsin Ave.

Georgetown University

Q St.

P St.

Florida Ave.

Columbia Ave.

29

16th St.

Dupont Circle

Georgetown

M St.

Rock Creek

New Hampshire Ave.

Massachusetts Ave.

Potomac River

VIRGINIA

Washington Memorial Pkwy.

Key Bridge

Whitehurst Freeway

Thompson's Boat House

Washington Circle

Pennsylvania Ave.

K St.

White House

Ave.

Theodore Roosevelt Island

Kennedy Center

| 0 | 1/2 Mi |
| 0 | .5 Km |

N

trips. For the latest stirrings, call the **Voice of the Naturalist** recording, updated weekly (☎ **301/652-1088**). The gift shop accepts Visa and personal checks.

✪ Rock Creek Nature Center

Rock Creek Park, 5200 Glover Rd. NW. ☎ **202/426-6829.** Free admission. Wed–Sun 9am–5pm. Directions: North on Connecticut Ave., turn right onto Military Rd., then turn right onto Glover Rd.

Plenty of self-guided nature trails and hands-on activities distinguish this facility in the District's largest park. Guided nature walks, films, planetarium shows, and live animal presentations are scheduled throughout the year. Call ahead for specifics and see "Gardens & Parks" in this chapter.

OUTDOOR SCULPTURE

If it hasn't already been done, someone should write a book on Washington's outdoor sculptures (please don't look at me). Here are a handful with special appeal for kids.

NATIONAL GALLERY OF ART'S SCULPTURE GARDEN   In 1999, this 6-acre sculpture garden opened on the Mall, just west of the gallery's West Building. You'll find it between 7th and 9th streets, Constitution Avenue, and Madison Drive NW. You'll practically trip over it during your Mall crawl. A pool (no swimming allowed) and large native shade trees provide battle-weary tourists a respite from the summer heat. And it's another place for the children to let off steam. The plantings are lovely, and all the heavy metal ain't exactly chopped liver. (For information on the sculptures, see chapter 6.)

ALBERT EINSTEIN   Nestled in the gardens of the National Academy of Sciences at 2101 Constitution Ave. NW, his comfortable-looking lap invites little ones to climb up and rest a while.

THE AWAKENING   Located at Hains Point in East Potomac Park, this is a sort of scary giant struggling to free himself from the ground. Don't worry, he can't hurt you.

In 1993, after a car ran into the reclining figure, the 17-foot arm had to be reattached. Doctor/sculptor Seward Johnson performed the extensive surgery.

GIANT COOTIE BUG   The cootie welcomes visitors to the Capital Children's Museum, 800 3rd St. NE. Be careful it doesn't catch you!

THE LANSBURG EAGLE   No relation to the bald eagle, the Lansburgh Eagle, all 800 pounds, landed with the help of a crane at 8th and E streets NW in March 1992. At last report it was still resting comfortably in the Pennsylvania Quarter's courtyard.

THE LONE SAILOR   He stands windblown at the U.S. Navy Memorial and Visitor Center at Market Square, Pennsylvania Avenue and 7th Street NW, where military bands give concerts on summer evenings.

LUNCHBREAK   Located at Washington Harbour, 30th and K streets NW in Georgetown, is an overalled workman enjoying lunch on a park bench, and he looks like he's for real.

MAN CONTROLLING TRADE   If I had sculpted this, I would have called it "Whoa, horsey." There are actually two of Michael Lantz's massive equestrian works mirroring each other on the east end of the Federal Trade Commission Building at Pennsylvania Avenue and 6th Street NW (the point of the Federal Triangle). One faces Constitution Avenue, the other Pennsylvania Avenue.

NATIONAL LAW ENFORCEMENT OFFICERS MEMORIAL   The bronze lions by Washington sculptor Ray Kaskey are grouped majestically around the Judiciary Square memorial to the officers who died on duty from 1794 to the present. The memorial is in the vicinity of the National Building Museum, 4th and F streets NW.

FARMS

Claude Moore Colonial Farm at Turkey Run

6310 Georgetown Pike, McLean, Va. ☎ **703/442-7557.** Admission $2 adults, $1 ages 3–12 and seniors; special events $3 adults, $1.50 ages 3–12 and seniors. Large groups should call ahead. Apr to mid-Dec Wed–Sun 10am–4:30pm. Closed mid-Dec to Mar, Thanksgiving, and rainy days. Directions: Beltway to Exit 13 (Route 193 east), go 2½ miles to the marked access road on the left to the farm, or take the G.W. Pkwy. to Rte. 123 south, go 1 mile, turn right to Rte. 193, then right into the marked access road to the farm.

If your kids complain that they have it rough, take them to see how their colonial forebears lived. Watch a poor colonial family (Park Service staff) in period dress split logs, make clothes, and tend livestock. The one-room house is a real eye-opener. Go on a weekday if possible. Special events are ongoing throughout the year, such as 18th-century market fairs in May, July, and October. If you live in the area, ask about the volunteer program for kids 10 and older.

✪ Oxon Hill Farm

6411 Oxon Hill Rd., Oxon Hill, Md. ☎ **301/839-1177.** Free admission. Daily 9am–5pm. Directions: Beltway to Exit 3A (Indian Head Hwy. south), turn right at first intersection, right onto Oxon Hill Rd., and follow it to the farm on the right.

Activities abound at this working farm from around 1900, operated by the Park Service. Little ones can pet the animals while older siblings learn about farm life by watching seasonal demonstrations of cider pressing, corn harvesting, and sheep shearing. A cow-milking demonstration is at 10am, 10:30am, and 3:30pm. The chicken feeding and egg gathering take place at 11am. A highlight of the self-guided nature walk is the stunning panorama of the Potomac River, Washington, and Virginia. For group reservations, call weekdays between 2:30 and 4pm (☎ **301/839-1176**).

2 Outdoor Activities

BIKING

The area abounds with off-road bike paths. The nicest thing to happen to local cyclists in many moons was the opening of the **Capital Crescent Trail** between Georgetown and Bethesda, Maryland. The route is paved and follows an old railroad right-of-way through scenic wooded areas. For more information, call ☎ **202/ 234-4874.** Other major trails include the **C&O Canal Towpath,** 23 miles from Georgetown to Seneca, Maryland; **George Washington Memorial Parkway,** from the Virginia side of Memorial Bridge through downtown Alexandria, ending at Mount Vernon; and **Rock Creek Park,** north from the famous and infamous Watergate through northwest D.C., past the zoo, and along Beach Drive into Maryland. Parts of the route along Beach Drive are closed to traffic on weekends (see the entry on Rock Creek Park in "Parks, Gardens & Other Wide-Open Spaces" in this chapter).

Bookstores and bicycle shops stock maps of local trails, or you can write to the **Washington Area Bicyclist Association** for trail information at WABA, Suite 640, 1819 H St. NW, Washington, DC 20006 (☎ **202/872-9830**). For free maps of the Rock Creek, C&O Canal, and Mount Vernon trails, write to the **National Park Service,** National Capital Region, Division of Public Information, 1100 Ohio Dr. SW, Washington, DC 20242 (☎ **202/619-7222**). Experienced cyclists who wish to tackle the entire C&O Canal (which takes about 3 days, averaging 61 miles a day) can write to C&O Canal, National Historic Parks, P.O. Box 4, Sharpsburg, MD 21782 (☎ **301/739-4200**).

Bike the Sites (☎ **202/966-8862;** www.bikethesites.com), offers participants professionally guided bike tours on Trek 21-speed hybrid bikes, March through November. They even provide helmets, water bottles, and a handlebar bag. In the Capital Sites Ride, cyclists visit 55 landmarks on an 8-mile circuit that takes around 3 hours and costs $35. Most of the terrain is flat on paved and gravel trails. The tours depart across from the Freer Gallery of Art, Jefferson Drive and 12th Street SW. The nearest Metro stop is the Smithsonian. Along the way, guides will feed you information (you supply the power bars). Children between 5 and 14 must be accompanied by an adult. Younger kids ride in trail-a-bikes attached to Mom or Dad's wheels. Families make up more than half of Bike the Sites business, and a majority of the adult riders haven't been on a bike in years.

If you prefer going it alone, bike rentals vary (depending on type) from about $15 to $25 per day, $4 to $7 per hour. Typically, 10-speed and hybrid bikes rent for $5 an hour or $25 a day, with a 3-hour minimum. **Big Wheel Bikes** has three locations: 1034 33rd St. NW in Georgetown (☎ **202/337-0254**); 2 Prince St., Alexandria, Virginia (☎ **703/739-2300**); and 6917 Arlington Rd., Bethesda, Maryland (☎ **301/652-0192**). **Fletcher's Boat House,** 4940 Canal Rd. NW (☎ **202/244-0461**) also rents bikes for a very reasonable $12 per day. You won't find a high concentration of restaurants around here, so you may want to tote snacks or brown bag lunch to enjoy at Fletcher's picnic area. Another place to rent bikes is at **Thompson's,** Rock Creek Parkway and Virginia Avenue NW (☎ **202/333-4861**).

If your kids are too young to pedal on their own, consider renting a bike child seat or trailer. Experts recommend that a second cyclist follow behind a bike with a child seat or trailer. Practice with the equipment before venturing out and stay on smooth surfaces away from traffic. *Always* helmet kids who are along for a free ride. The equipment rents for about $15 to $20 a day at area bike stores.

BOATING

Between late March and late November, there are at least four good reasons why you should rent a boat: (1) Kids love being on the water. (2) Your brood will gain a new perspective of the city. (3) They'll paddle while you relax. (4) Everyone will sleep like a baby afterward. Prices average $18 per boat per day; hourly rates vary. Most places are open from 9 or 10am to 5 or 6pm weekdays, with extended weekend and summer hours. Call first, because hours change seasonally. Arrive early on weekends.

Fletcher's, 4940 Canal Rd. NW (☎ **202/244-0461**), rents canoes, rowing shells, small sailboats, and rowboats. **Jack's Boats,** 3500 K St. NW in Georgetown (☎ **202/337-9642**), rents canoes, kayaks, and rowboats. **Thompson's Boat Center,** Rock Creek Parkway and Virginia Avenue NW (☎ **202/333-4861**), rents canoes, rowboats, shells, double shells, kayaks, and Sunfish. At the **Tidal Basin,** Ohio Drive and Tidal Basin (near the Jefferson Memorial; roughly 15th Street and Maine Avenue SW) (☎ **202/484-0206**), rent a pedal boat March through September ($7 per hour for a two-seater, $14 for a four-seater). Further afield (or, in this case, astream),

Atlantic Kayak, 1201 North Royal St., Alexandria, Va.(☎ **703/838-9072;** www.atlantickayak.com; e-mail: ackc@atlantickayak.com) rents canoes and kayaks and also offers kayaking classes and tours. If your kids are 7 or older, they can learn to paddle their own canoes summer evenings on the C&O Canal. Bless the National Park Service! They offer free evening classes during the summer at Fletcher's Boat House off Canal Road NW, and Swain's Lock, off River Road, west of Potomac, Maryland. Younger kids can ride with their parents, but the rule is: three to a canoe. Picnic tables are available at both sites for a light supper before the 6:30pm class begins (☎ **301/299-3613**).

FISHING

Besides being the nation's capital, a river runs through it. And, thanks to the Clean Water Act, there are fish—live fish—in that river. Every Friday, see the "On the Move" section of the *Washington Post's* "Weekend" magazine for a listing of what fish are running and biting where. Local anglers tell me mid-March until July is prime fishing time. Nonetheless you'll catch *something* (maybe an old tire?) from late February through October. Cast your line for catfish, bass, and stripers from the wall along the Washington Channel at Hains Point or Pentagon Lagoon; anywhere near Chain Bridge; or the seawall north of the Wilson Bridge in Alexandria, Virginia.

If you want to sink your line in the **Chesapeake Bay,** board a head boat for a half or full day. Try the *Tom Hooker* at the **Rod 'N Reel,** Route 261 and Mears Avenue in Chesapeake Beach, Maryland (☎ **800/233-2080**). It's about a 45-minute drive from D.C., and kids of all ages are welcome as long as someone is watching them. Prices in 1999 were $32 for adults, $29 for kids 12 and under. The boat goes out, weather permitting, twice a day: 8am to 3pm and 6pm to midnight. You can rent a rod for about $5. Oh, yes, a dozen bloodworms are included with the boarding fee. (My dad was squeamish and used to bait my hook with bologna. We caught an old shoe once.)

Be sure to wear nonskid shoes as the decks can get mighty slippery and slimey. Not up for negotiation are sunblock with an SPF of 15 or higher, a windbreaker or foul weather jacket, and two coolers—one for the fish you'll catch, one for lunch and drinks. If you're toting your own fishing gear, leave light tackle at home. Those prone to motion sickness should take an appropriate medication a half hour before boarding. I've found Bonine to work well without causing drowsiness.

Many area fishers favor casting off from Fletcher's Boat House at the intersection of Reservoir and Canal roads NW (☎ **202/244-0461**). Fletcher's sells bait and tackle, rents boats, and has a snack bar. With younger kids, I'd stick to the canal here. Conveniently, you can also pick up a fishing license at Fletcher's. The cost is $5 for residents and $7.50 for non-residents and is good for the day you purchase it through the rest of the calendar year. Short-term visitors will be better served by the $3 license, good for 14 consecutive days. For more information, call the D.C. Department of Health, Fisheries and Wildlife Division at ☎ **202/535-2260.**

Please be careful when you fish the Potomac. Every year several people drown in its unforgiving waters, especially treacherous and turbulent after heavy rains. Heed warning signs. They're posted for a reason. Be particularly cautious of slippery rocks along the shoreline.

HIKING

Many city and suburban parks have hiking trails (see the "Gardens & Parks" section in this chapter), and portions of the Blue Ridge Mountains and Appalachian

Trail are well within reach for a day trip. Some of the best local hiking for families is along the **C&O Canal** (184 miles!), **Theodore Roosevelt Island, Rock Creek Park,** and **the U.S. National Arboretum.** On the Maryland side of Great Falls Park, 11710 MacArthur Blvd., Potomac (☎ **301/299-3613**), the 4-mile **Billy Goat Trail** is a family favorite. The trail's entrance is off a towpath less than 2 miles south of the park's entrance. Nobody said you have to do the entire trail on your first try.

ICE-SKATING

Every few years Washington endures a severe winter (most recently the record-breaking 1995–96). One of the few pleasant aspects of this phenomenon is that the C&O Canal and Reflecting Pool (between the Lincoln Memorial and Washington Monument) and the pond in Constitution Gardens (near the Vietnam War Veterans Memorial) freeze over for skating. It's a scene straight from Currier and Ives, and one that your family won't want to miss.

Call the U.S. Park Service (☎ **202/619-7222**) to find out if the ice is thick—and safe—enough to support your flying feet.

An ice-skating rink opened in the National Gallery of Art Sculpture Garden Nov. 15, 1999. The season runs until mid-March, and hours are 10am to 10pm Monday through Thursday, 10am to 11pm Friday and Saturday, 11am to 10pm Sunday. Admission on weekdays is $5 for adults, $4.50 for students, $4 for seniors. Weekend prices are $5.50 for adults, $4.50 for students and seniors. You can rent skates for $2.50. Snacks are sold at the refreshment stand.

In the suburbs, the **Fairfax Ice Arena,** 3779 Pickett Rd., Fairfax, Virginia (☎ **703/323-1132**), is open year-round and offers skate rentals, lessons, and a pro shop. Don't be surprised if you run into a few Olympic hopefuls in training. In Maryland, there's an outdoor skating rink at **Bethesda Metro Center,** outside the Hyatt Regency Hotel. Parking is free for 3 hours with ice rink validation (☎ **301/656-0588**). Two covered outdoor rinks, **Cabin John Ice Rink,** 10610 Westlake Dr., Rockville (☎ **301/365-0585**), and **Wheaton Ice Rink,** at Arcola and Orebaugh avenues, Wheaton (☎ **301/649-2703**), attract scores of families. Both offer skate rentals and lessons. Cabin John has lockers and a snack bar and is open year-round. Skate rentals are $2.50. Admission is about $3 to $5, depending on the session.

IN-LINE SKATING

Surely nobody has to tell you in-line skating is a hot fitness trend for all ages. Local shops rent skates for about $15 to $20 per day (including elbow, knee, and wrist pads) and also sponsor clinics. Try the **Ski Center** at Massachusetts Avenue and 49th Street NW near American University (☎ **202/966-4474**); **City Bikes,** 2501 Champlain St. NW in Adams–Morgan (☎ **202/265-1564**); or **Metropolis Bicycles,** 709 8th St. SE, near Eastern Market (☎ **202/543-8900**). **Caravan Skate Shop,** 10766 Tucker St., Beltsville, Maryland (☎ **301/937-0066**), has free clinics weekly (for beginners who've purchased skates) and private and group lessons. Several others are listed under "Skating Equipment and Supplies" in the D.C., Maryland, and Virginia Yellow Pages.

According to reliable sources, the best skating sites are Rock Creek Park (when Beach Drive is closed to traffic Saturday and Sunday) and the C&O Canal trail between Georgetown and Fletcher's Boat House (about 1½ miles). Seasoned skaters may want to head for the pebble-infested Mall, but please don't try to blade through the museums. While I'm giving advice: Take a lesson first, and *please* don't skate without a helmet and pads.

KITE FLYING

The best kite flying in the capital area is in spring and fall. During most of the summer, a breeze attracts media attention, and in winter, well, it's too chilly. Look no further than the Mall for the optimum kite-flying space with no overhead impediments. Otherwise, head for the nearest schoolyard or playground. If you forgot to pack a kite, go to the **Air and Space Museum's gift shop** at 6th Street and Independence Avenue SW. If it flies, they have it.

Every year in late March, the Smithsonian sponsors a **kite festival** on the west side of the Washington Monument (☎ 202/357-2700). There are two hitches: the kite has to be homemade and it's supposed to remain airborne for at least 1 minute at an altitude of 100 feet or more. Ribbons are awarded to winners in different age groups, and trophies are given in several categories. If you're in town, try to catch it.

MINIATURE GOLF

Some of our family's biggest shared laughs have occurred playing miniature golf, due in no small part to the clumsiness of the senior members of the team. Here is one game that junior and senior tour hopefuls (and hopeless) can enjoy strictly for fun. It doesn't cost an arm and a leg to swing a club in the scenic surroundings of Hains Point in East Potomac Park. The **Circus Mini Golf Putt-4-Fun,** Ohio Drive SW, is open Sunday through Thursday from 11am to 9pm, Friday and Saturday from 11am to 10pm, weather permitting. It's $3 per game for anyone over 6; free for children 5 and under (☎ 202/488-8087).

There are numerous miniature golf courses outside the District. Here's a sampling of the closest: Monte Miniature Golf, College Park, Maryland (☎ 301/935-9821); Putt Putt Golf & Games, Rockville, Maryland (☎ 301/881-1663); Putt Putt Golf Course of Mount Vernon, Alexandria, Virginia (☎ 703/765-0707); and Upton Hill Regional Park Mini Golf, Arlington, Virginia (☎ 703/237-4953).

SAILING

The **Mariner Sailing School,** Belle Haven Marina, south of Alexandria, Virginia (☎ 703/768-0018), rents Windsurfers, Sunfish, and larger sailboats to experienced sailors. Canoes and kayaks are available for nonsailors. During the summer months, kids 8 to 15 can take a 5-day sailing course or windsurfing lessons. The **Washington Sailing Marina,** Dangerfield Island off the George Washington Memorial Parkway, Alexandria, Virginia (☎ 703/548-9027), rents sailboats and sailboards and runs a 1-week Red Cross sailing program for ages 10 to 16 during the summer. For information on sailing instruction on the Chesapeake Bay in Annapolis, Maryland (about 35 miles from downtown), see the Annapolis entry in chapter 10.

SWIMMING

In the good old summertime you're not completely out of luck if your hotel lacks a swimming pool. For the location of the public pool nearest you, call the D.C. **Department of Recreation Aquatic Program** (☎ 202/576-6436). Most pools are open from mid-June through Labor Day. The nicest pools are located at 25th and N streets, 34th Street and Volta Place NW in Georgetown, and East Potomac Park. But honestly, "nice" is a relative term and the pools are crowded beyond belief. Call for days of operation and hours.

If you live in the District, consider lapping up a family membership at one of the following hotel pools: Washington Hilton, 1919 Connecticut Ave. NW (☎ 202/

483-4100); Omni Shoreham, 2500 Calvert St. NW (☎ 202/234-0700); Loews L'Enfant Plaza, L'Enfant Plaza SW (☎ 202/646-4450); Quality Hotel Central, 1900 Connecticut Ave. NW (☎ 202/332-9300). Last one in's a rotten egg!

What if you want to test your water wings, but the weather is uncooperative? Head for Olney, Maryland's indoor pool, where the sun always shines. You don't have to be a county resident to take the plunge at the **Olney Indoor Swim Center.** The public pool, in Olney Manor Park at 16601 Georgia Ave., is about 15 miles north of downtown D.C. The center sports three diving boards, water slides, eight lap lanes, a kiddie slide, and large skylights that keep the area bright without artificial light most of the time. Adjacent to the heated pool are large "hydrotherapy pools" (hot tubs to you and me).

Kids 10 and older are admitted without a parent, provided they can prove their swimming mettle. The pool is open to the public year round with several sessions most days. Admission for noncounty residents is $5 for adults, $4 for everyone else (☎ 301/570-1210). For information on other public pools in suburban Maryland and Virginia, call the local county recreation department.

TENNIS

In Rock Creek Park, the tennis courts at 16th and Kennedy streets NW are open Monday through Friday from 7am to 11pm, Saturday and Sunday from 7am to 8pm. Courts must be reserved from April to November (☎ 202/722-5949). Or swing your racquet at one of the 24 courts (indoor, outdoor, lighted, and clay) in East Potomac Park, 1090 Ohio Dr. SW (☎ 202/554-5962). They're open spring through fall from 7am to 8pm with extended winter hours. Court time is $5 per hour. Inquire about instruction at each and information on USTA leagues and the Play Tennis America program (☎ 703/560-9480).

WINDSURFING

See "Sailing" above in this section.

3 Rides for Children

BALLOON RIDES

Go up, up, and away at several locations outside the Beltway. A balloon ride does not come cheaply, but if you're prepared to cough up $125 to $250 per person and there's not already enough hot air in Washington to suit you, call one of the following: **Adventures Aloft** (☎ 301/881-6262), **Aeronaut Masters** (☎ 301/869-2FLY), **Fantasy Flights** (☎ 301/417-0000), or **Balloons Unlimited** (☎ 703/ 281-2300).

BOAT RIDES

During the warm weather months, take advantage of Washington's wonderful waterfront setting and enjoy the city from offshore with your kids. They'll rate a boat ride as one of the high-water marks of their visit. Rent a pedal boat on the Tidal Basin or a canoe or rowboat on the C&O Canal or Potomac River. For details on several D.C. boating centers, see the "Boating" entry in the "Outdoor Activities" section of this chapter.

If you like the feel of the wind at your back, rent a small sailboat from **Fletcher's** (☎ 202/244-0461) or **Thompson's** (☎ 202/333-4861). If you're feeling more ambitious, less than an hour's drive from downtown you and your crew can learn to sail on the Chesapeake Bay. For more information on sailing off into the sunset, see the "Sailing" entry above and the "Annapolis" entry in chapter 10.

When boating, make sure there are PFDs (personal flotation devices—"life vests") onboard for each family member, and try them on for size before you leave the dock. If you prefer to sit back and let someone else play captain, board one of the many cruise boats that ply the Potomac's waters. The **Mount Vernon Cruise** is especially popular with families. See the "Cruises" section below.

CANAL BOAT RIDES ON THE C&O CANAL

Park Service guides in period dress will regale you with 19th-century canal lore and river songs as the mule-drawn boat makes its way slowly along the historic waterway. The *Canal Clipper* (☎ **301/299-2026**) departs from Great Falls in Potomac, Maryland, on Saturday and Sunday from mid-April through mid-June and mid-September through October; Wednesday through Sunday from mid-June to mid-September.

The *Georgetown,* berthed in the heart of Georgetown on the canal between 30th Street and Thomas Jefferson Street NW (☎ **202/653-5844**), operates mid-April through October, Wednesday through Sunday. During peak season (mid-June to mid-September), cruises depart three times a day; in spring and fall there's one cruise a day Wednesday through Friday and three a day on Saturday and Sunday. These two may look like barges, but they are actually boats, I was told by the Park Service, because they are steerable. The mules are the engine! A true barge has to be pulled and pushed; it cannot be steered. Live and learn. Anyway, the delightful and informative ride is 90 minutes long. Leave it to the Park Service. They carry boxes filled with old-fashioned toys for restless little girls and boys. The cost for either ride is $5 for adults, $3.50 for ages 2 to 12 and senior citizens 62 and over, and free for children under 2.

CRUISES

Since two sides of the Washington "diamond" front rivers—the Potomac and Anacostia—at least once during your stay you should cast off from terra firma and see the city from the water.

The 150-year-old riverboat *Nightingale II* (☎ **800/405-5511**) leaves from the Washington Harbour dock in Georgetown, 31st Street and the river, for a 50-minute narrated cruise departing hourly from noon to 7pm, April through October. The fare is $10 for adults, $5 for kids 3 to 12, and there's a snack bar onboard.

The luxurious 600-passenger *Spirit of Washington* (☎ **202/554-8000**) offers lunch, brunch, dinner, moonlight, and Mount Vernon cruises from Pier 4, 6th and Water streets SW. Forget the dinner and moonlight cruises with kids-too long, too expensive, and too boring for them. The 2-hour lunch and brunch cruises in the Washington Channel aboard the carpeted, climate-controlled ship are fine if your kids will do justice to the copious buffet and dessert. Live music and a show are included in the ticket price. Lunch cruises start at $30.85 for adults on weekdays, $35.55 weekends (less for kids 2 to 12). The 7-to-10pm dinner cruise is $59.70 Sunday through Thursday, $69.95 Friday, and $72.45 Saturday for adults and kids over 12. The Sunday jazz cruises feature live entertainment at brunch, noon to 2pm, and dinner, 7 to 10pm. Check the local papers for cost-saving coupons. Sometimes, kids 10 and under cruise free with a paying adult. For all cruises, reservations are a must (☎ **202/554-8000,** or 202/554-8013 for groups of 20 or more).

If food is secondary and you want to spend a fun-filled half day on the water and visiting a major sight, board the *Spirit of Mount Vernon* (☎ **202/554-8000**), where you can cruise down the Potomac to George Washington's beautiful estate.

Cruises depart Tuesday through Sunday at 9am and 2pm every month except for November and December. Tickets are $26.50 for adults, $17 for ages 6 to 11, free for children 2 to 5. Admission to Mt. Vernon is included in the ticket price. You'll have ample time to look around Mount Vernon before the return voyage. You may not bring food aboard, but rest assured there's a concession stand selling all the drinks and fast food kids' tummies can hold. There's also a restaurant at Mount Vernon. Arrive at the dock 1 hour before departure time.

A 45-minute cruise aboard the ***Potomac Spirit*** (☎ 703/780-2000) is another pleasant way to view the estate while enjoying a recorded narrative about George Washington's birthplace. Passengers board at Mount Vernon for the cruise that also takes in Piscataway Park and sumptuous riverfront homes. The cruise departs (and returns to) Mount Vernon every day but Monday, April through November, at 11:45am; weekends only October through March. Tickets are $5 and no reservation is required.

Glide by presidential monuments and the Iwo Jima memorial, the Kennedy Center, and Georgetown on the *Matthew Hayes*, which runs several times daily from May until early September; weekends only April, September, and October. There are two departure points: Georgetown (Washington Harbour dock, 31st Stret NW and the river) and Old Town, Alexandria (adjacent to the Torpedo Factory). The round-trip fare is $15 adults, $14 seniors, $7 kids 2 to 12.

The *Miss Christin* cruises the Potomac from Old Town Alexandria to Mount Vernon, from May until early September, Tuesday through Sunday. The cruise departs Old Town at 10am and 12:30pm, and leaves Mt. Vernon at 11am, 1:30pm, and 4pm. Fare (including admission to Mount Vernon) is $24 adults, $22 seniors, $12 children 6 to 10.

In the tradition of the Parisian bateaux on the Seine, the riverboat-restaurant ***Dandy*** (☎ 703/683-6090) plies the waters of the Potomac several times a week. Luncheon and dinner cruises depart Old Town, Alexandria, for a leisurely run up the Potomac past historic monuments and memorials, the Kennedy Center, Watergate, Rosslyn (Virginia), and Georgetown before heading back to port. Kids 10 and older with the palate and patience for a three-course lunch or five-course dinner with mostly adults will enjoy this cruise. I found the food plentiful but uninspired on the dinner cruise, and the magnificent scene doesn't come cheap. Prices range from $26 for the weekday lunch cruise, to $32 for the Sunday champagne brunch, to $63 for the Saturday dinner cruise (weeknights are less). Drinks are extra. For all cruises, knock $5 off adult prices for kids under 12. A family is allowed a maximum of three children (under the age of 12) at the reduced priced. Reservations are a must (☎ 703/683-6076).

Now here's a cruise worth diving for: **DC Ducks** (☎ 202/966-DUCK; www. historictours.com) utilizes amphibious vehicles, which transported troops and supplies during World War II, to ferry 30 visitors at a time around several downtown sights before dipping into the Virginia side of the Potomac at the Columbia Island Marina. After a short swim (lacking a rest room, it is legally restricted to a half-hour dunk), the Duck waddles ashore at Gravelly Point across from National Airport's main runway.

The keels-on-wheels tours depart from Union Station, 50 Massachusetts Ave. NE, daily from March to November, every hour on the hour from 10am to 4pm; more frequently at peak times. The narrated 90-minute ride (60 on land, 30 afloat) in the blue-awninged vessel/vehicle is $24 for adults, $14 for seniors 65 and older, $12 for children 12 and under.

Resembling a giant floating graham cracker gone berserk, the $6 million *Odyssey* (☎ 202/488-6010; www.odysseycruises.com) is docked at the Gangplank Marina, 600 Water St. SW. Designed to squeeze under the bridges spanning the Potomac, the glassed-in vessel accommodates 1,800 passengers. The 4-hour dinner cruise (actually, the first hour is spent tied up at the dock) starts Sunday through Thursday at 6pm (returning at 10pm), Friday and Saturday at 7pm (returning at 11pm). There's something going on every day and night of the week, from weekday lunch cruises ($33) to Saturday dinner ($83). Save $13 and take the dinner cruise Monday through Thursday ($70). In between are several other choices. All include a full-course meal, except for the Moonlight Cruise ($33), where hors d'oeuvres and drinks are served. A delightful way to wind down the weekend is the Sunday Jazz Brunch ($42). This is hardly young kids' fare, but you might want to try it if you're celebrating a special event or just won the lottery.

The *Admiral Tilp* cruises the Potomac from Old Town, Alexandria, Virginia (☎ 703/548-9000). For details, see "Old Town Alexandria" in chapter 10.

FERRY RIDES

About 30 miles northwest of the District of Columbia, the Gen. *Jubal Early,* an old cable ferry named after an even older Confederate general, crosses the Potomac from White's Ferry (☎ 301/349-5200) on the Maryland shore to just north of Leesburg, Virginia. Kids of all ages adore the *Jubal Early,* which operates daily from 5am to 11pm, weather permitting. The ferry makes several trips per hour ($3 one way, $5 round-trip), and the ride is 10 to 15 minutes long, depending on the current and weather. You can take your car on the ferry or go on foot. Take the Capital Beltway to I-270 to the Route 28 west exit, then continue on Route 28 west, and at Dawsonville take Route 107 and follow the signs.

If you have the time, consider a visit to Leesburg before returning to the Maryland side of the Potomac. The town oozes with charm and history. Market and Loudon streets run east and west and are transversed by King Street (north and south). Stop at the Loudon Museum, 14 Loudon St. SW (☎ 703/777-7427), for information and peruse the historic district with its brick sidewalks. Antique shops and restaurants abound in this gentle place, which is especially beautiful when the fall foliage flames in late October.

CAROUSELS

Families who enjoy going around together will want to take a ride on an antique carousel. Few excursions are as much fun or cost as little as these—only $1 per ride. The **Carousel on the Mall,** 1000 Jefferson Dr. SW., in front of the Smithsonian Castle (☎ 202/357-2700), operates from 10am to 6pm March through May, 10am to 7pm June through August, and 11am to 5pm September through February. The 1940s carousel, designed by Allan Herschell, sports 58 horses, two chariots, and a sea dragon.

If you're a carousel freak, check out the following in Maryland and Virginia:

Burke Lake Park, 7315 Ox Rd., Fairfax Station, Virginia (☎ 703/323-6600), is open the first 3 weeks of May, weekends only 11am to 6pm; late May until Labor Day, daily 11am to 6pm; after Labor Day, weekends only through September, 11am to 6pm.

Glen Echo Park, MacArthur Boulevard at Goldsboro Road, Glen Echo, Maryland (☎ 301/492-6282), has a classic 1921 Dentzel carousel, and it's our family's favorite. Ablaze with more than 1,200 lights, it has 52 carved wood figures and a 165-band Würlitzer organ. It operates from May through September on weekends from noon to 6pm, Wednesday and Thursday from 10am to 2pm. A park ranger gives a half-hour talk on the carousel's history Saturday at 10:30am.

Lake Fairfax Carousel, 1400 Lake Fairfax Dr., Reston, Virginia (☎ **703/471-5415**), opens Memorial Day weekend and closes Labor Day. You can ride from 10am to 6pm weekdays, noon to 8pm weekends.

Lee District Park Carousel, 6601 Telegraph Rd., Alexandria, Virginia (☎ **703/922-9841**), is open Memorial Day to Labor Day, Saturday and Sunday from noon to 4pm.

HAYRIDES

If you're visiting in the fall, especially around Halloween, treat your kids to a hayride. Afterward, stock up on apples, pumpkins, and fresh-pressed cider while you pick the hay out of each other's hair. Call for hours and special kids' activities. Here are two of the closer-in orchards offering hayrides as part of their all-out Halloween celebration: **Butler's Orchard,** 22200 Davis Mill Rd., Germantown, Maryland (☎ **301/972-3299**); and **Krop's Crops,** 11110 Georgetown Pike, Great Falls, Virginia (☎ **703/430-8955**).

Check the Maryland and Virginia phone books for bushels more.

PLANE RIDES

Roughly a dozen airports within an hour's drive of the District will clear you and your crew for takeoff, for a price. For a thrill, not much beats a bird's eye view of Washington and the environs. The *average* cost of an airborne sightseeing excursion is $100 per hour for a four-seater (with a pilot). The plane can accommodate up to 3 passengers, but it all depends on the weight (no fudging). You may be asked to step on a scale before boarding. Calling to reserve a day or more ahead is highly recommended. White-knucklers can call the National Transportation Safety Board for safety records (☎ **202/382-6538**). Here are a few of the airports closest to D.C.: **Lee Airport,** Edgewater, Maryland (☎ **410/956-2114**); **Montgomery Air Park,** Gaithersburg, Maryland (☎ **301/977-5200**); **Washington Dulles International Airport** (Squadron Aviation), Reston, Virginia (☎ **703/581-1600**).

TRAIN RIDES

If your youngsters have never been on a big choo-choo, board a northbound Amtrak train at Union Station, 50 Massachusetts Ave. NE (☎ **800/USA-RAIL**), and take a ride to New Carrollton, Maryland, one stop away. Because it's only a 10-minute hop, they won't have time to raid the snack car. Trains operate frequently throughout the day. Unfortunately, there isn't much to see or do in New Carrollton, so once you disembark you'll want to hop on the next train back. But, if you'd like to make a day of it, go to Baltimore, where there are plenty of kid-pleasing things to do. It's a 40-minute ride from Union Station. A one-way unreserved (off-peak) seat on Amtrak, Union Station to New Carrollton, is $11 for adults, $5.50 for kids 2 to 15. A one-way unreserved (off-peak) ticket from Union Station to Baltimore's Penn Station is $19 for adults, $9.50 kids. Reserved seats, business class, and the Metroliner cost more, as does travel at peak times (Fridays, Sundays, and holidays from 11am to 11pm).

Toddlers and preschoolers delight in riding the small-scale trains in the following regional parks: **Burke Lake Park,** 7315 Ox Rd., Fairfax Station, Virginia (☎ **703/323-6600**); **Cabin John Regional Park,** 7400 Tuckerman Lane, Rockville, Maryland (☎ **301/469-7835**); and **Wheaton Regional Park,** 2000 Shorefield Rd., Wheaton, Maryland (☎ **301/946-6396**).

Shopping for the Whole Family

8

Once upon a time D.C. was a remote shopping star and residents had to rocket to New York and other more worldly galaxies to find what they wanted. Now the most seriously addicted shopaholics can feed their habit at home. Flashy multilevel malls, dependable department stores, and trendy boutiques are as much a part of the D.C. scene as cherry blossoms and government red tape. In fact, shopping has become a highly competitive sport over the last several years as more discount stores have moved into the area, giving the full-price standbys a run for their money.

1 The Shopping Scene

Hecht's stands solitary guard over Washington's old downtown shopping area bordered by F, 7th, G, and 14th streets NW. Less than a mile away, along the Connecticut Avenue and K Street business corridor, branches of national chains and specialty shops nudge each other for elbow room. Due north, the neighborhood known as **Dupont Circle** attracts browsers and buyers with its many galleries and one-of-a-kind, sometimes left-of-center retail establishments.

Georgetown, long a haven for shopping mavens, fans out from Wisconsin Avenue and M Street NW and is best known for fashionable clothing, shoe, and housewares boutiques, T-shirt joints, and the ever-so-voguish **Georgetown Park Mall.** In recent years, many of the old-time establishments have been eclipsed by record, souvenir, and beauty shops and Levi's, Gap, and Banana Republic stores. Some things haven't changed, however, since I was a George Washington University student during the Middle Ages. Georgetown is still a numero uno draw for area teenagers, especially on weekends.

STORE HOURS   Most stores in the D.C. area are open Monday through Saturday from 9:30 or 10am to 5 or 6pm, and many are also open on Sunday and have extended hours one or more evenings. You should always call ahead.

SALES TAX   The sales tax in D.C. is 6%.

2 Shopping A to Z

ARTS & CRAFTS

✪ Indian Craft Shop
Department of the Interior, 18th and C sts NW, Room 1023. ☎ **202/208-4056.** Fax 202/219-1135. Metro: Farragut West or Smithsonian (then a 6-block walk from either).

More than 40 tribal areas are represented and an area of the shop is devoted to an Artist of the Month. Although not widely known, this is an excellent source (since 1938!) for authentic, top-quality Native American arts and crafts. Shop for weavings, sandpaintings, kachinas, fetish carvings, elaborate basketry and jewelry, and books on Indian art. Then stop at the Department of Interior Museum across the hall. To gain entrance to the building, you need photo ID—a passport, government ID, or driver's license. A cafeteria, on the lower level, is open for breakfast and lunch. Nonwalkers may find it a bit out of the way, so take a taxi. Street parking is limited. Open Monday through Friday from 8:30am to 4pm and on third Saturday of the month, 10am to 4pm. Closed federal holidays.

Pearl Art & Craft Supplies
5695 Telegraph Rd., Alexandria, Va. ☎ **703/960-3900.** Metro: Huntington, then a 5-minute walk.

One of the world's largest arts-and-crafts discount centers, Pearl has everything you need for any craft you can name, as well as a large selection of art materials. When it comes to craft supplies, Pearl is a gem.

Pearl has a second location in Federal Plaza, 12266 Rockville Pike, Rockville, Maryland (☎ **301/816-2900**). The hours in Alexandria are Monday, Friday, and Saturday from 9am to 8pm; Tuesday, Wednesday, and Thursday from 9am to 8:30pm; and Sunday 10am to 6pm.

Plaza Artist Materials
1019 19th St. NW, at K St. NW. ☎ **202/331-7090.** Metro: Farragut West or Farragut North.

Plaza Artist Materials has "everything your art desires," with a wide array of fine art, drawing, and drafting supplies and children's art kits. This is doodlers' paradise—hundreds of marking pens in enough colors to make a rainbow blush. Open Monday through Friday from 8am to 6pm and Saturday from 9am to 5pm. Branch stores in Bethesda, Rockville, and Laurel, Maryland, and Fairfax and Baileys Crossroads, Virginia.

Sullivan's Art Supplies
3412 Wisconsin Ave. NW. ☎ **202/362-1343.** Metro: Tenleytown, then take any No. 30 bus 1 mile south.

Sullivan's draws dabblers and professionals alike. The well-stocked space adjacent to Sullivan's Toy Store has all the basic oils, acrylics, watercolors, canvas, and brushes that a mini-Picasso or Cassatt could desire. Open Monday, Tuesday, Saturday from 10am to 6pm; Wednesday, Thursday, Friday 10am to 7pm; and Sunday noon to 5pm.

Torpedo Factory Art Center
105 N. Union St., Alexandria, Va. ☎ **703/838-4565.** Metro: King St.

Kids love watching the potters, sculptors, stained-glass artisans, and other craftspeople do their thing in this renovated World War I munitions plant, which also houses the City of Alexandria Archaeology Lab. Most items are for sale. Open daily from 10am to 5pm.

BALLOONS

Balloon Bouquets
☎ **202/785-1290.**

If you're celebrating a birthday or other special occasion during your visit, you can send a balloon arrangement of plain or imprinted latex or Mylar balloons with or without a toy, stuffed animal, cake, flowers, or a gift basket. One call to Balloon Bouquets and you'll have the world on a string. Some same-day delivery service is available. Orders are taken Monday through Saturday from 8am to 6pm.

Georgetown Paper Store
1803 Wisconsin Ave. NW. ☎ **202/333-3200.**

Blow up a plain or stamped balloon, or save your breath and let the Paper Store fill it with helium. They also carry a variety of plain and decorated Mylars and the biggest selection of party supplies and favors in the neighborhood. Open Monday through Friday 9am to 8pm, Saturday 9am to 7pm, and Sunday noon to 5pm.

BOOKS

While the stores listed below have a wonderful selection of children's books, don't overlook the following chains: **Barnes & Noble,** 3040 M St. NW (corner of Thomas Jefferson Street; ☎ **202/965-9880**); **B. Dalton Bookseller,** the Shops at National Place, F Street NW between 13th and 14th streets (☎ **202/393-1468**), also at Union Station, 1776 K St. NW, and 5345 Wisconsin Ave. NW; **Borders Books and Music,** 1800 L St. NW (☎ **202/466-4999**), **Crown Books/Super Crown,** 2020 K St. NW (☎ **202/659-2030,** also at 11 Dupont Circle, 1275 K St. NW, and 3335 Connecticut Ave. NW; **Trover Shop,** 1031 Connecticut Ave. NW (☎ **202/659-8138**), also at 221 Pennsylvania Ave. SE; **Waldenbooks,** Georgetown Park Mall, 3222 M St. NW (☎ **202/338-9331**).

A Likely Story Children's Bookstore
1555 King St., Alexandria, Va. ☎ **703/836-2498.** Fax 703/836-2498. E-mail: rdugan@ bellatlantic.net. Metro: King St.

More than 20,000 titles are shelved in this 2,000-square-foot children's bookstore just 2 blocks from the King Street Metro stop. Special programs include story times (Tuesday, Wednesday, and Saturday at 11am), workshops, and author appearances. There's a play area for younger kids so that older siblings can take their time making selections. Call to be placed on the mailing list for the store's newsletter showcasing new titles and upcoming events. Open Monday through Saturday from 10am to 6pm and Sunday from 1 to 5pm.

Audubon Naturalist Society Book Shop
8940 Jones Mill Rd., Chevy Chase, Md. ☎ **301/652-3606.**

Located at the Woodend Nature Center, on the site of the headquarters of the Audubon Society, the shop is just a wingbeat away from a nature preserve where youngsters can search for their favorite feathered friends. There's even a toy-filled room for your fledglings. It's open Monday through Wednesday and Friday from 10am to 5pm, Thursday 10am to 8, Saturday 9am to 5pm, and Sunday from noon to 5pm.

✪ Bookoo Books for Kids, etc.
4945 Elm St., Bethesda, Md. ☎ **301/652-2794.** Fax 301/652-6291. www. washingtonpost.com/yp/bookoobooks. Metro: Bethesda.

A favorite of young readers, this shop hosts a weekly story time Wednesday and Thursday at 10am for 2- to 5-year-olds. Monthly craft parties and reader-discussion groups are also fixtures in this family-friendly space. For a truly Bookoo birthday, local children enjoy picking a theme (Angelina Ballerina, Mystery/Detective, and Star Wars among the choices) and celebrating here. Parents like it too: no muss, no fuss. The basic party includes story time, face painting, a craft activity, games, cake and juice or soda, all paper ware and invitations, and a grown-up Bookoo host. Tack on extras (pizza, McDonald's Happy Meal, favors) if you like. Sounds good to me! Hours are Monday through Friday from 9:30am to 8pm, Saturday from 9:30am to 6pm, and Sunday from 11am to 5pm. Drivers take note: There's 2-hour free parking behind the store on Hampden Lane.

Washington, D.C. Shopping

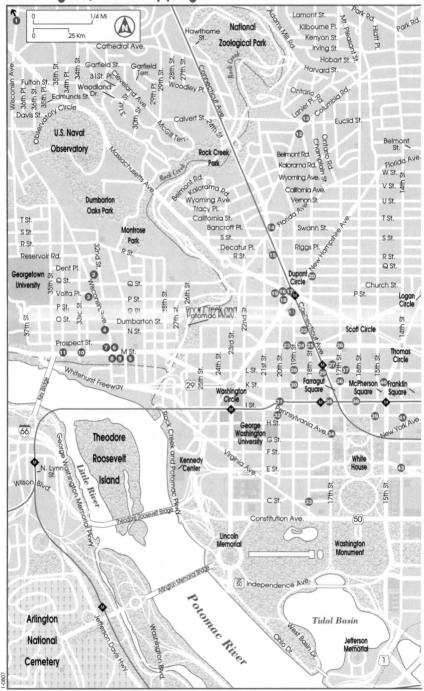

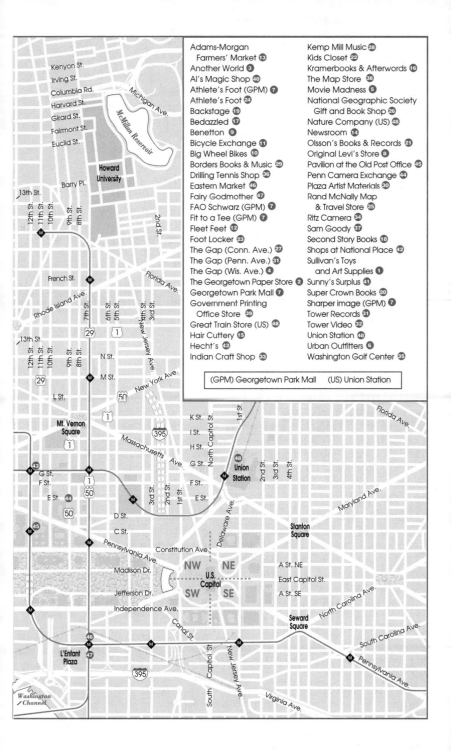

Adams-Morgan
  Farmers' Market ⑬
Another World ③
Al's Magic Shop ㊵
Athlete's Foot (GPM) ⑦
Athlete's Foot ㉔
Backstage ⑲
Bedazzled ⑰
Benetton ⑨
Bicycle Exchange ⑪
Big Wheel Bikes ⑩
Borders Books & Music ㉙
Drilling Tennis Shop ㊱
Eastern Market ㊻
Fairy Godmother ㊼
FAO Schwarz (GPM) ⑦
Fit to a Tee (GPM) ⑦
Fleet Feet ⑫
Foot Locker ㉓
The Gap (Conn. Ave.) ㉗
The Gap (Penn. Ave.) ㉛
The Gap (Wis. Ave.) ④
The Georgetown Paper Store ②
Georgetown Park Mall ⑦
Government Printing
  Office Store ㊴
Great Train Store (US) ㊽
Hair Cuttery ⑮
Hecht's ㊸
Indian Craft Shop ㉝

Kemp Mill Music ㉘
Kids Closet ㉒
Kramerbooks & Afterwords ⑯
The Map Store ㊳
Movie Madness ⑤
National Geographic Society
  Gift and Book Shop ㉖
Nature Company (US) ㊽
Newsroom ⑭
Olsson's Books & Records ㉑
Original Levi's Store ⑧
Pavilion at the Old Post Office ㊺
Penn Camera Exchange ⑭
Plaza Artist Materials ㉚
Rand McNally Map
  & Travel Store ㉕
Ritz Camera ㉞
Sam Goody ㊲
Second Story Books ⑱
Shops at National Place ㊷
Sullivan's Toys
  and Art Supplies ①
Sunny's Surplus ㊶
Super Crown Books ⑳
Sharper image (GPM) ⑦
Tower Records ㉛
Tower Video ㉜
Union Station ㊽
Urban Outfitters ⑥
Washington Golf Center ㉟

(GPM) Georgetown Park Mall   (US) Union Station

Borders Books, Music, & Café

1801 K St. NW, entrance on L St. ☎ **202/466-4999.** Metro: Farragut North or Farragut West.

This centrally located Borders carries 100,000 titles and an extensive selection of videos, tapes, and CDs. The popular Storytime program for preschoolers, held Saturday at 10:30am, gives parents 30 minutes to an hour to browse or enjoy a café latté and something sweet from the cafe/coffee bar. Hours are Monday through Friday from 8am to 10pm, Saturday from 9am to 9pm, and Sunday from 11am to 7pm.

✪ Borders for Kids (in Borders Books, Music & Café)

White Flint Mall, 11301 Rockville Pike, North Bethesda, Md. ☎ **301/816-1067.** Metro: White Flint.

This popular bookstore within a bookstore has a large play and performance area, and an expanded program of children's events, making Borders a popular family destination. Storytelling takes place Saturday at 11am and 1:30pm. The glass-enclosed coffee bar is the perfect place to unwind with a new book and espresso while the children are occupied. The hours are Monday through Saturday from 9am to 11pm and Sunday from 9am to 9pm. In Vienna, Virginia, there's a Borders at Tysons Square, 8311 Leesburg Pike, featuring an espresso bar (☎ **703/556-7766**).

✪ Fairy Godmother

319 7th St. SE. ☎ **202/547-5474.** Metro: Eastern Market.

This combination toy and bookstore on Capitol Hill is often overlooked, unfortunately. Stop in before or after you grab a bite at Eastern Market, a few doors away, or tour the Hill. In addition to a wide selection of kids' books (infants through young adults), the shop carries story tapes, toys for all ages, and an exceptional selection of hand and finger puppets. Inquire about story time and other special events. Hours are Monday from noon to 6pm (even fairy godmothers need a rest once in a while), Tuesday through Friday from 11am to 6pm, and Saturday from 10am to 5pm. Ask about extended hours pre-Christmas.

Government Printing Office

710 N. Capitol St. NW, between G and H sts. ☎ **202/512-0132.** Metro: Union Station.

Perhaps you didn't know, but the world's largest printer is right in the heart of li'l ole D.C. No matter how weird or way-out your kids' hobbies are, or if they're researching a term paper or trying to decide which CD player to buy, they can probably find a book or pamphlet on the subject here. With more than 17,000 titles currently in print, the GPO is a browser's heaven and also sells photographs, prints, lithographs, and posters. Open Monday through Friday from 8am to 4pm.

The GPO has another location at 1510 H St. NW (☎ **202/653-5075**), open Monday through Friday from 8am to 4pm, and a warehouse outlet in Laurel, Maryland (☎ **301/953-7974**).

Kramerbooks & Afterwords

1517 Connecticut Ave. NW, between Q St. and Dupont Circle. ☎ **202/387-1462.** Metro: Dupont Circle.

After making a purchase at this ever-popular Washington institution, you don't have to wait to get back to your hotel room to begin reading. Just step into the cafe-within-a bookstore ("Afterwords""—get it?) for a meal or snack and sink your teeth into a juicy new book. Owner David Tenney carries a very respectable selection of children's books ("but not *all* of them," he says), as well as quality paperbacks and major foreign works. Kids love this place. You will too. Open Monday through Thursday from 7:30am to 1am and round-the-clock Friday morning until 1am Monday.

National Zoo Bookstore

Education Building, 3001 Connecticut Ave. NW. ☎ **202/673-4967.** Metro: Woodley Park-Zoo or Cleveland Park.

Before or after visiting their favorite beasties, toddlers and preschoolers can browse through a selection of picture books while their older siblings peruse more sophisticated works on animal behavior, research, and conservation. Located near the zoo's main entrance, it's open every day but Christmas. Hours are 9am to 5pm daily, closed Dec. 25.

Nature Company

Union Station, 50 Massachusetts Ave. NE. ☎ **202/842-3700.** Metro: Foggy Bottom or Rosslyn.

I double dare you to walk out of one of these attractive, made-for-browsing stores (part of a national chain) without buying at least one exquisitely photographed nature volume to be enjoyed by the entire family. Open Monday through Thursday from 11am to 9pm, Friday and Saturday from 10am to 9pm, and Sunday from noon to 6pm.

Other branches are located at Fashion Centre at Pentagon City, 1100 S. Hayes St., Arlington, Virginia (☎ **703/415-3700**); and Tysons Corner Center, Vienna, Virginia (☎ **703/760-8930**). Call for hours and days.

Olsson's Books & Records

1307 19th St. NW, just off Dupont Circle. ☎ **202/785-2662** for records, or 202/785-1133 for books. Metro: Dupont Circle.

Olsson's is a class act. The hushed tones, knowledgeable staff, and classical music contribute to the soothing, nurturing atmosphere. Olsson's has an excellent selection of kids' books, including several shelves of classics. All recommendations are tagged. Open Monday through Saturday from 10am to 10pm and Sunday from noon to 7pm.

Additional locations include 1200 F St. at Metro Center (☎ **202/393-1853** for records, or **202/347-3686** for books); 418 7th St. NW in the Lansburgh building (☎ **202/638-7610**); 1239 Wisconsin Ave. NW, between M and N streets (☎ **202/ 338-6712** for records, ☎ **202/338-9544** for books); Bethesda, Maryland (☎ **301/ 652-3336**); and Alexandria, Virginia (☎ **703/684-007**7). All locations are open daily; call for hours.

✪ Politics and Prose

5015 Connecticut Ave. NW. (between Fessenden St. and Nebraska Ave.) ☎ **202/364-1919.** Metro: Van Ness, then L2 or L4 bus north ¾ mile.

After decades on upper Connecticut Avenue, the Cheshire Cat (one of the three oldest children's bookstores in the United States) went out of business. That's the bad news. The good news is that several of the friendly, helpful Chessy employees moved—along with the Cheshire Cat's inventory—down the road to Politics & Prose. Besides an extensive collection of titles for kids of all ages, Politics and Prose continues the Cheshire Cat's practice of hosting visits by children's book authors. The shop also fills mail and phone orders promptly. Open Sunday to Thursday 9am to 10pm and Friday, and Saturday 9am to midnight.

Super Crown Books

11 Dupont Circle, between P St. and New Hampshire Ave. NW. ☎ **202/319-1374.** Metro: Dupont Circle.

Of Crown's many branches, the Super Crown on Dupont Circle has the best selection of children's books. With 40% off *New York Times* hardcover best-sellers, 25% off paperbacks, and 10% to 20% discounts on everything else, how can you go wrong? Hours are daily from 9am to midnight.

In addition to the above, you'll find centrally located Crown branches, open daily, at 2020 K St. NW (☎ 202/659-2030) and 1275 K St. NW (☎ **202/ 289-7170**). Call for hours and the location of suburban branches.

Tree Top Toys

3301 New Mexico Ave. NW. ☎ **202/244-3500.** Metro: Tenleytown, then A.U. (American University) shuttle bus to campus. Cross Nebraska Ave. at New Mexico Ave. Directions: North on Massachusetts Ave. to Ward Circle, three-quarters way around circle to Nebraska Ave., left at New Mexico Ave.

Not *just* a toy store, Tree Top has expanded its book section twice in 3 years and added many kid-pleasing events to complement the well-stocked shelves. Monday and Wednesday mornings from 10:30 to 11am, preschoolers from 2 to 5 years old are invited to bring their favorite stuffed animal (bears preferred) to **Teddy Bear Storytime.** Throughout the year children's authors and costumed storybook characters pay a visit. No home with children should be without Tree Top's book catalog. Hours are Monday through Saturday from 9:30am to 5:30pm.

COMIC BOOKS

Another World

1504 Wisconsin Ave. NW, at P St. ☎ **202/333-8650** or 202/333-8651. Metro: Foggy Bottom, then take any no. 30 bus from Pennsylvania Avenue, or hoof it.

If comics nourish your kids' intellect, step into Another World in Georgetown and feed their need. You'll also find comic T-shirts and games. A recorded message lists all the new comics stocked since the previous week. Open Sunday through Thursday from 11am to 9pm and Friday and Saturday from 11am to 10pm.

Big Planet Comics

4908 Fairmont Ave., Bethesda, Md. ☎ **301/654-6856.** www.bigplanetcomics.com. Metro: Bethesda.

Cowabunga! Big Planet carries the latest X-Men, Disney, and Archie comics, along with vintage Nancy and Sluggo and Popeye for mom and dad. Comic cards are also available in Big Planet's quarters close to Bethesda Metro. Big Planet has opened a satellite at 426 Maple Ave. in Vienna, Virginia (☎ **703/242-9412**). The Bethesda Big Planet is open Monday through Friday from 11am to 7pm, Saturday from 11am to 6pm, and Sunday noon to 5pm. Plenty of parking in a public garage at the rear of the store.

COMPUTERS, CAMERAS & ELECTRONICS

Prices for audio/video equipment, cameras, and computers are very competitive. **Best Buy, Circuit City, CompUSA, Computer City,** and **Office Depot** are among the top computer purveyors, and all are manned by knowledgeable staff. The superstores will usually match a competitor's price within 30 days of a purchase, so hold onto your receipt. Also check the Yellow Pages and watch for ads in the *Washington Post* and *Washington Times.*

The best advice I can give if you're shopping for a home computer is to first check out the superstores because they have a large selection of competitively priced systems. Then consult the Yellow Pages, and visit one or two traditional retail stores, which sometimes sell used equipment. If the purchase is for your youngster and you can do without the latest bells and whistles, you can save big time. Here are a few names to get you started. **Computer Age,** Silver Spring, Maryland (☎ **301/ 588-6565**), also in Beltsville, Maryland, and Annandale, Virginia; **CompUSA,** Rockville, Maryland (☎ **301/816-8963**), and Tysons Corner, Virginia (☎ **703/ 749-4450**); and Computer City (owned by Tandy) in Rockville, Maryland, Fairfax, Virginia, and Tysons Corner, Virginia (☎ **800/633-8698**).

Circuit City
10490 Auto Park Dr., Bethesda, Md. ☎ **301/469-8028** (1905 Chain Bridge Rd., Tysons Corner, Virginia ☎ **703/893-6112,** also several other suburban locations).

For TVs, radios, stereo equipment, CD players, and VCRs, I have found Circuit City and Best Buy to be highly competitive. Every weekend, D.C.-area newspapers are stuffed with advertising supplements. It's a good place to begin your research. At the superstores, don't let the sometimes overzealous salespeople get to you. If they claim to be out of an advertised "special," ask for the manager. Call for directions and hours.

Penn Camera Exchange
915 E St. NW. ☎ **800/347-5770** or 202/347-5777. Metro: Metro Center or Gallery Place.

Those in the know swear by Penn Camera for its knowledgeable help, complete stock, and discounted prices on brand-name equipment. Penn not only sells new cameras but buys, trades, rents, and repairs used equipment. Check the Friday *Washington Post* "Weekend" section for announcements of special sales. Penn also has stores in Maryland and Virginia. Open Monday through Friday from 9am to 6pm and Saturday from 10am to 5pm.

Rent-A-Computer
4853 Cordell Ave., Bethesda, Md. ☎ **301/951-0811.** Metro: Bethesda, then walk north on Old Georgetown Rd. a few blocks, right at Cordell Ave. Directions: North on Wisconsin Ave. through Chevy Chase and into Bethesda, left at Old Georgetown Rd., right at Cordell Ave.

Here's a clever concept. Rent a computer short term or for the long haul while deciding if you want to buy. IBM equipment is a specialty, and Rent-A-Computer guarantees delivery service within 4 hours. Open Monday through Friday from 8:30am to 5:30pm.

Ritz Camera
1740 Pennsylvania Ave. NW. ☎ **202/466-3470;** nine other D.C. locations, including several in Maryland and Virginia. Metro: Farragut West.

This is a one-stop photo shop that sells and repairs equipment, and the salespeople are extremely helpful. Ritz offers 1-hour photofinishing and instant passport photos and sells frames, albums, and other cute, gimmicky photo holders. And you can enlarge your favorite photos on-site. Check the Yellow Pages for other addresses and phone numbers. Open Monday through Friday from 8:30am to 6pm and Saturday from 10am to 4pm.

Sharper Image
3276 M St. NW. ☎ **202/337-9361.** Metro: Foggy Bottom.

You can drop your offspring at the Sharper Image in Georgetown Park Mall in the morning, return several hours later, and they will not have missed you. If it's electronic, high-tech, or digital, and it also lights up, hums, and/or performs many functions simultaneously, it's waiting to be discovered at the Sharper Image. Open Monday through Saturday from 10am to 9pm and Sunday from noon to 6pm.

DEPARTMENT STORES
Although not in D.C., or even close by, two department stores worth noting are **Macy's,** the Galleria at Tysons II, 2255 International Dr., McLean, Virginia

(☎ **703/556-0000**), Pentagon City, 1000 S. Hayes St., Arlington, Virginia
(☎ **703/418-4488**); and **Nordstrom,** the Galleria at Tysons II, 2255 International
Dr., McLean, Virginia (☎ **703/761-1121**), Pentagon City, 1400 S. Hayes St.,
Arlington, Virginia (☎ **703/415-1121**), or Montgomery Mall, Bethesda, Maryland (☎ **301/365-4111**).

In D.C.

Hecht's
12th and G sts. NW, at Metro Center. ☎ **202/628-6661.** Metro: Metro Center.

Hecht's has been in business almost forever—for about a century, anyway. The flagship store, which opened its doors in 1985, is a five-story temple of chrome, glass,
and polished wood. The salespeople are still friendly and accommodating at
Hecht's, where the selection of children's clothing is abundant for all age groups and
moderately priced. If you forgot to pack something, you will find it here and not
get ripped off in the process. Hecht's also has a **TickeMasters** outlet. Open Monday
through Saturday from 10am to 8pm and Sunday from noon to 6pm.

　Besides the downtown store, Hecht's has 15 suburban stores.

Lord & Taylor
5225 Western Ave. NW. ☎ **202/362-9600.** Metro: Friendship Heights.

This smaller version of the famous Fifth Avenue store is located 1 block from the
Friendship Heights Metro stop near Chevy Chase, Maryland. You'll find high-
quality children's merchandise, and most is fairly priced. Lord & Taylor's frequent
sales are legendary. Open Monday through Friday from 10am to 9pm, Saturday
from 10am to 7pm, and Sunday from 11am to 6pm.

　There's also a store in the Fair Oaks Mall, Fairfax, Virginia (☎ **703/691-0100**).

Neiman Marcus
Mazza Gallerie, 5300 Wisconsin Ave. NW. ☎ **202/966-9700.** Metro: Friendship Heights.

I know people who shop for their kids' and grandkids' clothes at Neiman's. They
also feed them sirloin steak rather than hamburger. What can I say? The children's
departments tend to be low on merchandise and high on prices, and the salespeople
have become increasingly friendly and down-to-earth in recent years. Let Granny
do the buying here. (Why don't they accept MasterCard and Visa, like the rest of
the world?) Open Monday through Friday from 10am to 8pm, Saturday from
10am to 7pm, and Sunday from noon to 6pm. Two hours of free parking at underground garage; limited street parking.

　There is a Neiman Marcus branch at the Galleria at Tysons II in McLean, Virginia (☎ **703/761-1600**).

In the Suburbs

Bloomingdale's
White Flint Mall, North Bethesda (they can call it North Bethesda or Kensington, but it's still
Rockville to me), Md. ☎ **301/984-4600** (Tysons Corner, McLean, Va. ☎ 703/556-4600).
Metro: White Flint.

A Bloomie's is a Bloomie's is a Bloomie's. Taking a cue from their famous trendsetting mother in New York, these two suburban offspring do their best to satisfy the
buying appetites of material girls and boys. If you're unfamiliar with the store, I
think you'll be pleasantly surprised. Sure, there are plenty of overpriced imports, but
most of the prices are competitive. The White Flint store lost me when they redecorated and moved departments here, there, and everywhere several years ago. They
should hand out maps. Open Monday through Saturday from 10am to 9:30pm and
Sunday from noon to 6pm.

Saks Fifth Avenue

5555 Wisconsin Ave., Chevy Chase, Md. ☎ **301/657-9000.** Metro: Friendship Heights.

When my kids were very young, I loved shopping for them at Saks. But when their outfits began costing more than mine, I stopped shopping there—except when my mother came to town. Now I buy my grandson an occasional snazzy outfit at Saks. Kids grow up so fast. If yours will still tolerate your picking out special clothing for them, and you can tolerate the stiff prices, head for Saks. Metro is a short walk, and there's plenty of parking, free when you remember to validate the ticket in the store. Open Monday through Wednesday and Friday from 10am to 6pm, Thursday from 10am to 9pm, Saturday from 10am to 6pm, and Sunday from noon to 6pm.

DRUGSTORES

Washington's major drugstore chain, **CVS,** carries diversified merchandise that ranges from frozen foods to charcoal briquettes to items of interest to kids. There's a 24-hour CVS at 1211 Vermont Ave. NW (☎ **202/628-0720**), and another at 7 Dupont Circle (☎ **202/785-1466**), both with round-the-clock pharmacies.

FARMERS' MARKETS

A pleasant family activity is wandering through the many markets that sell seasonal produce, plants and flowers, homemade foodstuffs, and baked goods. Some are magnets for garage sale junkies. Here are a couple of the larger markets.

Adams-Morgan Market

Columbia Rd. and 18th St. NW (Perpetual Bank). Sat 7:30am–3pm. Metro: Dupont Circle, then walk.

Organically grown produce from Pennsylvania, as well as homemade baked goods and foods, and crafts are featured. The same goods are sold at the D.C. Market. Go early for the best selection.

D.C. Open-Air Market

Oklahoma Ave. and Benning Rd. NE (parking lot 6 near RFK Stadium). ☎ **202/678-2800.** July–Sept Tues 7am–5pm, Thurs and Sat 7am–6pm; Oct–June Thurs and Sat 7am–6pm. Metro: Stadium/Armory.

The same basic stuff as the Adams-Morgan Market is sold here but inside much larger quarters. Regulars tell me the produce is particularly fresh, and Saturday is the best and busiest day, with hordes flocking to the weekly flea market.

Eastern Market

7th St. SE, between North Carolina Ave. and C St. ☎ **202/543-7293.** Tues–Sat from 7am, closing hours vary. Metro: Eastern Market.

This is more like a bazaar. The market is jumping on Saturday with music and other entertainment. You'll find everything from hog jowls and oxtails to fresh produce and seafood. Teens love the secondhand clothes, knickknacks, and funky jewelry. On summer weekends farmers' stalls line the street.

FASHIONS

My college tuition was less than the cost of outfitting a young child these days. I took out a small loan to get my 2-year-old grandson jeans and T-shirts a few months back. And don't even talk to me about teenagers. Medical school is cheaper. You'll find everything from designer duds to awesome army surplus for kids from cradle to Corvette in the following listings.

Benetton

1200 Wisconsin Ave. NW, at M St. ☎ **202/625-0443** (Mazza Gallerie, 5300 Wisconsin Ave. NW ☎ 202/362-6970). Metro: Foggy Bottom.

This Italian-based company sells comfortable, trendsetting clothing through its franchise stores all over the world. Chances are your teenage daughters are familiar with it already. A separate section in the above-listed stores is devoted to kids from 6 months to 12 years. The two-story shop at Wisconsin and M devotes a large part of one floor to kids' wear.

Benetton 0-12

Georgetown Park Mall. Wisconsin Ave. and M St. NW ☎ **202/333-4140.** Metro: Foggy Bottom.

This is the only freestanding Benetton 0-12 in the D.C. area. You'll find the same stylish merchandise here as in the big people's store, but scaled down to fit kids from infancy to age 12. You can't argue with success; there are more than 150 Benetton children's stores across the United States. Hours are Monday through Saturday from 10am to 9pm and Sunday from noon to 6pm.

Full of Beans

5502 Connecticut Ave. NW. ☎ **202/362-8566.** Metro: Friendship Heights, then E2, E4, or E6 bus.

Full of Beans is full of garb for girls (in infant sizes to size 14) and boys (to size 10). The charming neighborhood shop, which draws from other D.C. neighborhoods and the 'burbs, carries its own line of cotton clothing that's durable, attractive, and well priced. You'll also find unusual gifts—one-of-a-kind items not found in the average toy store. Full of Beans is near Ramer's Shoes, so on upper Connecticut Avenue you can kill two birds with one stone. "Beans" is open Monday through Saturday from 10am to 5:30pm.

The Gap

1120 Connecticut Ave. NW. ☎ **202/429-0691** (Wisconsin Ave. NW, at N St. ☎ 202/333-2805; 2000 Pennsylvania Ave. NW. ☎ 202/429-6862; also about a dozen suburban stores).

To go with its large selection of jeans in many styles, colors, and weights for waists 28 inches and larger, The Gap carries color-coordinated shirts, sweaters, tees, and accessories. Merchandise is attractively displayed and prices are competitive. There are usually racks of amazingly low sale-priced items in the back of the store. In case you just moved here from Antarctica, the sweat suits and jeans wear like iron.

Gap Kids and Baby Gap

2000 Pennsylvania Ave. NW. ☎ **202/429-8711** (1267 Wisconsin Ave. NW ☎ 202/333-2805). Metro: Foggy Bottom.

The same classic, tough-wearing denim and casual wear made famous by the "senior" Gap is in D.C. for babies (newborn to 24 months) and kids (sizes 2 to 12). If your hometown doesn't have a Gap Kids, stock up on everything from denim diaper covers to tough-wearing jeans. There's another Gap Kids at 5430 Wisconsin Ave., Chevy Chase, Maryland (☎ **301/718-0886**), and several more in suburban malls. Open Monday through Friday from 10am to 8pm, Saturday from 10am to 6pm, and Sunday from noon to 5pm.

Kids Closet

1226 Connecticut Ave. NW. ☎ **202/429-9247.** Fax 202/429-9248. Metro: Farragut North or Dupont Circle.

For Absorba, Carter's, Christian Dior, OshKosh b'Gosh, and the like, stop at the Kids Closet. They have a plentiful selection of durable, attractive kids' wear for boys and girls in size 3 months to size 14. Kids Closet has expanded its selection of footwear and toys in recent days. Open Monday through Friday from 10am to 6pm and Saturday from 11am to 5pm.

Original Levi's Store

1220 Wisconsin Ave. NW, at M St. ☎ **202/338-8010.** Metro: Foggy Bottom, then a 15-minute walk, or take any no. 30 bus.

Older kids and adults will find every style and color garment made by Levi-Strauss in this three-level store. Those with waists not yet 26 inches will have to down an extra milk shake or two before shopping here. If you have trouble finding jeans that fit, you can order a custom-made Personal Pair at this store. The customer's measurements are fed into a computer, then sent to the factory. Three weeks later the one-of-a-kind jeans and a bill for $65 arrive. Hours are Monday through Thursday from 10am to 7pm, Friday and Saturday from 10am to 9pm, and Sunday from 11am to 6pm.

Sunny's Surplus

912 F St. NW (between 9th and 10th sts.). ☎ **202/737-2032.** Metro: Gallery Place or Metro Center.

For family shopping, give me a well-stocked Army-Navy store any day of the week. Sunny's sells boots, sneakers, work shoes, jeans, outerwear, socks (in larger sizes), and unisex T-shirts, sweatshirts, gloves, hats, and camping gear for creatures great and small. No wonder kids love to rummage through the goods and goodies here. They can pick up lots of colorful inexpensive items, like camouflage T-shirts, zany bandanas, backpacks, and maybe a canteen for those long hikes from the back door to the family car. Open Monday through Saturday from 8:30am to 6:30pm and Sunday from 11am to 5pm.

There is one other D.C. branch, in Georgetown at 3342 M St. NW (☎ **202/ 333-8550**), and several suburban stores.

Très Jolie

5232 44th St. NW. ☎ **202/237-8970.** Metro: Friendship Heights.

Sandwiched between the Doll & Toy Museum and Lord & Taylor near the D.C.–Chevy Chase line, Très Jolie is the spot to shop for fine-quality baby clothes, christening gowns, first communion dresses, and those difficult-to-find ring-bearer suits and flower girl dresses. Hours are Monday through Saturday from 10am to 6pm.

✪ Urban Outfitters

3111 M St. NW. ☎ **202/342-1012.** Metro: Foggy Bottom.

Attention all teens: If you like trendy, stylish clothing and funky but functional accessories for your room—all priced so they won't eat up next year's allowance— you'll love Urban Outfitters. They have a women's and men's department and carry some of the weird-looking shoes teens call fashionable. Don't overlook the large "renewal" section—a money-saving rather than a religious experience. Open Monday through Thursday from 10am to 10pm, Friday and Saturday from 10am to 11pm, and Sunday from 11am to 9pm.

✪ Why Not?

200 King St., Alexandria, Va. ☎ **703/548-2080.** Metro: King St., then bus for 1½ miles to King and Fairfax sts. and walk 1 block east toward river.

Why not, indeed! Be sure to include this upbeat shop in your visit to Old Town. In business for more than 25 years, Why Not? stocks infant to size 14 clothing for girls; infant through size 7 for boys. But it doesn't end there. A wide range of creatively displayed toys and books fill the two-story space and help to fashion a colorful and appealing environment. No wonder Why Not? continues to draw shoppers from around the Beltway. You'll feel good as soon as you walk in the door. Open Monday from 10am to 5:30pm, Tuesday through Saturday from 10am to 9pm, and Sunday from noon to 5pm. Shorter hours in winter.

FURNITURE

In addition to the stores below, try **Baby Depot** in Silver Spring, Maryland (☎ 301/589-3610; also in nine Burlington Coat Factory locations in Maryland and Virginia); **Baby-2-Teen** (Laurel, Maryland ☎ 301/953-9494; Arlington, Virginia ☎ 703/525-2972; Manassas, Virginia ☎ 703/631-2166); **Go to Your Room,** Gaithersburg, Maryland (☎ 301/417-9160); **Great Beginnings,** Gaithersburg, Maryland (☎ 301/417-9702); **Kids' Habitat,** Rockville, Maryland (☎ 301/231-6039); and **Great Northern Bunk Beds,** Jessup, Maryland (☎ 800/34-BUNKS).

Bellini Juvenile Designer Furniture

12141 Rockville Pike, Rockville, Maryland. ☎ **301/770-3944.** Metro: Twinbrook.

They're not kidding about the designer part. Bellini sells top-of-the-line, European-crafted cribs, bunk beds, trundles, and bedding accessories to furnish little princes and princesses with beautiful beginnings. Open Monday through Wednesday and Friday and Saturday from 10am to 6pm, Thursday from 10am to 8pm, and Sunday from noon to 5pm.

Buy Buy Baby

1683 Rockville Pike (Congressional Plaza), Rockville, Maryland. ☎ **301/984-1122.** Metro: Twinbrook (half mile).

What a gold mine! I can't imagine where parents-to-be and new moms and dads shopped before this fabulous one-stop emporium opened in 1996. On two floors you'll find everything, and I mean *everything,* for your bundle from heaven: layette items, strollers, cribs, diapers, clothing, toys, books, and then some. As a first-time grandparent, I'm glad I don't live closer to this store. It's positively addictive. Open Monday through Saturday from 9:30am to 9:30pm and Sunday from 11am to 6pm.

e.a.kids by Ethan Allen

4473 Connecticut Ave. NW, Washington, D.C. ☎ **202/364-2301.** www.ethanallen.com. Metro: Van Ness/UDC.

Ethan Allen, long a bastion of traditional, quality furniture, is targeting a new generation with the introduction of e.a.kids. Shop for youth furniture, bed coverings, and accessories at this location not far from the National Zoo. Other locations are in Rockville, Maryland (☎ 301/984-4360), Springfield Mall, Virginia (☎ 703/971-4504), and Tysons Corner, Virginia (☎ 703/356-6405). Open Monday through Friday from 10am to 7pm, Saturday from 10am to 6pm, and Sunday from noon to 5pm.

Lewis of London

12248 Rockville Pike, Rockville, Maryland. ☎ **301/468-2070** (7249 Arlington Blvd., Falls Church, Virginia). ☎ **703/876-9330.**

Lewis knows a thing or two about creating stylish furniture for children and teens. Besides several attractive lines of nursery furniture and accessories, the store sells juvenile furniture for older kids, plus strollers, high chairs, and infant clothing for tots up to 24 months. Open Monday to Wednesday and Friday and Saturday, 10am to 6pm, Thursday 10am to 8:30pm, and Sunday noon to 5pm.

HAIRCUTS

Cartoon Cuts

Eight locations in suburban Maryland and Virginia (call for the nearest one). ☎ **703/354-3801.**

One memory I'd like to erase: taking my kids for haircuts when they were toddlers. They screamed and carried on like they were undergoing open-heart surgery without anesthesia. At Cartoon Cuts, today's tots get trimmed while glued to the video monitors at each station. Elephant faucets have rinsing hoses for trunks so that shampooing becomes an event instead of a dreaded chore. The shops also host birthday and karaoke parties where little snippets can be made over into their favorite rock stars. Haircuts are $10.95, $11.95 weekends (entertainment included). Hours vary according to branch.

Hair Cuttery

1645 Connecticut Ave. NW. ☎ **202/232-9685.** (L'Enfant Plaza SW ☎ 202/863-9400; Metro: L'Enfant Plaza). Metro: Dupont Circle.

For a walk-in cut, wash, and blow-dry—still only $11—you can't beat the Hair Cuttery. Men, women, and children are equally welcome, regardless of hair length. Besides the two D.C. locations, there are several in the Maryland and Virginia suburbs.

JEWELRY & BEADS

Accents Jewelry

4930 Hampden Lane, Bethesda, Md. ☎ **301/656-7307.** Metro: Bethesda.

Come here for semiprecious beads (as little as 10¢ apiece), findings, and bead-stringing supplies. Accents also has jewelry-making classes. Open Monday through Wednesday and Friday from 10am to 5pm, Thursday from 10am to 7pm, and Saturday from 10am to 5pm.

Beadazzled

1322 Connecticut Ave. NW. ☎ **202/265-BEAD.** Metro: Dupont Circle.

Cute name, eh? There are plenty of baubles, bangles, and beads, plus everything in beadwork supplies and classes to keep you and yours from getting strung out. Open Wednesday through Saturday from 11am to 8pm, Sunday through Tuesday from 11am to 6pm. A second store is located at Tysons Corner Center in Virginia.

KITES

Air and Space Museum Gift Shop

6th St. and Independence Ave. SW. ☎ **202/357-1387.** Metro: L'Enfant Plaza.

Your kids will be walking on air when they see the selection of kites (from $5 to $120) sold here. Kites are color coded according to degree of difficulty. Mine ("for 7-year-olds") is a breeze to fly. Launch your purchase on the Mall just outside the museum. Open daily from 10am to 5:30pm with extended summer hours.

MAGIC SHOPS

Al's Magic Shop

1012 Vermont Ave. NW. ☎ **202/789-2800.** www.alsmagic.com. E-mail: Alcomagic@aol.com. Metro: McPherson Square.

If you're in the market for fake vomit, a squirt ring, or a bug in an ice cube, you've come to the right place. A Washington landmark for more than half a century, Al's is loaded with sleight-of-hand paraphernalia. Exploding cigar, anyone? Open Monday through Friday from 9:30am to 5:45pm, Saturday from 9am to 4:30pm, and closed Sunday.

MALLS

What did kids do before malls? I have *vague* recollections of hopscotch, marbles, and stickball, but hanging out at malls is the number one pastime of today's youth. Happily they trade natural for fluorescent light and exercise for just hanging out. You'll have no trouble keeping your little mall rats satisfied in the D.C. area. Just bring lots of money. Besides these listings, there are countless malls in suburban Maryland and Virginia. (Maybe you'll want to keep this bit of information to yourself.)

The Chevy Chase Pavilion

5345 Wisconsin Ave. NW, at Military Rd. ☎ **202/686-5335.** Metro: Friendship Heights.

Just a block away from the Friendship Heights Metro station, this bright and compact three-tiered mall is geared more to adults than children at the moment; however, there are some noted exceptions. There's a branch of **Sam Goody** for tapes and CDs, **B. Dalton Booksellers, Talbots and Talbots Petites, Sunglass Hut,** and several upper-end shops carrying women's and men's fashions. You'll also find a branch of the **Pottery Barn** and **Georgette Klinger** if you want to disappear for a massage, haircut, or makeover.

The **Limited Too** carries the same fashionable clothes as its big sister, The Limited, in sizes 4 to 16 for girls.

Between the **Atrium Cafes** on the Lower Level, **Cheesecake Factory,** and **California Pizza Kitchen,** you have no excuse to leave the Chevy Chase Pavilion hungry. Hours are Monday through Friday from 10am to 8pm, Saturday from 10am to 6pm, and Sunday from noon to 5pm. There is free parking in the building with validation.

Fashion Centre at Pentagon City

1100 South Hayes St., Arlington, Va. ☎ **703/415-2400.** Metro: Pentagon City.

My Virginia relatives and friends swear by the Fashion Centre (and I know some *big-time* shoppers on the other side of the Potomac). **Macy's** and **Nordstrom** are the anchors in this three-level mall with more than 160 stores. You'll find upscalers such as **Abercrombie and Fitch, Britches of Georgetowne** (the "e" wasn't my idea), the **Custom Shop,** the **Museum Company,** the **Coach Store, Georgetown Leather Design,** and **Joan and David.** One of the few area **Scribner's** bookstores is here, as well as **Brentano's.**

Of special interest to the *kinder* are the Athlete's Foot, Champs Sports, Foot Locker, the Game Keeper, The Gap and Gap Kids, Gymboree, KayBee Toys, The Limited Too, America!, the Disney Store, Sony Theatres (count 'em, six!), Sunglass Hut, and the Sweet Factory.

When you need a break or wear out your wallet, stop for a light bite in the Food Court, with a lucky 13 selections to choose from, or relax at one of seven restaurants. **Johnny Rockets** is always a family favorite with burgers, shakes, and other nutritious offerings that made America great. The **Grill at the Ritz-Carlton** holds up the high end of the spectrum; several cafes, **L and N Seafood Grill,** and **Ruby Tuesday**—all serving moderately priced fare—fall in between.

Hours are Monday through Saturday from 10am to 9:30pm and Sunday from 11am to 6pm, with extended hours during the Christmas season.

Georgetown Park Mall

3222 M St. NW., at Wisconsin Ave. ☎ **202/965-3415.** Metro: Foggy Bottom.

This handsome multilevel complex with more than 100 upscale shops invites browsers and buyers with its warm brick Victorian interior, complemented by skylights, fountains, chandeliers, and beautiful plantings. Shopping at Georgetown Park is an event. **FAO Schwarz, Benetton 0-12, Mrs. Field's Cookies, Fit to a Tee, Sunglass Hut, Record Town,** and **Waldenbooks** will please the kids most. Enjoy people-watching with a snack or meal from the **Canal Walk Food Court.** Open Monday through Saturday from 10am to 9pm and Sunday from noon to 6pm. Discounted parking with a $10 purchase.

Mazza Gallerie

5300 Wisconsin Ave. NW., between Western Ave. and Jenifer St. ☎ **202/966-6114** or 202/686-9515. Metro: Friendship Heights.

While **Neiman Marcus** and most of the boutiquey shops at this très chic four-level mall will be out of reach for little people's tastes and allowances, there are some exceptions, like **Filene's Basement** (for kids who fit into adult sizes). The **World of Science** carries educational books and games, telescopes, birdhouses, and gift items. **Record Town** is a popular source for tapes, CDs, posters, and celebrity buttons, and there's a **Foot Locker** store. Slip into **McDonald's** when a Big Mac attack hits, then dive into the divine "designer" chocolates at **Kron Chocolatier.** Open Monday through Friday from 10am to 8pm, Saturday from 10am to 6pm, and Sunday from noon to 5pm.

Montgomery Mall

7101 Democracy Blvd., Bethesda, Md. ☎ **301/469-6025**. Metro: Grosvenor, then no. 47 bus.

I am partial to this mall because, like the ideal chair in "Goldilocks and the Three Bears," it's not too big, it's not too small, it's just right! It's also clean, bright, attractive, and you don't need an atlas to find your way. Besides, it's where I shopped when my kids were growing up. Montgomery Mall is chock-full of family oriented stores that sell quality merchandise at (usually) bearable prices. And there's a **Nordstrom,** which needs no introduction and has a "Mothers' Room" with changing table and diaper vending machine.

Anyone who has ever shopped with kids knows how traumatic it can be for little ones who "have to go" but fear falling into an adult-size toilet. Well, Montgomery Mall has two family rest rooms (one on the Lower Level near Nordstrom; the other on the Upper Level near the Boulevard Cafés) with small-scale toilets and sinks, changing facilities, and a couch for nursing mothers who prefer privacy to performing in public.

Of interest to little people—other than the family rest rooms—are **Going to the Game** (athletic wear), the **Disney Store, Warner Bros. Studio Store, KayBee** (toys), **Babbage's** (software and computer games), **Gymboree** (kids' wear), **The Limited Too** (for girls sizes 4 to 16), **Kramer's** (clothing for growing girls and boys, camp supplies, gifts), **Gap Kids** (denim, and so on), **Stride Rite/Keds, Kids Foot Locker, My Room** (kids' furniture), **B. Dalton,** and **Waldenbooks.**

Take your pick of about a dozen eateries in the Boulevard Cafés, and five sit-down restaurants, including **California Pizza Kitchen, Slade's, Burger King,** and **Gifford's** beloved ice cream.

If you still think I'm talking through my hat, catch a flick at one of the three KB Montgomery Mall theaters (where my son worked one summer and always gave me extra butter on my popcorn), or drop older kids at the Game Room and Arcade across from the theater and enjoy some quality shopping time all by yourself. The mall is open Monday through Saturday from 10am to 9:30pm and Sunday from 11am to 6pm.

Pavilion at the Old Post Office

1100 Pennsylvania Ave. NW. ☎ **202/289-4224.** Metro: Federal Triangle.

It's nearly 200 feet straight up from the floor to the skylight canopy of this three-level complex of retail shops and restaurants housed in a 100-year-old office building. Don't expect to do major shopping here, but there are some novelty and souvenir shops.

Ride the glass elevator to the tower observation deck for a spectacular 360° view of downtown and the environs, then inspect the 10 massive bells (a bicentennial gift from England) that are rung on state occasions. If your blood sugar is running low, stop at **Candy Circus** or one of the numerous ice-cream and yogurt stands for a picker-upper.

Free entertainment is presented daily in the West Atrium. The shops are open March through August, Monday through Saturday from 10am to 9pm, Sunday from noon to 7pm and September through February, Monday through Saturday from 10am to 7pm, Sunday from noon to 7pm. The restaurants usually stay open an hour or two later than the retail shops. There are three entrances: 10th and 12th streets NW and Pennsylvania Avenue (at 11th Street).

Potomac Mills

Off I-95, Dale City, Va. ☎ **703/643-1770.** Directions: Drive south on I-95 into Virginia and the Dale City exit.

Would you believe Potomac Mills discount shopping mall is the top tourist attraction in Virginia? Well, it is. Not even Mr. Jefferson's Monticello, Mount Vernon, or Paramount's King's Dominion draws the numbers PM does. It's not unusual for more than 30,000 salivating shoppers, credit cards in hand, to lighten their wallets in the 1.2 *million*-square-foot mall daily. In addition to discount outlets for many nationally known department stores, you'll find scads of specialty shops, numbering 235 last count, and the warehouse-size **IKEA** where attractive, well-priced furniture (some assembly required), toys, and housewares are gobbled up. *A caveat:* Know ahead of time the average retail prices of the items you seek. It's not all bargains here and some of the merchandise is out of season or irregular. Hours are Monday through Saturday from 10am to 9:30pm and Sunday from 11am to 6pm.

Shops at National Place

Entrance on F St. NW, between 13th and 14th sts., or via the J.W. Marriott at 529 14th St. NW. ☎ **202/783-9090.** Metro: Metro Center.

Get out your credit cards in preparation for shopping at this attractive four-tiered complex in the renovated National Press Building. **Lids** (college and sport hats), **Electronique** (electonic gadgets), **Curious Kids** (toys), **Washington Kids** (newborn to size 8 clothing and accessories), **Capitol Image** (souvenirs), **Alamo Flags** (flags and souvenirs), **Best of Times** (clocks and watches), and **B. Dalton** (books) beckon. Have a meal or a snack in the Food Hall on the top level, where American, Chinese, Italian, Japanese, and other varieties of fast food and desserts are available throughout the day. Open Monday through Saturday from 10am to 7pm and Sunday from noon to 5pm.

Tysons Corner Center

1961 Chain Bridge Rd., at Route 7, Vienna, Va. ☎ **703/893-9400.** Metro: West Falls Church; from there you can catch a shuttle that runs every half hour in both directions.

This well-known mall is about 30 minutes from town in Vienna, Virginia (take the Beltway I-495 to Exit 11B and follow the signs). Among the 230 shops here are four major department stores—**Bloomingdale's, Nordstrom, Lord & Taylor,** and **Hecht's.** Other notable emporia of interest to kids include the **Nature Company,**

The Limited, Disney Store, Banana Republic, FAO Schwarz, Waldenbooks, Britches of Georgetowne, and **The Gap.** Once again—and very convenient—a U.S. Post Office. More than 30 restaurants run the gamut from **Magic Pan** to **California Pizza Kitchen,** and eight movie theaters make this a good choice for an afternoon shopping spree followed by a relaxing family dinner and a film. There's free parking for 10,000 cars. Open Monday through Saturday from 10am to 9:30pm and Sunday from noon to 6pm.

✪ Union Station
50 Massachusetts Ave. NE. ☎ **202/371-9441.** Metro: Union Station.

Since reopening in 1988 after extensive renovation, Union Station has become a top tourist draw. I still marvel at the magnificent architecture (the main halls were inspired by the Baths of Diocletian built in third-century Rome) and beautiful restoration. Hunker down for something good to eat at the lower-level Food Court, which can be entered via a majestic winding staircase. Nearly 75 shops are scattered between two levels. Of particular note: **B. Dalton** (local interest books, off Main Hall); the **Nature Company** (environmentally themed items, West Hall); **Accento** (handcrafted clothing and accessories for the whole family, West Hall), **Political Americana, Best of Washington, D.C.,** and **Made in America** (souvenirs, West Hall), **The Great Train Store** (model trains, railroad memorabilia, Main Floor Level); **Flights of Fancy** (toys, Main Floor Level); **Brookstone** (gadgets, electronics, Main Floor Level); and **Sam Goody** (records).

Time to kill? Catch nine different movies in the cinema complex. Open Monday through Saturday from 10am to 9pm and Sunday from noon to 6pm.

MAPS

ADC Map & Travel Center
1636 I St. NW. ☎ **202/628-2608.** Metro: Farragut North or Farragut West.

The center of the local cartophiles' universe for more than 40 years, the former Map Store (remodeled and renamed in 1998) has something for all age levels: wood puzzles of the continents and United States, inflatable and traditional globes, atlases, road and street maps, and even a world wastebasket for those who want to learn some geography while filing trash. Open Monday through Thursday from 9am to 5:30pm, Friday from 9am to 5:30pm, and Saturday from 11am to 5pm.

National Geographic Society Gift and Book Shop
17th and M sts. NW. ☎ **202/857-7588.** Metro: Farragut North.

Here you'll find the society's distinctive and finely detailed maps, as well as all National Geographic publications. You can also purchase back issues of *National Geographic* magazine, globes, games, and videos. Open Monday through Saturday from 9am to 5pm and Sunday from 10am to 5pm.

Rand McNally Map & Travel Store
1201 Connecticut Ave. NW. ☎ **202/223-6751.** Metro: Farragut North.

Expand your horizons at Rand McNally, where they have maps of places you've never heard of, many attractively displayed like museum prints. There are also travel guides, luggage, videos, travel-related gifts, and more than 30 globes, from a kid-size 6-incher to a special-order 6-foot motorized sphere. Branch stores are also in Montgomery Mall (Maryland) and Tysons Corner (Virginia). Open Monday through Friday from 9am to 6:30pm (until 7:30pm on Thursday) and Saturday from 10am to 6pm.

Travel Books & Language Center
4437 Wisconsin Ave. NW. ☎ **800/220-2665** or 202/237-1322. Fax 202/237-6022. E-mail: travelbks@aol.com. Metro: Tenleytown, and then walk a half block south.

Rochelle Jaffe moved her fantastic business from Bethesda to the District in November '97. Just a half block from the Tenleytown Metro, the store is the area's best source for maps, language aids, and, of course, travel books.

Take your pick of more than 17,000 maps at this unique travel bookstore, and let your kids help plan your next vacation. Whether you pine for Essex, Estonia, or Ecuador—or any point in between—Travel Books & Language Center has it. This is a must stop for accidental tourists, serious travel buffs, and geography freaks. Check out the "Destination of the Month"—all guides, maps, books, videos, and language materials of a featured destination are 15% off. Special events, featuring slide presentations and discussions on destinations around the globe, are held several evenings a month at 7pm. Open Monday through Saturday from 10am to 10pm and Sunday from noon to 7pm.

MUSEUM SHOPS
Museum shops are prime sources for educational books, gift items, crafts, and souvenirs (nothing tacky here; this is quality stuff) from all over the world. The Smithsonian museum shops are usually open daily from 10am to 5:30pm, sometimes with extended hours. Independent museum and gallery shops have varying hours, so call ahead. Don't forget a packet of freeze-dried ice cream for the kids!

Anacostia Museum, 1901 Fort Place SE (☎ **202/287-3414**). African books, toys, crafts.

Arthur M. Sackler and Freer Galleries, 1050 Independence Ave. SW (☎ **202/357-4880**). Asian and African art reproductions, crafts, books.

Arts and Industries Building, 900 Jefferson Dr. SW (☎ **202/357-1369**). Victoriana, miniatures, wooden toys, Smithsonian gift catalog.

Corcoran Gallery of Art, 500 17th St. NW (☎ **202/639-1790**). Art books, posters, jewelry.

Hirshhorn Museum, Independence Avenue and 7th Street SW (☎ **202/357-1429**). Art books and monographs, jewelry, some art supplies.

John F. Kennedy Center for the Performing Arts, 2700 F St. NW (☎ **202/416-8350**). Posters, videos, performing arts memorabilia.

Library of Congress, 1st Street SE, between Independence Avenue and C Street (☎ **202/707-0204**). Books, books, and more books, specialized journals, clothing accessories.

National Air and Space Museum, Independence Avenue and 7th Street SW (☎ **202/357-1387**). Flying toys (including kites); space-related books, memorabilia, jewelry, freeze-dried ice cream.

National Archives, Constitution Avenue and 8th Street NW (☎ **202/501-5235**). Books on genealogy, campaign buttons, famous documents (replicas only!).

National Building Museum, 401 F St. NW (☎ **202/272-7706**). Architectural toys, crafts, books, graphics.

National Gallery of Art, 4th Street and 6th Street at Constitution Avenue NW (☎ **202/737-4215**). Posters, art books, stationery, journals.

National Geographic Society, 17th and M streets NW (☎ **202/857-7588**). Maps, toys, globes, back issues of *National Geographic* magazine.

National Museum of African Art, 950 Independence Ave. SW (☎ **202/ 786-2147**). African-inspired accessories, crafts, toys, tapes.

National Museum of American Art, 8th and G streets NW (☎ **202/357-1545**). "Masterpieces of American Art" coloring book, picture frames, jewelry.

National Museum of American History, 14th Street and Constitution Avenue NW (☎ **202/357-1527**). Americana, books, games, toys, tapes.

National Museum of Natural History, 10th Street and Constitution Avenue NW (☎ **202/357-1537**). Crafts, jewelry, books.

National Museum of Women in the Arts, 1250 New York Ave. NW (☎ **202/ 783-7994**). Notepaper, books, calendars.

National Zoo, opposite 3000 Connecticut Ave. NW (☎ **202/673-4657**). Animal-inspired books, toys, crafts.

Phillips Collection, 1600 21st St. NW (☎ **202/667-6106**). Art books, toys, jewelry.

Renwick Gallery, 17th Street and Pennsylvania Avenue NW (☎ **202/357-1445**). Crafts, jewelry, how-to books.

U.S. Holocaust Memorial Museum, 100 Raoul Wallenberg Place (15th Street) SW (☎ **202/488-0400**). Books, tapes, Judaica.

NATURE TREASURES

National Museum of Natural History Gift Shops
10th St. and Constitution Ave. NW. ☎ **202/357-1535.** Metro: Federal Triangle.

Before or after your museum visit, stop at the recently expanded museum store on the ground floor. Some locals shop here for everyone on their holiday gift list. This is one of my favorite museum shops. You'll find an interesting collection of books—many geared to young people—on natural history and anthropology, as well as fossil reproduction kits, shells, minerals, and attractive and distinctive clothing, crafts, and jewelry. The smaller shop, also on the ground floor, sells puppets, activity books, puzzles, and plush animals. Open daily from 10am to 5:15pm, except December 25. Extended summer hours are determined annually.

Nature Company
Union Station, 50 Massachusetts Ave. NE. ☎ **202/842-3700.** Metro: Union Station.

It's hard not to love this place. Luring kids *out* of here can be as difficult as getting them into bed at night. But it's worth it. Everything sold in these shops, part of a national chain, is nature related: books, tapes, toys, prisms, bird feeders, posters, telescopes, and worlds more of stuff. Open Monday through Saturday from 10am to 9pm and Sunday from noon to 6pm. Nature story hours are scheduled throughout the year for different age groups. Call for details.

NEWSPAPERS & MAGAZINES

Newsroom
1753 Connecticut Ave. NW. ☎ **202/332-1489.** Metro: Dupont Circle.

Still going strong after more than 15 years, the Newsroom is a mainstay of the Dupont Circle area. They carry more than 200 domestic and foreign newspapers and numerous magazines in 20 languages. The foreign-language department has books and tapes for kids who want to learn other languages. Open daily from 7am to 9pm.

PERFORMING ARTS SUPPLIES

Backstage
2101 P St. NW. ☎ **202/775-1488.** Metro: Dupont Circle.

Anyone with an interest in the performing arts should take a cue from Washington thespians, musicians, and dancers and enter laughing at Backstage. Here is everything your family will need to get their act together: an award-winning selection of scripts, costumes, dancewear, makeup, sheet music, and books. Open Monday through Saturday from 10am to 6pm (Thursday until 7pm).

POSTERS

Movie Madness
1083 Thomas Jefferson Ave. (at M St.) NW. ☎ **202/337-7064.** Metro: Foggy Bottom.

Whether they're looking for a poster of their all-time favorite movie or new-wave group to decorate a bedroom wall, kids will find it at Movie Madness. The shop, which used to be next to the old Key Theater on Wisconsin Avenue, moved in 1998 when that building was sold. You'll find several hundred *original* posters, many reprints, and life-size stand-ups! There's a large selection of movie and rock star postcards to sift through, and plenty of oldie-but-goodie posters to accompany mom and dad down Memory Lane. Open Monday, Wednesday, Thursday noon to 8pm, Friday and Saturday noon to 9pm, and Sunday noon to 6pm. Closed Tuesday.

RESALE SHOPS

Davis Memorial Goodwill Industries Retail Store
2200 South Dakota Ave. NE. ☎ **202/636-4232.** www.dcgoodwill.org. Metro: Brookland, then H2 or H4 bus.

The location may be a bit out of the way, but there's no denying you'll find bargains galore here. Kids' clothing is available in sizes for infants on up. Between you and me, the parents of some very well-dressed Washington kids have been known to donate minidesigner duds marred by one eensy-weensy spot.

For 6 days every October Goodwill hosts its annual **book sale** (the largest on the entire East Coast!) at the D.C. Convention Center. It's a bibliophile's paradise, with rare and collectible books in numerous categories, including kids' books.

For more than 50 years, Goodwill has been sponsoring the annual **Embassy Tour,** usually the second Saturday of May. No passport is required, but advance tickets are. It will set you back $30 to visit the magnificent embassies of 8 to 10 countries. For more information, call ☎ **202/636-4225,** ext. 1257, or visit the Web site listed above.

For the 14 Goodwill stores in the Maryland and Virginia suburbs, call ☎ **202/ 636-4232.**

SHOES

Athlete's Foot
1150 Connecticut Ave. NW. ☎ **202/822-9406** (Georgetown Park, 3222 M St. NW. ☎ 202/ 965-7262; and several other locations). Metro: Farragut North.

Who would have thought such a funny name would grow to become the area's largest seller of athletic-type shoes? Although some styles are available in infant's size 3, the selection runs wild in larger sizes. They also carry hiking boots for older kids. Open Monday through Saturday from 10am to 9pm and Sunday from noon to 6pm.

Fleet Feet

1841 Columbia Rd. NW. ☎ **202/387-3888.** www.dcnet.com/fleetfeet. E-mail: Fleetdc@erols.com. Metro: Woodley Park then no. 42 Metrobus or walk.

Adams-Morgan's total sports/fitness shop carries all the top names for fleet-footed kids and adults, beginning with size 2. Open Monday through Friday from 10am to 8pm, Saturday from 10am to 7pm and Sunday from noon to 4pm. Limited street parking.

Foot Locker

3221 M St. NW. ☎ **202/333-7640** (1331 Pennsylvania Ave. NW. ☎ 202/783-2093; Mazza Gallerie, 5300 Wisconsin Ave. NW. ☎ 202/362-7427; and other D.C. branches). www.footlocker.com. Metro (M Street store): Foggy Bottom, then 10-minute walk west on Pennsylvania Ave. to M St.

All the big-name brands of athletic-type shoes for both first-stringers and bench-warmers are carried by this national chain. There are also several Virginia and Maryland branches.

The M Street shop is open Monday through Saturday from 10am to 9pm and Sunday from noon to 6pm.

Kids Foot Locker

Tysons Corner Center, Vienna, Va. ☎ **703/847-1843** (Montgomery Mall, Bethesda, Md. ☎ 301/365-0004; also several other suburban locations).

By the time you read this, there may be a Kids Foot Locker in Washington. If not, hotfoot it to Landmark or Fair Oaks Mall or Tysons Corner Center in Virginia; Landover, Prince George's, Montgomery Malls, St. Charles Towne Center, or Wheaton Plaza in Maryland for kids' shoes from newborn to size 6. Some clothing to size 20 is also featured at the Kids Foot Locker. It's never too early to pick up a wee-size Redskins jacket, sweats, T-shirt, or shorts. The Tysons, Virginia, store is open Monday through Saturday from 10am to 9:30pm and Sunday from 10am to 6:30pm.

Ramer's Shoes

3810 Northampton St. NW, off Connecticut Ave. ☎ **202/244-2288.** Metro: Friendship Heights, then take an E2, E4, or E6 bus.

Ramer's, the friendly neighborhood shoe store featuring Stride Rite shoes, is 1 block below Chevy Chase Circle. Come here for Keds, Sperry's, Sebago's, Little Capezio, and more in sizes 0 to 4½, widths AA to EEE. Open Monday through Friday from 9:30am to 6pm and Saturday from 9:30am to 5:30pm.

Also try **FR Richey Shoes,** Rockville, Maryland (☎ **301/881-3121**), and the dozen or so Stride Rite stores in suburban Maryland and Virginia malls.

SPORTS GEAR

Bicycle Exchange

4000 Wisconsin Ave. NW. ☎ **202/244-2800** (3411 M St. NW ☎ 202/337-8600). Metro: Tenleytown.

They carry a wide selection of recreational, touring, and racing children's bikes here, and free safety checks are given. Open Monday through Saturday from 10am to 9pm and Sunday from 11am to 6pm. There are also several Virginia branches.

Big Wheel Bikes

1034 33rd St. NW, at M St. ☎ **202/337-0254.** Fax 202/333-7035 (6917 Arlington Rd., Bethesda, Md. ☎ 301/652-0192; 2 Prince St., Alexandria, Va. ☎ 703/739-2300). Metro: Foggy Bottom.

If you're not interested in buying, Big Wheel rents kids' bikes (adults' bikes too). Open Monday through Friday from 10am to 7pm and Saturday and Sunday from 10am to 6pm.

Drilling Tennis and Golf Shop
1040 17th St. NW. ☎ **202/737-1100.** Metro: Farragut North or Farragut West.

The shop is owned by Fred Drilling, Washington Tennis Patrons' Hall of Famer, and the staff will see that your youngster comes out swinging the right racket from the store's selection for 2- to 12-year-olds. No kids' clothing here, but plenty of accessories. Open Monday through Friday from 9:30am to 6pm and Saturday from 10am to 4pm. If you must drive, parking is free.

Hudson Trail Outfitters
4530 Wisconsin Ave. NW. ☎ **202/363-9810.** Metro: Tenleytown.

Hudson Trail is a magnet for teens who are into hiking, biking, camping, and other outdoor activities. Quality gear, clothing, and accessories fill the rustic shop, and the youthful, healthy-looking salespeople are helpful and laid-back. Open Monday through Friday from 10am to 9pm, Saturday from 10am to 9pm, and Sunday from 11am to 6pm. Locations in Maryland and Virginia, too.

National Diving Center
4932 Wisconsin Ave. NW. ☎ **202/363-6123.** Fax 202/237-6538. E-mail: natdivcent@aol. com. Metro: Friendship Heights or Tenleytown.

Even the youngest snorkeler can be outfitted here. Manager Scott Vazquez says kids can snorkel as soon as they can swim, but potential scuba divers must be 12. Besides stocking snorkeling and diving gear, they offer lessons (with open-water checkouts in Pennsylvania rock quarries) and diving trips off the Atlantic coast and Caribbean. Open Monday 1 to 7pm, Tuesday through Friday 10am to 7pm, Saturday 11am to 6pm and closed Sunday. Call for specific details and schedules.

Play It Again Sports
11112 Lee Hwy., Fairfax, Va. ☎ **703/352-8284** (1094 Elden St., Herndon, Va. ☎ 703/471-5215; 642 Quince Orchard Rd., Gaithersburg, Md. ☎ 301/840-1122).

It was just a matter of time. Now you can purchase, sell, or trade *used* backpacks, hiking boots, roller and ice skates, baseball gear, ski equipment, and weight sets. What a swell idea! Where were they when my kids were outgrowing soccer cleats every other week? Call for hours and directions.

Ski Center
Massachusetts Ave. and 49th St. NW. ☎ **202/966-5413.**

Schuss down to the oldest ski shop in the South. The Ski Center has had an edge on ski stuff in the D.C. area for more than 30 years and can outfit all the younger members of your ski team with equipment and clothing. You can also buy or rent in-line skates here. Call for seasonal details. Open August through April. Hours vary.

Washington Golf Center
1722 I St. NW. ☎ **202/728-0088.** Metro: Farragut West.

Swing over here for kid-size clubs, bags, and practice equipment (but no clothes). Open Monday through Friday from 10am to 6pm and Saturday from 10am to 2pm. There are also several branch stores in Maryland and Virginia.

SPORTS TRADING CARDS

The following shops (plus close to two dozen more in the suburbs) sell trading cards and other sports-related memorabilia as well: **Another World,** 1504 Wisconsin Ave. NW (☎ 202/333-8651); **Star Chamber,** 1204 G St. NW (☎ 202/639-9447); **United Wholesalers,** corner of 4th Street and Florida Avenue NE (☎ 202/546-7020); **House of Cards** (☎ 301/933-0355); and **Card and Comic Collectorama** (☎ 703/548-3466).

TAPES, RECORDS & CDS

✪ Kemp Mill Music

1900 L St. NW. ☎ **202/223-5310** (1100 F St. NW ☎ 202/638-7077; also several suburban locations). Metro: Farragut North.

The largest retail record chain in the D.C. area carries everything from Winnie the Pooh to Alanis Morisette. Kemp Mill carries an especially boss selection of whatever's hot, making it a popular gathering place for area preteens and teens. Open Monday through Friday from 8:30am to 9pm, Saturday from 10am to 7pm, and Sunday from noon to 5pm.

✪ Olsson's Books & Records

1307 19th St. NW, off Dupont Circle. ☎ **202/785-2662** for records. Metro: Dupont Circle.

It isn't called Olsson's Books & *Records* for nothing. Most kids head for the neon ROCK ROOM sign, where there's always someone to give assistance. If your kids dig classical music, Olsson's has one of the best selections in the city; and if they don't have it, they'll order it. For hard-to-get items, Olsson's mail-order department is open from 9:30am to 7pm (☎ **800/989-8084**). Open Monday through Saturday from 10am to 10pm and Sunday from noon to 6pm. See listing under "Books," above, for additional locations.

Sam Goody

Union Station, 50 Massachusetts Ave. NE. ☎ **202/289-1405** (Chevy Chase Pavilion ☎ 202/364-1957; also numerous suburban locations). Metro: Union Station.

An offshoot of the long-popular New York record store, Sam Goody has numerous stores in and around D.C. The Union Station store is open Monday through Friday from 9:30am to 8pm, Saturday from 10am to 6pm, and Sunday from noon to 5pm.

✪ Tower Records

2000 Pennsylvania Ave. NW. ☎ **202/331-2400.** Metro: Foggy Bottom or Farragut West.

"Awesome" was my son's succinct appraisal of Tower Records on his first visit. It's a two-story, 18,000-square-foot supermarket of records, tapes, and CDs in Foggy Bottom on the campus of George Washington University. Tower carries standard Sesame Street and Disney fare plus several hundred kid-oriented selections for its discerning junior clientele. Everyone with kids should own a tape of Meryl Streep reading *The Tailor of Gloucester.* Open daily from 9am to midnight.

TOYS

Barstons Child's Play

5536 Connecticut Ave. NW. ☎ **202/244-3602.** Fax 202/244-3605. Metro: Friendship Heights, then a 10-minute walk.

Child's Play carries a wide selection of Playmobil (Germany), Lego, Lundby dollhouse furniture, and Gund stuffed animals. The software, book, and art sections have been expanded and a second location opened in the Baltimore 'burbs when you're up that way. This place is fun to visit, as many of the displayed toys invite touching—and you don't have to be under three feet tall to appreciate them. Free parking behind the shop. Open Monday through Wednesday and Friday from 9:30am to 7pm, Thursday from 9:30am to 8pm, Saturday from 9:30am to 6pm, and Sunday from noon to 5pm. There's also a Child's Play in Burtonsville and Gaithersburg, Maryland.

Fairy Godmother

See entry under "Books," above.

FAO Schwarz
Georgetown Park Mall, 3222 M St. NW. ☎ **202/342-2285.** Metro: Foggy Bottom.

The Tiffany's of toys, FAO Schwarz (no "t") is the offshoot of the famous New York City store featured in the movie *Big*. Only top-quality playthings are sold here, with prices to match. They have a very large Nintendo selection and more than 100 Madame Alexander dolls. Hours are Monday through Saturday from 10am to 9pm and Sunday from noon to 6pm.

Granny's Place
303 Cameron St., Alexandria, Va. ☎ **703/549-0119.** Metro: King St., then DASH bus to Old Town.

With a name like Granny's, you know the place will be cute and inviting before you walk in the door. Wooden playground equipment, unusual games, toys, puppets, and dolls are featured, along with clothing for infants to size 14. Granny's always had a way with kids. Open Monday through Saturday from 10am to 5:30pm and Sunday from noon to 5:30pm. Call for directions.

✪ Great Train Store
Union Station, 50 Massachusetts Ave. NE. ☎ **202/371-2881.** Metro: Union Station.

"All aboard!" That's what the store manager chants conductor-style from the entrance of this neat store. Bachmann, Lionel, Mantua, and Marklin are but some of the model choo-choos carried at this unique shop on the main floor of the Concourse at—where else—Union Station. The store also sells books, videos, railway-inspired toys, and railroad novelty items like signs and T-shirts. It's a fascinating place to browse and take an imaginary railroad journey. Open Monday through Friday from 8am to 9pm, Saturday from 10am to 9pm, and Sunday from noon to 6pm.

✪ Sullivan's
3412 Wisconsin Ave. NW. ☎ **202/362-1343.** Metro: Tenleytown, then take any no. 30 bus.

If a film crew were scouting for a typical neighborhood toy store, Sullivan's would be the ideal. A feeling of comfortable disarray pervades the Cleveland Park shop. Kids of all ages will find plenty to toy with on the well-stocked shelves. There's a huge selection of art supplies, too. The most fun can be had up front, where 60 glass jars are filled with 99¢ toys. Open Monday through Wednesday and Friday from 10am to 6pm, Thursday from 10am to 7pm, Saturday from 9:30am to 5:30pm, and Sunday from noon to 4pm.

Toys "R" Us
11810 Rockville Pike, at Old Georgetown Rd., Rockville, Md. ☎ **301/770-3376.**

Santa's Workshop doesn't hold a candle to this warehouse of discount-priced toys, games, seasonal sports gear and outdoor equipment, juvenile furniture, and party supplies. Shop early or late unless you have nerves of steel and can withstand hundreds of tiny voices whining "I want!" a cappella. Open Monday through Saturday from 9:30am to 9:30pm and Sunday from 10am to 6pm. There are several other branches in suburban Maryland and Virginia.

✪ Tree Top Toys
3301 New Mexico Ave. NW. ☎ **202/244-3500** (Langley Shopping Center, 1382 Chain Bridge Rd., McLean, Va. ☎ 703/356-1400). Fax 202/966-0848. E-mail: TTToys@aol.com. Metro: Tenleytown, then American University bus to campus and cross street.

Congratulations to Tree Top for amending its name (and merchandise) to include "and books, and clothes" and adding a second location in suburban Virginia. This charming toy store near the campus of American University is known for its large selection of imported French dolls and baby toys. Tree Top Toys, growing faster than an adolescent, carries clothing in sizes zero to six. The toy area was expanded a few years ago, and books fill more than 2,000 square feet of space. Special events include visits by costumed book characters—Madeleine and Peter Rabbit among them—and story time for preschoolers. Ask for a copy of the shop's colorful toy and book catalogs. You'll find everything from infants' crib toys to big kids' games and models. Kids who enroll in the Birthday Club are entitled to free balloons and 20% off their favorite item on their special day. Open Monday through Saturday from 9:30am to 5:30pm. One-hour free parking with validation in garage.

Washington Dolls' House and Toy Museum
5236 44th St. NW. ☎ **202/244-0024.** Metro: Friendship Heights.

This magical museum (see chapter 6) also sells a wonderful assortment of doll- and dollhouse-related books and magazines, furniture and accessories, and consignment items in the second-floor shops. For the avid collector, there are even miniature quilt kits. The women who work here obviously love what they're doing. Open Tuesday through Saturday from 10am to 5pm and Sunday from noon to 5pm.

T-SHIRTS

For a souvenir or gift T-shirt, check out the museum shops and numerous vendors blanketing the area around the National Mall.

Fit to a Tee
Georgetown Park Mall, 3222 M St. NW. ☎ **202/965-3650.** Metro: Foggy Bottom or Rosslyn.

Every year I buy my little brother a birthday T-shirt at Fit to a Tee. My brother is 49, but who's counting? His favorite one—now threadbare—is emblazoned with the skeletal structure of the torso, with all parts labeled. The shop is crammed with oodles of souvenir and message shirts for kids under and over 40, in sizes infant through XXX large. If you're in a bad mood, a visit here will cheer you up. Open Monday through Saturday from 10am to 10pm and Sunday from noon to 6:30pm.

VIDEOS

Videotapes may be the next best thing to a baby-sitter—an ideal way to calm the kids after a frenetic day of sightseeing and buy a bit of quiet time for yourself. A lot of the neighborhood mom-and-pop stores are going under because of fierce competition from the national chains. Stay tuned.

✪ Blockbuster's
2332 Wisconsin Ave. NW, Georgetown. ☎ **202/625-6200** (1639 P St. NW, Dupont Circle, ☎ 202/232-2682; Georgia Ave. NW, Howard University, ☎ 202/234-6100; 3519 Connecticut Ave. NW, Van Ness ☎ 202/363-9500). Metro: Foggy Bottom.

This chain has come on like, well, blockbusters in the last decade, and there seems to be no stopping 'em. All the branches have a special kids' section and rent VCRs that attach easily to a TV for around $15 for 3 nights (plus a $100 deposit). Call the desired branch for hours and directions.

Tower Video
2000 Pennsylvania Ave. NW, 20th St. entrance. ☎ **202/223-3900.** Metro: Foggy Bottom.

In the heart of Foggy Bottom just 4 blocks from the White House, Tower has hundreds of children's videos, one of the largest selections in the city. On the opposite end of this enclosed minimall is Tower Records. Open daily from 9am to midnight.

9

Entertainment for the Whole Family

Children's tastes in entertainment are as varied as their parents'. Some kids like watching the pros shoot hoops; others enjoy seeing lions and tigers jump through them. Some junior culture-vultures are transported by *Swan Lake,* while their middle-brow siblings think it's far duckier to yuck it up in a comedy club. Whether your family's musical appetite runs to Beethoven, bluegrass, or the Smashing Pumpkins, you won't leave the table hungry after sampling Washington's cultural smorgasbord.

Once a sleepy southern town that died at 9pm (on a good night!), D.C. now hosts so many events simultaneously that you'll be hard-pressed to choose from among them. We're second only to New York in the quality and quantity of our theatrical productions, musical offerings, and dance performances. That's why we try harder!

If you have tickets to an evening event, consider ending your sightseeing midafternoon and enforce a rest period—with extra points for napping—so that everyone will be "up" for a night on the town.

Check the *Washington Post* "Style" section Monday through Saturday, *Children's Events* in the "Weekend" magazine on Friday, and the "Show" section on Sunday to find out what's doin'. *Washingtonian* magazine and the *City Paper* are other good sources.

TICKETS

Depending on availability, you can pick up tickets to future performances and half-price tickets to most events the day of the performance *only* at **TICKETplace** on the mezzanine of the Old Post Office Pavilion at 12th Street and Pennsylvania Avenue NW. More than 60 institutions participate in the service cosponsored by the Kennedy Center and the Cultural Alliance of Greater Washington. The walk-up counter is easily accessible by Metro. The Federal Triangle and Metro Center stations are closest. It's cash only for half-price tickets, plus a 10% service charge, but credit cards are accepted for full-price tickets to future events. TICKETplace is open Tuesday through Saturday from 11am to 6pm. Tickets for Sunday and Monday events are sold on Saturday.

Full-price tickets to most performances and sporting events are also sold through **TicketMaster** (☎ **202/432-SEAT**), with outlets at all Hecht's department stores. Hecht's flagship store is at 12th and G streets NW. If you know before you leave home there's something special you want to see, call ahead.

The **Kennedy Center** has several reduced-ticket programs in its ongoing effort to make performances more accessible to everyone. Besides the same-day, half-price tickets on sale at TICKETplace in the Old Post Office Pavilion, **Pay-What-You-Can** tickets are offered for selected performances at whatever price the patron can comfortably afford. Watch for ads in local newspapers. **SPTs** (specially priced tickets) refers to the 10% of seats set aside for half-price sale to full-time students, persons with disabilities, and seniors. Same-day **Rush SPTs** are available at noon for matinees and 6pm for evening performances.

When you can't get what you want through ordinary channels, there are several ticket brokers in town. They don't like being called "brokers," but that's what they are. Independent ticket brokers buy blocks of premium seats and resell them, usually with a hefty service charge attached. One that's been around a long time and is centrally located, just 4 blocks from the White House and near the Foggy Bottom Metro, is **Top Centre Ticket Service** at 2000 Pennsylvania Ave. (☎ **202/452-9040**). Also, try **Great Seats** (☎ **301/985-6250;** www.greatseats.com). Check the Yellow Pages for others.

1 Theater

The John F. Kennedy Center for the Performing Arts and the Washington Performing Arts Society have the highest visibility as presenters of family events, but numerous other cultural organizations and independent producers excel at delivering high caliber entertainment suitable for young people. Don't overlook them! The Kennedy Center, Arena Stage, National Theatre, and Shakespeare Theatre offer student discounts. (It wouldn't hurt to ask the other presenters about student tickets when you call.)

Many D.C.-area theaters provide **backstage tours,** where visitors can enter rehearsal studios and dressing rooms, enjoy a demonstration of the sound and lighting equipment, and watch the hand-cranked fly lines raise and lower scenery. For youngsters a behind-the-scenes tour is, in many instances, more fascinating than a live performance. Don't be surprised during your tour if the curtain goes up and your family is center stage in the spotlight. At the Kennedy Center, hour-long tours of the theaters and public spaces are offered weekdays every 15 minutes between 10am and 1pm (☎ **202/416-8341**). Same for the National Theatre, but you must call ahead (☎ **202/783-3370**). Some of the below-listed theaters offer tours and occasionally escort visitors backstage by special arrangement.

✪ Adventure Theatre
Glen Echo Park, MacArthur Blvd. at Goldsboro Rd., Glen Echo, Md. ☎ **301/320-5331.** Fax 301/320-5331. All seats $5. Take Massachusetts Ave. north into Maryland. Left at Goldsboro Rd. Left at MacArthur (park located at this intersection). Follow signs to parking.

A mix of original and familiar children's plays for 4- to 12-year-olds is presented year-round on Saturday and Sunday at 1:30 and 3:30pm. The 1999–2000 season features eight productions, from the classic *The Secret Garden* to a locally scripted *Dinosaur!*

The distinctive theater was once a penny arcade on the grounds of the former amusement park. Cap the afternoon off with a ride on the Dentzel carousel, across from the theater. With the Six Tix Pack ($27) you can use all six tickets for one show, three each for two shows, or any other combo you can come up with. These must be ordered in advance, not at the box office! Call to reserve tickets to individual performances.

Alden Theatre

McLean Community Center, 1234 Ingleside Ave., McLean, Va. ☎ **703/790-9223.** Prices vary with performance.

The "McLean Kids" series is a potpourri of kid-pleasing productions presented from September to June in the state-of-the-art Alden Theatre. Plays, puppet shows, music, and dance are performed various weekends during the school year, and the theater is only a 20-minute ride from downtown. Call for specific show times and directions.

Arena Stage

Maine Ave. and 6th St. SW. ☎ **202/488-3300.** www.arenastg@shirenet.com. E-mail: arenastg@shirenet.com. Tickets $27–$50, 35% discount for full-time students except Sat evening. Metro: Waterfront Station.

Many hit plays make it big at Arena Stage before moving to Broadway, and a roster of Arena "graduates" reads like a who's who in American theater. If you want to introduce older children to drama at its finest, look no further. Since some productions are not suitable for young people, call the theater for an educated opinion and check the reviews in local papers.

Adults with tickets for the four-part Saturday matinee series can drop their kids, ages 5 to 12, in the Old Vat Theater, where storytelling, behind-the-scenes demonstrations, and improv keep youngsters amused. The Kidsplay series (for kids 5 to 11) is $100 per child for four sessions (☎ **202/488-4377**). Students 5 to 12 pay $25 per regular performance with proof of age. Box office hours are 10am to 7pm.

I applaud Arena Stage's past policy of allowing subscribers a rebate of $15 per production toward baby-sitting expenses, and I hope they continue this practice well into the millennium.

BAPA's Imagination Stage at White Flint

White Flint Mall (top floor), 11301 Rockville Pike, N. Bethesda, Md. ☎ **301/881-5106.** Fax 301/881-7083. www.bapaarts.org. Tickets $6.

Established in 1990, the Bethesda Academy of Performing Arts (BAPA) presents a handful of shows by academy students plus four or five performances by outside companies every year. The academy also offers classes and summer programs in the performing arts and classes for children with special needs. BAPA is planning a move to a new 450-seat, pull-out-all-the-stops theater in Bethesda in mid- or late 2000.

Children's Theatre of Arlington

Thomas Jefferson Community Theatre, 125 S. Old Glebe Rd., Arlington, Va. (near Rt. 50 and Glebe Rd.). ☎ **703/548-1154.** Tickets at the door $8 adults, $6 students, seniors, children.

Three plays *for* and *by* children are staged annually by this community theater group. *Winnie the Pooh* and *Mary Poppins* are among the four productions, suitable for kids 3 and up, during the 1999–2000 season. CTA also offers summer workshops for kids of all ages and classes during the school year.

✪ Discovery Theater

Smithsonian's Arts and Industries Building, 900 Jefferson Dr. SW. ☎ **202/357-1500.** Tickets $5. Metro: Smithsonian.

Discovery Theater is still packing them in with a varied selection of plays, storytelling, puppetry, and mime on Tuesday through Saturday, every month but August. Show times are Tuesday through Friday at 10 and 11:30am and Saturday at 11:30am and 1pm. Reservations are required. Productions are geared to the 12-and-under set.

Folger Theatre (at the Folger Shakespeare Library)

201 E. Capitol St. SE. ☎ **202/544-7077.** www.shakespeare-etc.org. Tickets $8–$40; student discounts. Metro: Capitol South or Union Station.

All the world's a stage in this intimate 243-seat Elizabethan-style theater in the shadow of the U.S. Capitol. Although the Folger has been upstaged since the Shakespeare Theatre group packed its bags to take up residence in the Lansburgh Building at 450 7th St. NW nearly a decade ago, please don't let that dissuade you from visiting or attending a performance. Wouldn't you love to ham it up with Hamlet? Shake up Your Saturdays refers to performance workshops for kids 8 to 14 on select Saturdays from 10:30am to 12:30pm (☎ **202/544-7077**).

Full-scale renditions of *Hamlet* and *Julius Caesar* are among the offerings for the 1999–2000 season. Lectures, poetry and fiction readings, and family and education programs also fill the playbill at the Folger. It's also home to The Folger Consort chamber ensemble and annual Pen-Faulkner Awards for literature. Frolic at the annual celebration of the Bard's April 23 birthday, usually held the Saturday closest to the 23rd. The gift shop sells "Romeo & Juliet for Kids" and other watered-down versions of the classics, as well as tapes, CDs, videos and posters. The library is open for research Monday through Saturday from 10am to 4pm; the box office from 10am to 5pm. Closed Sunday.

Ford's Theatre

511 10th St. NW., between E and F sts. ☎ **202/347-4833.** Fax 202/347-6269. www.fordstheatre.org. E-mail: onstage@fordstheatre.org. Tickets $27–$43; ask about student and senior discounts. Metro: Metro Center.

From late November to early January, historic Ford's is the site of Dickens's *A Christmas Carol.* Many of the musical productions staged throughout the rest of the year are also suitable for families. As a rule of thumb, most productions are suitable for well-behaved kids 6 and older. But check first. Box office hours are Monday, 10am to 6pm; Tuesday to Friday 10am to 8pm and Saturday and Sunday noon to 8pm.

✪ Imagination Celebration

Kennedy Center for the Performing Arts, at the southern end of New Hampshire Ave. NW and Rock Creek Pkwy. ☎ **800/444-1234** or 202/467-4600. Tickets $40 (4-performance series); individual tickets vary. Metro: Foggy Bottom, then free Kennedy Center shuttle bus.

These series of family performances are designed for age groups from preschool to teens. Past offerings included taiko drums from Japan, a new musical by Emmy-winning director/choreographer Debbie Allen, and National Symphony Orchestra Kinderkonzerts. At $40 for four performances, the series of top-flight family entertainment, which evolved from a month-long project a few short years ago, is a steal. As a subscriber, you can also travel backstage in "From Page to Stage" and learn how productions are developed through the Performance Plus series. For an additional $70, series subscribers can attend Performance Plus events, which are held prior to or immediately following performances (☎ **202/416-8500**).

As part of the Kennedy Center's **Millennium Stage** project, free performances take place daily at 6pm, unless otherwise noted, in the Grand Foyer (☎ **202/467-4600**).

Mount Vernon Children's Community Theatre

Heritage Presbyterian Church, 8503 Fort Hunt Rd., Alexandria, Va. ☎ **703/360-0686.** Prices vary with the performance.

Three major performances are presented annually by this noted ensemble in Virginia's Mount Vernon area. Classes and workshops are offered also. Reservations are advised a week or two in advance.

✪ Now This!

Blair Mansion Inn, 7711 Eastern Ave., Silver Spring, Md. ☎ **202/364-8292.** Tickets (includes tax and tip) $17.75 lunch and show, $11 dessert and show. Metro: Takoma or Silver Spring, then taxi.

Every Saturday at 1:30pm families fill the historic Blair Mansion Inn for a delightful spin-off of the adult dinner theater concept. *Now This* includes lunch and interactive musical entertainment, so audience participation is key. A musical comedy improv group performs the show, especially suited to young people. Reservations are a must! Show up at 1pm if you're lunching, at 1:30pm if you're having dessert. Plenty of on-site parking.

Pavilion at the Old Post Office

1100 Pennsylvania Ave. NW. ☎ **202/289-4224.** www.oldpostofficedc.com. Free admission. Metro: Federal Triangle.

There's family entertainment most days as clowns, jugglers, musicians, puppets, and dancers do their thing from lunch time on.

Publick Playhouse

5445 Landover Rd., Hyattsville, Md. ☎ **301/277-1710.** Ticket prices vary.

This Prince George's County center for the performing arts has grown like Topsy in recent years, and offers a wide array of theater, music, and dance events. Saturday's Finest Family Matinees has presented everything from *A Christmas Carol* to "Meet the Musicians: Mozart," in which an actor/pianist in period costume ever so painlessly educated his young audience through music and stories. The Midweek Matinees, usually on Wednesday and Thursday, are targeted at school-age audiences.

Round House Theatre

12210 Bushey Dr., Silver Spring, Md. ☎ **301/933-1644.** Fax 301/933-2321. www.round-house.org. E-mail: info@round-house.org. $10–$28; students $10.

While most productions are geared toward adults, Montgomery County's professional resident theater company presents a children's show series for kids from 3 to 12 on six Saturday afternoons during the school year at 1 and 2:30pm. The Round House Theatre School has classes and workshops for kids from first grade through high school and a teen touring company. Students 30 and under can purchase tickets for $10 with an ID. The Wheaton Metro Station is a short cab ride away.

✪ Saturday Morning at the National

National Theatre, 1321 E St. NW, at Pennsylvania Ave. NW. ☎ **202/783-3372.** Free admission. Metro: Federal Triangle.

October through April, two free shows are given Saturday at 9:30 and 11am. The well-attended weekend series is as good as kids' entertainment gets, so arrive early. It's strictly first-come, first-seated.

Scandal Tours

By telephone only. ☎ **202/783-7212.** Tickets $30.

This tour/show is squeals on wheels that will leave all but your youngest rolling in the aisles. Board a bus for an irreverent tour of the Vista International, Tidal Basin, the Capitol steps, and many other sites of notorious escapades. Performed by members of the highly touted Gross National Product comedy troupe, the scandalous 75- to 90-minute ride departs the Old Post Office Pavilion at 11th Street and Pennsylvania Avenue on Saturdays at 1pm. It's suitable for older kids who are used to the type of humor dished out on *Saturday Night Live.*

Shakespeare Theatre

450 7th St. NW. ☎ **202/393-2700.** Metro: Archives. Tickets $12–$45; seniors 20% off; students 50% off 1 hour before curtain. Metro: Archives.

Introduce your kids over 10 to one of the well-produced plays by Shakespeare and his contemporaries, and other cultural events, in the 447-seat venue that opened in the Lansburgh Building in March 1992. In recent years, Stacy Keach, Kelly McGillis, and Richard Thomas have starred. Every September at an open house, kids can see what goes on behind the scenes. The free summertime **Shakespeare Free for All** productions are always a big hit at the Carter Barron Amphitheater, and the theater looks forward to presenting more Shakespeare in Rock Creek Park in future summers. Your kids may get hooked on the Bard after a performance here.

✪ Theater for Young People

Kennedy Center for the Performing Arts, at the southern end of New Hampshire Ave. NW and Rock Creek Pkwy. ☎ **202/416-8830.** Tickets $5–$12. Metro: Foggy Bottom.

Hour-long programs include puppet shows, storytelling, and plays for kids 3 and up. More than 250 performances are held on Friday, Saturday, and Sunday during the school year in the Terrace Theater and Theater Lab. A special Preschool Series is designed for families with children 3 to 6. Call for a current brochure.

✪ Wolf Trap Farm Park for the Performing Arts

1624 Trap Rd., Vienna, Va. ☎ **703/255-1868.** Fax 703/255-1916. www.wolf-trap.org. E-mail: wolftrap@wolf-trap.org. Tickets $7–$70, some free.

The best in music, opera, and dance play on the stage of the sylvan 6,900-seat **Filene Center II** during the summer. Riverdance, *Rent,* Garrison Keillor, Seal, and numerous pop, jazz, and country stars appeared at Wolf Trap in 1999. A goodly number of the music and dance events are suitable for those with kids in tow. Many families pack a picnic and blanket and opt for less expensive lawn seats where little children's whispering is better tolerated.

For nearly 30 years **Children's Theatre in the Woods** has been entertaining youths in July and August with free plays, stories, puppet shows, and clowning. Two acts appear each week. Shows are at 10 and 11am on Tuesday through Saturday. The performer from the 10am program gives a hands-on workshop for kids 4 and older on Tuesday, Thursday, and Saturday at 11am. Reservations are required for all shows and workshops (☎ **703/255-1827**). Food is not allowed in the theater, but plenty of tables and grassy hillsides accommodate picnickers.

The **International Children's Festival,** held in September, features oodles of performances and workshops for kids of all ages (☎ **703/642-0862**). The 1999 ticket prices for the festival were $10 for adults, $8 for kids and seniors, free for children under 3. On weekends in October through May, the **Barnstorm series** for children is a potpourri of story theater, folk music, puppetry, mime, ethnic dance, and storytelling in the prerevolutionary 350-seat German barn. Call ☎ **703/ 938-2404** for information.

The Wolf Trap box office is open Monday through Friday from 10am to 6pm, weekends and holidays from noon to 5pm. Everyone, regardless of age, must have a ticket.

If you don't have wheels, take Metro to the West Falls Church (Virginia) station. In summer, the Wolf Trap Express Shuttle bus ($3 round-trip) runs from the Metro to the Filene Center every 20 minutes starting 2 hours before the performance for all events, except opera. Be advised that the last bus leaves Wolf Trap at 11pm or 20 minutes after the last performance. If you come by car, take I-495 to Exit 12B

(Dulles Toll Road); stay on the local exit road, then Route 267 west to Exit 6 until you come to Wolf Trap. Space is somewhat limited for free on-site parking, so get here early if you're driving.

2 Dance

Washington draws the top professional ballet, modern, folk, and ethnic dance companies from all over the world. The Kennedy Center and Washington Performing Arts Society are leading presenters. In addition, the acclaimed Washington Ballet, numerous modern and postmodern dance groups, and several student companies—many of which are springboards for tomorrow's professionals—are headquartered here. All perform regularly in the area. Tickets for performances by local groups are usually nominally priced, often below $15. Most of the local performing groups are affiliated with schools that offer a wide range of children's dance classes and workshops.

Capitol Ballet Company
1200 Delafield Place NW. ☎ **202/882-4039.** Prices vary with the performance.

The performing group of the Jones-Haywood School of Ballet dances in D.C. at different locations.

✪ Dance Place
3225 8th St. NE. ☎ **202/269-1600.** Fax 202/269-4103. www.danceplace.org. Tickets $5–$15; kids free at Family Series performances. Metro: Brookland.

Under Carla Perlo's guiding light, Dance Place has been D.C.'s leading presenter of contemporary and ethnic dance for nearly 20 years. Dance Place pulsates year-round with performances, classes, and workshops. Kids feel comfortable in the informal atmosphere of the performance space and are especially welcome at the Sunday afternoon family performances. The June week-long Dance Africa DC Festival is a multisensory treat celebrating African culture through food, crafts, music and dance, and master classes. Other highlights include the January Tap Dance Festival, performances by Carla's Kids (Dance Place's junior company) and the Youth Festival showcasing local talent.

Fairfax Ballet
14119-O Sullyfield Circle, Chantilly, Va. ☎ **703/803-1055.**

The Fairfax Ballet, directed by Ilona and Thomas Russell, performs in the spring, as well as the Christmas season when it presents *The Nutcracker* annually. The Russells are former professional dancers who established the company's affiliated school, the Russell School of Ballet, more than 30 years ago.

Glen Echo Dance Theatre
Glen Echo Park, 7300 MacArthur Blvd., at Goldsboro Rd., Glen Echo, Md. ☎ **301/229-6022.** Prices vary with performance.

Weekend performances by local and visiting dance groups are held in the old Spanish Ballroom at this former amusement park. Glen Echo also has dance classes for the whole family.

✪ Maryland Youth Ballet
7702 Woodmont Ave., Bethesda, Md. ☎ **301/652-2232.** Prices vary with performance. Metro: Bethesda.

The MYB, under the direction of Hortensia Fonseca and Michelle Lees, presents a polished family concert series every spring and holiday *Nutcracker* in December featuring advanced ballet students. Numerous former MYB students have gone on to become members of well-known professional companies. Two of American Ballet Theatre's current principal ballerinas—Susan Jaffe and Julie Kent—trained at the

MYB. Not a bad track record, eh? Get your tickets early for this spirited production of *The Nutcracker*, suitable for kids 3 and older. It's frequently standing room only, and deservedly so. Box office hours are 9:30am to 7:30pm.

Metropolitan Ballet Theatre

10076 Darnestown Rd., Rockville, Md. ☎ **301/762-1757.** Prices vary with the performance.

Former New York City Ballet ballerina Suzanne Erlon established the MBT. Many of the young dancers are students at Erlon's North Potomac Ballet Academy and appear with visiting guest artists in *The Nutcracker* and other seasonal performances throughout the year. Performances are held at the Performing Arts Center of Montgomery College, Rockville Campus, Manakkee Street (off Route 355/Rockville Pike). Take Metro to Rockville Metro Center, then Ride-On Bus no.46 or no. 55 to Performing Arts Center.

The Primary Movers

4201 16th St. NW. ☎ **202/722-1595.** E-mail: primmove@erols.com. Prices vary with the performance; student discounts.

Rima Faber, who trained with Anna Sokolow and Martha Graham, has taught students from 3 to 103 during a long and illustrious career as a dancer, teacher, and choreographer. She directs this unique company of young people who dance with infectious enthusiasm and abandon. Performances, suitable for kids 2 and older, are held at theaters and festivals throughout the D.C. metropolitan area.

Virginia Ballet Company

8001 Forbes Place, Springfield, Va. ☎ **703/321-8009.** Prices vary with the performance.

Now in its 30th season, Virginia Ballet performs *The Nutcracker* annually at Northern Virginia Community College's Cultural Center in Annandale and has ongoing classes at its Springfield studio. The company's artistic directors, Oleg Tupine and Tania Rousseau, are well-respected former dancers who teach at the company's school, which they founded.

Washington Ballet

3515 Wisconsin Ave. NW. ☎ **202/362-3606.** Prices vary with the performance. Tickets can be purchased by calling TicketMaster (☎ 202/432-SEAT) or by going to TicketMaster locations (including Hecht's), or to the theater box office. Tickets to performances at the George Mason University Center for the Arts can be purchased over the phone (☎ 703/993-8888). Groups of 10 or more can purchase discounted tickets (☎ 202/362-3606, ext. 120).

Washington's resident professional ballet company, directed by Septime Webre, presents a fall, winter, and spring series at the Kennedy Center. The mixed classical and contemporary programs are suitable for children over 8 who usually find a few short works easier to digest than a full-length ballet. *The Nutcracker*, a holiday staple, is presented at George Mason University in suburban Virginia and at the Warner Theatre each December. **Ballets from Within** features works by student choreographers, and "The Young Dancers" is an apprentice ensemble that performs in the community. Founder and longtime artistic director Mary Day is credited with nurturing the talents of many professional dancers (Kevin MacKenzie and Amanda McKerrow to wit) and putting the company on the map.

3 Music

CLASSICAL MUSIC

Washington is home to the National Symphony Orchestra, the Washington Opera, and numerous first-rate chamber orchestras and choral groups that give family and children's performances throughout the area. Guest artists also appear year-round at many sites in and around the city. Consult the *Washington Post* and *Washington Times* or call the individual presenters for performance dates, times, and ticket prices, which vary widely. Family performances, especially around holidays, are often free.

✪ Concerts for Young People

Concert Hall, Kennedy Center for the Performing Arts. ☎ **202/452-1321.** Ticket prices vary.

The Washington Chamber Symphony (WCS), under the baton of "The Magic Maestro," Stephen Simon, annually presents four pairs of concerts on Saturday and Sunday afternoons for families with kids from 6 to 12 years old. The WCS numbers 30 to 40 musicians, depending on the program. One past program, *Piano on Fire!*, consisted of highlights from three great piano concertos. I doubt you'll find a better way to introduce your children to classical music. No one under 6 is admitted. Ticket prices for the 1999–2000 concerts ranged from $12 to $37.50 per ticket. Call for subscription prices.

✪ Concerts on the Canal

Foundry Mall, between 30th and Thomas Jefferson sts. NW (just below M St.). ☎ **202/653-5190** or 703/866-7150. Free admission.

While away a lazy summer Sunday afternoon on the C&O Canal and listen to classical, folk, pop, R&B, or country-western music. Concerts usually run from 4 to 6:30pm on six Sundays from early June through August. Watch toddlers especially carefully; the canal is a very real threat.

D.C. Youth Chorale

Duke Ellington School of the Arts, 35th and R sts. NW. ☎ **202/282-0096** or 202/282-0123.

Concerts by this citywide student chorus are held at various locations. Although most of the repertoire is classical, a healthy sprinkling of popular and folk selections is included.

D.C. Youth Orchestra

Coolidge High School, 5th and Sheridan sts. NW. ☎ **202/723-1612.** Tickets under $5.

Close your eyes and this youth orchestra sounds as harmonious as many professional ensembles. The spirited and impressive group of young people 5 to 19 years old has toured 15 countries and played for six U.S. presidents since its founding in 1960.

Fairfax Choral Society

4028 Hummer Rd., Annandale, Va. ☎ **703/642-0862.** Fax 703/642-1773. www.fairfaxchoralsociety.org. Tickets $18 adults, $12 seniors, $9 youths.

Concerts in the metropolitan area by the children's 65-voice chorus, as well as the "parent" groups—an 80-voice chorus and 25-voice chorale—always draw an admiring crowd. Although not easily accessible by public transportation, there's plenty of free parking.

✪ National Symphony Orchestra

John F. Kennedy Center for the Performing Arts, at the southern end of New Hampshire Ave. NW and Rock Creek Pkwy. ☎ **202/467-4600.**

Young People's and Family Concerts are important ingredients in the NSO's menu of about 200 concerts annually. During the summer, NSO treats families to free concerts on Memorial Day weekend, the Fourth of July, and Labor Day on the West Lawn of the U.S. Capitol. You can also catch them at Wolf Trap's Filene Center in Virginia and the Carter Barron Amphitheatre, 16th Street and Colorado Avenue NW, in the summer.

Washington Performing Arts Society (WPAS)
2000 L St. NW. ☎ **202/833-9800.**

Besides a full schedule of concerts by internationally acclaimed orchestras, soloists, chamber groups, and dance companies, Washington's first presenter of cultural events, WPAS, sponsors the Parade of the Arts Family Series, designed for families with children 6 to 12.

✪ Young Performers Series
Kennedy Center for the Performing Arts. ☎ **202/467-4600.**

Free musical performances by talented young people from the D.C. area are featured on alternate Wednesdays in the Grand Foyer. You may hear a Peabody Conservatory pianist, classical guitarist, or university voice students performing operatic excerpts.

BAND CONCERTS

One of the perks of visiting Washington in the summer is enjoying the free band concerts held at several downtown venues. Call first to double-check times, as scheduling varies from year to year. Watch local newspapers for information on military band concerts the rest of the year.

✪ Marine Corps Friday Evening Parades
U.S. Marine Barracks, 8th and I sts. SE. ☎ **202/433-6060** or 202/433-4011 for a 24-hour recording.

Dress parades Friday evenings from mid-May through August get underway at 2045 hours (8:45pm). Arrive no later than 8pm. It's a show and a half. That's why you have to call for reservations on the *Monday* 3 weeks before the parade you want to attend. You may also write for reservations; address your request to Adjutant, Marine Barracks, 8th and I streets SE, Washington, DC 20390.

Military Band Summer Concert Series
U.S. Capitol (West Terrace), the Ellipse (behind the White House). ☎ **703/696-3399.** www.army.mil/armyband. Free.

Attend a free outdoor concert by a U.S. military band Tuesdays at the Ellipse (behind the White House) or Thursdays at the U.S. Capitol (West Terrace), beginning at 8pm from Memorial Day through August. In past years concerts were almost every evening. Who knows what the new millennium will bring, so call first.

Sunset Parade
Iwo Jima Memorial, near Arlington Cemetery. ☎ **202/433-4497** or 202/433-4173.

It's first-come, first-served for lawn seats at the Marine Corps War Memorial, where you'll hear the 80-member Marine Drum and Bugle Corps and see precision drills Tuesday evening at 7pm from late May through August. Shuttle buses run from the Visitor Center at Arlington Cemetery, starting at 6pm.

Twilight Tattoo
The Ellipse, south of the White House. ☎ **703/696-3718.**

Enjoy intricate military drills and precision marching along with selections by the U.S. Army Band on Wednesday from mid-July to mid-August at 7pm. Arrive early to get a good seat.

U.S. Navy Concerts on the Avenue Series
U.S. Navy Memorial, 701 Pennsylvania Ave. NW, between 7th and 9th sts. ☎ **202/737-2300,** ext. 768. Fax 202/737-2308. E-mail: sales@lonesailor.org. Metro: Archives/Navy Memorial.

Beginning Memorial Day at 8pm, and thereafter until Labor Day on selected Tuesday evenings, get in tune with the U.S. Navy, Air Force, and Marine bands. Concerts are free and all ages are welcome. Call for a schedule.

U.S. Navy Summer Pageant
Washington Navy Yard waterfront, 9th and M sts. SE. ☎ **202/433-2218.**

Every Wednesday from the last Wednesday in May through August, a multimedia presentation showcases the history of the U.S. Navy at 9pm. Reservations are required; call the number listed above.

BLUES & JAZZ

The Barns of Wolf Trap
1624 Trap Rd., Vienna, Va. ☎ **703/938-2404,** or 703/218-6500 to charge tickets. www.wolftrap.org. Tickets $10–$25; kids pay full price. Free parking.

Jazz, pop, country, and bluegrass predominate from October to May on the grounds of this cozy center for the performing arts. The 200-year-old barn has been restored and the horses are long gone. Former unknowns Mary Chapin Carpenter, Harry Connick Jr., and Vince Gill entertained here in their salad days. Though not a place to bring babies, the Barns invites school-agers to come with their parents and soak up a little history with the music, dance, and performance art in this charming, rustic setting. Take Metro to the West Falls Church station, then a taxi. Also plenty of free parking.

✪ Blues Alley
1073 Wisconsin Ave. NW, in an alley behind M St. ☎ **202/337-4141.** Fax 202/337-7946. www.bluesalley.com. Tickets $14–$40 depending on the performer (students pay half Sun–Thurs, some shows), plus $7 food or drink minimum and a $1.25 surcharge for the Blues Alley Music Society. Metro: Foggy Bottom, then 10-block walk.

Washington's first and foremost jazz club for more than a quarter of a century has played host to Charlie Byrd, Eartha Kitt, Nancy Wilson, Wynton and Branford Marsalis, and hundreds of other jazz greats. There are two shows (8 and 10pm) weeknights, sometimes three on Friday and Saturday. Reservations are taken up to 2 weeks in advance, and seating is first-come, first-served. Box office hours are noon to 10pm. Anyone well behaved over the age of 6 is welcome.

Dinner begins at 6pm, and you'll have no trouble gobbling up the minimum. For kids there are burgers and sandwiches in the lower registers ($6 to $10), main courses (mostly beef and Creole dishes) from $15 to $20 in the upper. Most drinks cost $3 to $7.

COUNTRY & FOLK

The Barns of Wolf Trap
See listing under "Blues & Jazz" above.

Concerts on the Canal
See listing under "Classical Music" above.

✪ Dubliner
520 N. Capitol St. NW. ☎ **202/737-3773.** No cover charge or minimum; food $6–$11 at lunch, $7–$16 at dinner.

The Dubliner is so fond of kids they even have high chairs, so wee leprechauns can enjoy the spirited Irish music (but not the Killian's Red) along with Mom and Dad.

4 Films

For film reviews, check the daily newspapers. The *Washington Post* has synopses of current movies in the Friday "Weekend" section. Happily for movie lovers, the number of discount movie houses in D.C. is on the rise, and at many theaters tickets to matinees and/or the first evening show are greatly reduced. One place you won't find bargains is at the refreshment stand. The prices are outrageous. You can buy a meal at a fast-food restaurant for what some theaters charge for a bucket of popcorn. Naturally, theater managers frown on patrons bringing in outside food, but if you're discreet and stuff your purse or pockets with candy before you enter, there's not a thing they can do. Maybe if enough family moviegoers boycott the stale, overpriced popcorn and $1.50-and-up candy and drinks, theater owners will be forced to price snacks more realistically.

✪ Air and Space Museum

Samuel P. Langley Theater, Independence Ave. and 7th St. SW. ☎ **202/357-1686** or 202/357-1675. Tickets $5.50 adults, $4.25 ages 2 to 21 and seniors 55 and older. Metro: L'Enfant Plaza.

If you're visiting the museum, stop at the box office first, preferably when it opens around 9:45am. Tickets may be purchased up to 2 weeks in advance. The breath-taking films shown on the five-story IMAX screen frequently sell out, and after you've seen one you'll know why. *To Fly,* the first Langley Theater presentation in 1976, still packs 'em in. It's an aerial journey of America from an 1800s-era hot-air balloon, barnstormer, and Saturn rocket that is guaranteed to raise goose bumps on the toughest flesh. *Mission to Mir* explores life aboard Russia's giant Space Station Mir (the one that had an accident in 1997). *Cosmic Voyage* examines the outermost galaxies as well as the minutest parts of our world. The films alternate, sometimes with a third and fourth film, and each is shown from one to four times daily. Don't sit too close to the screen, as the huge images and booming sound track may frighten younger children. Although popcorn is not allowed, I doubt that you'll miss it.

American Film Institute Theater

Kennedy Center, New Hampshire Ave. NW and Rock Creek Pkwy. ☎ **202/416-7815.** Tickets $6.50 for nonmembers, $5.50 for members (AFI memberships cost $20), senior citizens, and students under 18 with ID. Metro: Foggy Bottom.

Some of the American Film Institute's (AFI's) regular series of classic and new films, both foreign and domestic, will appeal to movie buffs 8 and older, depending on the subject matter. Movies are shown weeknights with some weekend matinees. The box office is open only on days when there is a showing.

Underground parking at the Kennedy Center is $8 for the entire evening after 5pm.

Discovery Channel Theater

MCI Center, 7th and F sts., NW. ☎ **202/639-0908.** www.flagshipdiscovery.com. Metro: Gallery Place/Chinatown.

Stop and see the 15-minute film about D.C. when you're in the neighborhood visiting Ford's Theatre, the FBI, or Chinatown. The sweeping aerials of familiar and lesser-known sights in this "unofficial" tour of Washington are stunning. You'll pick up some interesting trivia about the capital city from its infancy to the present, like the role walnuts play in preserving bronze statuary. The movie plays every half hour Monday through Saturday from 10am to 8:45pm and Sunday from noon to

5:45pm. The cost is $2.50 for adults, $1.50 for children 6-11, free for kids 5 and under and $1.50 seniors 55 and older.

Hirshhorn Museum

Independence Ave. at 7th St. SW. ☎ **202/357-2700** or 202/357-3235. Free admission. Metro: L'Enfant Plaza.

The Hirshhorn hosts a free film series for kids under 12 several Saturdays during the school year at 11am in the lower-level auditorium. Call to find out what's on the big screen.

Martin Luther King Jr. Memorial Library

901 G St. NW. ☎ **202/727-1248.** Free admission. Metro: Metro Center.

Films for preschoolers are shown throughout the year every Friday at 10:30am.

National Museum of African Art

950 Independence Ave. SW. ☎ **202/357-2700.** Free admission. Metro: Smithsonian.

Call for a schedule of animated and regular films on daily life, folktales, and the art of Africa's rich and diverse culture. Films, suitable for kids 6 to 15, are usually shown Saturdays at 2pm in the Learning Center Lecture Hall on the second level.

✪ Screen on the Green

Washington Monument grounds, 15th St. and Constitution Ave. NW. ☎ **877/262-5866** (toll-free). www.screenonthegreen.com. Free. Metro: Smithsonian.

In summer 1999, the lawn surrounding the Washington Monument carpeted the District's newest theater. For 5 Monday evenings in July and August vintage films—*Citizen Kane* and *Casablanca* among them—played at sunset on a 20-by-40-foot screen. (Does this remind anyone out there of drive-ins?) One hopes that this happening becomes a permanent bloom in the local landscape.

5 Puppet Shows

Puppet shows are given throughout the year, most frequently by the Puppet Co. at the Puppet Co. Playhouse in Glen Echo Park, by various presenters in the Smithsonian's Discovery Theater and through the Kennedy Center's Theater for Young People. See "Theater" earlier in this chapter for addresses and phone numbers. For a current listing of performances, check the Friday "Weekend" section of the *Washington Post.*

Several top-notch puppeteers live and work in the D.C. area. They have a knack for captivating and entertaining kids, while slipping in important messages on social and moral issues. Most performances are timed for 45 minutes or less, just the right length for restless tykes. Like stand-up comedians, the puppeteers warm up their audiences first, and some perform cloaked in black in the Bunraku style. Call the following puppeteers to see if they'll be presenting a show during your visit. No strings attached.

August Puppet Theatre

1202 S. Washington St., Alexandria, Va. ☎ **703/549-6657.**

Utilizing hand puppets primarily, the August Puppet Theatre works audiences with original scripts and fairy tales.

Blue Sky Puppet Theatre

4301 Van Buren St., University Park, Md. ☎ **301/927-5599.**

Blue Sky has been pulling strings since 1974 and performs at numerous venues in and around the city. Wolf Trap Park for the Performing Arts usually hosts them in the summer. Call for dates as they vary from year to year.

Bob Brown Puppet Productions

1415 S. Queen St., Arlington, Va. ☎ **703/319-9102.**

Bob Brown has been presenting puppet shows in D.C.-area theaters and schools for more years than a marionette cast has strings.

○ The Puppet Co.

The Puppet Co. Playhouse, Glen Echo Park, 7300 MacArthur Blvd., Glen Echo, Md. ☎ **301/ 320-6668.** www.thepuppetco.org. Tickets $5. From Washington: Massachusetts Ave. north into Maryland. Left at Goldsboro Rd. Left at MacArthur Blvd. and park entrance. Follow signs to parking. From suburbs: I-495/95 to Exit 39 (River Rd.) East (toward D.C.). Right at 5th traffic light (Goldsboro Rd.) to end. Right at MacArthur, follow signs to Glen Echo Park parking.

If you don't do another entertaining thing, take your family (I don't care how old you or your children are) to a performance by the Puppet Co. in the Puppet Co. Playhouse, a 200-seat theater carved from Glen Echo Park's historic Spanish Ballroom. Award-winning codirectors Christopher Piper and Allen Stevens and their troupe produce shows that win fans from 2 to 102. Each show runs about 6 weeks. Performances are Wednesday, Thursday, and Friday at 10 and 11:30am; Saturday and Sunday at 11:30am and 1pm. Call to reserve tickets. *Be forewarned:* Seating is on the carpeted floor.

For kids who would like to learn more about this ancient craft, puppet-making classes are offered by the Puppet Co. at Glen Echo Park (☎ **301/492-6229**), Bethesda Academy of Performing Arts (☎ **301/320-2550**), the Kennedy Center's Adventures in the Arts program (☎ **202/416-8810**), and the Smithsonian Residents Associates (☎ **202/357-3255**).

6 Story Hours

Story hours at the public library or area bookstores are fun and quiet times for preschoolers and young scholars-and their parents.

Martin Luther King Jr. Memorial Library

901 G St. NW. ☎ **202/727-1151** for hours and information, or 202/727-1248 for children's activities.

The main branch of the D.C. Public Library has story hours for preschoolers year-round on Tuesday mornings at 10:30am. Although the program is a magnet for day-care and preschool groups, a spokesperson for the library said, "There's always room for visitors." To play it safe, call first. The "Saturday Special" program at 11am during the school year is for preschoolers and kids in grades 1 to 3. Lasting 30 to 45 minutes, it may include stories, films, songs, games, or crafts.

A monthly calendar of events is available at all library branches around the first of every month. Ask your hotel concierge for the branch nearest you. To find out about the many free summer programs available to residents and visitors, call ☎ **202/727-1248.**

Besides the Martin Luther King Jr. Memorial Library, from time to time visiting authors speak at the following children's bookstores, which also have story hours: **A Likely Story,** 1555 King St., Alexandria, Virginia (☎ **703/836-2498**); **BooKoo Books for Kids, etc.,** 4945 Elm St., Bethesda, Maryland (☎ **301/652-2794**); **Borders Books and Music,** 1800 L St. NW (☎ **202/466-4999**); **Borders for Kids,** White Flint Mall, North Bethesda, Maryland (☎ **301/816-1067**); **Cheshire Cat,** 5512 Connecticut Ave. NW (☎ **202/244-3956**); **Fairy Godmother,** 319 7th St. SE (☎ **202/547-5474**); and **Tree Top Toys,** 3301 New Mexico Ave. NW (☎ **202/244-3500**). Many of the **Nature Company** stores have story hours for different age groups. Call the individual stores for details (see the "Books" section in chapter 8). Check the monthly Literary Calendar that appears the third or fourth Sunday of every month in the *Book World* magazine of the Sunday *Washington Post.*

7 The Circus

While many circuses pitch their tents in Washington from time to time, only one— "The Greatest Show on Earth"—arrives as regularly as the daffodils every spring.

✪ Ringling Bros. and Barnum & Bailey Circus
Feld Bros. Enterprises, Vienna, Va. ☎ **703/448-4000** or 202/432-SEAT. Tickets $10–$20.

The world's only three-ring circus takes over the D.C. Armory at 2001 E. Capitol St. SE (adjacent to RFK Stadium) in late March and early April for 2 weeks. If the 2½-hour spectacular is too long for your little ones, consider leaving at intermission. You remember that old saying, "Half a circus is better than none." While ticket prices are fair, most food and souvenirs are through the roof, er, tent. To cut costs and avoid arguments, eat before you go and put a lid on what kids spend on the extras.

For many kids, the best part of the circus takes place before the opening performance—and it's free! The parade of animals from the circus train to the Armory is even more exciting than their antics in the ring. There's something extra special about watching lions, tigers, and elephants promenading down city streets. Watch local newspapers for the time and route.

Easy Excursions 10

If time permits, you may want to plan a side trip to one or more of the following attractions. Using your hotel as a base, you can visit most of these in a day and be back in D.C. for the nightly news on TV.

1 Theme Park Thrills

Six Flags America is only 15 minutes from the Beltway in Prince George's County, Maryland. If the kids plead long and loud enough, you're bound to give in (I know I did). Farther afield is **Paramount's Kings Dominion,** near Richmond, Virginia, about a 75-minute drive from the District. It may seem like a waste of time and money to lose your lunch on a giant roller coaster, but remember, your kids are only young once.

I read recently that amusement parks depend on food and beverage, games, and souvenir sales for half their revenues. Although you're a captive audience once you arrive, with a little advance planning you don't have to feel like a human ATM machine once you've paid the staggering admission. One solution is to pack a cooler with drinks and snacks and picnic outside the parks—*after* the roller coaster, of course.

✪ Six Flags America

13710 Central Ave., Largo, Md. ☎ **301/249-1500.** www.sixflags.com. Admission $30 ages 9 and up; $15 ages 4–8, free kids 3 and under. Weekends only May and Oct, daily Memorial Day to Labor Day. Hours vary. Metro: Addison Rd. (not a great neighborhood), then taxi. Directions: Take I-495/I-95 to Exit 15A (Rte. 214 east). The park is 5 miles on the left. Ages 2–14.

Only 12 miles from D.C., the former Adventure World features many water-based rides and one of the world's largest wave pools. Comprised of several miniparks—all with rides, games, and food stands; many with shows—on a 115-acre site in Prince George's County, Six Flags is just minutes from the Beltway. The park has a reputation for satisfying visitors' thrill-seeking needs and different tolerances for saturation and motion. New attractions include two roller coasters—The Joker's Jinx and Two-Face: The Flip Side, and an action-packed stunt show, the Batman Thrill Spectacular. Kids of all ages like to explore Looney Tunes Movie Town, where they'll meet their favorite cartoon characters.

On 10-acre **Skull Island,** the big draw is the $12 million **Typhoon Sea Coaster.** Waiting an hour to ride the wet-and-wild roller coaster is not unheard of, so if at all possible, visit on a weekday and arrive early.

The **Paradise Island Water Park** has more than a dozen water slides. For younger kids (accompanied by an adult), **Kids' Cove** is on its own lagoon, with an octopus water slide and other tamer fare for young children. The newest addition to Paradise Island is a five-story tower of geysers, waterfalls, and slides known as **Crocodile Cal's Outback Beach House.** To board the wilder rides, including the Rainbow Falls, Black Hole, and Bonzai Pipeline, you must be 54 inches (tall, not wide).

A Day at the Circus, with 13 rides geared to kids, has an Aerial Elephant, Kiddie Bumper Boats, and a Circus Train, along with two shows several times a day. The **Moroccan Village** features the infamous **Python** vertical-looping roller coaster, the Wild One (an old-fashioned wooden roller coaster), games, and a private picnic area for large groups only (call to reserve). **Pirates Cove** is home of the popular **Shipwreck Falls,** a thriller of a ride that leaves a wall of water in its wake.

An entertaining Wild West stunt demonstration show takes place several times a day in Coyote Creek, where you'll also find oldies but goodies such as bumper cars and a tilt-a-whirl.

Bathing suits are required for the water slides and pool; stow your dry duds in rental lockers. Outside food may not be brought in. The park's offerings are plentiful, though expensive. **Jerry's Pizza** and **Boardwalk Fries** are sure bets. The other 15 or so stands hawk everything from frozen yogurt to hamburgers and fried chicken, but it is all overpriced. A box of popcorn and large soda will set you back $5.

Lockers are available for $3 (almost as steep as the roller coaster, don't you think?), so you don't have to stay in a wet bathing suit all day. Several rest rooms and baby-changing stations are strategically located.

Note: We'd be remiss if we didn't tell you about(1) the traffic jams in and out of Six Flags during its 1999 inaugural season, and (2) the scores of disgruntled visitors who stood in long lines to purchase tickets and food and board rides. We have our fingers crossed that Six Flags management has smoothed over these rough spots and left the bumps to the roller coasters.

Paramount's Kings Dominion

Doswell, Va. (about 80 miles south of D.C.). ☎ **804/876-5000.** www.pkdthrills.com. Admission $34 ages 7–54, $25 ages 3–6, $29 ages 55 and older, free for children 2 and under. $6 parking. Late Mar to Memorial Day, Sept–Oct weekends only; Memorial Day to Labor Day open daily, hours vary. Directions: Take I-95 south to Exit 98 (Doswell). You can't miss it from there. Ages 4–14.

Note: Coupons are sometimes available at area supermarkets to reduce the cost of admission.

The eight roller coasters, close to 40 other rides in six theme areas, water park, numerous shows, shops, and attractions could keep your family busy for a fortnight or two.

Visit **KidZville,** inhabited by Hanna-Barbera offspring. Explore **Yogi's Cave** and ride the **Taxi Jam Coaster** (billed as "a child's first coaster"). Youngsters can romp in the Kidz Construction Company, a huge play area, and board a dump truck or cement mixer hauling unusual cargo. **The Busytown Café** is a cutesy place to eat, decorated with characters from the pen of popular kids' author Richard Scarry.

A word of caution: Don't ride the newest roller coaster, **Volcano, The Blast Coaster,** after a full meal. Traveling at speeds up to 70 miles per hour, it turns upside-down four times and simulates an active volcano eruption. (Guess what: You're the eruption!)

When it comes to thrilling rides, the **Avalanche, Anaconda, Grizzly, and Rebel Yell** still pack 'em in, but you may need a Dramamine beforehand. (Factoid to stash in your box of caramel corn: The **Grizzly** was modeled after Coney Island's famous Wildcat.)

At WaterWorks, dip into Big Wave Bay, a gigantic wave pool, or swim over to The Surf City Splash House, with more than 50 wet and wild ways to get drenched.

If, like me, you get motion sickness riding in an elevator and your kids are old enough to do the rides unescorted, pass the time in one of the air-conditioned shows or souvenir shops, selling mostly shlocky, overpriced gewgaws. I can't say it enough: Lines for rides can be incredibly long on weekends and holidays.

2 Mount Vernon

16 miles S of Washington, D.C.

George Washington's estate, just 16 miles from the District, has been lovingly restored to its original appearance, down to the paint colors on the walls. No visit to Washington, D.C., is complete without a visit here.

GETTING THERE

BY CAR   Take any of the bridges over the Potomac into Virginia to the George Washington Memorial Parkway going south. The parkway ends at Mount Vernon.

BY TOURMOBILE   Tourmobile buses (☎ **202/554-5100**) depart daily from Arlington National Cemetery and the Washington Monument. Round-trip fare is $20 for adults, $10 for children 3 to 11 and free for kids 2 and under. The fare includes admission to Mount Vernon. Payment is in cash or traveler's check *only*. Call ahead for departure hours.

BY RIVERBOAT   Every month but November and December, the *Spirit of Mount Vernon* riverboat travels down the Potomac from Pier 4, at 6th and Water streets SW (☎ **202/554-8000** for departure hours). There are two sailings daily. Round-trip fares are $21.50 for adults, $19.25 for senior citizens, $12.75 for ages 6 to 11, free for children 5 and under. Fares include admission to Mount Vernon. Sightseeing cruises aboard Potomac Spirit depart the Mount Vernon dock April through October, at 11:15am. The 45-minute ride is a pleasant way to break up a visit and catch some cool breezes off the water. The fare is $5 adults, $4 seniors and military, $3 kids 6 to 11 and free for 2 and under (☎ **202/554-8000**).

INFORMATION

Mount Vernon is owned and maintained by the **Mount Vernon Ladies' Association.** For a brochure, write to them at Mount Vernon, VA 22121 (☎ **703/780-2000;** www.mountvernon.org). Mount Vernon is open daily, including December 25, April through August from 8am to 4pm; March, September, and October from 9am to 5pm; and November through February from 9am to 4pm. Admission is $8 for adults, $7.50 for seniors 62 and older, $4 for ages 6 to 11, and free for children under 5.

SPECIAL EVENTS

Washington's birthday is celebrated the third Monday in February with a memorial service open to the public, and every December the mansion is decorated for

Christmas. Also for Christmas, during the three weekends preceding the big day, a candlelight tour is available from 5pm to 8pm.

EXPLORING MOUNT VERNON

If you've ever wondered how an aristocratic 18th-century family lived, this is how. (There's one exception: In 1998, air-conditioning was added to cool this hot attraction. Before air-conditioning, the upstairs bedrooms often reached a sweltering 100°.) Some of the furnishings are original, and the rooms are arranged as if they were still inhabited. About 500 of the original 8,000 acres still exist as part of the estate, and 30 are yours to explore. The plantation dates from 1674 when the land was granted to Washington's great-grandfather. Washington spent 2 years in retirement here before he died in 1799.

As you tour at your own pace, docents are on hand to answer visitor queries. They take pride and a personal interest in Mount Vernon's story and are extremely knowledgeable, so don't be bashful with your questions. Children are usually less interested in the period furnishings than the family kitchen and outbuildings where everyday tasks—baking, weaving, and washing—took place.

In the **Hands-on-History tent** (next to the mansion), children take part in such activities as carding and spinning wool, trying on colonial clothing, playing corncob darts, and rolling hoops. The tent is open May through September from 10am to 1pm. A special weekend program from Memorial Day through Labor Day helps re-create the ambience of 18th-century plantation life.

April through October, head to **George Washington: Pioneer Farmer,** the working farm site down by the riverside. Depending on the season, kids can watch a sheep shearing, ride in a wagon, or talk to the animals. They may even assist in harvesting. Let's not forget that George was, first and foremost, a farmer who planted new crops and experimented with new farming techniques at Mount Vernon. Ask at the barn for an Activity Pack, a guide to the hands-on activities here.

A short walk from the mansion is the tomb where George, his wife, Martha, and other family members are buried. On the third Monday of February, a memorial service commemorating Washington's birthday is held at the estate.

Also of interest is the slave burial ground and 30-minute walking tour describing slave life in Mount Vernon. The tour is available April through October at 10am, noon, 2pm, and 4pm. Tours of the gardens are given April through October at 11am, 1pm, and 3pm. In the museum, you can view the family's personal possessions. Allow time for a stroll through the grounds and gardens. Wait until you see the view from the front lawn. Talk about prime waterfront property!

DINING

Just outside the main gate are a **snack bar,** open for breakfast, lunch, and light fare, and the **Mount Vernon Inn** restaurant, open daily for lunch from 11am to 3:30pm and Monday through Saturday for dinner from 5 to 9pm (☎ **703/780-0011**). Reservations are recommended at the Inn. You can picnic 1 mile north of Mount Vernon at Riverside Park, or on your way back to D.C., stop in Old Town Alexandria, where there are scores of restaurants. If you choose the *Spirit of Mount Vernon* as your mode of travel, there's a snack bar onboard.

3 Old Town Alexandria

6 miles S of Washington, D.C.

Everyone enjoys a visit to Old Town, the once-thriving colonial port on the western shore of the Potomac River. About 6 miles south of D.C., it's a picturesque parcel that invites walking. The area is steeped in history, with many fine restorations of 18th- and 19th-century buildings dotting its cobblestone streets. If possible, plan your visit for any day but Monday, when some attractions are closed.

George Washington was a teenage surveyor's assistant when Alexandria became a city in 1749. The original 60 acres now comprise Old Town. During your visit, allow time to explore the waterfront and board a tall ship, watch artisans at work in the Torpedo Factory Art Center, and shop for up-to-date merchandise in old-style buildings.

GETTING THERE

BY METRO   The easiest way to get to Old Town is via Metro. Old Town's narrow streets become traffic choked on weekends, and you won't need your car to sweep through the neighborhood. *Most* of the sights are contained within a 36-square-block grid. Board any Yellow line train bound for National Airport to the King Street station. From the King Street station, board a DASH bus to King and Fairfax—right to the door of the Visitor Center. If you ask for a transfer, you can board any DASH bus within a 3-hour period. It's a short ride from the station; on a nice day, you may want to hoof it.

BY CAR   If you're driving, take the Arlington Memorial or 14th Street Bridge to the scenic George Washington Memorial Parkway, which will take you right into King Street, Alexandria's main thoroughfare. It's about a 6-mile trip. In rush hour, however, those 6 miles will feel like 60. Parking permits are available for out-of-towners from the Ramsay House Visitor Center (see below). A permit will allow you to park free at 2-hour meters all over town.

INFORMATION

Make the **Ramsay House Visitor Center,** 221 King St. (☎ **703/838-4200**), your first stop. A faithful reconstruction of Alexandria's first house, it is open every day but Thanksgiving, December 25, and January 1, from 9am to 5pm. Pick up a brochure (available in several languages), **Discovery Sheets,** outlining self-guided walking tours for families with kids in three age groups, and **Cheap Treats,** suggestions for stretching your vacation dollars. If your kids are old enough to appreciate such things, you can purchase admission tickets to historic homes and sights here. For information on costumed historic tours, call Doorways to Old Virginia (☎ **703/548-0100**). Of special interest to kids is the Graveyards and Ghosts tour, available in the fall by appointment.

SPECIAL EVENTS

Inquire about special events, some of which require tickets, at the Visitor Center. There's always something doing in Old Town! If you're planning ahead and can't reach the phone numbers listed below, call the Visitor Center (☎ **703/838-4200**).

JANUARY   The **birthdays of Robert E. Lee** and his father, **"Light Horse Harry"** Lee, are celebrated with house tours, music, and refreshments.

FEBRUARY   Festivities marking **George Washington's birthday** include the nation's largest George Washington Day parade, a 10-kilometer race, and special tours in honor of Alexandria's most famous former resident.

MARCH   Alexandria's origin may be Scottish, but you wouldn't know it when **St. Patrick's Day** rolls around. The town grows greener than a field of shamrocks, and there's a parade and plenty of entertainment.

APRIL   Tours of historic homes and gardens are featured during **Historic Garden Week.**

MAY   From May to September, narrated **Lantern Tours** leave from the Visitor Center on Saturday at 8pm. Purchase your tickets right before the tour. School-age kids on up enjoy the anecdotal narration about Alexandria's history. For information, call ☎ 703/838-4200 or 703/548-0100.

JUNE   Don't miss the **Red Cross Waterfront Festival,** an outstanding family event held the second week of June. Boat rides and races, historic tall ships, children's games, entertainment, and food are featured at the harbor. Since the event draws around 100,000 people, arrive early. For information, call ☎ **703/838-4200.**

Drive or taxi it over to Fort Ward on selected days for Civil War drills, concerts, and lectures.

JULY   Alexandria's Scottish heritage is celebrated with **Virginia Scottish Games** the fourth weekend of the month. Athletic events, a parade of tartan-clad clans, Highland dancing, and storytelling are some of the events. For information, call ☎ 703/838-4200.

AUGUST   An 18th-century tavern is the scene for music, entertainment, food-1700s style-during **August Tavern Days.** For information, call ☎ **703/838-4200.** **Union Army Garrison Day** features authentically dressed military units in drills. Call ☎ /03/838-4848.

SEPTEMBER   Storytellers, jugglers, crafts, and people in period dress are featured at the **Colonial Fair.** Kids especially like the glassblowing demonstration. For information, call ☎ **703/838-4200.**

OCTOBER   The competition is stiff at the **War Between the States Chili Cookoff** in Waterfront Park. For a small admission fee you can sample all the entries and enjoy fiddling contests and country music. For information, call ☎ **703/548-0100.**

Take your ghouls and boys (over the age of 10, please) to the 1-hour Ghost Tours, conducted evenings around Halloween. Call ☎ **703/548-0100** for details.

NOVEMBER   Maybe your older kids will accompany you willingly to the **Historic Alexandria Antiques Show,** with dozens of dealers from several states showing their wares. For information, call ☎ **703/838-4554.**

DECEMBER   The **Annual Scottish Christmas Walk** heralds the holiday season with bagpipers, a parade of the clans, puppet and magic shows, and, of course, food. Children's games and Scottish dogs and horses (probably not in kilts) will please the bonnie ones.

Visit historic Alexandria homes and a tavern, decked with holly and other seasonal decorations, during the **Old Town Christmas Candlelight Tour,** usually the second week of the month.

EXPLORING OLD TOWN

Take younger children to Waterfront Park, where they can run loose, feed the pigeons, and look at the boats. Board the 125-foot schooner *Alexandria,* a classic Scandinavian cargo vessel berthed here. Tour the decks, main salon, and a stateroom of this tall ship Saturday and Sunday from noon to 5pm. The tour is free, but donations are appreciated.

Bring your lunch if you wish and take a 40-minute narrated cruise of the Alexandria Waterfront aboard the *Admiral Tilp,* which casts off from the dock at the foot of Cameron Street, behind the Torpedo Factory (☎ **703/548-9000**). Departures are several times daily from May until early September; weekends only in April, most of September, and all of October. Tickets are $8 for adults, $7 for seniors, $4 for kids 2 to 12. Call for information on longer cruises, between Old Town and Georgetown (Washington Harbour, 31st and K Streets NW) aboard the *Matthew Hayes,* and to Mount Vernon on the *Miss Christin.* All operate seasonally. Also see "Cruises" in chapter 7.

Everyone enjoys a stroll through Old Town's quaint streets to browse in the area's enticing shops. Of special interest to kids are **Granny's Place,** 303 Cameron St., and **Why Not?,** 200 King St.

Note: Some properties are closed on Monday.

Boyhood Home of Robert E. Lee

607 Oronoco St. ☎ **703/548-8454.** Admission $4 adults, $2 ages 11–17, free for children under 11. Mon–Sat 10am–3:30pm, Sun 1–3:30pm. Ages 10–14.

This Federal-style mansion, home to "Light Horse Harry" Lee, and his wife and brood of five, was built in 1795 by John Potts whose family had a metal business in Pennsylvania. The period furnishings are frozen in time in 1820. In the kitchen, you'll see the original fireplace and oven imported from England. A docent swears that after 200 years the oven would still work. Visitors walk on the original floors upstairs where George and Martha Washington stayed in the West Bedroom. It is said that George enjoyed one of his last meals in this house. A portrait of Martha as a young woman hangs in the Morning Room. An Adams-style mantel can be seen in Mrs. Lee's bedroom. Children are intrigued by the homemade toys and arrowheads (the area was once an Indian hunting ground!) displayed in the nursery. Speaking of children, if one of yours is doing research for a school project, the docents will take extra time to answer questions. Docent-led tours are ongoing and last from 30 to 45 minutes.

Fort Ward Museum and Park

4301 W. Braddock Rd. ☎ **703/838-4848.** Free admission; donations appreciated for special events. Park daily 9am–sunset; museum Tues–Sat 9am–5pm, Sun noon–5pm. Ages 2–14.

This 45-acre park, a short drive from Old Town, boasts an extensive Civil War research library and is the site of one of the forts erected to defend Washington during the Civil War. Explore the fort, six mounted guns, and reproduction of an officer's hut. Civil War weapons and other war-related exhibits are displayed in the museum. Picnic areas surround the fort, and outdoor concerts are given Thursday during the summer. Every year during **Living History Day** (usually on the hottest day in August), visitors flock to the Civil War encampment where uniformed regiments perform drills. Tell the kids, no battles allowed.

Gadsby's Tavern Museum

134 N. Royal St. ☎ **703/838-4242.** Admission $4 adults, $2 ages 11–17, free for children 10 and under with paying adult. Apr–Sept Tues–Sat 10am–5pm, Sun 1–5pm; Oct–Mar Tues–Sat 11am–4pm, Sun 1–4pm. Ages 10–14.

For a unique Old Town experience, I suggest a stop at the tavern visited (but not recently) by Washington, Madison, and Jefferson. Originally two buildings, which were joined in 1796 by innkeeper John Gadsby, it is now a museum of colonial furnishings and artifacts.

Half-hour tours are conducted 15 minutes before and after the hour. October through March, the first tour is at 11:15am, the last at 3:15pm. April through September, the first tour is at 10:15am and the last at 4:15pm. Sunday tours are between 1:15 and 4:15pm year-round.

As part of the **Time Travels** program, docents garbed in period dress assume the identity of a worker or tavern guest and interact with visitors. They particularly enjoy engaging children in conversation, and the results can be hilarious.

In the hands-on dormer room in the 1770 section of the museum, kids can try out the straw mattresses and rope beds, like the ones tavern guests slumbered on. How did they ever sleep?

Gadsby's Tavern, on the newer building's first floor, offers half-price children's portions of some entrees, and strolling musicians entertain evenings and during Sunday brunch.

In the past, school-age "ladies," their dolls, and chaperones enjoyed 18th-century tea dances while sharpening their social skills. Hopefully, Gadsby's will continue to offer this white-gloved opportunity.

Lee-Fendall House

614 Oronoco St. ☎ **703/548-1789.** Admission $4 adults, $2 ages 11–17, free for children under 11. Tues–Fri 10am–4pm, Sat 10am–4pm, Sun 1–4pm. Ages 6–14.

Many Lees have called this home over the years, but Robert E. never hung his clothes in the closet. Alexandria's only Victorian house-museum was built in 1785. The original structure was renovated in 1850. Kids like the antique dollhouse collection and boxwood garden better than the home, which serves as a museum of Lee furniture and memorabilia. The half-hour tour paints an impressionistic picture of family life in the Victorian age.

Stabler-Leadbeater Apothecary Shop

105-107 S. Fairfax St. ☎ **703/836-3713.** Admission $2.50 adults 18 and older, $2 students 11–17, free for children 10 and under. Mon–Sat 10am–4pm, Sun 1–5pm. Ages 8–14.

Stop here on your travels and look for the handwritten request for cod-liver oil, signed by "Mrs. Washington"—not Martha, as many think, but Mrs. Bushrod Washington, the wife of George Washington's nephew. On display are hand-blown medicine bottles and bloodletting paraphernalia. Parts of the shop may have to close during restoration, slated to begin some time in 2000. Self-guided tours with audio are available.

✪ Torpedo Factory Art Center

105 N. Union St. ☎ **703/838-4565.** Free admission. Torpedo Factory: daily 10am–5pm. Alexandria Archaeology and Research Lab: Tues–Fri 10am–3pm, Sat 10am–5pm, Sun 1–5pm. Closed Thanksgiving, Dec 25, Jan 1, Easter, July 4. Ages 4–14.

This is a must-see for all ages. In a navy-built torpedo shell-case factory, circa World War I, the only thing fired these days is the clay. Catch sculptors, painters, weavers, potters, and numerous other craftspeople and artisans in the act of creating. Since most items are priced reasonably, it's an excellent opportunity to stock up on one-of-a-kind gifts. Kids seem most fascinated watching clay take shape on the potter's wheel. Self-guided tours, available at the information desk, will help you structure your visit. Alexandria Archaeology is also centered here, and many unearthed artifacts are on display.

ACCOMMODATIONS

Old Town Holiday Inn

480 King St., Alexandria, VA 22314. ☎ **703/549-6080.** 227 units. A/C MINIBAR TV TEL. From $169 double; ask about Great Rate packages based on availability. AE, DC, DISC, MC, V.

Alexandria

To National Airport and Washington, D.C.

Powhatan St.

First St.

Canal Center Plaza

Potomac River

Montgomery St.

Madison St.

Wythe St.

Pendleton St.

① ② Oronoco St.

Princess St.

Queen St.

Founders
Quay St. **Park**

Cameron St. ③

King St. ④

⑤

⑥

**Waterfront
Park**

Prince St.

Duke St.

Wolfe St.

Wilkes St.

← To I-95 and 1

Gibbon St.

→ From I-95 and 1

To Mount Vernon,
Woodlawn,
Gunston Hall
↓

Franklin St.

Henry St. (Rte. 1 South)

Patrick St. (Rte. 1 North)

Alfred St.

Columbus St.

Washington St.

St. Asaph St.

Pitt St.

Royal St.

Fairfax St.

Lee St.

Union St.

Boyhood Home of Robert E. Lee ②   Ramsay House Visitors Bureau ④
Fort Ward Museum   Stabler-Leadbeater Apothecary Museum ⑤
  & Park ⑦   Torpedo Factory/
Gadsby's Tavern Museum ③   Alexandria Archaeology ⑥
Lee-Fendall House ①

If you want to stay overnight in Old Town, you can't get any closer than this. There's a large indoor pool open year-round. **The 101** is a somewhat formal restaurant serving breakfast, lunch, and dinner. Try **Annabelle's Lounge** for a snack or quick bite. Complimentary coffee and Danish in the morning and afternoon tea are included in the room rate Monday through Friday. Cocktails and hors d'oeuvres are gratis Wednesday from 5:30 to 7pm.

DINING
EXPENSIVE
Chart House Restaurant
1 Cameron St. ☎ **703/684-5080.** Reservations recommended. Main dishes $16–$23. AE, DC, DISC, MC, V. Mon–Thurs 5–10pm, Fri–Sat 5–11pm, Sun 10:45am–2:15pm (brunch) and 4–10pm. SEAFOOD/BEEF.

I've been disappointed by Chart House restaurants in several other locales. This one is an exception, and, though expensive, is a cut above the rest. The waterfront setting doesn't hurt. Neither does the professional and attentive but not too buddy-buddy wait staff. An ideal setting for a special-occasion dinner, the Chart House welcomes kids of all ages, but personally I don't think it's appropriate for kids under 5 or 6. When our family splurges, we don't want to be caught in the middle of a food fight or serenaded by a tantrum-plagued toddler.

The fried coconut shrimp is sensational, and the Chart House also turns out tasty fish and beef. Unlimited trips to the copious salad bar, with about 40 items, and bread are included in the main course price. The mud pie—cookie crust with coffee ice cream and a mound of fudge, topped with whipped cream and almonds, is a worthwhile splurge, even if you're full. It's huge-enough for two or three generous samplings.

The children's menu for kids under 12 features chicken fingers and spaghetti. High chairs and booster seats abound.

MODERATE
Warehouse Bar & Grill
214 King St. ☎ **703/683-6868.** Reservations recommended. Sandwiches $5.95–$7.95; dinner main courses $12.95–$21.95. AE, DC, DISC, MC, V. Mon–Thurs 11am–10:30pm, Fri 11am–11pm, Sat 8:30am–11pm, Sun 10am–9:30pm (brunch 10am–4pm). SEAFOOD/STEAK.

The fried shrimp and clams are done to a turn—crunchy and greaseless—at this popular seafood house, but more ambitious fish selections sometimes fall flat as a flounder. Fish haters crying "Where's the beef?" are in luck—the steaks are surprisingly good. Ask for the kids' menu featuring pasta, chicken, or fish nuggets in pint-sized portions. On Sunday, you can enjoy a hearty breakfast before beginning your tour of Old Town. High chairs and boosters are available.

INEXPENSIVE
Chadwick's
203 S. Strand St. ☎ **703/836-4442.** Fax 703/836-6780. Reservations accepted. Main courses $5.95–$16.95. AE, DC, DISC, MC, V. Sun 10am–midnight, Mon–Thurs 11:30am–midnight, Fri–Sat 11:30am–1am. AMERICAN. Metro: King Stret, then Dash bus or mile-plus walk.

Eat in or carry out at good old reliable Chadwick's, a stylish pub opposite the waterfront, between Duke and Prince streets. The salads, burgers, homemade soups, and Sunday brunch are all standouts, and kids always receive VIP treatment. Diners under the age of 10 can order from their own menu, which includes pizza, grilled cheese, and chicken tenders. The tender price is $2.95. Kudos to Chadwick's for fighting inflation. High chairs and booster seats are available. There's some street parking, and a pay lot ($5) across the street.

Hard Times Cafe

1404 King St. ☎ **703/683-5340.** Reservations for 10 or more. Main courses $3.95–$6.50. AE, MC, V. Sun–Thurs 11am–10pm, Fri–Sat 11am–11pm. AMERICAN. Metro: King Street, then Dash bus; or walk.

You could live on the onion rings here, but it'd be a shame not to leave room for the chili. Kids usually prefer the milder, tomatoey Cincinnati variety to the spicy, mostly meat Texas style. There's also veggie chili, the weakest of the three. The chili burger is sensational. Kids can order from their own menu. Plenty of high chairs and boosters. There's some metered street parking, and free evening and weekend parking in the rear lot. Don't forget the Hard Times when in Herndon or Arlington, Virginia, or Rockville, Maryland.

Union Street Public House

121 S. Union St. ☎ **703/548-1785.** Reservations not accepted. Main courses $5.50–$14. AE, DISC, MC, V. Mon–Thurs 11:30am–10:30pm, Fri–Sat 11:30am–11:30pm, Sun 11am–10:30pm. AMERICAN.

Try the burger topped with cheddar on toasted rye, ribs, or small fillet on an English muffin at this lively pub known for consistently good food and service. Sample one of the local beers while you're here. Little ones can order from the kids' menu and settle into a high chair or booster seat.

4 Annapolis

35 miles NE of Washington, D.C.

Set off with your crew for Annapolis, the 300-year-old jewel of the Chesapeake, less than an hour's drive—as the gull flies—from downtown D.C. Explore the many facets of this friendly and charming 18th-century seaport on the Severn River, dubbed "the sailing capital of the United States." Annapolis is home to the U.S. Naval Academy, Maryland State House, St. John's College, beautifully maintained historic homes, fine shops and restaurants, and about 30,000 pleasure crafts.

GETTING THERE

BY BUS   Bus transport is available Monday through Friday via Dillon's Bus Service (☎ **410/647-2321**), which picks up passengers at several points throughout the District and makes three stops in Annapolis, including the Navy-Marine Corps Stadium parking area. One-way fare is $3.35. Call for departure times and to find the most convenient departure point.

BY CAR   Annapolis is easily reached in about 40 minutes by car via U.S. 50, an eastern extension of New York Avenue. Take the Rowe (rhymes with cow) Boulevard exit and follow signs.

PARKING   If you can't find a metered spot near the City Dock, or want to avoid the hassle of looking, try the Hillman Garage (closest to the downtown action) with entrances on Duke of Gloucester Street and Main Street, or Gott's Court Garage, Northwest Street off Church Circle (behind the West Street Visitor Center). Both are 50¢ an hour. If you strike out, head back to the Navy-Marine Corps Stadium (Rowe Boulevard and Taylor Avenue), where all-day parking is $4 and includes a shuttle to downtown between 10am and 9pm (extended hours during special events).

INFORMATION

Stock up on brochures at the **Visitor Information Center** booth at the City Dock in the heart of town. It's open daily from 9am to 5pm. More comprehensive information is available from the walk-in **Visitor Center** at 26 West St., off Church Circle, open daily from 9am to 5pm (☎ **410/280-0445**). Here, the "Whiz Bang Machine," a touch screen video guide, dispenses information about sights and special events that include Fourth of July festivities, Navy football, and the annual Christmas Parade of Lights in the harbor.

For a list of upcoming events, lodging, and restaurants, write to the Annapolis Visitor Center, 26 West St., Annapolis, MD 21401. If you want to see Annapolis from the sea, stop at the City Dock or call for information on **Chesapeake Marine Tours'** cruises (☎ **410/268-7600**). *Hint:* To see Annapolis at its best, avoid summer Saturdays and Sundays, unless you plan on arriving before noon. Afterward it's a zoo.

The **area code** for Annapolis is 410.

SPECIAL EVENTS

JANUARY   Kids 10 and older (with a parent) can attend Opening Day of the **Maryland General Assembly** at the State House on State Circle (☎ **410/ 841-3810**).

APRIL   The Easter Bunny will greet kids 8 and under at the annual **Easter Egg Hunt** at Sandy Point State Park on Route 50 near the Chesapeake Bay Bridge. Prizes are given for finding specially marked eggs (☎ **410/280-0445**). On several Friday afternoons this month and next, attend the colorful **Weekly Parades** by the Brigade of Midshipmen at Worden Field on the U.S. Naval Academy grounds. The Mids step off at 3:30pm (☎ **410/263-6933**). You may also attend practice on Wednesday afternoons. The Ballet Theatre of Annapolis presents its spring **Dance Concert** at this time of the year (☎ **410/263-8289**).

MAY   The first Sunday of this month the **Bay Bridge Walk** attracts families by the thousands. Bring strollers for young ones as the walk is about 4½ miles. Park at the Navy-Marine Corps Stadium on Rowe Boulevard or Anne Arundel Community College on College Parkway in Arnold. Buses ferry walkers to Kent Island at the east end of the bridge. Afterward, walkers are whisked to Sandy Point State Park for a **Bayfest** celebration with lots of food and entertainment before being shuttled back to the family buggy. Go early! (☎ **410/260-8730**). The **Waterfront Festival** features sailing minilessons, Chesapeake Bay retriever obedience demonstrations, sea chanteys, crafts, and food booths galore (☎ **410/268-8828**). The **Clyde Beatty–Cole Brothers Circus** pitches its tents for several days at the Navy-Marine Corps Memorial Stadium on Rowe Boulevard (☎ **410/268-TOUR**). During Commissioning Week in late May at the Naval Academy, the public is invited to dress parades and a stunning air show by the Blue Angels, celebrating the graduation of the Naval Academy's first class (seniors to us civvies). Walk tall and bring bottled water, as it's usually hot (☎ **410/263-6933**). A festive **Memorial Day Parade** wends its musical way through the streets of the Historic District to the City Dock (☎ **410/280-0445**). **Discover Nature** is geared to kids 3 to 5 and their parents, at the 6-acre Helen Avalynne Tawes Garden (she was a former First Lady of Maryland). Reservations are required (☎ **410/260-8189**).

JULY   Bring lawn chairs or a blanket and enjoy the waterfront **Summer Serenade Concert Series** at the City Dock, most Tuesday evenings at 7:30pm through mid-August (☎ **410/280-0445**). A **Fourth of July Celebration** with oodles of family

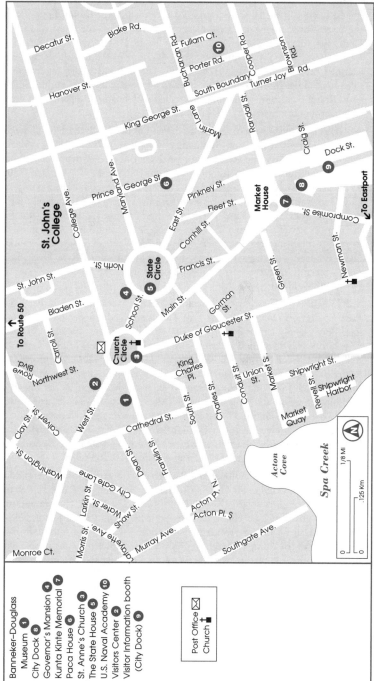

Banneker–Douglass
Museum **1**
City Dock **8**
Governor's Mansion **4**
Kunta Kinte Memorial **7**
Paca House **6**
St. Anne's Church **3**
The State House **5**
U.S. Naval Academy **10**
Visitors Center **2**
Visitor Information booth
(City Dock) **9**

⊠ Post Office
✝ Church

fun takes place at the City Dock and Naval Academy. At 9:15pm, fireworks over the Severn River cap the 4th. Crab pickers by the bushel scuttle over to the **Rotary Crab Feast** (the world's largest crab feast was featured in the August 1988 *National Geographic* magazine!) the third or fourth Saturday of the month, at the Navy-Marine Corps Stadium (☎ **410/280-0445**). The Ship and Soldier Shop's semiannual **Toy Soldier Show** convenes at Loews Hotel on West Street on July 8, 2000 and December 9, 2000 more than 150 tables of miniatures, representing dealers from all over the country (☎ **410/268-1141**).

AUGUST   Pooch lovers of all ages are invited to the **All-Breed Dog Show and Obedience Trials** at the Navy-Marine Stadium (☎ **410/280-0445**). Also this month, the **Maryland Renaissance Festival** kicks off in Crownsville (20 minutes from downtown Annapolis) and runs through October (☎ **410/266-7304**). At the annual **Kunta Kinte Festival,** held the second weekend of the month at the City Dock and St. John's College, the life of this African slave (inspiration for his descendant Alex Haley's *Roots*) is celebrated. Artists paint kids' faces with tribal markings as a griot tells stories about life during slavery, and dancers and musicians perform African-inspired works (☎ **410/349-0338**). Head for the City Dock or Naval Academy waterfront for a front-row seat at **Annapolis Race Week,** Labor Day weekend, sponsored by the Chesapeake Bay Yacht Racing Association (☎ **410/269-1194**).

SEPTEMBER   The **Maryland Seafood Festival** takes over Sandy Point State Park the first weekend after Labor Day. This is a splendid opportunity to sample local fare; family entertainment—other than eating—is ongoing (☎ **410/974-2149**). **Navy Football** kicks off this month in the Navy-Marine Corps Stadium. After several lackluster seasons, the Mids have had winning teams the past few years. Even when they lose, the games and half-time shows are colorful and inspiring. Your kids (and you) are sure to enjoy the march-on by the Brigade of Midshipmen before the game and the precision drills and entertainment between halfs (☎ **410/ 268-6060**). Hi-ho, come to the **Anne Arundel County Fair** at the county fairgrounds in Crownsville (☎ **410/923-3400**). A crisp fall afternoon is the ideal time to warm the bleachers at Worden Field while watching a **Dress Parade** by the 4,000-member Brigade of Midshipmen (☎ **410/263-6933**).

OCTOBER   The **U.S. Sailboat and Powerboat Shows** draw boating enthusiasts from all over the world to the City Dock on succeeding weekends. Not for tiny tots, and strollers are discouraged (☎ **410/268-8828**). The **Ballet Theatre of Annapolis,** comprised of local young dancers, presents its annual fall performance at Maryland Hall for the Creative Arts (☎ **410/263-8289**). The **Annapolis Symphony Orchestra Youth Concert** features works accessible to young people. Prior to the performance, players from the brass, wind, string, and percussion sections demonstrate the range of their instruments for little ears (☎ **410/263-0907**). The annual **Ghosts and Goblins Concert,** hosted by the Naval Academy, invites kids and adults to arrive in costume for a Halloween sampling of spooky organ selections at the Naval Academy Chapel (☎ **410/263-6933**).

NOVEMBER   Late in the month none other than **Santa Claus** himself arrives (by boat, of course) at the City Dock (☎ **410/280-0445**).

DECEMBER   To get in the holiday spirit, set aside time to see the **Greening of Annapolis,** when downtown and West Annapolis businesses are gussied up for the holidays. Charles Dickens, eat your heart out (☎ **410/280-0445**). Treat your kids to a performance of *The Nutcracker* and *Santa's Workshop* by the Ballet Theatre of

Annapolis (☎ 410/263-8289) or *Messiah* by the Annapolis Chorale (☎ 410/263-4309), both at Maryland Hall for the Creative Arts. An especially festive production of *A Christmas Carol* is presented annually by the Colonial Players (☎ 410/268-7373). March up West Street to the Annapolis **Christmas Toy Soldier Show** at Loews Annapolis Hotel (☎ 410/268-1141). The Christmas **House and Boat Tour** is a December highlight when visitors are welcomed into holiday-bedecked homes, B&Bs, and luxury yachts. Enjoy a **Child's Colonial Christmas** at the London Town Publik House and Gardens in Edgewater (☎ 410/222-1919). At the **Governor's Open House** on State Circle you may shake hands with the governor (☎ 410/974-3531). Take part in the **Grand Illumination** at the City Dock when the community Christmas tree is lit and carolers do their holiday thing (☎ 410/280-0445). Bundle up and go early to the **Christmas Lights Parade,** sponsored by the Eastport Yacht Club and visible from several spots in and around City Dock. Scores of local boat owners spend months festooning their rigs with lights, greenery, and costumed mates for the well-attended event (☎ 410/267-8986). End one year and begin a new one on an upbeat at the alcohol-free, family oriented **First Night Annapolis** celebration, featuring performances by musicians, mimes, choral groups, and dancers in storefronts and public buildings throughout downtown, the Naval Academy, and St. John's College. Special kids' entertainment starts at 4pm on New Year's Eve, and at midnight fireworks light up the harbor. It's great fun, and you won't wake up in the morning with a hangover (☎ 410/974-9332).

EXPLORING ANNAPOLIS

Weekends and holidays, bench seats are scarce at **Susan Campbell Memorial Park,** fronting Ego Alley, Spa Creek, and the Chesapeake Bay. Even so, it's a great place to stroll and enjoy the panoramic view of the harbor and beyond. Unwind on the seawall with an ice-cream cone from **Storm Bros. Ice Cream Factory,** 130 Dock St., and plan your day as pleasure craft parade up Ego Alley. A ceremony commemorating the arrival of *Roots* author Alex Haley's ancestor, Kunta Kinte, aboard the slave ship *Lord Ligonier* on September 29, 1767, is held annually at City Dock, and a life-size statue of Mr. Haley was unveiled in December 1999.

Despite a small-town population of 35,000, Annapolis encompasses 16 miles of waterfront. Not surprisingly, one of the best vantage points is from the water, so board one of the **charter boats** or water taxis berthed at the dock or **learn to sail**—it's a breeze at one of the area's sailing schools. Sightseeing, shopping, and restaurants are all an easy walk from the heart of the historic district.

For an overview and excellent introduction to this "city by the bay," **Discover Annapolis Tours** offers visitors 350 years of history and architecture aboard minibuses with big windows. Bring your camera for the stop at Governor Richie Overlook with its sweeping views of the Severn River and Naval Academy. Tours depart from the Visitors Center, 26 West St. (half a block from St. Anne's Church), several times a day, and last 1 hour. The cost is $10 for adults, $3 for kids 12 and under, and free for preschoolers. Call for departure times (☎ 410/626-6000).

Take an **audio tour** (lasting about 1 hour and 15 minutes), narrated by none other than Walter Cronkite, from the Welcome Center at 77 Main St. (☎ 410/268-5576), or **African American Heritage tour.** For a **guided walking tour** of the historic district, State House, Naval Academy, and St. John's College, led by knowledgeable tour leaders in period dress, call the **Historic Annapolis Foundation** (☎ 410/267-7619) or **Three Centuries Tours** (☎ 410/263-5401).

Rickshawlike **pedicabs** have proliferated in recent years on downtown streets. A young and robust team of drivers will take you anywhere you want to go, so you can tailor your own tour, then sit back and relax while the cyclist huffs and puffs. Hail one on the street—in truth, they'll probably hail you first!—or stop at the pedicab booth at the Marriott Waterfront Hotel. The drivers work solely for gratuities—and your pleasure.

Hike up **Main Street** from the City Dock to Church Circle. Regrettably, over the past 10 years the national chains have moved in with a vengeance, and many of the old-time mom-and-pop stores bit the dust, unable to cope with the soaring rents. A few exceptions remain: **A. L. Goodies** is still at 100 Main St. for souvenirs, T-shirts, fudge (skip the cookies; they look better than they taste), and the largest and most entertaining greeting card and novelty notepad selection for miles around (on the second floor). **Avoca Handweavers,** at 141 Main, stocks beautiful, but not inexpensive, woolens from the British Isles, many of which are hand knit. **Snyder's Bootery,** facing Conduit Street, has the biggest selection of once-exclusive boat shoes (now worn by everyone with feet) ever assembled under one roof. Across from Snyder's is **Chick and Ruth's Delly,** an Annapolis institution since the 1950s, and open round-the-clock. Do drop in for breakfast, lunch, dinner, or a snack and soak up the atmosphere with your chocolate malt (see "Dining," below).

Encircling the Maryland State House on **State Circle** are some of the town's premier shops and galleries, often overlooked by visitors. At **Annapolis Pottery,** where browsers can catch potters at work, a dazzling assortment of attractive, well-priced dishes and accessories is for sale, and special orders are taken. A few doors away is **Nancy Hammond Editions,** where the award-winning local artist sells her striking limited-edition silk-screen prints of Chesapeake Bay scenes, the Naval Academy, and the Caribbean. The note cards, T-shirts, and sweatshirts make wonderful souvenirs and gifts. Another gem is the **Maryland Federation of Art Gallery,** housed in a restored building dating from 1840, at 18 State Circle. Solo and small group exhibits of multimedia works change every 4 weeks and include three national shows per year.

Maryland Avenue, with its many home design and accessory boutiques, antique shops, and galleries, is more reminiscent of "old" Annapolis and therefore worthy of investigation. A top draw for casual lookers and serious shoppers, the commercial section runs from State Circle to Prince George Street. A standout along the bricked street is the **Aurora Gallery** (no. 67), a few doors from the State House, with a well-chosen array of American-made crafts, pottery, jewelry, and paintings— some created by the artist-owners. Try as I might, seldom have I been able to exit Aurora empty-handed. Across the street is the **Briarwood Book Shop** (no. 88) for used and out-of-print books. The **Dawson Gallery** (no. 44) is valued (by those who know about such things) for its 18th-, 19th-, and early 20th-century American and European paintings. A couple were purchased by Harrison Ford while filming *Patriot Games* in Annapolis several years ago. Funny, I would have pegged him as a lover of contemporary art.

Annapolis Sailing School

601 6th St. ☎ **800/638-9192** or 410/267-7205. Admission $190 and up; packages with hotel room available. Late Mar–Oct. Ages 4–14.

Before you go overboard for sailing, this is a good place to start. In 2 days of concentrated instruction alternating between the classroom and the school's fleet of 24-foot Rainbow sloops, families can learn enough to skipper a small boat. Honest! I've done it. **KidShip** offers sailing instruction-basic, intermediate, and advanced— for kids 4 and up in weekend, 3-day, and 5-day sessions, from May through September. KidShip also has beginning windsurfing and safe boating courses.

Banneker-Douglass Museum

84 Franklin. ☎ **410/974-2893.** Free admission. Tues–Fri 10am–3pm, Sat noon–4pm. Ages 8–14.

You'll find this little-known museum off Church Circle, in a Victorian gothic church built in 1874 by former slaves. Anyone interested in American history and the black American experience should take a few minutes to visit the edifice named for Benjamin Banneker (1731–1806), astronomer, farmer, surveyor, and mathematician. Changing exhibits are devoted to African-American history in Maryland. Banneker is best known for assisting Major Andrew Ellicott, the surveyor chosen by President George Washington to establish the boundaries of the District of Columbia in 1791.

Banneker's English grandmother taught him to read and write at his boyhood home outside of Baltimore. A farmer, he developed an interest in mathematics and became a self-taught astronomer. From 1791 to 1796, he penned an almanac of his own astronomical and tide calculations and weather predictions. He sent a copy to Thomas Jefferson along with a letter advocating the abolition of slavery. Jefferson was so impressed that he forwarded the almanac to the Royal Academy of Sciences in Paris. The almanac was used by opponents of slavery, here and abroad, as evidence of black achievement.

Chesapeake Children's Museum

2331D Forest Dr. (Festival at Riva Shopping Center). ☎ **410/266-0677.** Admission $3; free for children under 1 year old. Note: Children must be accompanied by an adult. Thurs–Tues 11am–6pm; Wed is for groups only. Directions: Rte. 50 east to Aris T. Allen Blvd. (Rte. 665) to Riva Rd. exit. Left at Riva Rd. to shopping center on right. Ages 2–10.

I hate to be the one to drag your family away from the waterfront, but this hands-on museum is a natural detour for those traveling with young children, especially preschoolers. In the unlikeliest of settings—a storefront next to Chuck E Cheese in a strip shopping center 10 minutes from City Dock—young children don foul weather gear and climb aboard a securely anchored minitug. They can also peer into an osprey nest and fashion clay molds of duck tracks. The setting may be Lilliputian, but there are multiple ways for little ones to learn while doing.

Near the entrance, a follow-the-rainbow sign directs kids to nine age-appropriate areas. Most exhibit areas change themes every 2 months. In "Body Works," 20 feet of vacuum cleaner hose is cleverly labeled: "A human's small intestine—20 feet." The Minnows room, for infants and toddlers, is filled with soft, safe playthings.

The museum holds story times, special events, and classes in art and movement; talks for parents on child-related topics are sponsored here, too. With a little help from their friends (and the state), the founders hope to find a larger, permanent home before the current crop of visitors enter college.

Chesapeake Marine Tours

City Dock. ☎ **410/268-7600,** or 301/261-2719 from D.C. Admission $6–$33 (St. Michael's). Daily May–Oct 11am–dusk. Ages 2–14.

Board the *Harbour Queen* for a 40-minute Severn River cruise, leaving on the hour, spring through fall. Ninety-minute Severn River and Thomas Point Lighthouse cruises are offered at several times during the week. When time permits, you may want to take an all-day trip to historic and scenic St. Michael's on the Eastern Shore. There are snack bars aboard all boats, music on some. Reservations are required for the St. Michael's cruise.

If you're first-timers, the 40-minute narrated cruise on the double-decked *Harbour Queen* provides a pleasing introduction to the waterfront sights including the

Bay Bridge and Naval Academy. May through September, daily departures are hourly beginning at 11am, ending at 7pm Saturday, Sunday, and holidays, and earlier on weekdays; April and early October, departures are at noon, 1, and 2pm. The 90-minute cruises run less frequently. There's full bar service and snacks onboard. Admission is $6 for adults, $3 for ages 2 through 11 on the 40-minute cruise; $12 for adults, $6 for children 11 and under on the 90-minute ride.

Jug Bay Wetlands Sanctuary

1361 Wrighton Rd., Lothian. ☎ **410/741-9330.** Admission $2.50 adults, $2 seniors, $1.50 under age 18. Year-round Wed and Sat 9am–5pm; Dec–Feb by reservation only 9am–5pm. Directions: From D.C., take the Beltway to Rte. 4 east/south, 10½ miles to right at Plummer Lane, right on Wrighton Rd. Go half a mile to entrance on left. Call for directions from Annapolis. Ages 4–14.

This is an incredible spot for anyone with an interest in the natural world in general and/or Chesapeake Bay ecology. It's about a half hour from Annapolis, but well worth the ride. Seasonal outdoor workshops on 7 miles of hiking paths take place weekends as part of the **Discover Program,** and special summer kids' programs are always well attended. Monday through Friday tours begin on the hour and half hour. The times for weekend tours vary. The cost is $6 for adults, $3 for children 11 and under.

By the time you read this, work should be completed on the transformation of the old exhibit room into a visitor-friendly, laboratory-like setting. In the new space, hands-on activities will be encouraged in the wetlands learning room, and visitors can interact at work stations in seven environmentally themed areas.

I suggest calling ahead no matter when you plan your visit as this is primarily a research facility and not always open to the public.

Maryland Hall for the Creative Arts

801 Chase St. ☎ **410/263-5544.** www.mdhallarts.org. Admission varies with activity. Year-round. Ages 6–14.

Workshops in the fine arts, demonstrations, exhibits, and performances take place year-round in the former school building, a 5-minute ride from the City Dock. The Annapolis Symphony (☎ **410/269-1132**), Ballet Theatre of Annapolis, and Annapolis Youth Orchestra all make their home here. You can catch them several times annually.

Maryland State House

State Circle. ☎ **410/974-3400.** Free admission. Daily 9am–5pm. Ages 8–14.

The oldest state capitol in continuous legislative use served as the nation's capitol from November 1783 to June 1784. In this building, George Washington resigned his commission in 1783, and the Treaty of Paris was ratified. Half-hour tours are scheduled at 11am and 3pm daily.

Miss Anne or *Miss Anne II*

City Dock. ☎ **410/268-7600.** Admission $6 adults, $3 age 11 and under. Daily 12:15–9:45pm. Ages 2–14.

These smallish sightseeing boats cast off every half hour for a tour of the harbor and Spa Creek.

Newman Street Playground

Newman and Compromise sts. Free admission. Daily during daylight hours. Ages 2–10.

Local school kids helped to plan the humongous wooden structure that attracts toddlers to teens. You can picnic here or seek shade and rest during your tour of Annapolis. The park is diagonally across from the Annapolis Marriott Waterfront hotel.

William Paca House and Gardens
186 Prince George St. ☎ **410/263-5533.** www.annapolis.org. Adults $7 (house and gardens), $5 (house only), $4 (gardens only); half price for ages 6–18. Mon–Sat 10am–4pm, Sun noon–4pm. Closed Thanksgiving, Dec. 24, and Dec 25. Ages 8–14.

William Paca, a signer of the Declaration of Independence and governor of Maryland during the Revolution, built this five-part Georgian mansion between 1763 and 1765. In the early 1900s, the house became a hostelry for legislators and visitors to the U.S. Naval Academy. When the wrecker's ball threatened in 1965, the Historic Annapolis Foundation stepped in and restored the house and 2-acre garden to their former grandeur. While older kids generally find the house of interest, *everyone* delights in the garden with its intricate parterres, terraces, and waterway. The flower enclosure is abloom from March to November. A self-guided audio tour is only $1. Metered street parking nearby; garage within walking distance.

Helen Avalynne Tawes Garden
Behind Department of Natural Resources, 580 Taylor Ave., at Rowe Blvd. (across from the stadium). ☎ **410/974-3717.** Free admission. Garden daily sunrise–sunset. Lobby exhibits Mon–Fri 8am–5pm (closed holidays). Ages 4–14.

The delightful 6-acre garden depicts Maryland's varied landscape, from the Appalachians in the western part of the state to the ocean beaches of the Eastern Shore, and is a reminder of the necessity to value and conserve our precious natural resources.

Weekdays, pick up a booklet at the garden display in the lobby and check out the great blue heron and Baltimore oriole (here the state bird, not a baseball player) before beginning your walk. More than likely, the most interesting thing to younger kids will be the Texture, Taste and Fragrance Garden, which invites visitors to "taste and see if you can identify" certain herbs.

◑ U.S. Naval Academy
Visitor Gate at foot of King George St. ☎ **410/263-6933.** Free self-guided tour; guided tour $5.50 adults, $4.50 seniors, $3.50 for children in first–sixth grade, free for children under first grade. Academy grounds daily Mar–Nov 9am–5pm, Dec–Feb 9am–4pm. Group tours by appointment year-round. Directions: Rte. 50 east to Rowe Blvd. exit. Proceed on Rowe about 1 mile to left at College Ave., right at King George St. to Gate 1 and parking adjacent to the Halsey Field House. Ages 6–14.

It's only a 5-minute walk from the City Dock in downtown Annapolis to the Naval Academy, founded in 1845. Hours change seasonally for the hour-long tour that departs from the Armel-Leftwich Visitor Center adjacent to the Halsey Field House inside Gate 1 on the academy grounds. Try to see the short film *To Lead and to Serve* before you begin your tour. The interactive exhibits and gift shop bear checking out, as well as the view of downtown from the riverfront promenade behind the building. Upstairs, kids can ogle over David Robinson's basketball.

Guided tours, of interest to kids 8 and above, are offered year-round. Call for times as they change seasonally. During the academic year, the noon tour leaves at 11:45am to take in noon meal formation (weather permitting) in Tecumseh Court, in front of Bancroft Hall.

You may also visit several buildings on your own. In **Lejeune Hall,** across from the Visitor Center, you'll find cases of trophies and photographs of the academy's athletic achievements and maybe catch some action in the Olympic-size pool. Close by is **Dahlgren Hall,** where a chrome yellow biplane "flies" from the ceiling. The navy's ice hockey team plays here, and from time to time it is the site of figure skating competitions and a New Year's Eve ice show, part of First Night Annapolis. Pick up a hockey schedule along with a snack at the Dry Dock Restaurant. It's a hop, skip, and jump across the Yard, as the academy grounds are called, to the awesome **Navy Chapel** and **John Paul Jones's crypt.** Nearby is the Naval Academy Museum, **Preble Hall,** filled with 200 years of naval art and artifacts. The ground-floor **Gallery of Ships** delights all ages. Many of the ships are original builder's models (☎ **410/293-2108**). From the seawall at the **Robert Crown Sailing Center,** you may see boatloads of plebes learning to sail. Even though they may never board a sailboat at any other time in their lives, they are all required to learn the basics.

Bancroft Hall is the "dormitory" for all 4,000 midshipmen. If you're touring on your own, arrive at Bancroft Hall a few minutes before noon (weather permitting) for **noon meal formation** (about 12:10pm weekdays, 12:20pm weekends)—in my mind the highlight of an academy visit. Would your kids be willing to line up like this for their macaroni and cheese? There's usually plenty of activity in the afternoon on the fields behind Bancroft. Stroll the beautiful grounds, walk along the **Dewey seawall** for a wide-angle view of the harbor, and, in season, catch a band concert in the gazebo. After **Commissioning Week,** in late May or early June, it's fun to watch the procession of weddings (one an hour!) from the lawn opposite the chapel.

Many athletic events are free. Most are open to the public. For information and tickets, call the Naval Academy Athletic Association (☎ **800/US-4-NAVY**).

ACCOMMODATIONS

If you're planning an overnight stay, take your pick of historic inns, B&Bs, and luxury hotels. Hotels outside the historic district often offer complimentary shuttle service. For a brochure describing B&Bs in Annapolis, write the **Annapolis Association of Licensed Bed and Breakfast Owners,** P.O. Box 744, Annapolis, MD 21404, or contact **Bed & Breakfasts of Maryland** (☎ **410/269-6232**).

Annapolis Marriott Waterfront
80 Compromise St., Annapolis, MD 21401. ☎ **800/336-0072** or 410/268-7555. 150 units. A/C TV TEL. $160–$300 (waterfront suite) single or double. AE, DISC, MC, V. Ask about special packages and promotions. Parking $10 per day.

Overlooking the harbor and Spa Creek, the Marriott enjoys a prime downtown location as well as **Pusser's Landing** restaurant and dockside bar/lounge. A children's menu at lunch and dinner offers a handful of reasonably priced items; or they can fill up on one of the light fare offerings. Scores of Annapolis eateries (not to mention shopping and sightseeing) are within a few blocks. Room service is available, and the hotel has an exercise room with fitness equipment. I'm sure they have their reasons, but I think they goofed when they deep-sixed the swimming pool several years ago. When there are big doin's at the Naval Academy, and during the boat shows in October, this place is booked a year ahead.

Chez Amis B&B
85 East St., Annapolis, MD 21401. ☎ **410/263-6631.** www.chezamiz.com. 4 units. A/C TV. $105, $115, $130 per room. $15 for child, kids over 10 only. Special off-season rates. MC, V. Parking $4 per 24 hours in nearby garage.

Chez Amis is a family friendly B&B carved from a corner store on a quiet block in the heart of the historic district. The original tin ceilings, pine floors, and oak counters are retained, and quilts, pieced by the proprietor's grandmother, decorate the walls. All four rooms have private bathrooms (one with a claw-foot tub). Guests enjoy a full breakfast with a hot entree, juices, homemade breads, fresh fruit, coffee, and tea. Children over 10 are welcome and can bunk in the same or a separate room. You'll find terry robes and fresh flowers in all rooms.

Private Pleasure

Annapolis City Marina, Severn Ave. (behind Carrolls Creek Café restaurant), Annapolis, Md. 21403. ☎ **800/877-9330** or 410/267-7802. www.harborviewbnb.com. 2 staterooms. A/C TV. $230 per room; $400 for both. Rates include an evening cruise (weather permitting) and continental breakfast. AE, DISC, MC, V.

This would be my choice if I were visiting from out of town. But I live down the road. Guests enjoy a continental breakfast with congenial hosts in the paneled main salon or aft deck of this beautifully appointed 1947 Trumpy yacht. CD players and VCRs are available. Watch the sunset over Annapolis harbor and enjoy the marina's pool and cafe in season. Gourmet catering and captained cruises are also available. The Giardinis welcome families with kids 6 and older who are well supervised, as unscheduled midnight swims are a concern.

Scotlaur Inn

165 Main St., Annapolis, MD 21401. ☎ **410/268-5665.** www.scotlaurinn.com. 10 units. A/C TV TEL. $59.95–$99 per room. Ask about special midweek rates. MC, V. Garage parking $8 per night.

Roll out of bed onto Main Street—literally! Stay at what may be the world's only "Bed and Bagel" and enjoy a full complimentary breakfast in **Chick and Ruth's Delly** downstairs. Small pets are welcome at this family owned and operated establishment, but they won't receive a free breakfast. The 10 distinctive rooms all have private bathrooms (some with shower only, so be sure to ask if you must have a tub). Rooms are charmingly done in turn-of-the-century furnishings. The walls are so thick, you'll think you're in the country. Hair dryers and complimentary soap and shampoo await guests, and cable TV should be installed by the time you read this. If you wake up hungry for a sandwich and a milkshake in the middle of the night, phone downstairs and someone will deliver your snack. When you go downstairs for breakfast, ask Ted to do magic tricks for your kids. You won't have to ask twice.

DINING
MODERATE

Cafe Normandie

185 Main St. ☎ **410/280-6470.** Reservations recommended. Lunch and dinner main courses $5.95–$19; breakfast less. AE, MC, V. Sun–Thurs 8am–10pm, Fri–Sat 8am–11pm. COUNTRY FRENCH.

I would have no problem dining at this cozy, plant-filled bistro three times a day. Don't try all these at one sitting, but the cream of crab soup, Caesar salad, veal and fish main courses, crepes, and fresh fruit tarts are especially noteworthy. If your kids are finicky, they're bound to dig the crepes.

Cantler's Riverside Inn

458 Forest Beach Rd. ☎ **410/757-1311.** Reservations not accepted Sat–Sun. All items $4–$20 (not including crabs). AE, DC, MC, V. Sun–Thurs 11am–11pm. Fri–Sat 11am–midnight. SEAFOOD.

If you're visiting Annapolis in the summer, it'd be a crime not to dig into the local delicacy, steamed Maryland blue crabs (in season from May to October), at this wonderful restaurant on Mill Creek. Depending on the weather, grab a seat on the deck, covered patio, or inside. Get here early on the weekends—that means by 12:30pm for lunch and 6pm for dinner. We were devastated when we arrived with out-of-town friends on a sultry July evening at 7pm, and there were no more crabs. Ever seen four grown people cry? The crabs and steamed clams (when available) are the best around. After that, try the crab-vegetable soup, soft-shell crab sandwich, or fried chicken. There's hot dogs, hamburgers, chicken, fried or steamed shrimp, or a crab cake sandwich for the kids. *Note:* The steamed crabs are heavily doused with Old Bay seasoning, which may be too spicy for little ones.

Before or after your crab feast, take the kids underneath the restaurant for a peek into the dockside shedding boxes. This is where the Maryland blue crabs do their striptease (with no privacy) to become the sought-after delicacy, soft-shell crabs. Call for directions—less than a 10-minute ride from downtown Annapolis.

INEXPENSIVE

Chick and Ruth's Delly

165 Main St. ☎ **410/269-6737.** Reservations not accepted. Most items $1–$7.50. No credit cards. Daily, 24 hours. Closed Thanksgiving and Dec 25. DELI.

Ruth and Chick Levitt moved from Baltimore and established their deli restaurant on Main Street back in the 1950s, before Annapolis became a yuppie outpost. Since Chick's greatly mourned passing in January 1995, his son Ted runs the place (when he isn't entertaining customers with sleight of hand), and the grandchildren are in training. The **Dellyland Delight kids' menu** (for those 7 and under) offers breakfast fare and sandwiches with potato chips or french fries. Of course you'll treat them to one of the oversized sodas or shakes they won't be able to finish (that's where you come in). I love the well-seasoned home fries on the breakfast platters, which are served all day. The 44 tasty sandwiches (try the Main Street if you can't decide) are named for Maryland pols and locals. You'll love the funky 1950s decor, fountain treats, and cheeky waitresses at this friendly eatery that has served three generations of Annapolitans. I introduced my grandson to Chick and Ruth's when he was 6 months old (not years) and he loves it.

Riordan's

26 Market Space. ☎ **410/263-5449.** Reservations not accepted. All items $4.25–$17; sandwiches $6–$8. AE, DC, MC, V. Daily 11am–2am. Brunch Sun 10am–1pm. AMERICAN.

Close your eyes and picture a friendly neighborhood saloon with lots of wood, brass, and tchotchkes on the walls—that's Riordan's. No wonder locals introduce their children early on to the potato skins with the works, burgers, sandwiches (especially the roast beef and Reuben), and such. The food is consistently good, and the friendly servers know how to hustle. Sunday brunch is an Annapolis tradition ($6.95 to $10.95 for grown-ups, $5 for kids). Riordan's children's menu for the 10-and-under set offers burgers, chicken tenders, spaghetti, and Cajun popcorn shrimp, each for $4 or less.

Tony's Pizza-N-Pasta

36 West St. ☎ **410/268-1631.** Reservations not accepted. Main courses $3.95–$12.95. MC, V. Mon–Thurs 10:30am–8:30pm, Fri 10:30am–9pm, Sat 10:30am–4pm. ITALIAN.

I can't figure out why this place isn't mobbed all the time. Tony's is a neighborhood joint in the best sense. The help is accommodating, everything's cooked to order, and the pizza is a prizewinner with its perfectly textured crust that's made fresh daily. We're partial to the "Vegetale" topped with onions, green peppers, mushrooms, and black olives. Try one of the pasta or seafood dishes if you're not in a pizza frame of mind. The eggs margarita and frittata are standouts at Saturday brunch, served all day. At Tony's, prices are 1950s low, and it's only a 5-minute walk to Main Street. There's a children's menu, high chairs, and boosters. Wonderful old photos of Annapolis adorn the walls.

5 Baltimore

38 miles NE of Washington, D.C.

Where to start? Only an hour's drive or 40-minute train ride from D.C., Charm City offers families such an abundance of sights and experiences that you could easily spend several days and leave begging for more. Home of Babe Ruth, H. L. Mencken, and birthplace of our national anthem and Baltimore clipper ships, the city is enlivened by its rich ethnic heritage. Baltimore is also a big sports town, supporting both the Baltimore Ravens (NFL Football) and Orioles baseball.

A myriad of activities are centered at the **Inner Harbor,** a revitalized complex of businesses, sightseeing attractions, shops, restaurants, and hotels built around the city's natural harbor. The Baltimore Orioles play in Oriole Park at Camden Yards (see "Exploring Baltimore" later in this chapter), frequently to sell-out crowds. The Baltimore Ravens (NFL football team) play at PSI Stadium next to Oriole Park. (see "Spectator Sports," in chapter 7).

Not the least of Baltimore's claims to fame are steamed blue crabs, harvested spring through fall from the Chesapeake Bay, and the best corned beef between New York City and Miami Beach (harvested year-round). Don't leave without sampling both.

GETTING THERE

BY TRAIN   Frequent daily train service via Amtrak (☎ **800/USA-RAIL**) is available between Washington and Baltimore. Fare is $19 one way unreserved; business class (reserved and roomier seat) is $27; $9.50 for children 2 to 15 traveling with an adult; $16.50 for seniors. The trip takes 40 minutes and links D.C.'s Union Station and Baltimore's Penn Station, about 15 blocks or a short taxi ride from the Inner Harbor.

Less expensive (and less sexy) than Amtrak is the **MARC commuter train** (☎ **800/325-RAIL;** www.mtamaryland.com). It's a glorified subway car, but the price recommends it and it is, after all, a train. The fare from D.C.'s Union Station to Baltimore's Penn Station is only $5.75 one way, but bear in mind that it operates weekdays only.

BY BUS   Greyhound (☎ **800/231-2222**) provides frequent service between the Washington bus terminal at 1st and L streets NE and 2110 W. Fayette St. in Baltimore. The current fare is: Monday through Thursday $9 one way, $15 round-trip; Friday through Sunday $10 one way, $16 round-trip. Children 2 through 11 pay half price (one child per paying adult).

BY CAR   To get to Baltimore, take I-95 to I-395 north to Pratt Street; make a right and another right at President Street. You'll find many parking lots near the harbor.

INFORMATION

For maps and information on sightseeing and walking tours, contact the **Baltimore Convention and Visitor Association,** 300 W. Pratt St., Baltimore, MD 21201 (☎ **800/282-6632** or 410/837-4636; www.baltimore.org). Another informative Web site is www.ci.baltimore.md.us. For information on city tours, contact **About Town Tours** (☎ **410/592-7770**). A **Visitor Center** is located at the Inner Harbor opposite the Pratt Street Pavilion, near the USS *Constellation*.

SPECIAL EVENTS

JANUARY   Ring in the New Year at the Inner Harbor where you'll be dazzled by a stunning pyrotechnic display at midnight (☎ 410/837-4636). For a chilling experience, watch ice carvers create spectacular sculptures (☎ 800/HARBOR-1).

FEBRUARY   Bring older kids to the **Baltimore Craft Show.** More than 500 artisans sell their wares in Festival Hall at one of the largest and most prestigious craft shows in the country (☎ 410/659-7000).

MARCH   In past years a **Children's Fair,** geared to 3- to 12-year-olds, has been held at the State Fairgrounds in Timonium, north of the city (☎ 410/225-0052). Musicians and other performers entertain at Harborplace around **St. Patrick's Day.**

APRIL   Watch **street performers audition** for summer performance spots in the Harborplace Amphitheatre. It's a hoot! For information, call ☎ 800/HARBOR-1. The Aberdeen Proving Grounds (about half an hour north of the city) is the site of an **Armed Forces Day Open House** the third Saturday of the month. State police K-9 dog demonstrations, jousting competitions, and tours of the complex are highlights (☎ 410/278-3807). Storytelling, face-painting, and hayrides take place at the **Children's Spring Festival** hosted by the Rose Hill Manor Museum (☎ 301/694-1646). Enjoy contemporary band music at the **Easter Sunday Music Fest** in the Harborplace Amphitheatre (☎ 800/HARBOR-1). The Easter Bunny greets children throughout Harborplace and the Gallery on Easter Sunday afternoon.

MAY   The **Preakness** (part of the Triple Crown) is celebrated with concerts, parades, and balloon festivals the third week of May preceding the race at Pimlico (☎ 410/542-9400). Area school bands and choirs serenade at Harborplace all month long (☎ 800/HARBOR-1).

JUNE   **Summer Ethnic Festivals** take place June to September, but not every weekend. Admission is free, but bring your wallet and appetite. Call for the dates of the Polish, German, Italian, and other festivals (☎ 800/Harbor-1). Enjoy music Friday, Saturday, and Sunday all summer at the Harborplace Amphitheatre's **Summer Concert Series** (☎ 800/HARBOR-1). Head for **Citysand** in the Harborplace Amphitheatre where architects work with kids to sculpt elaborate sand creations (☎ 800/HARBOR-1). Pay tribute to the Stars and Stripes on **Flag Day** (June 14) at **Fort McHenry** (☎ 410/962-4290). Baltimore is one of seven ports to host a flotilla of tall ships as part of **Opsail 2000,** June 23 to 29, 2000. The festivities take place in and around the Inner Harbor (☎ 800/HARBOR-1).

JULY   Baltimoreans celebrate the **Fourth of July** in grand style with daytime entertainment and a dazzling fireworks display at the Inner Harbor. A summer concert series takes place every Friday, Saturday, and Sunday night in the amphitheater. As part of Baltimore's Festival of the Arts, **Artscape** is usually held the third weekend of the month along Mt. Royal Avenue. Artwork by youngsters is displayed as well as visual arts-and-craft exhibits at this happening enlivened by jugglers, mimes, music makers, and street theater (☎ 410/396-4575).

AUGUST   Who can resist the free entertainment dished out by fire-eaters, unicyclists, jugglers, and clowns at the Inner Harbor (☎ 800/HARBOR-1)?

SEPTEMBER   Bookworms from several states wriggle over to the annual **Baltimore Book Festival** held 1 weekend at Mt. Vernon Place (☎ 800/HARBOR-1).

OCTOBER   The **Fells Point Funfest** (first weekend) attracts kids of all ages to its colorful street festival. Clowns, jugglers, and musicians entertain, and children's

Baltimore

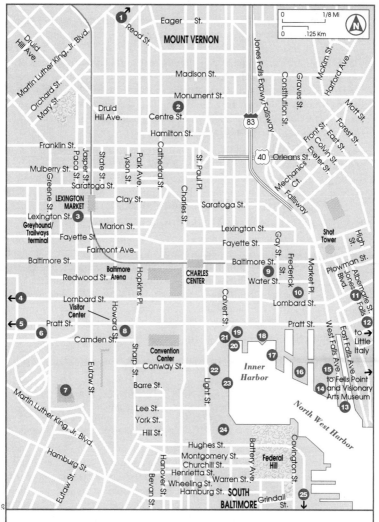

Babe Ruth Birthplace/Maryland Baseball Hall of Fame ⑥
Baltimore City Life Museums ⑪
Baltimore International Culinary College ⑨
Baltimore Maritime Museum ⑰
Baltimore Museum of Art ①
Baltimore and Ohio (B&O) Railroad Museum ⑤
Columbus Center ⑮
Festival Hall ⑧

Fort McHenry ㉕
H.L. Mencken House ④
Harbor cruises ㉓
Harborplace ㉑
Holocaust Memorial ⑩
Lexington Market ③
Light Street Pavilion ㉒
Marine Mammal Pavilion ⑭
Maryland Science Center ㉔
National Aquarium ⑯

Oriole Park at Camden Yards (baseball) ⑦
Pier 6 Concert Pavilion ⑬
Pratt Street Pavilion ⑲
Star-Spangled Banner Flag House and 1812 Museum ⑫
Top of the World ⑱
U.S. Frigate Constellation ⑳
Walters Art Gallery ②

games, tempting snacks, and crafts are always within easy reach (☎ **410/ 837-4636**). Learn something about the Chesapeake Bay while watching watermen race wooden boats at the **Watermen's Festival** at Cox's Point Park in Essex (☎ **410/887-0251**). Celebrate Baltimore's rich maritime history at **Kids on the Bay,** held at the Inner Harbor as part of the 2-week Baltimore on the Bay festival. Plenty of kid-pleasing activities will delight your little swabs (☎ **410/837-4636**). During the annual fall **Port Fest,** visitors can tour the Dundalk Marine Terminal, the U.S. Navy Reserve Center, historic schooners, and a ship or two at one of the country's busiest ports (☎ **410/837-4636**).

NOVEMBER   What would Thanksgiving be without a parade? Follow the floats and cartoon characters from Camden Yards to Market Place on the Saturday before Turkey Day for the **Thanksgiving Parade** (☎ **410/837-4636**). Harborplace and the Gallery are spruced up for the holidays. Choirs herald the season and Santa's Place and Santa's Petting Zoo open (☎ **800-HARBOR-1**).

DECEMBER   At the **Annual Lighted Boat Parade** illuminates the harbor as more than 50 boats in holiday finery file past (☎ **800/HARBOR-1**). In a **Merry Tuba Christmas,** traditional carols are played by an orchestra of tubas and euphoniums in the Harborplace Amphitheatre (☎ **800/HARBOR-1**). Enjoy a carriage ride and caroling at the **Fells Point Old-Fashioned Candlelight Christmas,** several weekend evenings before the 25th (☎ **410/276-6287**). **New Year's Eve Extravaganza** at the Baltimore Convention Center is a perfect way for the entire family to bid adieu to the old year: no booze and plenty of entertainment, with fireworks at midnight over the Inner Harbor (☎ **800/282-6632**).

EXPLORING BALTIMORE

American Visionary Art Museum
800 Key Hwy. ☎ **410/244-1900.** Fax 410-244-5858. Admission $6 adults; $4 age 5 and older, students, and seniors; free for children 4 and under. MC, V. Tues–Sun 10am–6pm. Closed Mon, Thanksgiving, Christmas. Directions: Take I-95 north to Exit 55, left onto Key Hwy. Continue 1½ miles to Covington St. Parking across from main entrance ($3 all day).

There's some really weird stuff going on here, and it's utterly captivating. I imagine if Hieronymus Bosch and Monty Python joined forces to create an art museum, this is what it would like. There's little rhyme or reason to the creative off-the-walls explosion celebrated here. Most of the self-taught artists are outsiders—jailbirds, religious visionaries, and certifiable wackos. Because most of the paintings, drawings, sculptures, and assemblages are so off-center that they're in the next galaxy, they grab children with their stripped-bare honesty and lack of pretension. No climbing, please, on the 55-foot Whirligig in the outdoor plaza.

When was the last time you took in works by artists who believe human life sprang from Easter Island after the flood or received messages from the Pleiades via a "mental radio"? Recline on a cot to view through binoculars the Book of Revelations (here 300 feet long) by Thomas Thompson, then wing it. Check out the museum shop for stuff you won't find in the Smithsonian.

Baltimore and Ohio Railroad Museum
901 W. Pratt St. (at Poppleton). ☎ **410/752-2490.** Admission $6.50 adults, $5.50 seniors, $4 ages 3–12, free for children 2 and under. Daily 10am–5pm. Directions: Take I-95 north to Russell St. exit, left at Lombard, go 3 blocks to left at Poppleton to museum parking. Ages 4–14.

Train buffs make tracks for this museum on the site of the country's first train station, where the first passenger ticket was issued in 1830. Check out the HO gauge train display on the second floor. The detail is astounding. In the roundhouse you can wander through the locomotives, freight and passenger cars, and cabooses. The comprehensive exhibits are a must-see for little toots who get steamed up over trains and railroad history. In the backyard, train rides on the diesel Montclair Express are offered Saturday, Sunday, and holidays. Half-hour movies on railroad history run on weekends, and a gift shop stocks books, train memorabilia, and whistles. All aboard!

Baltimore Museum of Art

Art Museum Dr., at North Charles and 31st sts. ☎ **410/396-7100.** Admission $6 adults 19 and over, $4 seniors and full-time students, free for age 18 and under; free admission Thurs. Wed–Fri 11am–5pm, Sat–Sun 11am–6pm. Closed major holidays. Directions: Rte. 295 north to Russell St. exit. Right at Pratt, left on Charles to Art Museum Dr.

Maryland's largest art museum is noted for its decorative arts, furniture, and paintings. The Cone Collection is one of the world's outstanding modern art collections, with works by Matisse, Picasso, Cézanne, van Gogh, and Gauguin. The Levi and Wurtzburger outdoor sculpture gardens brim with contemporary pieces.

Comprised of 16 galleries, the new modern art wing houses a prestigious collection of 20th-century art. Changing exhibitions augment the permanent collection. Summer jazz performances take place in the sculpture garden where picnicking is welcome (☎ **410/396-6314**). Special family programs are ongoing.

Baltimore Museum of Industry

1415 Key Hwy. ☎ **410/727-4808.** Fax 410-727-4869. www.thebmi-org. E-mail: bmi@charm.net. Admission $5 adults, $3.50 seniors and students, free for children 6 and under. Workshops extra. Labor Day to Memorial Day, Wed 7–9pm, Thurs–Fri noon–5pm, Sat 10am–5pm, Sun noon–5pm; Memorial Day to Labor Day, Tues, Thurs, and Fri noon–5pm, Wed 6–9pm, Sat 10am–5pm, Sun noon–5pm. Ages 4–14.

Every weekend in the Children's Motorworks section of this innovative museum, dedicated to the industrial history of Baltimore, youngsters as young as 5 work on an assembly line for 45 minutes to turn out cardboard vans. Kids can role-play in the Oyster Cannery where children 10 and up punch a time clock and become workers in an 1883 Baltimore cannery for an hour. The young shuckers use real oyster shells with white clay oysters, before moving on to a skilled task such as making or labeling cans. Kids are paid with brass tokens they can then use in the company store. Children gravitate to the turn-of-the-century drugstore, a replica of George Bunting's apothecary (he invented Noxzema, in case you didn't know) complete with soda fountain. In other parts of the museum, visitors encounter a meat-packing exhibit and a 1920s garment loft workshop.

Tickets can be purchased at the door for the Cannery ($3.50), Saturday at 11am and 2pm, Sunday at 2:30pm; and the Children's Motorworks ($2), Saturday and Sunday at 1pm. (It's advisable to call ahead, I was told. Don't want to disappoint the kiddies!) Housed in the former Platt Oyster Cannery on the Inner Harbor, the museum is distinguished by a large red crane out front.

✪ Baltimore Zoo

Druid Hill Park. ☎ **410/366-LION,** or 410/396-7102 for special events. Admission $9 adults 16–61, $5.50 ages 2–15 and seniors 62 and over, free for children under 2. Mon–Fri 10am–4pm, Sat–Sun 10am–5:30pm. Directions: Take I-95 north to 695 west (toward Towson) to I-83 south (Jones Falls Expressway). Exit 7 west off the Expressway to Druid Park Lake Dr. and follow signs to the zoo. Ages 2–14.

Home of the nation's number-one rated children's zoo, the innovative Baltimore Zoo has long been trading cages for natural habitats that enable animal lovers to come face-to-face with their favorite creatures. After a visit, kids come away with a greater appreciation of an animal's point of view and the interrelationship of all living things.

Especially noteworthy are the wildlife in the **Maryland Wilderness** section of the Children's Zoo, inhabited by more than 100 local species. In the bog turtle exhibit, fashioned from a portion of restored wetland, visitors learn about the bog's role in the overall "health" of the Chesapeake Bay. By studying the turtle's adaptability, researches can use the habitat as a model for future restoration of Bay wetlands. Your little bipeds can also climb into a huge oriole's nest, scale a tree like a bear, or crawl woodchuck-style through an acrylic tunnel under a dam. In the **Maryland Farmyard,** kids are invited to ride a pony, pet a sheep, breeze down the silo slide, or watch a demonstration of cow milking. Lunch with the Kodiak bears at 2pm or watch the African black-footed penguins dive for an early dinner of raw fish at 3pm.

In the **Chimpanzee Forest,** designed as part of a species survival plan, you and your little monkeys can watch the chimps swing from a fire hose vine and frolic in their very own play area. Due to the clever construction and well-placed observation platforms, visitors are made to feel like part of the chimps' world.

From May to September, junior explorers (2 to 15) can trade their pith helmets for a bundle of summer fun, which includes a free copy of the Zoofari Adventure Guide, a clever exhibit-related activity book with catchy titles, like "Shake, Rattle, and Ouch!" (for the page devoted to porcupines). Kids and adults can scale the Siberian Summit, a 24-foot wall with varying surfaces and degrees of difficulty. Saturdays from 4 to 8pm, May through September, catch the sunset with the animals and enjoy live entertainment and food in the Village Green.

Cap your visit with a ride on the antique carousel and train.

Columbus Center for Marine Biotechnology Research and Education
701 E. Pratt St., Piers 5 and 6 (next to National Aquarium). ☎ **410/576-5700.** Admission $7 adults, $6 seniors, $5 ages 4–11, free for children 3 and under. Sat–Thurs 10am–5pm, Fri 10am–8pm. Closed Thanksgiving and Dec 25. Directions: Take Rte. 295 north to Baltimore, Russell St. exit. Right at Pratt St. to Inner Harbor. Follow signs to Pier 5/6 parking. Ages 6–14.

The Columbus Center is the newest addition to the flourishing Inner Harbor scene. Designed primarily as a research and educational facility, with labs, classrooms, and lecture halls, the **Hall of Exploration** opened in May 1997. In 257,000 square feet of futuristic space in a circuslike tent, lab researchers rub shoulders with state-of-the-art displays promoting marine biotechnology.

Concrete stairs shaped like the double helix of a DNA strand, miles of glass piping, and natural light streaming through four gigantic roof "eyes" create a stunning environment for inquiring minds.

You'll find 48 interactive workstations in five themed areas and plenty of hands-on activities and multimedia presentations. All are created to topple the wall between abstract science and everyday phenomena. A walk-through waterfall, underwater microscope for observing life in the Chesapeake Bay, and 45-foot-long walk-through rockfish (also known as striped bass) focus on nurturing a better understanding of local seafood harvesting. The audience becomes a predator—here, a hungry sand tiger shark—in **Shark Attack,** a multimedia sensory experience in the theater, which is shaped like a horseshoe crab. Visitors are invited to peer into some work areas where researchers study marine animal and plant biology.

The third-deck **Overlook Cafe** has a limited menu and free Internet access stations. In the Real Science Store, full of games and exhibit-related books, visitors can pick up certificates for winning interactive games.

✪ Fort McHenry National Monument and Historic Shrine
East Fort Ave. (at the very end). ☎ **410/962-4290.** Free admission to the park; Star Fort: $5 age 17 and over, free for age 16 and under. Daily 8am–4:45pm. Ask about extended summer hours. Directions: Take I-95 north to Exit 55 (before the tunnel) and follow signs. Ages 4–14.

Francis Scott Key was so moved on the night of September 11, 1814, as the British fired on Fort McHenry (missing their target repeatedly, I might add), he wrote a poem that became our national anthem in 1931. Visit the spot where the bombs were "bursting in air" while Key was waxing poetic on a boat in the harbor. A 16-minute orientation film plays on the half hour from 9am to 4pm. The gun collection and underground dungeons are of special interest to most kids. The waterfront park is an idyllic spot for watching boats (passing tankers are a common sight) and reflecting.

Harborplace and The Gallery

200 E. Pratt St. Pratt, Light, and Calvert sts. at the Inner Harbor. ☎ **410/332-4191.** ☎ 800/HARBOR-1. www.harborplace.com. Mon–Sat 10am–9pm, Sun 11am–7pm; some extended summer hours. Directions: Take I-95 north and follow signs to Inner Harbor. Ages 2–14.

I haven't yet met the kid who dislikes shopping, unless it's for dress shoes or eyeglasses. During your visit to the Inner Harbor, browse through this pleasant, not too big, four-level mélange of shops and restaurants. Unlike many malls, with their claustrophobic, tomblike ambience, the Gallery has a soaring, light-filled atrium that evokes the outdoors. The big draws for children are the **Discovery Channel Store, The Disney Store, World of Science,** the **Sharper Image,** and **Gap Kids** for stylish, durable clothing.

When hunger strikes, you can drop some major bucks at **Planet Hollywood** (across the street at the Pratt Street Pavilion) or head for The Gallery's fourth-level food court, where the **Ocean City** fries and burgers are sure kid-pleasers. You'll also find **Bain's Deli, Steak Escape, Salad Creations, Sbarro,** and **China City.** Dig diners? Slip into **Eat at Joe's** (3rd level) for your favorite diner fare. **Donna's Coffee Bar & Café** (2nd level) serves soups, salads, sandwiches, pizza. For dessert, dip into a some rich and creamy **Ben & Jerry's.**

✪ Harborplace

Pratt, Light, and Calvert sts. ☎ **410/332-4191.** Shops and Food Hall: Mon–Sat 10am–9pm, Sun 11am–7pm (extended weekend hours in summer); restaurants with separate entrances stay open later. Directions: Take I-95 north and follow signs to Harborplace. Ages 2–14.

Baltimore's top tourist draw at the Inner Harbor consists of two pavilions that do their seductive best to lure visitors into their shops, restaurants, and food stalls. The **Light Street Pavilion** is primarily food oriented. Kids love the second-floor Food Hall, which draws locals and visitors with a wide array of American-style and ethnic fast food. Weather permitting, chow down on a bench overlooking the harbor. For sit-down service, try **Capitol City Brewing Co., Johnny Rockets** (50's style diner), or **Paolo's.** **Lee's Ice Cream** is made locally. Wind up in the toy store **All Wound Up. Accento** sells attractive handcrafted clothing and accessories for the entire family. At the **information kiosk,** find out about special events, which in the past have included rowing regattas, band concerts, and crab races.

Shoppers head for the **Pratt Street Pavilion,** filled with big-name retail stores, one-of-a kind boutiques, and more restaurants. Check out **Dapy** for wacky electronic playthings and **Big Dog Sportswear.** Flip a coin then pig out at the following sit-down restaurants: **California Pizza Kitchen, Pizzeria Uno, Cheesecake Factory, Planet Hollywood, Tex Mex Grill,** or **Waynes Bar-B-Que.** Even on dismal nonholidays, the air is festive around Harborplace. Without spending a cent, you can have a rich time watching the other tourists, strolling the waterfront promenades, and window shopping.

Inner Harbor Ice Rink

Rash Field off Key Hwy. ☎ **410/837-4636.** Admission $4–$5 adults, depending on session, $3 for children under 12. Hours vary.

Skate daily from December through early March at this outdoor rink with the Inner Harbor as a backdrop. The view is particularly stunning after dark. Please, please remember hats and gloves for the kiddies, and keep a tight rein on youngsters under 5. Skate rentals are $2.

Lexington Market
West Lexington St. (between Paca and Eutaw). ☎ 410/685-6169. Mon–Sat 8:30am–6pm. Directions: Take I-95 north to Russell St. exit. Russell runs into Paca; continue 5 blocks. Ages 2–14.

Skip breakfast; it's pig-out time! Eat your way through this former open-air market that blew out 200 birthday candles in 1982. The oldest continuously open U.S. market began humbly in 1782 when farmers in Conestogas arrived from outlying areas to barter produce, game, fowl, and dairy goods. The first shed was raised in 1803, and the market grew in fits and starts until it was wiped out by fire in 1949. The bulk of the market, as you see it today, reopened in 1952.

More than 130 merchants hawk produce, seafood, poultry, and a variety of pre-pared foods and baked goods from row upon row of stalls in two buildings. An information kiosk is located in the center of the Arcade, the sight of entertainment and special events such as the annual chocolate and ice-cream festivals. Seating for 500 is available on the Arcade's second level. Recommendations (diligently researched over many years) include **Polock Johnny's sausage sandwiches** (with the works), **Barron's Deli** for corned beef, **Faidley's** for seafood, **Utz potato chips,** and **Berger's** for cookies and doughnuts. Who remembered the Tums?

Baltimore Maritime Museum
Lightship Chesapeake and 7-Foot Knoll Lighthouse, USS *Torsk* submarine, and USCG Cutter *Taney,* Pier 3, Inner Harbor, Pratt and Gay sts. ☎ 410/396-3453. Admission $5.50 adults, $4.50 seniors, $3 ages 5–12, free for children 4 and under. Daily, summer 10am–6pm, winter 10:30–5pm. Closed major holidays. Directions: Take I-95 north and follow signs to Inner Harbor. Ages 4–14.

Kids will get an idea of how sailors live and work on this guided tour of a lightship, lighthouse, submarine, and 327-foot cutter.

Maryland Science Center
Inner Harbor, 601 Light St. (at Key Hwy). ☎ 410/685-5225. Admission $9 adults, $7 ages 4–17 and seniors, free for children 3 and under. Mon–Fri 10am–5pm, Sat–Sun 10am–6pm. Closed Thanksgiving and Dec 25. Directions: Take I-95 north and follow signs. Ages 2–14.

Time passes quickly in this facility established by the Maryland Academy of Sciences. Scores of hands-on exhibits invite kids of all ages to touch, to explore, to learn. Enter a distorted room, make friends with a computer, and delve into physics, geology, and the human mind.

The third-floor **Kids' Room** features a jungle gym and slide, plant and animal specimens, and a dress-up corner. It's open daily from 12:30 to 4:30pm.

Watch a movie on the five-story-high **IMAX** screen or reach for the stars in the **Davis Planetarium.** Both are recommended for kids 4 and over. Two movies alternate in the IMAX theater, and planetarium shows air twice a day on weekdays, numerous times on weekends. Friday and Saturday at 7:30pm, a double feature is shown in the IMAX. Timed tickets are sold at the box office.

While tickets may seem steep, admission includes all exhibits, one IMAX movie, and a planetarium show. The exhibits alone are worth the price of admission. Strollers are not allowed in the theaters.

Weather permitting, a carousel next to the science center goes round and round weekends throughout the year, with extended summer hours. The figures on this

1912 Herschell-Spillman creation include horses, dogs, pigs, and roosters. Rides are $1 (☎ **410/964-0055**).

✪ National Aquarium

Pier 3, 501 E. Pratt St. (adjacent to Harborplace). ☎ **410/576-3800.** Timed-entry tickets required. Admission $14 adults, $10.50 seniors 60 and over, $7.50 ages 3–11, free for children under 3. Purchase advance tickets after 3pm a day ahead through TicketMaster (☎ **202/432-SEAT**). Sun–Thurs 9am–6pm, Fri–Sat 9am–8pm. Closed Thanksgiving and Dec 25. Directions: Take I-95 north and follow signs to Inner Harbor. Ages 2–14.

You'll feel like you're underwater the minute you enter this multistory aquarium that towers over the harbor. Set aside at least 2½ to 3 hours *early in the day* to do justice to the main Aquarium Building and Marine Mammal Pavilion. I once made the mistake of visiting in the afternoon, and the experience was totally frustrating because of the crowds. To avoid disappointment, order tickets ahead (see above).

Moving ramps and escalators transport visitors through various aquatic habitats. The various ring tanks contain rays, tropical fish, and sharks. The **Maryland Exhibit** follows a raindrop from pond to ocean. Kids like to hunt for protectively colored species in **Surviving Through Adaptation** and inspect horseshoe crabs and sea stars in the touch pool in the **Children's Cove.** Hands down, the steamy and exotic **Rain Forest,** where small animals and tropical birds roam freely, is the most popular exhibit. The **Atlantic Coral Reef** has over 800 species. The coral is plastic, but the fish don't mind.

Very young kids may bore easily in the main Aquarium, especially if their view is blocked by tourists three deep, but they'll surely wake up in the **Marine Mammal Pavilion.** The exploration station includes many interactive displays. One allows you to mimic whale sounds. Bottlenose dolphins entertain several times a day during half-hour shows. Unlike shows at many other seaquariums, which are strictly for entertainment's sake, these are highly instructional. The 1,300-seat $40 million pavilion features two multiscreen video monitors that strikingly supplement the antics in the pool.

Outside the main Aquarium, the seals are fed several times a day. Call for feeding times, as they are not "sealed" in stone. Check the sign over the lobby information desk to find out when the sharks (mercifully, indoors) dine.

National Historic Seaport of Baltimore

Baltimore Inner and Outer Harbor. ☎ **1-877-NH-CPORT.** Admission: $15.75 adults, $10.50 youth 6–14, $2 kids 5 and under. Open: year-round. Closed major holidays. Hours vary.

Adults can save $8 by purchasing a pass card covering admission to the USS *Constellation*, water taxi, USS *Torsk,* USCG Cutter *Taney,* Chesapeake Lightship, Knott Lighthouse, Top of the World, and Baltimore Museum of Industry.

Oriole Park at Camden Yards

333 W. Camden St. ☎ **401/685-9800.** Admission $5 (SRO on day of game, if a sellout); $7 (bleachers); several tiers of medium-priced seats up to $30 (club box); free for children 2 and under. Tours of the stadium are offered daily (when there's an evening game). Call for times, which vary (☎ **410/685-9800**). To charge tickets in D.C., call ☎ **202/432-SEAT.** Early Apr to early Oct (unless the O's get really lucky and make the playoffs). Directions: Take I-95 north to Rte. 395/Downtown or I-295 north. Follow signs to stadium. Ages 6–14.

Take them out to an Orioles ball game, *if* your young ones are old enough to sit still through nine or more innings. Even when the game is lackluster, it is a thrill to be in this magnificent structure, which opened in spring 1992, replacing worn-out Memorial Stadium. For my money, the view of downtown Baltimore, so perfectly framed beyond the outfield, is better than an O's ninth-inning home run with the bases loaded. If the game is boring, check out the overflow memorabilia from the Babe Ruth Museum (see entry below).

You could do worse than to patronize the numerous and varied food concessions, but a word of warning: The food is tasty but pricey. You'll save by packing a picnic to be enjoyed pregame at one of the tables provided for such purposes on the Eutaw Street corridor, between the warehouse and ballpark. For your family's comfort, the seats are roomy, and, best of all, there are abundant rest rooms. Tickets are a hot commodity, so order early whenever possible. Ask about special events and promotional giveaways, many of which are geared to young people. For information on public transportation to the games, call ☎ **800/543-9809** or 410/539-5000.

Babe Ruth Museum

216 Emory St. ☎ **410/727-1539.** Admission $5 adults, $3 seniors, $2 ages 5–16; reduced admission for AAA members. Daily 10am–5pm (until 7pm on Oriole home-game days). Closed Thanksgiving, Dec 25, Jan 1. Directions: Take I-95 north to Rte. 395/Downtown. At fork, take Martin Luther King Jr. Blvd. Turn right on Pratt, go 2 blocks, and then turn right on Emory. Go 1 block to museum. Ages 6–14.

Stand in the very room where George Herman Ruth Jr. drew his first breath in 1895. The sultan of swat's career record of 714 homers remained unbroken for more than 40 years until Hank Aaron settled the score in 1974. Displays in this downtown row house chronicle the Babe's life, and there's a healthy dose of Baltimore Oriole memorabilia, too. Don't miss the photo of the 3 year old slugger playing ball. At the **Second Saturdays** programs (second Saturday of each month), special guests regale visitors with baseball stories and reminiscences.

Port Discovery

35 Market Place (at Lombard St.). ☎ **410/727-8120.** Admission $10 adults, $7.50 kids 3–12, free 2 and under. Daily 10am–5:30pm.

Trace your kids against the "magic" wall of a glass booth, coax them through a house full of sensory illusions, and cheer them on as they explore Kid Works, a maze full of opportunities for climbing, jumping, and sliding. Along with these, the Dreamlab, Sensation Station and other innovative interactives are garnering wide attention from area families. While this high-tech children's play house is devoted to the 5 and under set, it is not unusual for teenagers and other older relatives to get involved. Occupying a former fish market near the Inner Harbor, Port Discovery is stimulating, educational, and fun. Give shopping and eating a rest and walk the few blocks from the waterfront to this kid-pleasing attraction.

Star-Spangled Banner Flag House

844 E. Pratt St. ☎ **410/837-1793.** Admission $5 adults; $4 seniors, military (with ID); $2 ages 6–18; free for children under 6. Group rates. Tues–Sat 10am–4pm. Ages 6–14.

Almost everyone has heard of Francis Scott Key. But how many of you know who Mary Pickersgill was? If you visit this brick row house built in 1793 at the corner of Pratt and Albemarle streets, a short walk down Pratt from the Inner Harbor, you'll find out. Seems Mary, from a prominent Philadelphia family, was entrusted with creating a garrison flag 30 feet by 42 feet by the commander of Fort McHenry during the War of 1812. The order was for a flag the British would have no trouble seeing from a distance. When the flag outgrew Mary's bedroom, she pieced it on the floor of a nearby malt house. Mary delivered the goods in about 6 weeks, and it inspired Key to write our national anthem in 1814. Now you know the rest of the story.

Visitors will see many of her personal possessions and can view a video in the adjacent museum building. Call about special programs, held monthly (such as Flag Day in June). If you want to see the flag, it's hanging in the Smithsonian's National Museum of American History.

Top of the World

Inner Harbor, 27th floor of World Trade Center, 401 E. Pratt St. ☎ **410/837-VIEW.** TOTW@charmnet,BOP.org. Admission $3 adults, $2 ages 5–15 and seniors 60 and over, free for children 4 and under. Mon–Sat 10am–5pm, Sun noon–5pm; extended summer hours. Directions: Take I-95 north and follow signs to Inner Harbor. Ages 4–14.

On a clear day you can see forever; well, almost. Would you settle for the harbor, the O's new stadium, and north to Towson 13 miles away?

CRUISES

Of the numerous cruise boats plying the Inner Harbor during the warm-weather months, here are a few that are particularly appealing to tiny tars.

Baltimore Patriot

Pratt St. side of Harborplace. ☎ **410/685-4288.** Admission $6.50 adults, $3.30 ages 2–11. May–Sept daily, hourly 11am–4pm; Apr and Oct daily 11am, 1, and 3pm. Ages 4–14.

In a 1½-hour tour, travel the 8-mile length of the harbor on the *Baltimore Patriot,* which sails from Constellation Dock daily from April or May through October. Cruise past Fort McHenry, Fells Point, Federal Hill, and Fort Carroll (a six-sided island in the middle of the Patapsco River), before returning to port. A cruise to Ft. McHenry operates during the warm-weather months between 11:30am and 4:30pm, every hour on the half hour. The ride is 30 minutes each way and costs $5 for adults, $3.75 for kids 2 to 11.

Clipper City

Light St. Finger Pier at Harborplace. ☎ **410/575-7930.** Admission varies according to cruise. Apr–Oct 15. Ages 4–14.

This 150-foot replica of a 19th-century top-sail schooner leaves port almost daily from April through mid-October. Cruises are of varying lengths, and you must call for reservations a week or more in advance.

Half Shell

Harborplace. ☎ **410/522-4214.** Call for prices and departure times.

The *Half Shell,* a 54-foot working oyster boat built in 1928, clears its deck of oyster shells to ferry groups (no walk-ons) around the harbor. Call for reservations.

Minnie V

Harborplace. ☎ **410/685-0295.** Admission $12 adults, $3 for children under 12. May–Sept weekends, 11am–5pm, every 2 hours on odd hour. Ages 4–14.

Shiver me timbers, the *Minnie V.,* a classic skipjack built in 1906, will take your family—gulls and buoys of all ages welcome—for a narrated 1½-hour tour of the Inner Harbor under sail. Learn a thing or two about Baltimore's maritime history while enjoying gentle breezes off the Patapsco.

USS Constellation

Inner Harbor. Pier 1, Pratt and Light sts. ☎ **410-539-1797.** www.constellation.org. Admission $6 15 and older, $4.75 seniors, $3.50 kids 6–14, free kids 5 and under. Hours: daily 10am–6pm. Closed major holidays.

After 3 years in dry dock where it underwent major refurbishment (to the tune of $7.5 million), the USS *Constellation* sailed to its Inner Harbor berth in 1999 amid friendly cannon fire. Built in 1854 and retired in 1945, it was the last navy ship powered entirely by sail. Landlubbers are granted permission to come aboard and tour the majestic sloop of war.

ACCOMMODATIONS

Days Inn
100 Hopkins Place, Baltimore, MD 21201. ☎ **800/325-2525** or 410/576-1000. 250 units. A/C TV TEL. $99–$199 double. Age 18 and under stay free in parents' room; age 12 and under eat free with paying adult. Ask about special family and weekend packages. AE, DC, DISC, MC, V. Parking $8.50.

Just 3 blocks from the Inner Harbor, 2 blocks from Oriole Park at Camden Yards, and 4 blocks from the Aquarium, the Days Inn is still a good buy for families, especially if you're able to take advantage of one of several special packages usually offered on weekends (depending on availability).

A free refrigerator is available on request to cut down on the cost of snacking and eating out. **Ashley's,** the hotel's restaurant, is informal and family friendly, serving breakfast, lunch, and dinner weekdays, breakfast and dinner on weekends. Kids 12 and under can eat free with a paying adult. Tickets for the enormously popular Aquarium are on sale at the front desk. This could save you valuable time, unless you enjoy standing in line. An outdoor pool is open from Memorial Day to Labor Day. The biggest negative about this hotel is trying to reach it by phone.

✪ Renaissance Harborplace
202 E. Pratt St., Baltimore, MD 21202. ☎ **800/535-1201** or 410/547-1200. 622 units. A/C MINIBAR TV TEL. Weekdays from $240 double; weekends from $215. Ask about special family packages and discounts (depending on occupancy). Children 16 and under stay free in parents' room. AE, DC, DISC, MC, V. Self-parking $10, valet $14.

Go for it! The Renaissance's location is prime, and rooms are spacious and nicely appointed. Morning coffee and a newspaper are gratis; turndown service as well, if you so desire. **Windows,** the hotel's restaurant and lounge overlooking the harbor, welcomes families. There's an indoor pool, Jacuzzi, sauna, and Nautilus equipment on the seventh floor, and the hotel is attached to the Gallery, a multilevel mall with scores of shops, restaurants, and food stands. Harborplace is just across Pratt Street, and reachable by a skywalk from the hotel. The concierge will secure tickets for local attractions and arrange a bonded baby-sitter if you want to enjoy Baltimore's nightlife *sans* kiddies.

DINING
MODERATE

Chiapperelli's
237 S. High St. ☎ **410/837-0309.** Reservations recommended. Lunch main courses $6.95–$14.95. Dinner main courses $10–$20. AE, CB, DC, MC, V. Mon–Thurs 11am–10pm, Fri–Sat 11am–midnight, Sun 11am–10pm. ITALIAN.

Bring the bambinos for heartily sauced pastas (nothing subtle or bland here), seafood, and veal (such as veal Neapolitan) at this Little Italy fixture, still going strong after 50 years. The ravioli and tortellini Alfredo are *bellissimo,* and the hot antipasto appetizer is an appetizing meal in itself. *Be forewarned:* The portions are huge, especially the pasta. You may have trouble finishing your entree after the large house salad, deliciously drenched in a creamy garlicky dressing. Go ahead: Force yourselves to try the homemade bread. Child's portions are available.

Gunning's Crab House

3901 S. Hanover St. ☎ **410/354-0085.** Reservations required for 8 or more. Main courses $7.95–$17.95; crabs $25 and up a dozen, depending on size. AE, DISC, MC, V. Daily noon–10pm. SEAFOOD.

This is Brooklyn, Maryland, which is hard-shell crab territory, so roll up your sleeves and dig into a pile of steamed crabs, while the waitresses "Hon" you to death. If picking crabs seems too much like work, try Gunning's award-winning crab cakes or one of several other seafood offerings. Gunning's is also known for its fried green pepper rings. Try 'em (you'll thank me). A kids menu features popcorn shrimp, minihot dogs, and hamburgers. Eat in one of the dining rooms or the large enclosed "garden" room, or outdoors in the crab garden when the weather cooperates. Crabs are also available for carryout. *A friendly tip:* Buy the largest-size crabs—less work and more meat.

Paolo's

Light St. Pavilion at Harborplace, Pratt and Light sts. ☎ **410/539-7060.** Reservations not accepted. Main courses $6.95–$16.95. AE, DC, DISC, MC, V. Daily 11am–1:30am. ITALIAN/AMERICAN.

This place has plenty going for it: atmosphere, friendly service, reasonable prices, and very good food to boot. Children are given crayons while waiting for pizza, spaghetti, grilled chicken, or chicken fingers from the kids' menu. You won't go wrong with pizza, pasta, or a giant salad, but the chicken (grilled or oven roasted) is really special. Come for brunch on Saturday and Sunday.

INEXPENSIVE

Al Pacino Café

609 S. Broadway (Fells Point). ☎ **410/327-0005.** Reservations not accepted. $1.50 (french fries) to $13.95 (large pizza with the works). CB, DC, MC, V. Sun–Thurs 11am–midnight, Fri 11am–2am, Sat 11am–2am. Directions: Take I-95 to I-395 north to Pratt St., right on Pratt, pass Inner Harbor, right on President or Albermarle, left on Eastern Ave., right on Broadway. PIZZA/MIDDLE EASTERN.

Drop in after you've soaked up some maritime history and local color in Fells Point. The atmosphere is homey—some might say homely—but the pizza has been praised and prized by the *Baltimore Sun, City Paper,* and *Baltimore Magazine.* If you need more of an endorsement, our family loves it despite the grungy decor. The connection with Al Pacino is tenuous. The word on the street is that the owners selected the cafes name 'cause they dig the actor. There are 29 varieties of pizza baked in the wood-burning oven. For something different, I suggest the Egyptian pizza topped with falafel and cilantro. Some of the other choices are simple, some exotic (the "Taba" features squid and mushrooms. Your kids will love it. *Not!*). Free refills on sodas, lemonade, tea, and coffee; and they have high chairs. Other locations are at 542 E. Belvedere Ave., 900 Cathedral St., and 6080 Falls Rd. in Mt. Washington.

'Food Hall

Light St. Pavilion at Harborplace, Pratt and Light sts. ☎ **410/332-4191.** Most items $1–$6. No credit cards. Spring–summer daily 10am–10pm; fall–winter Mon–Fri 9am–5pm, Sat–Sun 10am–8pm. FOOD COURT.

Pizza, french fries, milk shakes, sandwiches, tempura, cookies, roast beef, crab cakes, hot dogs, gyros, fried chicken, fruit drinks, sushi, egg rolls, tacos, oysters, calzone, barbecue, ice cream. Did I skip something? Eat lunch early or late or you may have to stand. Can't decide? Try Thrasher's french fries well done with plenty of vinegar and salt. Take your ticket to heartburn city outside, and grab a seat with a harbor view.

Lenny's

1150 E. Lombard St. ☎ **410/327-1177.** Reservations not accepted. Most items $2–$5. AE, DISC, MC, VISA. Mon–Sat 7:30am–6pm, Sun 8am–5pm. DELI.

Lenny's location may leave something to be desired, but such a minor irritation disappears with the first bite into a corned beef sandwich. It comes two ways: regular, with a little fat for flavor and moistness for true corned-beef lovers ($4.15), and lean for sissies ($5.15). Someday nutritionists will add this (along with egg creams and chopped chicken liver) to their list of essential foods. In the meantime, don't forget a pickle—half done or well done (sour)—to go with your corned beef. Lenny's also offers a selection of sandwiches and platters. Who wants to eat a platter when you can eat corned beef? The original Lenny's is still thriving in Owings Mills.

Index

See also Accommodations and Restaurant indexes, below.

ACCOMMODATIONS

FROMMER'S® COMPLETE TRAVEL GUIDES

FROMMER'S® DOLLAR-A-DAY GUIDES

Australia from $50 a Day
California from $60 a Day
Caribbean from $70 a Day
England from $70 a Day
Europe from $60 a Day
Florida from $60 a Day

Hawaii from $70 a Day
Ireland from $50 a Day
Israel from $45 a Day
Italy from $70 a Day
London from $85 a Day
New York from $80 a Day

New Zealand from $50 a Day
Paris from $85 a Day
San Francisco from $60 a Day
Washington, D.C.,
  from $60 a Day

FROMMER'S® PORTABLE GUIDES

Acapulco, Ixtapa &
  Zihuatanejo
Alaska Cruises & Ports of Call
Bahamas
Baja & Los Cabos
Berlin
California Wine Country
Charleston & Savannah
Chicago

Dublin
Hawaii: The Big Island
Las Vegas
London
Maine Coast
Maui
New Orleans
New York City
Paris

Puerto Vallarta, Manzanillo
  & Guadalajara
San Diego
San Francisco
Sydney
Tampa & St. Petersburg
Venice
Washington, D.C.

FROMMER'S® NATIONAL PARK GUIDES

Family Vacations in the
  National Parks
Grand Canyon

National Parks of the
  American West
Rocky Mountain

Yellowstone & Grand Teton
Yosemite & Sequoia/
  Kings Canyon
Zion & Bryce Canyon

FROMMER'S® GREAT OUTDOOR GUIDES

New England
Northern California

Southern California & Baja
Washington & Oregon

FROMMER'S® MEMORABLE WALKS

Chicago
London

New York
Paris

San Francisco
Washington D.C.

FROMMER'S® IRREVERENT GUIDES

Amsterdam
Boston
Chicago
Las Vegas

London
Los Angeles
Manhattan

New Orleans
Paris
San Francisco

Seattle & Portland
Vancouver
Walt Disney World
Washington, D.C.

FROMMER'S® BEST-LOVED DRIVING TOURS

America
Britain
California

Florida
France
Germany

Ireland
Italy
New England

Scotland
Spain
Western Europe

THE UNOFFICIAL GUIDES®

Bed & Breakfast in
  New England
Bed & Breakfast in
  the Northwest
Beyond Disney
Branson, Missouri
California with Kids
Chicago

Cruises
Disneyland
Florida with Kids
The Great Smoky &
  Blue Ridge
  Mountains
Inside Disney
Las Vegas

London
Miami & the Keys
Mini Las Vegas
Mini-Mickey
New Orleans
New York City
Paris
San Francisco

Skiing in the West
Walt Disney World
Walt Disney World
  for Grown-ups
Walt Disney World
  for Kids
Washington, D.C.

SPECIAL-INTEREST TITLES

Born to Shop: France
Born to Shop: Hong Kong
Born to Shop: Italy
Born to Shop: New York
Born to Shop: Paris
Frommer's Britain's Best Bike Rides
The Civil War Trust's Official Guide
  to the Civil War Discovery Trail
Frommer's Caribbean Hideaways
Frommer's Europe's Greatest Driving Tours
Frommer's Food Lover's Companion to France
Frommer's Food Lover's Companion to Italy
Frommer's Gay & Lesbian Europe
Israel Past & Present
Monks' Guide to California

Monks' Guide to New York City
The Moon
New York City with Kids
Unforgettable Weekends
Outside Magazine's Guide
  to Family Vacations
Places Rated Almanac
Retirement Places Rated
Road Atlas Britain
Road Atlas Europe
Washington, D.C., with Kids
Wonderful Weekends from Boston
Wonderful Weekends from New York City
Wonderful Weekends from San Francisco
Wonderful Weekends from Los Angeles